A Church of Our Own

A Church of Our Own

Disestablishment and Diversity in American Religion

R. STEPHEN WARNER

RUTGERS UNIVERSITY PRESS

NEW BRUNSWICK, NEW JERSEY, AND LONDON

LIBRARY OF CONGRESS CATALOGING-IN-PUBLICATION DATA

Warner, R. Stephen.
   A church of our own : disestablishment and diversity in American religion /
R. Stephen Warner.
       p. cm.
   Includes bibliographical references and index.
   ISBN 0-8135-3622-7 (alk. paper)—ISBN 0-8135-3623-5 (pbk. : alk. paper)
   I. United States—Religion.   2. Christian sociology—United States.   I. Title.
BL2525.W385 2005
306.6′773—dc22.   2004025320

A British Cataloging-in-Publication record for this book is available from the British Library

Manufactured in the United States of America

CONTENTS

A Note on the Text   vii

Retrospect: Looking Backward and Inward   1

PART ONE
Identifying the New Paradigm
of Constitutive Disestablishment

1   Starting Over: Reflections on American Religion (1991)   13

2   Work in Progress Toward a New Paradigm for the Sociological
        Study of Religion in the United States (1993)   18

3   A Paradigm Is Not a Theory (1997)   63

4   New Paradigm Histories of American Religion   69

    Roger Finke and Rodney Stark on American Religion after
    Disestablishment: A Review of *The Churching of America,
    1776–1990* (1993)

    Grant Wacker on the First Generation of Pentecostals:
    A Review of *Heaven Below* (2003)

    Joel Carpenter on the Second Generation of Fundamentalists:
    A Review of *Revive Us Again* (1999)

    Donald Miller on "New Paradigm Churches": A Review of
    Reinventing American Protestantism (1997)

5   Religion, Boundaries, and Bridges (1997)   83

6   Enlisting Smelser's Theory of Ambivalence to Maintain
        Progress in Sociology of Religion's New Paradigm (2004) 105

PART TWO
Close-ups and Overviews
of Diverse Congregations

7   Mirror for American Protestantism: Mendocino Presbyterian
        Church in the Sixties and Seventies (1990)   125

8   The Place of the Congregation in the Contemporary American
        Religious Configuration (1994)   145

9   The Metropolitan Community Churches and the Gay Agenda:
        The Power of Pentecostalism and Essentialism (1995)   183

10 Seeing the Word in a Church for the Deaf (with James S.
        Pappas, 1993)   209

11 Elizondo's Pastoral Theology in Action: An Inductive
        Appreciation (2000)   213

12 Pentecostal Immigrants and the Making of the Sun
        Belt (1993)   226

13 Religion and New (Post-1965) Immigrants: Some Principles
        Drawn from Field Research (2000)   232

14 Interpreting "Asian American Religion" for a Non-American
        Audience (2003)   253

15 The De-Europeanization of American Christianity (2004)   257

16 Changes in the Civic Role of Religion (1999)   263

        Prospect: Looking Forward and Outward   278

        Appendix: List of Author's Cited Works   293

        Index   299

A NOTE ON THE TEXT

Chapters 1 through 16 are reproduced from the publications in which they originally appeared between 1990 and 2004. I am grateful to the respective publishers for permission, acknowledged in each chapter, to reprint these works. As far as practicable, the chapters are reprinted as originally published, but a few changes have been made. A handful of typographical and other errors have been corrected. Usage has been standardized. Publication data for sources originally referenced as "forthcoming" or "in press" have been updated. Except for the three chapters (7, 8, and 11) originally published using humanities-style endnote- or footnote-referencing formats, referencing of literature has been standardized in the format used in sociology journals. The most significant editorial change in this edition is that references to my own work, including coauthored work, cited in chapters 2, 3, 4, 5, 6, 9, 13, and 16 have been gathered together in an appendix. I am grateful for the comments and suggestions of Nancy Ammerman, Joy Charlton, Anne Heider, and Kristi Long and for the careful copyediting of Bobbe Needham in the preparation of this book.

R. Stephen Warner
Evanston, Illinois
December 3, 2004

A Church of Our Own

Retrospect

Looking Backward and Inward

Twenty-five years ago, I was among the scholars who brought news to the academy of the evangelical subculture flourishing in the midst of our modern society. I had encountered this subculture in 1975 while doing research in a distinguished, historic Presbyterian church in Mendocino, California, and I initially thought such a church an unlikely home for what I took to be an impossibly old-fashioned and down-market brand of religion. It took me ten years to understand what I had stumbled upon.

For most of those ten years, I was teaching at the University of Illinois in Chicago, but most of the reading I did to prepare for my classes in sociology of religion gave me little help in figuring out what I had come across in Mendocino. In contrast, going with my students to their churches, synagogues, mosques, and temples did prove helpful. Chicago was another place where religion flourished, primarily as a consequence of its being—both in the past and in the present—a city of immigrants. Immigrants, or more broadly, people on the move, try to build in their new setting a cultural space they can feel at home in, and I found that in our society religious institutions often serve them as spaces to fill that need. I reflected on something I had noticed about the church people of Mendocino: most of them were new to town, having moved there precisely to immerse themselves in small-town life. (I called them "elective parochials.") The evangelical theology their pastor taught resonated with the small-town values they had adopted. In the same way, the staggering variety of churches and other religious institutions across metropolitan Chicago enshrined the cultures of the people who had built them.

My book about the Mendocino church, *New Wine in Old Wineskins*, was finally ready for press in 1986. In the conclusion, reflecting on what I had seen in California and in Chicago, I wrote (Warner 1988a, 290): "The U.S. is a country where men and women on the frontier had to set up their own churches if they were to have any public worship, and where immigrants found that religion was the one part of their traditional cultures that American society would allow them to keep." This need, and freedom, for grassroots involvement was the result of the rules for religion written into American constitutional law: "U.S. religiosity is strong because of, not despite, our separation of church and state, and rates of religious participation increased dramatically as the early colonial church-state establishments were abolished and religion became subject to a free market of opinion." In the history of the United States, religious disestablishment, religious diversity, and religious vitality go hand in hand.

I learned these lessons from Will Herberg's *Protestant, Catholic, Jew*, and having finished the book on evangelicalism in Mendocino, I decided that the time had come for an update of Herberg's book and that, drawing on what I'd learned in writing my book, I was the person to undertake it. The articles, chapters, essays, and reviews brought together in this book are the result of that intention.

Homage to Will Herberg

Protestant, Catholic, Jew: An Essay in American Religious Sociology, first published in 1955 but better known in its second edition (Herberg 1960), is still one of the most valuable and stimulating treatments of American religion I know of. Writing in the midst of the post–World War II boom in U.S. religion, Herberg astutely sensed that something else was afoot than sheer piety. He discovered that religion, as the most purely voluntary of American institutions, was the culturally favored way for people in the United States to be both indisputably American and legitimately loyal to some pre- or supra-American identity. Americans were expected to be religious, but it was largely a matter of indifference what religion they adhered to. Herberg had put his finger on the pluralistic spirit at the heart of U.S. religion.

Unlike many interpreters of American religion, Herberg looked more to the nineteenth century than to the seventeenth to appreciate religion's popular appeal and its internal diversity. Instead of assuming that the Puritans had provided the mold for U.S. religion, he focused on the religious awakenings early in the nineteenth century and the ever-increasing flow of immigration throughout the century. In the ever-expanding West, where the upper-crust heirs of the Puritans were increasingly incapable of speaking to their long-lost old-stock Protestant cousins, people on the frontier were evangelized instead by Baptists, Methodists, and Disciples, who made religion a popular cultural idiom for the non-elite Anglo-Saxon population. Among later-arriving Catholics and Jews (and some Protestants), religion was the increasingly precious cultural legacy of the immigrant forebears as collective memories of the old country faded, the only legacy, in fact, that their grandchildren could appropriate. As Herberg put it, ethnic identities "transmuted" over time into religious ones.

Having witnessed a Protestant religious awakening in northern California in the 1970s and, toward the end of that decade, having come to teach in Chicago, a city built by immigrants in the nineteenth century and being rebuilt by them before my eyes in the twentieth, I found Herberg an insightful guide. If some

Protestant groups decline, as did the Presbyterians and Methodists after 1965, that does not mean that Protestantism itself is declining. If post-1965 immigrant parents despair that their children are losing the ability or desire to speak their mother tongue, favoring English instead, they work all the harder to pass on their religion.

Of course Herberg had his blind spots. Attuned to the importance of evangelical Protestantism before the Civil War, he (along with most observers of his time) did not see that evangelicalism in the 1950s was rebounding from its defeats of the 1920s. Knowing that immigration had profoundly shaped U.S. religion, he (along with most observers of his time) could not imagine that within a decade U.S. immigration law would be unshackled from the racist restrictions written into it in the 1920s. He could say little about the Black Church and even less about Hispanics, recognizing the racial factor in their identities that placed them outside the white Protestant-Catholic-Jewish "triple melting pot." Along with most observers of his time, he took heterosexuality and the nuclear family for granted.

What he did see and did tell about was that religion allowed and encouraged Americans, who derived from an astonishing array of often antagonistic backgrounds, to be both different and assimilated. By Herberg's time in the middle of the twentieth century, to be Protestant, or Catholic, or Jewish were three equally legitimate ways of being American. Ecumenical Protestantism emerged in the 1950s out of nineteenth-century competitive evangelism. U.S. Catholicism was forged out of struggles especially between the Irish, who won, and the Germans, whose demand for ethnic particularity was defeated. U.S. Judaism came fitfully together out of mutually disdainful German and Russian immigrant streams. Herberg may not have appreciated how temporary were the truces internal to each of his three great religious communities, but he recounted the processes that led to them with sufficient clarity and detail to suggest their fragility. He did not pay sufficient attention to racial minorities, but he did see how the astonishing mélange of peoples who came to be known as "white" appropriated acceptable but differentiated American identities through their embrace of religion.

Throughout the 1980s, sociology of religion students in Chicago brought me (or served as) examples of religious processes that, with Herberg's account of the nineteenth century fresh in mind, seemed strangely familiar. Presbyterians and Methodists were few and far between, but many students were eager to identify themselves as "Christian." Black students stood out in class, both for the rhetorical skills they had been encouraged to develop in church and for the distinctive, religiously tinged language they learned there. As the years went by, more Muslim women wearing *hijab* and Jewish men wearing yarmulkes came to class, and Asian American students used the student union to publicize their Bible study meetings. My class went on field trips and found that Catholic churches left empty by the flight of their white parishioners to the suburbs were being refilled by immigrants from Mexico. We discovered that other Catholic churches were finding ways to be distinctively and differently religious in their musical, liturgical, and ideological demeanor, as older ethnic identities faded among Chicagoland's whites. In 1985, one student proposed a class visit to a gay church in his neighborhood. (That visit was my introduction to the Metropolitan Community Church.) In the part of America I taught in, much societal difference assumed a religious expression, as Herberg would have expected.

Riding home on the "L" after class one day in 1986, I sketched an outline of the book in which I would update Herberg. Beefed up, that outline became the heart of a successful sabbatical proposal. Chapter 1 would set forth the thesis that, being disestablished, religion is America's traditional way of expressing allowable difference. Chapter 2 would detail the sources of my information, the same sorts of literature—quantitative and qualitative sociological treatises, histories, and magazine articles—that Herberg relied on, as well as my experience teaching sociology of religion in Chicago. Chapter 3 would cover the Protestants, arguing that loyalty to denominations was giving way to Left/Right faction fighting within them.

Pieces of that early outline have been reshuffled over the years, but the projected Chapter 5 still stands out in my mind. Its topic was religion among post-1965 immigrants, especially the Koreans, Indians, and Mexicans I was coming to know and know of, for whom their religion was highly salient. I gathered whole boxes of material for that chapter: newspaper clippings, students' theme papers, honors theses, conference papers, a very few social science journal articles and monographs, and field notes and local newsletters that I collected on my own visits to immigrant religious institutions.

The only chapter that actually got written during the sabbatical year (1988–1989) was the one on the gay church (the basis of Chapter 9 here), but I was inspired in the following years to be alert for religious expressions among other subcultural groups in America: the deaf (Chapter 10), Mexican Americans in Texas (Chapter 11), and "Okies" in California (Chapter 12).

Two things impeded my progress on the book—the lack of literature and the theoretical inadequacy of what literature there was. I was especially stymied by the dearth of studies of new immigrant religious institutions to draw on for Chapter 5. I had a theoretical frame that I could decorate with colorful stories from my first-hand observations. But to write a chapter in a book that my fellow social scientists as well as a wider public would take seriously, I would need to call on the authority of full-blown ethnographic studies of such churches, temples, and mosques, studies written by scholars fluent in their languages and cultures. As a monolingual English-speaking white Protestant, I could not do this research myself even if I had the time.

So in 1993 I used the boxes of stuff I had gathered as the basis for a proposal to the Lilly Endowment and the Pew Trusts. I asked them to fund a fellowship program that would identify, train, and support twelve scholars with the requisite fluencies to conduct the needed research. I called it the New Ethnic and Immigrant Congregations Project, and I asked Judith Wittner, of Loyola University, to join me in conducting the training seminar and supervising the fellows' reports. When our book, *Gatherings in Diaspora* (Warner and Wittner 1998a), came out, promising new careers were launched (see Chapter 5 here) and I finally had a critical mass of the literature I needed to write the 1986 outline's chapter, which appears here as Chapter 13.

The second stumbling block was that so much of the literature I did find and wanted to cite was flawed by bad theory. Accounts of flourishing evangelical Christian, charismatic Catholic, and Orthodox Jewish groups were framed as if the main issue facing the group was how to maintain its deviant beliefs in the face of hegemonic secular rationalism. Focused so much on this basically defensive problem, the analyst typically neglected to consider how the group's energy might have an impact on the surrounding society. It was as if assertive religion could only be a relic, sooner or later doomed to fade away. I am not above citing someone's work for purposes other than he or she intends—that is a risk one takes with scholarly publication—but too often the conclusion I wanted to draw from these studies flew directly in the face of what the author wanted to say. Unhappy with the prospect of too many distracting disclaimers—"Yes, I recognize that this is not how the author interprets her/his quite compelling data"—and thinking I might be able to root out the bad theory, I spent much of the next year that I had on leave in launching a full-scale theoretical attack, the article on the new paradigm that is reprinted as Chapter 2 here.

The "bad theory" I speak of came from a quite brilliant book by the young Peter Berger (1969) that I had myself found cogent before encountering real live religion in California in the 1970s. Himself an immigrant from Europe, Berger synthesized the ideas of social theorists Emile Durkheim, Max Weber, Alfred Schutz, and others into a precociously influential social constructionist theory of religion. Because I already had tenure on the basis of my work in theory and was not constrained to prove that I had paid my sociological dues, I did not need to pay homage to the reigning theory in sociology of religion. Because I had not studied sociology of religion in graduate school, I was free to learn it on my own, with Herberg and my students as unwitting mentors. Only later did I recognize that this choice put me more in touch with historians and sociologists of American religion and immigration than with the European social theory to which my adopted field was oriented (and which I continue to teach every spring semester). Herberg drew on William Warren Sweet, Sidney Mead, Oscar Handlin, Marcus Hansen, Liston Pope, Richard Niebuhr, Joseph Fichter, Thomas McAvoy, Marshall Sklare, and Nathan Glazer, among many, many others, but he did not draw on Durkheim, Weber, or Schutz. Herberg's religion was recent and noisy, not faded and far-off.

Herberg did not celebrate American religion. A theologian as much as a sociologist, he drew on the European-inspired neoorthodoxy of Paul Tillich and Reinhold Niebuhr to cast scorn on what he (along with Berger) saw as its deeply idolatrous tendencies. He also drew heavily on the seminal, Weberian-inspired account of American religious fragmentation by Reinhold's brother H. Richard (Niebuhr 1929). He may have known that Weber himself came to America in 1904 and, astonished by what he saw and heard, insightfully portrayed the distinctive properties of American religion (Weber 1946, 1985). Whatever the cause, Herberg, unlike the theoretically inclined sociologists of religion I encountered in the late 1970s, saw American religion through an American lens. I am fortunate that, although I never met him, he was my teacher.

The Book in Front of You

Although I did not write all the chapters on my 1986 outline, it has animated much of my work over the intervening years, brought together in this book. Part I is devoted to the set of ideas that I proposed to replace the previously dominant theory in the sociology of religion; the key idea is that American religion is constitutively disestablished. Part II presents the congregational template by which most American religious communities have been organized, whether or not officially, and portrays some of the diversity of American congregations.

Realizing that the older theory took the established state churches of Europe as its explicit or implicit starting point—the imagined sacred past to which the allegedly secularized present was contrasted—I proposed that we needed a "new paradigm" to accommodate the fact that since the founding of the Republic, religious institutions in America have grown and prospered under the rule of "disestablishment." The state cannot recognize religious authority or compel religious observance, but neither can it hinder the free exercise of religion. Unlike Republican France, which made itself secular in order to overturn the power of the Catholic Church, Republican America allowed religion in general to flourish while promoting no one religion in particular. The state may not support religion, but it also has no right to determine what is an acceptable religion. American churches did not experience the trauma of losing their privileges; with one or two exceptions, they were born in, and adapted well to, the condition of disestablishment.

Chapter 2, the centerpiece of Part I, reprints the 1993 article in which I elaborated on the lens—what I prefer to call the "paradigm"—through which American religion must be understood. Herberg introduced me to the historically oriented scholars who had, I claim, been interpreting American religion adequately for some time, people like Sidney Mead and Seymour Martin Lipset. As I worked on the ideas that went into the article, I was thrilled to find that some of my sociological colleagues, especially Roger Finke and Rodney Stark, were perceptively seeing and forcefully saying some of the same things. This external confirmation encouraged me to believe, and to claim, that a paradigm shift was under way.

But I did not fully endorse the economic slant of Finke and Stark's thinking. What was crucial to American religion, I claimed, was that disestablishment allowed groups in the society to avail themselves of religion as a vehicle of mobilization. What came to be called the "religious economies theory" or the "rational choice theory of religion" is full of insights about American religion (as I acknowledge in the book review included in Chapter 4), but it may not be the best way of under-standing religion in general. The point of the new paradigm, as I articulated it, is that American religion is different from the religion of Europe, where religion was historically established. Explaining what I meant by speaking of a "paradigm" is the burden of Chapter 3, originally published in 1997 as a "reply" to the estimable but, I felt, mistargeted critique of my 1993 article published at the same time by sociologist Frank Lechner.

Chapter 1, "Starting Over," contains the first of several quasi-autobiographical accounts in the book that recount processes of discovery. The essay reflects on my first visit to Europe (near the end of my sabbatical year in 1989), when I was struck by the sheer age of historically significant churches in England compared to those I was familiar with in America. From this perception I drew a contrast between religious organization as a thing of the past in Europe and religious organization as a recent accomplishment in the United States. This contrast is overdrawn, but it helped me understand why Europeans might be attracted to the old paradigm secularization theory that, in its application to the United States, I was trying to overcome. Traveling to Europe convinced me that American religion was consti-tutively different.

Chapter 4 collects reviews of four books that I appropriate as historical new paradigm case studies, doing no violence to their authors' intentions. Finke and Stark's "churching of America" was especially the work of nineteenth-century Bap-tists, Methodists, and Catholics. Grant Wacker portrays the culture of the rank-and-file Pentecostal movement as it took form just after the turn of the twentieth century. Joel Carpenter shows how the heirs of early twentieth-century fundamen-talists brought their carefully nurtured religious counterculture back into Ameri-can public life by the middle of the century. Donald Miller's "new paradigm churches" developed an anti-bureaucratic organizational style in the late twenti-eth century to reach out to another counterculture, that of post-1960s young Americans. A recurrent theme in these reviews—that the book in question was "long-awaited"—is an offhand acknowledgment that my thinking had already been shaped by the respective authors' preliminary reports. In that sense, these reviews are lengthy footnotes to Chapter 2.

Chapters 5 and 6 present different attempts to add depth to the psychological underpinnings of the new paradigm. Consistently perceiving morale-building power in the American religions I had studied, I have never been satisfied to think of religious men and women as consumers of a commodity, rational or otherwise. In my view, religion connects too intimately with the emotions for such rational-actor presumptions to be satisfactory. Chapter 5 theorizes how religious ritual involving music and motion can create powerful feelings of solidarity among unacquainted individuals. Chapter 6 theorizes how, depending on the way it is organized, religion can promote feelings of freedom and exhilaration or entrap-ment and anger on the part of its constituents. Consistent with the new paradigm, both chapters examine the creative, emergent role of religion and explain why religious choice, which the old paradigm thought inimical to religious commitment, can be a source of religious passion.

The chapters in Part II sample the enormous diversity of American religious communities, with disestablishment as a background. Because the government neither provided religion as a public service nor dictated what religions could stand for, Americans were free to set up their own churches. The diversity of the American people could be mirrored in the diversity of their religious institutions.

The organizational vehicles through which American religion accommodates difference have varied over time. From the Civil War to World War II, "denominations" gave many Americans a meaningful but nonthreatening subcultural identity (Swatos 1981), but by the last third of the twentieth century, as Robert Wuthnow (1988) ably documented, denominations had lost much of their significance as markers. Old paradigm theorists, inclined to privilege religious establishments, tended to see in this decline signs of the secularization that was well under way in Europe. Recognizing that religious structures have taken many forms in the United States, the new paradigm noticed thriving congregations that engaged their local cultures even within declining denominations. Chapter 7, the earliest written in the book, summarizes my study of Mendocino Presbyterian Church, where I made this discovery.

I originally conceived the research in Mendocino as a study of conflict and consensus, but the failure of this frame required me to become proficient in the sociology of religion. Chapter 7 was written after it became clear that *New Wine in Old Wineskins* had touched many nerves, and it was funded by a small grant that allowed me to extend the temporal scope of that book by two years and to draw some conclusions for a mainline Protestant audience. It serves as background to Chapter 8, the centerpiece of Part II, which argues that congregations are increasingly the organizational heart of American religion. Others had come to similar conclusions at about the same time, and Chapter 8 was commissioned in 1990 by a project devoted to writing congregational histories and analyzing the place of the congregation in American religion with the tools of theology, history, and sociology (Wind and Lewis 1994). The chapter served as an outlet into which I could pour much of the research I had done for the Herberg update.

Congregations are the religious institutions that best represent the dizzying array of local, ethnic, racial, sexual, and other communities that make up the American mosaic. Mendocino Presbyterian Church in the 1970s expressed a local spirit I called elective parochialism. The first congregation of the Metropolitan Community Church (Chapter 9) was started by a few Los Angeles gay men who came out of the closet together in 1968 to express the gay and Christian identities that their previous churches said could not be reconciled. Chicago Catholic Ephpheta (Chapter 10) and the cathedral parish of San Antonio, Texas (Chapter 11), serve Catholics—respectively, deaf and Mexican American Catholics—whose cultures had previously been overlooked, even scorned by their church. The leadership portrayed in Chapter 9 is entrepreneurial, taking advantage of religious disestablishment to set up a previously unimaginable church. The two Catholic parishes are led by articulate, passionate priest-advocates who represent their people in front of a hierarchy whose members know well that, because of disestablishment, the people are free to leave the church.

Herberg's book and Chicago's population alerted me to the role of international immigration in religion, but Martin Marty (1984) and Frances FitzGerald (1986) helped me appreciate the broader importance in American religion of motion across society—from one place to another or one status to another (Warner 1998e). People who move across state lines and cultural boundaries, as well as those who migrate from one country to another, must reconstruct their lives in the new setting. Chapter 12 calls attention to an unjustly neglected book, Dan Morgan's *Rising in the West*, which narrates how Pentecostalism became prominent in California through the depression-era migration of people from Oklahoma and Arkansas.

Chapters 13 through 15 treat different religious aspects of the new immigration. As already recounted, Chapter 13, written for a journal in the hybrid discipline of American studies, takes general stock of what on-site field researchers have learned about immigrants' religions, how their religion affects migration, and how setting up in America affects their religious institutions. Chapter 14, originally published in a Jordanian journal, explains why "Asian American Religion" is not what European, Middle Eastern, and Asian audiences might expect. Chapter 15, written for a mainline Protestant audience, explains that immigration is making American Christianity more theologically conservative (while politically liberal) and less white.

Chapter 16, originally written for a project that examined what increasing sociocultural diversity portends for the United States, speculates that the major public impact of the new American religious diversity is "subcultural reproduction." In a period of U.S. history when alienation from popular culture is a widespread sentiment—when no one seems to embrace or be willing to take responsibility for the cynical, trivial, sex-and-violence-drenched sensationalism of television and videos; when parents of all political orientations despair of the effect this sensationalism has on their growing children; when in their own land more and more Americans share the immigrant experience of feeling like strangers—the multitude of American religious communities are increasingly serving as nuclei of expressively modest, socially bonded, civic-minded counterpublics, which, when one looks closely at them, may be more alike than they are different. In its own unique way, each is doing what the others would broadly applaud.

The book concludes with "Prospect," looking ahead to new studies of American religion.

REFERENCES

(References to writings of the author are found in a separate listing at the back of the book.)

Berger, Peter L. 1969. *The Sacred Canopy: Elements of a Sociological Theory of Religion.* Garden City, N.Y.: Doubleday Anchor.

FitzGerald, Frances. 1986. *Cities on a Hill: A Journey Through Contemporary American Cultures.* New York: Simon and Schuster.

Herberg, Will. 1960. *Protestant, Catholic, Jew: An Essay in American Religious Sociology.* 2d ed. Garden City, N.Y.: Doubleday Anchor.

Marty, Martin E. 1984. *Pilgrims in Their Own Land: 500 Years of Religion in America.* Boston: Little, Brown.

Niebuhr, H. Richard. 1929. *The Social Sources of Denominationalism.* New York: Henry Holt.

Swatos, William H., Jr. 1981. "Beyond Denominationalism? Community and Culture in American Religion." *Journal for the Scientific Study of Religion* 20 (September): 217–227.

Weber, Max. 1946. "The Protestant Sects and the Spirit of Capitalism." In *From Max Weber: Essays in Sociology,* ed. Hans H. Gerth and C. Wrights Mills. New York: Oxford University Press.

———. 1985. " 'Churches' and 'Sects' in North America: An Ecclesiastical Sociopolitical Sketch." *Sociological Theory* 3 (Spring): 7–13.

Wind, James P., and James W. Lewis, eds. 1994. *American Congregations.* 2 vols. Chicago: University of Chicago Press.

Wuthnow, Robert. 1988. *The Restructuring of American Religion: Society and Faith since World War II.* Princeton, N.J.: Princeton University Press.

PART ONE

Identifying the New Paradigm of Constitutive Disestablishment

1

Starting Over

Reflections on American Religion (1991)

On a recent trip to England, I made a discovery about American religion. More precisely, my glimpse of some English churches led me to understand the American religious experience in ways that much theorizing about religion—theorizing based on the European experience—fails to capture. In brief: religion in England presents itself as a residue of premodern history, whereas religion in the United States is a concomitant of modernization.

My tour began in Warwick, where my sister was posted on a three-year assignment with IBM. She took us on an all-day tour of the Cotswolds before we picked up our rental car in Coventry and began a northward swing toward Yorkshire. I quickly noticed something peculiar about Birmingham. It is a vast and sprawling industrial city much like Chicago, with factories and working-class housing near the highway and skyscrapers in the distance, but with a difference. When one looks out across Chicago from an elevated train or highway, the most prominent buildings outside the Loop are ecclesiastical ones. All over the city, standing above the ubiquitous three-flats, are huge, steepled stone churches. This is not the case in Birmingham. The grand churches we saw were nestled instead in quaint villages like Lower Slaughter in the Cotswolds or swallowed by downtown development in cathedral cities like Coventry (both the modern cathedral and its bombed-out predecessor). Religion appears in this respect to be quite literally a thing of the past.

This impression was complicated but not confounded by subsequent architectural and liturgical impressions. With the signal exception of Coventry's noble postwar cathedral, what was noteworthy was almost by definition what was old, including two tiny thousand-year-old Saxon chapels in Wiltshire. We toured the cathedrals in York and Wells, the abbeys of Bath and Westminster, and parish churches in Gloucestershire, Yorkshire, Somerset, and Avon. The grandest churches were the work of the late Middle Ages.

These churches varied liturgically and theologically, to judge from the services we attended and the literature racks we perused. The congregation at St. Michael le Belfrey in York, immediately across the street from the great Minster, was evidently evangelical, whereas St. Cuthbert's in Wells seemed socially concerned. But in every case, historical stewardship had obvious priority. Notices requested donations from visitors for the upkeep of the property. In some cases, the very work of maintenance and restoration had inspired major educational displays; we learned a lot about English history by touring the awesome archeological crypt under Yorkminster, developed within the last twenty years as a byproduct of shoring up the building's foundations. In other cases, as at Westminster Abbey, it was hard to avoid the impression that the religious service itself was an artifactual restoration.

Architecturally, these English churches have implicated themselves in bygone political glories. Epochs of pride and prosperity left their mark in the ambitious architectural concepts of the thirteenth century (in York) and the rich ornamentation of the eighteenth (in Bath). Visionary medieval bishops lie in effigy around quires, and lavish tablets memorializing distinguished parishioners' sacrifices for God, king, and empire crowd the walls of naves. Insofar as today's parishes are not rich, such past glories must constitute present burdens.

American church architecture is lean by comparison. Our oldest church buildings—hand-hewn meetinghouses in the Northeast and adobe missions in the Southwest—are modest in size and decor, and our grandest ones are seldom more than a century and a half old, most of them much less. Indeed some, like National Cathedral in Washington and Grace Cathedral in San Francisco, are newly completed, and others, like St. John the Divine in New York, are still under construction.

This is in part a function of the brevity of our Christian history. The invasion of this continent by Christians is a relatively recent thing. The newness of American church magnificence is also due to the coincidence of industrialization and immigration with the building of great cities between the Civil War and the depression. While nationalist and romantic movements in Europe were appropriating their respective classic, Gothic, and Moorish legacies, transplanted kinsfolk in the United States had the cultural incentive, the stonemasons' skills, and the economic wherewithal to build ecclesiastical shrines to their rediscovered heritages. The results are evident in the skylines of cities like Chicago, Philadelphia, New York (the outer boroughs), Pittsburgh, Cleveland, Detroit, and San Francisco. Church building resumed after World War II in new cities and suburbs, when great laminated wooden arches put in place overnight by huge cranes defined the space of new sanctuaries for cross-country migrants to places like Los Angeles and San Jose. More recently, one of the outstanding architectural landmarks of the San Francisco Bay Area is the Mormon temple, built in the 1960s high in the Oakland hills.

The zenith of American religion, if indeed we have yet passed it, came only a quarter of a century—not three-quarters of a millennium—ago. In Europe, Christianity achieved a state monopoly in the fourth century, a religious establishment that was consolidated over the next thousand years. Recent centuries in Europe have seen the erosion of this establishment, an erosion properly known as "secularization." In the United States, secularization, or disestablishment, took place soon after the Revolution, when the First Amendment prohibition of a federal religious establishment was extended to the states. Since then, religion has been a voluntary institution, yet the proportion of the population claiming membership in religious bodies grew steadily from the beginning of the nineteenth century up to the time of JFK's New Frontier in the twentieth.

Whereas the modern history of religion in Europe consists of variations on the theme of secularization, the story of religion in the United States is one of voluntary organization on a massive scale. Just when the religious establishments of Europe were struggling fiercely to maintain their legal privileges (or gracefully to relinquish them), American denominations were starting from scratch, most successfully the Baptist, Methodist, and Disciples bodies emerging from the Second Great Awakening. It is understandable that European-oriented theorists, like the Austrian-born sociologist Peter Berger, look back to the era of religious monopoly memorialized by great medieval cathedrals as the normative state of religion (Berger speaks of a "sacred canopy"), a state from which we have, it is argued, inexorably declined. But the religious history of the United States, as recently told by Jon Butler and Nathan Hatch, demands a different paradigm, one highlighting not a sacred canopy but a steady cacophony of would-be religious leaders competing for the allegiance of followers free to walk the other way.

Students who approach contemporary American religious communities using the sacred canopy framework are inclined to ask, "How can they keep it up?" What they should be asking is, "What are they doing with it?" The hallmark of American religion is not preservation but mobilization. American religious leaders have typically found themselves in the position of ministering to mobile clienteles: immigrants coming from across the sea, homesteaders trekking to the frontier, farmers' children making their way in big cities, black sharecroppers seeking decent treatment in the urban North, middle-class families moving to the suburbs, northerners fleeing the Rust Belt for the Sun Belt. People's religious commitments are put at risk by such motion, and those who would be their shepherds have often used the rhetoric of nostalgia to mobilize their loyalties. But we who would understand these phenomena, the waning as well as waxing of religious vitality, will be misled if we invoke the theory of secularization and look to a premodern religious past as the benchmark of religious change. In America, religion and modernity have always gone hand in hand.

Since immigration law was radically reformed in 1965, whole new constituencies have played variations on the American theme of religious organizing. The evidence is in new architectural monuments, from the newly dedicated mosque on upper Third Avenue in New York to the twin 135-foot minarets of the Islamic Center of Greater Toledo, the 78-foot white concrete tower of the Hindu Temple outside Chicago, and the magnificent Hsi Lai Temple in Hacienda Heights east of

Los Angeles. I have observed other immigrant religious groups, earlier in their process of organization, adapt available spaces to sacred ends: Wat Dhammaram (Thai Buddhist), using what had been a Burbank, Illinois, public school building; the Muslim Community Center of Chicago in a former supper club on the north-west side; Kwan Um Sa (Korean Buddhists) appropriating a converted Masonic hall in downtown Los Angeles. Innumerable immigrant congregations use space currently occupied by mainline congregations, meeting later (or earlier) in the day than their hosts. In all cases, these groups are starting afresh in America.

Beginning with the Great Awakening and the War of Independence, Americans have felt entitled to start over, as Frances FitzGerald has argued in her conclusion to *Cities on a Hill*. African Americans and Jews have added communal, peripatetic, and sojourner layers of meaning to this American proclivity, and immigrants from all cultures have modeled starting over in their very actions. The spirit of starting over surely contributes to the willingness of American congregations to sell inner-city properties to up-and-coming immigrant groups and move to new quarters in the suburbs. Having visited many such places where newcomers have made loving use of sturdily built edifices of generations back—an 1890s Reform synagogue that is now the home of a distinguished African American Baptist church, a 1900s German Lutheran *kirche* equipped with a full-immersion baptistry by Puerto Rican Protes-tants, a 1920s Presbyterian sanctuary filled with gorgeous icons by a Syrian Orthodox congregation, a 1940s synagogue put to busy use by Korean Seventh-Day Adven-tists—I imagine that the pain felt by those who relinquished the properties is com-pensated by the joys of those who now worship in them.

English churches are fine places to visit, but most Americans would not want to live with them. The spirit of American religion seems antagonistic to the palpable history they enshrine. Willow Creek Community Church, the suburban Chicago megachurch, exemplifies this spirit. Meeting originally in a movie theater to serve a mobile clientele in one of the fastest-growing regions of the country, Willow Creek claims a Sunday attendance of twelve thousand. People enter through a "lobby" to worship in a technologically first-rate but religiously neutral "auditorium," which looks out through plain glass windows onto the spacious, pastoral "campus." In the words of a church brochure: "Even as new facilities are built to accommodate ever-increasing crowds, the church remains committed to serving each person," helping people "fulfill their personal and relational needs." Church is more a matter of activ-ity than place.

Evangelicals have their own brand of nostalgia for "old-time religion," but what they hanker for is not institutional continuity. They have been ready to start over—often with an appeal to primitive Christianity. The modern Pentecostal movement, which traces its brief history to the first day of the twentieth century in Topeka, Kansas, epitomizes the American religious wish to leapfrog between the Acts of the Apostles and the deeds of latter-day saints. As Martin Marty said recently in these pages: "All through American history, especially Protestant history, the winners of disputes seem to be those who have best made the case that they represent the authority and purity of the simple Bible and the primitive Christian generation. Intervening history not only does not matter; it corrupts."

While studying a Presbyterian congregation in Mendocino, California, that has the distinction of occupying one of the oldest, most-photographed, and best-maintained church buildings on the West Coast, I sometimes heard whispered the half wish that the Victorian Gothic sanctuary of native redwood might burn down to free the congregation of the limits set in 1868. I hope that does not happen. But it is not my job to keep the place in repair.

American believers' willingness to start over, to shrug off their institutional baggage, has its drawbacks. It leads us to ignore the historical particularity of our condition. It obscures the wisdom of living religious traditions. It isolates and burdens the stewards of historic religious properties. It tempts us to think that present cultural enthusiasms represent eternal principles. Nevertheless, this characteristic trait has saved us from the despairing sentiment that God must have looked more kindly upon our ancestors than upon us. It has freed generations of people to look to the future and organize in the present.

2

Work in Progress Toward a New Paradigm for the Sociological Study of Religion in the United States (1993)

In every scientific venture, the thing that comes first is Vision. That is to say, before embarking upon analytic work of any kind, we must first single out the set of phenomena we wish to investigate, and acquire "intuitively" a pre-liminary notion of how they hang together or, in other words, of what appear from our standpoint to be their fundamental properties. This should be obvious. If it is not, this is only owing to the fact that in practice we mostly do not start from a vision of our own but from the work of our predecessors or from ideas that float in the public mind.

—Joseph A. Schumpeter, *History of Economic Analysis*

Introduction

The sociology of American religion is undergoing a period of ferment, interpreted herein as a paradigm shift in process. This article is at once a partial review of a vast, rapidly growing literature and an attempt at theoretical integration that draws tendentiously on certain strains within that literature. Thus the article is part of the very process it heralds. The older paradigm—identified here with the early work of Peter Berger (1969, 1970)—is still cited by a great many researchers in the field and remains useful for understanding aspects of the phenomenology of religious life. However, those who use the older paradigm to interpret American religious organization—congregations, denominations, special purpose groups, and more—face increasing interpretive difficulties and decreasing rhetorical con-fidence. The newer paradigm—consciously under development by only a handful of independent investigators—stands a better chance of providing intellectual coherence to the field.

The newer paradigm stems not from the old one (Tschannen 1991), which was developed to account for the European experience, but from an entirely indepen-dent vision inspired by American history. Thus, rather than fully documenting the alleged deficiencies of the older paradigm (see Hadden 1987), this article will only briefly recount some recent developments in American religion that are anomalous from its perspective before turning to an exposition of the emerging new paradigm. Section I sketches the crisis in the old paradigm, and Section II presents the presuppositional key to the new paradigm, the idea that religious institutions in the United States operate within an open market. The balance of the article is a series of corollaries to this idea. Section III argues that institutional religion in the United States is constitutively pluralistic, Section IV that American religious institutions are structurally flexible, Section V that they can serve as vehicles of empowerment for minorities and otherwise subjugated people, and Section VI that recent individualistic tendencies in American religion are consistent with its history. A conclusion considers benefits to be gained from future research oriented to the new paradigm.

The focus throughout is sociological, on religion as an institutional sector (Friedland and Alford 1991) rather than a primarily cultural or psychological phenomenon, and comparative in conception, focusing on the distinctive parameters of religion in American society, rather than on the evolution of "religion" as a generic phenomenon. Unless otherwise indicated, "America" refers to the United States and, for stylistic convenience, "American" to things pertaining to the society, government, or people of the United States.

I. Anomalies and Crisis

In *Protestant, Catholic, Jew*, a product of the 1950s, Will Herberg (1960) influentially portrayed a society suffused by religion. At that time, when cultural elites took liberal Protestant hegemony for granted, Reinhold Niebuhr and Paul Tillich appeared on the cover of *Time*, and the claim of the National Council of Churches to represent nearly forty million Americans still seemed credible (Herberg 1960, 134), it was not particularly striking that the majority of the leaders of the civil rights movement were clergymen. But a generation later, when many educated Americans had come to believe that religion was inconsequential, the fact that the movement that had produced the most sweeping progressive social change in modern U.S. history was led by Protestant preachers (Morris 1984) struck many intellectuals as anomalous (Wills 1990).

The surprise that news of American religion has occasioned in the past fifteen years—the incomprehension that met Jimmy Carter's confession as a born-again Christian; the embarrassment occasioned by Jesse Jackson's public prayers; the near panic that greeted the emergence of the New Religious Right; the incredulity met by regular reports that more that 90 percent of Americans believe in God and 70 percent in an afterlife, that nearly 90 percent report they pray and the majority of those pray daily, that 70 percent claim church membership and 40 percent attend weekly (Gallup 1990; Davis and Smith 1991); the derision earned by Oral Roberts's reports of conversations with God; the patronizing response given to the National Conference of Catholic Bishops' pronouncements on peace and

justice—testifies not so much to the state of American religion as to its misunder-
standing by those who have been too deeply schooled in the conventional wisdom
of social science. "The learned have their superstitions, prominent among them a
belief that superstition is evaporating" (Wills 1990, 15).

This conventional social science wisdom is rooted in a paradigm that conceived religion, like politics, to be a property of the whole society, such that the
institutionalized separation of state and church in modern society offered religion
only two alternatives: either religious values would become increasingly generalized so that they could remain the property of the whole, increasingly pluralistic,
society, or, if they remained resolutely particularistic, they would devolve to an
inconsequential private sphere. The former alternative was theorized by Talcott
Parsons (1960, 1967, 1969); the latter, by Peter Berger (1969). We shall see that religion in the United States has typically expressed not the culture of the society as a
whole but the subcultures of its many constituents, that it should not be thought
of either as the Parsonian conscience of the whole or as the Bergerian refuge of the
periphery, but as the vital expression of groups.

For the older paradigm, insofar as religion had a place in the lives of conventional Americans, it merely supported, or only decorated, the status quo; insofar
as religion was obstreperous, it was likely found only on the margins of society.
Thus, writing on the basis of his observations at midcentury, Talcott Parsons
(1960, 1967, 1969) proposed that religion in modern society, to the extent that it
was viable, was likely to be ascriptive in recruitment, generalized in content, and
consensual in appeal. Yet by the 1980s previously descriptive designations like
"Christian" and "humanist" became divisive labels, and arguments over the particular statuses of Jesus and the Bible took on renewed urgency. On the one hand,
nearly one out of ten Americans no longer professed a religion at all (Gallup 1988,
47). But on the other hand, proselytizers were busy: one out of three persons
reported that, sometime during the year ending in March 1988, they had been
invited to join someone else's church (Gallup 1990, 29).

Conversely, Peter Berger said in 1970, defiant assertions of supernaturalism
were "likely to be restricted to smaller groups, typically those whose social location (in 'backward' regions, say, or in the lower classes) gives them little interest
or stake in the world of modernity" (1970, 21), but less than a decade later Mary Jo
Neitz (1990, 91) "met lawyers and business executives . . . speaking in tongues and
practicing faith healing" at a huge Roman Catholic charismatic prayer-group
meeting every Monday night in an affluent Chicago suburb (see also Neitz 1987).
Pentecostalism was no longer peculiar to the down-and-out: Gallup (1988, 56) estimated that 9 percent of all Americans, including 8 percent of all U.S. college
graduates, took part in a charismatic group in the years 1986–1988. A startling
phenomenon to those who expect religion to be innocuous and conventional is an
energetic new Christian denomination of twenty-two thousand members, the Universal Fellowship of Metropolitan Community Churches, which ministers to gays
and lesbians on the basis of an orthodox Trinitarian theology with echoes of

Pentecostalism (Perry and Swicegood 1990, esp. chap. 4; Warner 1989b; Jacquet and Jones 1991, 262). Alongside the UFMCC are gay and lesbian congregations standing on their own (Thumma 1991) and operating within conventional Protestant denominations, as well as Catholic and Jewish communities (Gorman 1980). The sheer variety within American religion is staggering (Melton 1989).

Many scholars studying these developments—assertive particularism, resurgent traditionalism, creative innovation, and all-round vitality in American religion—have attempted to frame their reports using the "sacred canopy" perspective (Berger 1969), which is, after all, their disciplinary cultural capital. Yet inconclusive results have become chronic in the field (Ammerman 1987, esp. 1–3; Christiano 1987, chap. 7; Davidman 1991, 28–29, 203–204; Poloma 1989, 93; Prell 1989, 161–165, 270). Others (e.g., Bender 1991; Finney 1991; Gilkes 1985; Gorman 1980; Kaufman 1991; Preston 1988; Rose 1987; Stacey 1990), especially feminist scholars, drawn to the field by interests more topical, moral, political, or personal than the theoretical interests defined by the sociology of religion, have produced reports unframed by either paradigm, and thus subject to appropriation by both. That the reigning theory does not seem to work has become an open secret. Indeed, a sociological observer from abroad reports "the impression that, at least in the United States, it is the antisecularization thesis that has become the accepted wisdom" (Sharot 1991, 271). "Antisecularization," however, is a mere negation; it is not yet a paradigm.

Advocates of the older paradigm have by no means retired from the scene and, indeed, have counterattacked (Lechner 1991; Tschannen 1991). Using the apparatus of secularization, they have attempted to account for apparent anomalies such as the resurgence of fundamentalism (Lechner 1985) and the persistence of evangelical (Hunter 1983) and liberal (Roof 1978) Protestantism. They have reformulated "secularization" to make it conform better to the American experience (Chaves 1991c). Yet much of secularization theory's best evidence and most forceful advocacy comes from Europe, where secularization is arguably a historical fact as well as a theory (see Hadden 1987, 589–591, 599).

The debate is unsatisfactory and will likely remain so until the opponents of the secularization paradigm develop their own paradigm. In the last few years, they have begun to do so.

II. The Crux of the Matter: Disestablishment and Religious Mobilization in the United States

The emerging paradigm begins with theoretical reflection on a fact of U.S. religious history highly inconvenient to secularization theory: the proportion of the population enrolled in churches grew hugely throughout the nineteenth century and the first half of the twentieth century, which, by any measure, were times of rapid modernization. Whereas about 10 percent of the population were church members at the time of the American Revolution, about 60 percent are so today, with particularly rapid growth registered in the fifty years preceding the Civil War and the Great Depression (Herberg 1960, 47–50; Caplow, Bahr, and Chadwick 1983, 28–29; Finke and Stark 1986; Stark and Finke 1988). One naive glance at the numbers is bound to give the impression that, in the experience of the United States, societal modernization went hand in hand with religious mobilization.[1] The end result is that with the exception of "a few agrarian states such as Ireland and Poland" "the United States has been the most God-believing and religion-adhering, fundamentalist, and religiously traditional country in Christendom," as well as "the most religiously fecund country" where "more new religions have been born . . . than in any other society" (Lipset 1991, 187).

In default of census data on individual religious affiliation, which the government may not inquire into, sociologists of religion employ what can be called "poll" data (sample surveys done by Gallup, NORC, etc.) and "roll" data (reports of internal counts by religious bodies themselves). Measured in terms of poll data, the current rate of adult church membership is between 69 percent (Gallup 1990, 43) and 61 percent (Davis and Smith 1991, 399); in "roll data" terms, the figure is 59 percent (Jacquet and Jones 1991, 303, 265).[2] While mainline Protestant denominations have lost members since peaking in the mid-1960s and individually reported church membership has declined four or five percentage points from the 73 percent registered in polls at that time, it stretches these points mightily to see this slight and uneven decline over three decades as evidence for secularization theory, in view of about ten previous decades of strong and positive zero-order correlations between church membership and industrialization, urbanization, immigration, and most of the other processes that are thought to cause secularization.[3]

The research of historians helps us understand what is distinctive about American religious institutions (Hackett 1988). Despite the impression on the part of today's conservative Christians that the United States was founded as a Christian nation, the early decades of American independence were times of eclectic spiritual ferment but thinly distributed church membership. Jon Butler (1990), in *Awash in a Sea of Faith*, emphasizes widespread religious indifference in colonial New England and documents flourishing non-Christian strains of magic, astrology, and spiritualism in the antebellum years. In *The Democratization of American Christianity*, Nathan Hatch (1989) chronicles the strenuous efforts of early nineteenth-century revivalists to bring into religious fellowship the masses of common people who had been ignored by colonial religious establishments.

The great antebellum revivals, or the Second Great Awakening (ca. 1790–1830), have accordingly been interpreted by historians not as exercises in nostalgia but as strenuous, and largely successful, efforts at social organization (Mathews 1969; Smith 1968). "Worried about colonial spiritual lethargy since the seventeenth century, concerned about the rise of deism and skepticism among the political and social elite, propelled by a republican ideology to secure Christian foundations of American political virtue, and seeing in independence new opportunities to win adherents, religious leaders rushed to proselytize citizens in a growing nation"

(Butler 1990, 274). The enormous growth of the Catholic Church in the United States later in the nineteenth century was similarly not merely a matter of the importation of preexisting religious commitments but the result of strenuous effort by revivalists worried about apostasy of spiritual kinsfolk in a dominantly Protestant culture (Dolan 1978; Finke 1988).

The analytic key to the new paradigm is the disestablishment of the churches and the rise of an open market for religion, the process that intervened between colonial lethargy and antebellum fervor. Establishment was not uniform across the colonies and disestablishment did not occur overnight in 1789, for the First Amendment prohibited only Congress (not the states) from establishing religion. Disestablishment was the fruit of an ironic alliance between deistic political elites and insurgent evangelical firebrands (Littel 1962; Mead 1963; Finke 1990), and it had two profound implications for the institutional order of religion: first, protection for the free exercise of religion in general; second, no protection for any religious organization in particular. For the people, there was freedom of worship. For the churches, it was sink or swim, and the market share of Congregationalists started quickly to sink, whereas the Baptists and Methodists swam expertly (Herberg 1960, 103–107; Finke and Stark 1989a). The long-term result of disestablishment was a far higher level of religious mobilization than had existed before.

Thus, rather than viewing American religion as a mere exception to or negation of the pattern of European establishment, new-paradigm sociologists have learned from historians to view U.S. religion as institutionally distinct and distinctively competitive. Table 2.1 dramatizes the difference between the new and old paradigms.

The use of economic imagery is widespread among students of American religion. The historian Butler writes of Baptists developing "national spiritual markets" and observes that denominational leaders on the postrevolutionary frontier "read maps with an intensity that challenged land speculators" (1990, 275–276). The historian Terry Bilhartz (1986, 139) focused on "the marketing skill of . . . competing venders" in his monograph on religion in early national Baltimore, and he casually introduced "supply side" imagery to the discussion. This imagery was later developed by Hatch into a theory of "competition in the religious marketplace" among spiritual "entrepreneurs" in a "divine economy" (1989, 15, 67, 101). Anthropologists Irving Zaretsky and Mark Leone (1974, xxxvi) write that American religion "is the last voice for decentralization and the free enterprise system." Sociologist Richard Lee (1992, 6) claims that "both religious and economic behavior are shaped by a common independent variable, reward," and Andrew Greeley (1989, 122) agrees that "a 'rational choice' theory does much to explain the persistence of religion in the United States." Rodney Stark and William Bainbridge (1985, 1987) developed an elaborate theory of "the religious economy," and Finke and Stark (1992) have used the theory to account for two hundred years of organizational success and failure of U.S. religious bodies. Economist Laurence Iannaccone found an early statement of the market theory of religion in Adam Smith's

TABLE 2.1

Schematic Comparison of New and Old Paradigms

	New	Old
Paradigmatic situation	Competition	Monopoly
Best historical fit	Second Great Awakening	Medieval Catholicism
Place and time	United States, early 19th c.	Europe, 500–1500 C.E.
Master narrative	Revival and routinization	Linear secularization
Secularity threatens	Irksome demands	Implausible beliefs
Elite prototype	Entrepreneur	Prebendary
View of pluralism	Constitutive	Degenerative
Social base	Social groups	Whole society
Typical organization	Denomination, congregation	Universal church, parish
Function of religion	Solidarity, morale	Explanation, meaning
Identity	Contested	Taken for granted
Recruitment	Emergent, achieved	Primordial, ascribed
Today's figures	Stark, Finke, Greeley	Berger, Lechner, Hunter
Classic texts	"Protestant Sects"; *Elementary Forms*	*Protestant Ethic*; *Division of Labor*

Wealth of Nations and tested it with cross-national data. He found that, "among Protestants, at least, church attendance and religious belief both are greater in countries with numerous competing churches than in countries dominated by a single church" (Iannaccone 1991, 157).

The new paradigm is not *defined* by economic imagery, however, but by the idea that disestablishment is the norm. For instance, Berger's statement that in contemporary America "religious institutions become marketing agencies and the religious traditions become consumer commodities" (Berger 1969, 138) is an often-cited observation (see also Hammond 1986). Still, Berger represents the older paradigm, dominated by the scenario of European secularization, not the emerging one, which is based on and specifically describes and explains the American experience. For Berger, the *modern* American market situation is a degenerate one of "loss," "rupture," "deprivation," "fragility," "tenuousness," and "crisis" (1969, chap. 6), whereas the paradigmatic, durable, *traditional* situation is one in which religions are "authoritatively imposed" as "monopolies" by the "coercive support" of the state (1969, 138, 135, 131). According to Berger, the market situation of religion in modern society deprives religious institutions of the support of coerced monopoly; above all they lack the support of being "taken for granted" that arises in the absence of ideological competition.

Accordingly, when Bergerians are confronted with some old-fashioned religion thriving in modern America, they feel constrained to account for it as a kind of deviant case. Thus the analyst focuses on the surrogate supports, called "plausibility structures," that the group provides itself. Such framing of the research usually requires that the ethnographer concentrate on the sociological commonplace that members of the group in question surround themselves with likeminded others. The reader learns indeed how the group cognitively defends itself, but, unless other theoretical sources are drawn upon, little of how it organizationally expresses itself (Wuthnow 1986).

Contrary to the sacred canopy concept, ethnographers (e.g., Snow and Machalek 1982) have argued that maintaining supernatural religious beliefs in U.S. society is not particularly difficult, and opinion pollers have found high levels of self-reported belief in God and devotional and attitudinal religiosity (praying daily, reading the Bible, etc.) among the "unchurched" (those who do not regularly participate in a religious body; see Gallup 1988; Davis and Smith 1991). This suggests that other factors than "implausibility" (e.g., anger at church pronouncements on birth control) are at work in whatever religious disaffection does exist in the United States (Greeley 1989).

Thus one result of the older paradigm was that relatively too much attention was paid to the question of maintaining deviant religious cognitions and too little to what the religion in question did for its adherents and they for it in the real world. The work of James Davison Hunter is a case in point. Hunter devoted his first two monographs (Hunter 1983, 1987) to the quandaries and compromises modern America poses for conservative Christians, leaving for a third (Hunter 1991) the question of the cultural challenge that conservative Christians pose for modern America. Since Hunter is an intelligent, energetic, resourceful, and empirically responsible scholar, his work can be appropriated for the new paradigm despite his Bergerian presuppositions.

Another result of taking the monopolistic situation as the norm is an illusory focus on the shock posed to religious organizations by their adjustment to the circumstances of pluralism. It is said that churches can "*no longer* take for granted" the loyalty of clients. Their ideas, "which *previously* could be authoritatively imposed," now must be marketed. In the pluralistic situation, religious activity "*comes* to be dominated by the logic of market economics" (Berger 1969, 138; emphases added). Thus does Peter Berger account for the secularizing, homogenizing, psychologizing tendencies of religion in the contemporary United States, as if a few gigantic, previously privileged suppliers had been suddenly confronted a few decades ago by hordes of price-conscious consumers (see also Luckmann 1991, 176–179). Yet it has been nearly two centuries since religion in the United States could be coercively imposed. Very few of the hundreds of religious organizations flourishing in the United States today—arguably only the Episcopal Church

(Swatos 1979)—have had to adjust to a pluralistic situation. Most of them were born into it.

The adjustment-to-pluralism model is not groundless. It matches the personal and familial experience of some groups from which religion scholars derive. Eastern European Jews came to the United States from encapsulated, religiously monolithic communities, and their offspring are aware of the contrast of traditional and modern worlds (Davidman 1991, 34–37; Furman 1987, 130–131). Bergerian theory narrates the psychological experience of intellectuals who emerge from religiously conservative families to the religiously indifferent world of the academy, where they learn that religion is socially constructed and that theirs is only one of many systems of meaning (Wacker 1984). People with such biographies have undergone psychologically the perforation of a sacred canopy that the old paradigm attributes sociologically to Western society as a whole. Bergerian theory can thus succeed as a phenomenology of religious lives where it fails as a theory of American religious organizations.

Contributors to the new paradigm have not reached consensus on all matters. Historians (Marsden 1990; Michaelson 1990) might well be surprised to hear the work of Jon Butler (1990) and Nathan Hatch (1989) attributed to the same "new paradigm," for the former's long-standing focus on religious authoritarianism is known to contrast with the latter's equally persistent stress on consumer sovereignty. Yet not only does each endorse the other's book, both agree on the fundamental point that, however it is to be evaluated, the Christianization of the United States was neither a residue of Puritan hegemony nor a transplantation of a European sacred canopy but an accomplishment of nineteenth-century activists.[4] This fundamental point is itself hardly new to historians and was central to those upon whom Herberg relied (e.g., Mead 1963). Indeed, more recent in religious historiography are challenges from European-oriented Marxian and Foucauldian perspectives. But Butler and Hatch join forces with the new-paradigm sociologists in stressing the distinctive properties of U.S. religion against such challenges.[5]

Those who use economic imagery do not agree on the full logic of market analysis as applied to religion or on all its empirical corollaries. For example, the rational consumer of religious commodities is as often imagined to be fickle as to be brand loyal. Analysts as different as Finke and Stark, Bellah and associates, and Berger look for signs of individual religious mobility as evidence of religious rationality, whereas Iannaccone, Greeley, and Lee model steadiness of religious identity as a means of reaping rewards of investments in religious cultural capital.[6] On the organizational side, the free marketplace of religion is expected by Stark and Bainbridge (1985) to exhibit inexhaustible variety and by Iannaccone (1986) to offer sectarian as well as churchly alternatives, whereas Berger (1969, 148) expects to find "standardization and marginal differentiation." A paradigm is not yet a theory but a set of ideas that make some questions more obvious and urgent than others. Much remains to be specified.

In particular, debate has arisen in the literature over the effects of pluralism on religion. Finke and Stark, the most outspoken exponents of the new paradigm, assert categorically that "the more pluralism, the greater the religious mobilization of the population" (1988, 43). The exchange began when Finke and Stark (1988) argued that they had successfully tested that claim using turn-of-the century census data. These data had previously been analyzed by Kevin Christiano (1987), who had expected consistency with the older paradigm but was surprised by mixed results. Kevin Breault (1989b) then defended the older paradigm's expectations with both a critique of Finke and Stark's methods and an analysis of another, contemporary, dataset. More recently, Judith Blau, Kenneth Land, and their associates have entered the fray, testing elaborate models on data from 1910 to 1930 (Land, Deane, and Blau 1991) and from 1850 to 1930 (Blau, Redding, and Land 1991). They reject Finke and Stark's pluralism theory with the conclusion: "It may be true that America has exceptionally much religious diversity and also exceptionally high rates of religious membership, but the two are not causally related—at least not positively" (Blau, Redding, and Land 1991, 36).

The debate on pluralism is unresolved and the issues are complex, having to do with measures of religious diversity, proper units of analysis, the adequacy of various datasets, the possibility that causal forces differ for Protestant and Catholic contexts and that causal relationships may have changed over time, and other matters. But resolution seems close on two issues. The older expectation (see Christiano 1987) that cities are necessarily inimical to religion has been refuted; indeed, U.S. cities and their modern economy evidently provide resources and conditions conducive to religious mobilization (Finke and Stark 1988; Blau, Redding, and Land 1991; Olson 1993). Score one for the new paradigm.

On the other hand, Finke and Stark (1988, 1989b) have conceded what Christiano (1987) earlier found, that religious concentration, in the sense of numerical predominance of one denomination in a geographical area, does not necessarily militate against religious vitality, particularly if that denomination is Catholic. Iannaccone (1991, 171) reports that this theoretical complication was also recognized by Adam Smith for Catholic countries in the eighteenth century. If, as in the case of Ireland and Poland, the church is allied with a sense of submerged nationalism (Lipset 1991), or—as in the American instances of Utah Mormons, turn-of-the-century urban Catholics, and postbellum Southern Baptists—the geographically concentrated group perceives itself to be a minority surrounded by a hostile culture (Shipps 1985; Finke and Stark 1988, 44–46; 1989b, 1054–1056; Wacker 1991), the regionally dominant church is less likely to lapse into the complacency that a protected position invites. Conversely, if, as in France, a monopolistic church is allied with the widely despised losing side in a nationwide struggle, it will languish.

Finke and Stark, Iannaccone, and Blau and Land and their associates all employ a measure of monopoly/competition that is based on the relative homogeneity/diversity of religious affiliation within a given unit, but Iannaccone (1991) argues that neither models of pure monopoly (literally, a single supplier of religion) nor pure competition (countless small suppliers) is realistic in the discussion of religion. Instead, he suggests (Iannaccone 1991, 160–163) that religious disestablishment should be measured by the relative prevalence of government subsidies to or interference in religion. Chaves and Cann (1992) take up his suggestion; measuring state regulation directly, they provide more evidence for the proposition that an open market conduces to religious vitality.

Such is the contribution of Hatch's supply-side imagery: what is important about religious markets from this perspective is not so much the diversity of alternatives available to consumers as the incentive for suppliers to meet consumers' needs, which is maximized when the religious economy is wide open to energetic entrants, none of whom has a guaranteed income. Consider the phenomenally influential Oral Roberts, whose career is a key to Pentecostalism's breaking out of its class-, race-, and region-based boundaries in the second half of this century. Roberts was ordained at age eighteen as a preacher in the Pentecostal Holiness denomination, which, "like most new sects, had a vast oversupply of ministers" (Harrell 1985, 20). The ambitious Roberts soon outgrew his denomination and at age thirty invested $60,000 in his own infrastructure: a truck-and-trailer rig, portable organ, piano, sound system, folding chairs, and a tent with room for 3,000. Four years later, he bought a tent big enough for 12,500 and soon began broadcasting (these biographical details come from Harrell 1985, esp. 20–21, 51). For Roberts and entrepreneurs like him, ordination was not a sinecure but a license with a built-in incentive to reach out to new audiences through innovative means.

Accordingly, the concept of a competitive religious market entails neither that religious organizations pander to a lowest common denominator of spiritual commitment nor that religious consumers constantly compare competing suppliers' responses to their fixed demands (cf. Scherer 1988, 481; Wuthnow 1991, 6–7). For example, evangelical Protestants are currently worried about the presumed mass defection of inner-city African Americans to Islam (e.g., Guthrie 1991), and Catholic bishops are concerned about the reported defection of Hispanics to Pentecostalism (e.g., National Conference of Catholic Bishops 1984). No matter that, because the U.S. Census Bureau may not inquire into individuals' religion, hard data on such trends are lacking: widely repeated anecdotes and case studies help mobilize countermeasures that initially take the form of paying more attention to the client at risk, where the supplier changes the distribution of its effort, not its basic teaching (e.g. Fitzpatrick 1990). Thus, research indicates that recent denominational growth and decline patterns are largely explained by patterns of new church plantings (foundings of new congregations, parishes, and missions; see Hadaway 1990; Marler and Hadaway 1992). Religious organizations cannot succeed in the market unless they bring their services to consumers, but the new paradigm does not claim that religious entrepreneurs are insincere about their product. Quite the contrary.

If the paradigmatic situation for Bergerians is the sacred canopy, the religious monopoly inaugurated in Europe by Constantine in the fourth century, then for market theorists it is the furious competition to evangelize North America in the nineteenth, the revivalism of the Second Great Awakening and later (Warner 1991a). The competitive patterns that emerged two centuries ago in the United States constitute "an institutionally specific cultural system" (Friedland and Alford 1991, 234) that minimizes state interference in religion and permits adaptation to an always changing society.

III. The Master Function of Religion in the United States: Social Space for Cultural Pluralism

Unity is a normative ideal for Christian ethicists, and an analytic presupposition for their old-paradigm cousins. But from the beginning, religion in the United States has been associated with societal differentiation, and pluralism has tended in this society to take on a religious expression. During colonial times, New England was the stronghold of Congregationalism; New York, New Jersey, Pennsylvania, and Delaware of the Presbyterian and Reformed churches; and Virginia of Anglicanism. Religion and region are associated to this day (Stump 1984; Hill 1985). But already by the time of the American Revolution, the Anglicans were relatively stronger on the coast and the Baptists in the hinterland, and another axis of variation—urban-rural—came into play, with a distinct social class component soon overlaid upon it as the Methodists and Baptists swept across the frontiers of upstate New York, the Ohio River valley, and the Appalachian Piedmont. At the present time, Episcopalians, the successors to the Anglicans, still outrank Baptists and Methodists not only in income and education but also in the likelihood of urban residence.

These three demographic factors—region, social class, and urbanism—at first served to differentiate from each other a dozen or so denominations of mostly white, Anglo-Saxon Protestants, but by the middle of the nineteenth century, religion in the United States became much more multicultural, with race, ethnicity, and national origin added to the demographic differentiators of religious denominations. The immigration of masses of Catholics and Jews (as well as more Lutherans) from Germany and Catholics from Ireland increased the sociological salience of religious identity itself, the Civil War intensified religious sectionalism, and the rapid rise of African American churches after the war added a color line between the churches (instead of simply within them). At the turn of the nineteenth century, immigration from Scandinavia gave language and national identity renewed religious significance for Lutherans and Baptists, and that from eastern and southern Europe strengthened minority religious groups—Catholics, Jews, and eastern Orthodox—whose claims on constituent loyalties were as least as strong as those of the older Protestant bodies.

These social factors in religious differentiation—class, race, ethnicity, language, urbanism, region, and the like—are not simply templates on which religious association is modeled, nor are they merely identities people carry as individuals from one locale to another, identities destined to fade as the carriers die. Religion itself is recognized in American society, if not always by social scientists, as a fundamental category of identity and association, and it is thereby capable of grounding both solidarities and identities (Herberg 1960).

First of all, religion is constitutive for some American subcultures. From early colonial days to the present many groups came to this country to practice their religion unmolested: English Puritans and French Huguenots, German Mennonites and Russian Jews, Tibetan Buddhists and Iranian Baha'is. Others, like Mormons, Seventh-Day Adventists, and Jehovah's Witnesses, began in America, withdrew from the wider culture into their own geographical and associational enclaves, and then brought their new ideas back to the world. Originally a protest movement of American whites, Jehovah's Witnesses have recruited substantial numbers of African Americans to their cause (Cooper 1974) and expanded the social space available for other religious protest movements (Fields 1982); Seventh-Day Adventism created a worldwide health-oriented religious culture (Bull and Lockhart 1989); and Mormonism became "a separate and distinct religious tradition in its own right" (Shipps 1985, xi), the first world religion created in the United States.

Second, religion in America has historically promoted the formation of associations among mobile people. Many frontier settlements were consolidated when the pioneers set up churches. The principle of voluntary congregational church membership made "a concrete social contribution [that] was to provide a means for hitherto complete strangers, migrants on the frontier, to establish close personal relations quickly" (Miyakawa 1964, 214). The same was true of transatlantic migrants. "Immigrant congregations . . . were not transplants of traditional institutions but communities of commitment and, therefore, arenas of change. Often founded by lay persons and always dependent on voluntary support, their structures, leadership, and liturgy had to be shaped to meet pressing human needs" (Smith 1978, 1178). In a system where religious institutions comprehend not the whole society but subcultures, modernity, migration, and mobility make it possible for people to found religious associations that are at once self-selected and adapted to present circumstances (Olson 1992).

Third, religion in America serves as a refuge of free association and autonomous identity, a "free social space" (Evans and Boyte 1986). Throughout its history, the United States has been a dynamic, rapidly changing society, particularly in its economic aspect, with a political constitution that protects minority religious rights at the same time that it stifles minority political representation (Wuthnow 1991, 295). In such a setting, religion is a refuge for cultural particularity. Such was the heart of Will Herberg's theory of American religion.

> Of the immigrant who came to this country it was expected that, sooner or later, either in his own person or through his children, he would give up virtually everything he had brought with him from the "old country"—his

language, his nationality, his manner of life—and would adopt the ways of his new home. Within broad limits, however, his becoming an American did not involve his abandoning the old religion in favor of some native American substitute. Quite the contrary, not only was he expected to retain his old religion, as he was not expected to retain his old language or nationality, but such was the shape of America that it was largely in and through his religion that he, or rather his children and grandchildren, found an identifiable place in American life. (Herberg 1960, 27–28)

Later I shall cite Herberg's own qualification of the notion that "old country" religion is simply "retained." Yet his argument helps us to understand why religion remains the preeminent voluntary associational form in our society (Curtis, Grabb, and Baer 1992).

Yet such constitutive pluralism is foreign to the older paradigm. Religious prophets scorn the social functions of particularistic religious participation in the United States and they long for signs of religious unity. The theologian H. Richard Niebuhr (1929) was scandalized by the denominational particularism he did so much to analyze. Will Herberg, as much a theologian as a sociologist, celebrated the "triple melting pot" that transmuted multitudinous nationalities into three nationwide religious communities, and he openly cheered the victory of the (Americanizing and mostly Irish) Roman Catholic hierarchy over the (particularly German) movement for ethnic dioceses within the American church (1960, 144–145). Both Niebuhr and Herberg appreciated the role that genuine religion played for communal identity in a rapidly modernizing, pluralistic society, but the fact that mass migration, one of the major and arguably least illegitimate sources of American religious pluralism, was all but shut down in the years they wrote made the persistence of pluralism seem all the more perverse.[7] Their moralistic attitude influenced others to interpret pluralism—beyond the legitimate Protestant-Catholic-Jew trinity—as evidence of weak religion (Berger 1961; 1969, 108, 200) rather than the paradigmatic situation of religion in America.

Recent immigration has given a new boost to religious pluralism, which is just starting to receive the attention of students of religion (e.g., Christiano 1991; Denny 1987; Hurh and Kim 1990; Kivisto 1992; Numrich 1992; Warner 1990b; Waugh 1992; Williams 1988). The religious experiences of immigrants from the 1840s through the 1920s—Protestants, Catholics, Eastern Orthodox, and Jews, overwhelmingly European—have been analyzed by historians central to the new paradigm (e.g., Dolan 1975, 1985, 1988; Smith 1971, 1978), but since 1965 there has been a whole new stream of immigration. Nearly as many people entered the country in the past quarter century (1966–1990) as did between 1890 and 1914 (fourteen million compared to seventeen million; see Keeley 1991). Moreover, the "new" immigrants are racially, ethnically, linguistically, and religiously more heterogeneous than those of a century ago. One result is that the purely religious boundaries of American religious pluralism have expanded with the recent addition of about as many Muslims and Buddhists to the U.S. population as there are adherents of the Eastern Orthodox churches, and a significant number of Hindus have arrived as well (Kosmin and Lachman 1991). Yet despite the novelty of these beliefs, many of the processes of immigration and religious settlement today are similar to those of the past.

Because of restrictions on the U.S. Census Bureau, firm data are hard to come by on the religious profile of the new immigrants and other expanding minorities. We do not know for certain the religious affiliations of the 22.4 million Hispanics, 1.6 million Chinese, 1.4 million Filipinos, 897,000 Indo-Pakistanis, 848,000 Japanese, and 799,000 Koreans recorded by the 1990 census (*Asian American Handbook* 1991, 9.61), nor the 919,000 refugees admitted from Southeast Asia between 1975 and 1989 (Rutledge 1992, 37). However, locally based studies have recently been conducted of some new immigrant religious identities and associations: Asian Indians in Atlanta (Fenton 1988), Chicago, Houston, and elsewhere (Williams 1988); Sri Lankans in New York City, Washington, D.C., and Los Angeles (Blackburn 1987; Numrich 1992); Muslims in Toledo (Denny 1987), rural Alberta (Waugh 1992), and three unnamed locations in the northeastern United States (Haddad and Lummis 1987); Iranians in Los Angeles (Bozorgmehr et al. 1990); Thai Buddhists in Chicago (Numrich 1992); Vietnamese in Oklahoma City (Rutledge 1982); and Koreans in Chicago and Los Angeles (Hurh and Kim 1990; Warner 1990b; Yu 1988)—and patterns seem to be consistent with the experiences of earlier immigrants.

First, today as in the past, ethnic and religious mobilization and minority consciousness often begin in the home country, "amidst complex economic and cultural rivalries" (Smith 1978, 1165). Vietnam is culturally divided along Buddhist, Catholic, and other lines, and so are immigrant Vietnamese (Rutledge 1982, 1992). "Asian Indians" are united by a U.S. census category, but elsewhere they are divided by religion into Hindus, Muslims, Sikhs, Jains, Christians, and other groups, and by language into Hindi, Punjabi, Malayalee, Gujarati, and others. Urdu-speaking Muslims may be Pakistani or Indian in national origin (Williams 1988). Neither in the homeland nor in the United States are these identities "taken for granted" in the manner of the older paradigm.

Second, immigrant identities are not fixed after migration to the United States (Smith 1978; Sollors 1988). National, regional, linguistic, religious, and other country-of-origin affiliations vary in their contribution to the emigration process and become more or less salient in the United States (Williams 1988). A critical mass of the respective grouping may or may not be present in the U.S. locality; when it is absent, solidary groups may be broader in recruitment but thinner in commitment. The host culture itself contains "proximal hosts" (Mittelberg and Waters 1992), preexisting ethnic and racial groupings into which the host society places the immigrants, who, in turn, may reject their ascription. Group consciousness is also affected by the vagaries of interaction with agents of the host society: federal immigration authorities and census takers stress national origin, local school districts and potential employers are concerned with language, a few underfunded networks focus on gender, and some resettlement agencies care about religion (Gold 1987).

Third, because religion in the United States "is an accepted mode both of establishing distinct identity and of intercommunal negotiation" (Williams 1988, 3) and because migration itself is "often a theologizing experience" (Smith 1978, 1175), religious association may be more salient for both individuals and the group after immigration than it had been before immigration. This effect seems to pertain particularly for contemporary Indian, Pakistani, and Korean immigrants (Williams 1988; Haddad and Lummis 1987; Hurh and Kim 1990; Lee 1991). Perhaps the most distinctively religious new immigrant group is Korean Americans, half of whom, as sampled by Hurh and Kim (1990), report premigration membership in Christian churches but another quarter of whom affiliate with Christian churches after arriving in this country. By 1988, Korean immigrants had established some two thousand congregations in the United States (Lee 1991). Religion does not always take on increased salience. In Los Angeles, for example, ethnic Muslim refugees from the Iranian Islamic revolution have shied away from mosques during their relatively brief residence in the United States (Bozorgmehr et al. 1990). But religion is widely available to new immigrants as a legitimate institutional form (Williams 1988).

Fourth, the institutions established by immigrants are affected by generational succession. Early in the experience of the first generation, the immigrant congregation approximates a gemeinschaft within the gesellschaft, a remembrance of Zion in the midst of Babylon, and for that among other reasons Muslim women are more visible in American mosques than in Middle Eastern ones (Waugh 1992; Haddad and Lummis 1987) and competition increases among men for positions of clerical and lay leadership in Korean American congregations (Hurh and Kim 1990; Shin and Park 1988). For the first generation, religion is in part a refuge from America. But the arrival of a second generation, now as in the past (Niebuhr 1929), suggests to many participants that some home country ways, in particular language, must be sacrificed in order to maintain the attention of the children (Numrich 1992). Conducting worship in the English language is one of the classic paths by which America transmutes ethnicity into religion, where what gives the group its identity is no longer Urdu, for example, but Islam (Hathout, Osman, and Hathout 1989; Williams 1988, 282–283), not Japanese but Buddhism (Mullins 1988; Kashima 1990), not Yiddish but Judaism (Herberg 1960, 31).

In addition to international migration as a factor in religious pluralism, there is internal migration, particularly that impelled by culture, of which the migration of gay men to major cities since World War II is prototypical. Frances FitzGerald (1986, 27) cites a late 1970s report that more than three-fourths of the population of the Castro, San Francisco's gay district, had moved to that city within that decade. With such massive population shuffling in mind and a view of the Bay Area in front of her as she stood on one of the city's hills, FitzGerald conceived a new metaphor for the social mechanism at work in contemporary American cultural life, "*not a melting pot but a centrifuge* that spun [people] around and distributed them out again across the landscape according to new principles," including income and lifestyle (1986, 16, emphasis added). On the basis of such social sorting into a gathered community (and his own energy and imagination), the religious entrepreneur Troy Perry founded the Metropolitan Community Church in Los Angeles in 1968 (Dart 1969, 1991; Perry 1972; Warner 1989b). Thus, the grounds on which Americans gather and find one or another religious message compelling, grounds that have historically included geography, social class, race, national origin, generation, ethnicity, and language, now also include gender, sexual orientation, "lifestyle," and moral culture.

The work of Daniel Olson (1989, 1993) has shed light on the anomaly (to the older paradigm) that religious institutions flourish in this most mobile of societies. On the one hand, it is a well-established generalization that geographical mobility is inversely correlated in the short run with religious participation (Wuthnow and Christiano 1979; Finke 1989). It seems that mobility disrupts the social networks that support regular church attendance. On the other hand, as we have seen, transatlantic migrants invigorated American religious life in the nineteenth century and at least some of the post-1965 immigrants are doing so today. Moreover, churches located in growing communities—particularly suburbs—have a better chance of growing in membership than those in stable or declining areas (see, e.g., Roof et al. 1979). Furthermore, denominations grow when they "plant" new churches and decline when they do not (Marler and Hadaway 1992). Assuming that one of the motivations for religious participation in the United States is the desire for friendly and culturally supportive associations, Olson argues that members of old and stable churches tend to have all the friends they want, but that new churches are likely to have many members whose demand for church-based friendships are not yet satiated. They therefore make room in their lives for newcomers (Olson 1989). Claude Fischer's work (1982) suggests that larger communities facilitate cobelievers' spending time with each other, so that urbanism can promote religious communalism rather than homogenization. Locations with high rates of in-migration thus offer attractive markets for aggressive religious organizations.

IV. Structural Adaptability

Religious forms are typically sacralized. For example, "apostolic succession" in the leadership structure of Catholic and Episcopal churches is a hallowed doctrine traced to Jesus' laying his hands on Simon Peter, and the "divine liturgy" in the Orthodox Church is claimed to represent an unbroken patriarchal tradition well over a thousand years old. The older paradigm theoretically privileges religious establishments and is inclined to take their word for what is truly "religious" and what is "worldly." But because of disestablishment, U.S. religious forms have historically been malleable. Thus in America today there are Roman Catholic parishes pastored, de facto, by women (Wallace 1992), and Orthodox churches where scriptures are read (with an American accent) also by women (Warner 1992b). Religious forms change in the United States, and Herberg (1960, 83) knew better than to say that they are only "retained" from historical patterns: "religion in America has tended toward a marked disparagement of 'forms,' whether theological or liturgical." But the new paradigm does not regard religious change as presumptive evidence of "worldliness."

From the perspective of Europe, where the universal "church" was the social and theoretical norm against which the radical "sect" perennially protested, the American "denomination"—making little claim to inclusiveness yet also working within the world—was a structural innovation (Niebuhr 1929; Smith 1968; Swatos 1979). The voluntarism of the U.S. religious system has also facilitated the development, since early in the nineteenth century, of parachurch "special purpose groups" (Wuthnow 1988, chap. 6), both bureaucracies (e.g., the American Bible Society) and collegia (e.g., the Full Gospel Business Men's Fellowship International). Another pervasive American pattern is the congregational model of local church organization, whether or not sanctioned by the hierarchy (Silver 1990; Warner 1994a).

Long-term centralization and bureaucratization characterize much of organizational life in modern societies (Powell and DiMaggio 1991), but the institutional history of U.S. religion is better seen as an alternation of centripetal and centrifugal tendencies.

The centripetal tendency comprises bureaucratization and professionalization of denominational and ecumenical staffs, where material and especially human resources flow upward toward headquarters and greater attention is paid to edicts of the center, whether or not such a flow is legitimated by the respective religious doctrines. In the history of mainline Protestantism from the Civil War to the Vietnam War, centripetal processes produced denominational bureaucracies and ecumenical agencies (notably the National Council of Churches) and tended to substitute professional expertise and political ideology for religious orthodoxy as a source of organizational power (Hadden 1969; Pratt 1972; Carroll, Hargrove, and Lummis 1983, chap. 2; Wuthnow 1988; Ammerman 1990; Chaves 1991b; Olson and Carroll 1992). At its height in the first half of this century, centripetalism in mainline Protestantism took the form of an order that felt like, to both its own fiduciaries and excluded minorities, a protected establishment (Hutchison 1989); the recent erosion of this "establishment" centripetalism is interpreted by some participants as the long-delayed process of secularization predicted by the older paradigm. One result of this temporary establishment was that, for a generation, mainline Protestant leaders were in general more liberal than their laity (Hadden 1969; Hoge 1976; Takayama 1980; Wood 1981; Warner 1988a). More recently, the centripetal flow in mainline Protestantism has ebbed, indeed reversed, as denominational and ecumenical budgets have been slashed and symbolically significant mainline headquarters have been moved from New York to places like Cleveland

and Louisville (McKinney and Roof 1990). Undoubtedly, the most influential attempt to delineate recent centrifugal processes is found in Robert Wuthnow's (1988) chapter on "the declining significance of denominationalism," which analyzes both the blurring of individual denominational identities and the weakening of denominational organizations. Wuthnow's evidence suggests that since World War II denominations have become less distinct from each other but more diverse within themselves in member attitudes and demographics. For instance, the old nominal-level variable "Catholic-Protestant" has ceased to have predictive power for most sociological studies of individual beliefs and behavior and is instead being replaced by frequency of church attendance. Wuthnow documents declining interdenominational antagonism and increasing cross-denominational intermarriage and membership switching. Perhaps because of the success of ecumenism, denominational loyalties have declined and church shopping has increased. In important mainline Protestant bodies, fewer clergy confine their training to their denominational seminaries, and local churches send a declining share of their resources to organizational headquarters.

Wuthnow intends none of this to say that religious boundaries have disappeared or that religion has no further power as a sociological variable. The social centrifuge, as FitzGerald (1986) would have it, not only spins things out from the center but also reshuffles them into new combinations. Wuthnow's (1988) "restructuring" spotlights an organizational shift along a new cultural fault line of American religion, comparable to that which took place early in the nineteenth century (see Wuthnow 1988, xiv). Wuthnow sees denominations fading relative to nationwide special purpose groups on each side of the divide between Religious "Left" and "Right" (see also Liebman and Wuthnow 1983; Roof and McKinney 1987; Diamond 1989; Jorstad 1990; Hunter 1991). On the left are such organizations as People for the American Way, Witness for Peace, and Clergy and Laity Concerned; on the right are the Moral Majority, Focus on the Family, and Religious Roundtable.

Another centrifugal conceptualization is "de facto congregationalism" (Warner 1994a), that is, labeling an institutionalized bias of American religious life toward affectively significant associations under local and lay control, beginning with observations of differences between congregations within the same denomination (Warner 1983, 1988a; see also Carroll and Roozen 1990). De facto congregationalism implies that the local religious community is in fact constituted by those who assemble together (which is the etymological root of "congregation") rather than by the geographic units into which higher church authorities divide their constituents, which is what "parishes" historically are. Since Vatican II, the Catholic Church seems to be quietly relaxing the geographic parish concept of local church affiliation in the direction of the more cultural gathered-congregation concept, accommodating itself to members' cultural values. Music, architecture, preaching, liturgy, and sexual orientation are thus joining language and national origin as principles of intra-Catholic differentiation (Warner 1994a; Christiano 1991). The historian Jay Dolan indicates that Catholic de facto congregationalism has deep roots in America. "The post-Vatican II era has rightly been called the age of the emerging laity, but history reminds us quite clearly that, even in the brief past of Catholic America, lay people at one time had a major responsibility for the growth and development of the local church" (Dolan 1985, 192; see also Smith 1971).

The normative congregationalism of Judaism has long facilitated adaptability, and at the present time it is women who are causing the greatest changes in that ancient tradition by claiming professional opportunities as cantors and rabbis and demanding that they ought to be counted as members of the minyan for prayer. The resulting adaptations include ordination for women in Reform and Conservative branches, the synagogue reform movement known as Egalitarian Minyan, and the house-based groups known as Havurot (Wertheimer 1989, 96, 104, 129–134, 136, 141, 154–157; Prell 1989). Beginning in the middle of the nineteenth century, an earlier congregationally based innovation was mixed gender, or "family," seating (Sarna 1987).

Congregational patterns seem to be emerging among non-Christian religious groups. Among immigrant Muslims, the mosque, established in Islamic countries as a place for prayer, has become an educational and service center to meet the needs of the Muslim community—a congregation, in other words—with adult classes, potlucks, and coffee hours. The imam, who, according to Sunni Islamic practice, is simply the prayer leader, has become in America a religious professional who celebrates marriages, counsels families, visits the sick, conducts funerals, and represents his people among the local clergy, modeling himself in the process on pastors, priests, and rabbis (for details, see Chazanov 1991; Denny 1987; Fenton 1988, 187–197; Haddad and Lummis 1987; Waugh 1992; see also Kashima 1977 on Japanese-origin Buddhists and Fenton 1988 on Hindus).

The adaptability of religion in the United States does not mimic liberal democracy or necessarily bring "progress." American religious institutions respond to both consumer demands and supplier initiatives. Today, many lay people make claims in the name of democratic and, increasingly, feminist values that are discovered by insiders to reside in the religious tradition itself; one result is such innovations as Egalitarian Minyan. But other democratic tendencies tend to be theologically conservative: the Christian charismatic movement, in which individuals feel themselves to be directly in touch with the deity, and evangelicalism, whose tradition of biblical literalism and literacy mean that the ultimate charter of the group is at the disposal of any member (McGuire 1982; Neitz 1987; Warner 1988a; Bender 1991). Market incentives induce religious elites to maximize the appeal of their organizations to potential constituencies, and one result is entrepreneurial but authoritarian religious institutions—for example, fundamentalist missions to Hispanics (e.g., Montoya 1987) and Buddhist centers catering to European American converts (Fields 1991, 1992; Preston 1988).

While in medieval Europe there was only one "the" Church, in America religion has taken many forms, denominational and congregational among them.

Since the new paradigm recognizes the historic popularity of American religion, it is more generous than the old paradigm in crediting such forms as genuinely religious.

V. Individual and Group Empowerment

The older paradigm expects religion to be increasingly privatized and invisible when it is not generalized (see Sec. I). Moreover, those most interested in promoting social change, scholars affiliated with the Left, have been long disinclined to think that religion could play a positive role from the point of view of their values (Hannigan 1991, 317–318; Fields 1982). Thus, the role of religion in social change has been widely overlooked.

Yet religious involvement in the United States has historically been one way that groups have improved their lot. The 1960s would not have been the same without American churches, and Aldon Morris (1984, 4) reminds us that "the black church functioned as the institutional center of the modern civil rights movement." Nor would the outspoken moral conservatism of the 1980s have been the same without churches. The Moral Majority was mobilized by entrepreneurial pastors of local churches, largely independent Baptists, who represented not an establishment, but an insurgency (Liebman 1983, 72; see also Guth 1983; Ammerman 1990). But moral conservatives are not the only recent players, since Sanctuary, the movement challenging U.S. immigration policies toward Central American refugees, is also "firmly rooted in religious groups" (Wiltfang and McAdam 1991, 1003; see also Matters 1992).

Remarkably, the gay liberation movement is itself a practitioner of the art of church-based mobilization. Troy Perry, some of his allies in the gay rights movement, and his severest conservative critics all credit the Metropolitan Community Church with being the organizational center of the attempt to legitimate gay culture in the United States (Perry and Swicegood 1990, chaps. 9–10; Humphreys 1972, 149–153; Rueda 1982, 270–296). Dennis Altman, a radical theoretician of the gay movement, observes that "in many places the church is the only form of the gay movement that exists," and he characterizes Perry as "perhaps the most charismatic leader yet produced by the American gay movement" (Altman 1982, 123, 27).

That churches can play this empowering role is due in part to the pluralism that Christian ethicists deplore and the old paradigm misconstrues, which is embodied in the widely cited observation that eleven o'clock on Sunday morning is the most segregated hour of American life. The obverse of this unpleasant truth is that any group can have its own church. Churches, synagogues, mosques, and the like, as human institutions dedicated to spiritual matters, also inherently have access to the worldly; they combine the symbolic and the material, the cultural and the structural, group morale and social networks. Insofar as a subordinated group requires for its emancipation access to financial and social resources, churches in the United States are a convenient and legitimate means of organization, and in some cases—the classic example may be found among African Americans—they may be the only such means available. "Churches provided the [civil rights] movement with an organized mass base; a leadership of clergymen largely economically independent of the larger white society and skilled in the art of managing people and resources; an institutionalized financial base through which protest was financed; and meeting places where the masses planned tactics and strategies and collectively committed themselves to the struggle" (Morris 1984, 4). Jesse Jackson recently testified that "church was like my laboratory, my first actual public stage, where I began to develop and practice my speaking powers" (as quoted in Frady 1992, 59). Empowerment is partly a function of pluralistic social organization.

But the special potency of religious institutions comes from answers they give to a group's need for faith in the justice of its cause and the inevitability of triumph. Such faith depends on the conviction, misleadingly called "otherworldliness," of the existence of a religious reality. If one assumes a sacred/secular dichotomy, supernatural beliefs can seem irrelevant to this-worldly action at best, antagonistic at worst (cf. Fields 1982; Hannigan 1991). In this view, shared by many social scientists and some liberation theologians, the most progressive religions must be the most demythologized; thus, for their own good, oppressed groups must slough off their superstitions. But on the model of the African American experience, where sacred and secular are inextricable, the new paradigm expects otherwise. To insist that rebels be iconoclasts is to deprive them of one source of their courage.

Eric Lincoln and Lawrence Mamiya state, in their recent comprehensive study of the black church, that "other-worldly religious transcendence can be related dialectically to the motivation, discipline, and courage needed for this-worldly political action" (Lincoln and Mamiya 1990, 234). Based on a textual analysis of spoken sermons, Bruce Rosenberg writes that African American preachers know that there are "sacred texts that cannot be altered. . . . David must always slay Goliath, Christ is always the Son of God, and always in the beginning God makes the heaven and the earth" (Rosenberg 1988, 145). Pastor James Henry Harris adds: "Black folk expect the preacher to reassure them of God's power, not to question or doubt it. They expect the pastor to help them cope with joblessness, poverty and discrimination by transforming their despair into hope" (Harris 1990, 599). As Garry Wills puts it: "Hope welling up from the darkest places remains the miracle of African American Christianity" (Wills 1990, 204). Thus numerous empirical studies attest that the black church is historically *both* theologically conservative *and* a resource for social change; it contributes to *both* group solidarity *and* personal well-being (Ellison 1991). African Americans who leave the church in disgust in effect distance themselves from the black community and its struggle as much as from religion (Sherkat and Ellison 1991).

Other communities have manifested the power of combining autonomous organization with theologically conservative beliefs and practices. Dwight Billings's theory of "religion as opposition" argues that among Appalachian coal miners in

Holiness and Baptist congregations independent of company control, "the repetition of collective symbols and their ritualized expression in sermons, prayers, and group singing helped to sustain miners' commitment to the sacred cause of unionism and solidarity" (Billings 1990, 20). By segregating themselves into a denomination, the members of the Metropolitan Community Church are able both to organize their own ministries and to celebrate Troy Perry's Pentecostally inspired conviction that he was created gay by a beneficent personal God (Perry 1972, III; Perry and Swicegood 1990, 30; Warner 1989b). Although the analyst must in each case elucidate the mechanisms by which supernatural religion facilitates social strength, experience teaches us to look for such a link.

Thus it is to be expected that the empowerment functions of religion are latent. At an individual level, those who seek well-being in religion tend not to find it; those who gain well-being from religion are not those who seek it (Althauser 1990). At a communal level, the New Religious Right of the early 1980s harnessed individual religious convictions to political ends, but the process did not work in the other direction, that is, individual political ends did not take religious forms. Those who watched the politicized TV preachers were more interested in their religious than their political messages (Shupe and Stacey 1982). Something similar is true of African American religion: Wilcox and Gomez (1990) argue on the basis of data from the 1979–1980 National Survey of Black Americans that the significant effect of religion on political participation and political attitudes is indirect and is mediated through the contribution of religion to group identification. In other words, political empowerment appears to be a by-product of religion, not its manifest goal (see also Sherkat and Ellison 1991).

Therefore, although we can notice stirrings of collective public participation stemming from the religious institutions of new immigrants in the United States, it would be grossly premature to test the political empowerment hypothesis on their current level of outspokenness. As Lincoln and Mamiya observe, in reference to the black church and political action: "Both forms of protest and electoral politics are only made possible by the *prior* foundation of community building activity" (1990, 199; emphasis added). Studies of conservative Protestants, who seemed to have emerged out of nowhere in the 1970s (cf. Herberg 1960, 123), reveal that their recent vociferousness was preceded by generations of institution building away from the attention of the broader public (Brereton 1991; Carpenter 1980; Marsden 1987).

The role of religious organizations for the empowerment of women presents a rich test case for the new paradigm. Given the role of religion in the construction and maintenance of patriarchy, it is no surprise that, with few exceptions, the more an American woman identifies with feminism, the less she identifies with organized religion (Wuthnow 1988, 226–230). Yet it is also true that, by nearly any measure, American women are more involved in religion than are their male counterparts—more likely than men to attend church, to read the Bible, to pray, to say that religion is salient to their lives, and less likely to profess nonbelief

(Wuthnow 1988; Wuthnow and Lehrman 1990). Some theoretical approaches see women's religiosity as so much false consciousness, an extension of patriarchal control. Those oriented to the new paradigm, however, are inclined to agree with feminist theories that women's cultures—whether or not feminist (Cott 1989)—represent women's attempts to make the best of their historical circumstances (Kandiyoti 1988), and they have learned to look to U.S. social history for evidence.

The mid-nineteenth-century social movement for "moral reform," arguably the first public social space for American women as a whole and, in turn, the organizational matrix out of which first-wave feminism emerged, was a direct outgrowth of the evangelical Second Great Awakening. During that era, roughly the first third of the nineteenth century in the United States, the modern gender order of "separate spheres" was developed, which in turn ruled relations between the sexes until only a generation ago.[8] As social organization in the years between the Revolution and the Civil War moved away from home-centered production toward the differentiation of industrial production and family consumption, the vocational education of young men no longer took place in apprenticeships at their fathers' sides, and American Protestant women joined with their pastors to construct an essentialist doctrine of womanhood as custodian of culture and protector of morality. Business and politics were men's business, but culture and morality were spheres belonging to women. Seeing that their interests and values were distinct from those of men, women soon came together in local, regional, and national associations for the promotion of "moral reform." Insisting that home was woman's place, they did not limit woman's place to the home but also opened a public arena of women's action (Cott 1977; Ryan 1979, 1981; Epstein 1981; Smith-Rosenberg 1985).

The lesson for the new paradigm is pointed. The very pluralism of American religion that gives it power to promote group solidarity also makes it the more likely that the voices of those subordinated within the group are silenced. If the religious community simply mirrors the local patriarchy (or the local gerontocracy), women (or young people) will have reason to escape it (Gilkes 1985; Burdick 1990; Billings 1990). Yet insofar as the relationship between domestic and religious institutions is orthogonal—that is to say as along as there is a structural church-family differentiation—"institutional contradiction" (Friedland and Alford 1981) can allow women to play one patriarchal institution against another. Women's associations provide such differentiation. "Using religion to develop extra-domestic roles, [women] created powerful local and nationwide single-sex organizations expressive of women's particular angers, anxieties, and demands" (Smith-Rosenberg 1985, 142).

Successors to moral reform organizations provided avenues of women's influence in mainline Protestantism until a generation ago, when, in a program of gender desegregation and ecumenism, they were absorbed into denominational agencies (Brereton 1989) at about the same time that openings accelerated for women in seminary education and mainline Protestant and liberal Jewish ordination (Carroll,

Hargrove, and Lummis 1983; Wertheimer 1989, 104, 130–134, 141). Thus, although ordained women's career opportunities are not the equal of men's, it is probably no accident that among Presbyterians, Episcopalians, and Jews, there is no inverse correlation between feminist consciousness and women's religious participation (Wuthnow 1988, 229–230).

Yet with only the minimal organizational leverage of being extra-familial, religion has long provided moral leverage to American women when other power resources are lacking. Among Catholics in the years between the depression and the 1960s, devotion to Saint Jude led women to feel "empowered in new ways. They broke off relationships with 'mean' boyfriends [and] rejected unwanted medical treatments" (Orsi 1991, 159; see also McGuire 1982, 179–182; Neitz 1990, 101–104). Among Pentecostals in rural Missouri, "religious life provided the *only* opportunity for young girls to leave home and travel. . . . Young girls who could go virtually nowhere else could hardly wait to don their best dresses and hurry down to the tent" (Lawless 1988, 73, 75; see also Lawless 1983). In today's neoevangelical and charismatic movements, women often convert before their husbands do; in this they are like their sisters of the Second Great Awakening and today's Latin American evangelicals, who gain the moral leverage that comes with entering the religious community of their own volition (Warner 1988a: 118–127, 143–145, 292–293; Ryan 1981; Brusco 1986). Precisely because of the power of its God, Pentecostalism gives some women opportunities as religious entrepreneurs (Lawless 1988; Kwilecki 1987).

Women committed to marriage and motherhood find moral support and interpersonal leverage in many evangelical and charismatic fellowships, in which relational values and androgynous images of God are increasingly endorsed (Hunter and Stehlin 1987; Neitz 1987, 149–150). In a modern Orthodox synagogue, Lynn Davidman observed that "one of the aspects of family life in this Orthodox community that was highlighted by several women was that the men seemed to be involved in child care, both within the synagogue and outside of it" (Davidman 1991, 117). On the basis of field research with "postfeminist" converts to evangelicalism, Stacey and Gerard (1990, 111–112) write that such women's "turn to evangelicalism represents . . . a strategy that refuses to forfeit, and even builds upon, the feminist critique of men and the 'traditional' family," and provides them with "effective strategies for reshaping husbands in their own image."

Proponents of both the newer paradigm (Iannaccone and Miles 1990) and the older one (Hunter and Stehlin 1987) have recognized that much of contemporary conservative religion in the United States, particularly evangelicalism and neo-Pentecostalism, has been affected by feminism, which indeed is a fact that the public needs to know (see Stacey 1990). But this fact can be interpreted as representing the capitulation of religion to secular currents—as ultraconservatives, radicals, and the older paradigm are inclined to see it—or as a mobilization of latent feminist currents in religion itself—a view consistent with much recent historical research. For example, the stringent patriarchy of contemporary

Protestant fundamentalism, which the new evangelicals are relaxing, the dictum that no woman may hold authority over any man, far from being "traditional" was itself a turn-of-the-century reaction against feminist currents in nineteenth-century evangelicalism (Caldwell 1991; Barfoot and Sheppard 1980; Zikmund 1979).

Ideological leverage inheres in religion (Fields 1982). Jewish and Christian feminists have good reason to see adumbrations of their ideals lying near the heart of the traditions they wish to alter, for example, in the Gospel testimonies that the Resurrection was first revealed to Jesus' female disciples. The affinity of Korean Americans for Christianity, and more particularly for Presbyterianism, is partly due to the heroic role played by Presbyterian missionaries and converts in Korea's turn-of-the-century struggle against Japanese colonialism (Kitano and Daniels 1988, 113–114). Troy Perry's moment of inspiration to establish the Metropolitan Community Church came when he realized that the God whom he had not ceased to love and fear wanted Perry to take his gospel of innate homosexuality into the gay community (Perry 1972, 8; Perry and Swicegood 1990, 30).

VI. The "New" Voluntarism

The preceding four sections have developed four distinctive and perennial aspects of American religion that, under different rubrics, have received the attention of contemporary researchers and that, considered theoretically, pose an alternative to the older paradigm. With appropriate complications and qualifications, religion in the United States is and has long been (a) disestablished, (b) culturally pluralistic, (c) structurally adaptable, and (d) empowering. My final topic is the recent (i.e., post-1960s) complex of individualized religious identification—including conversion to new religious identities and assertive embrace of old ones, as well as apostasy on a wide scale—that I will follow Roof and McKinney (1987) in referring to as "the new voluntarism."[9] The contemporary scene seems sufficiently discontinuous with the patterns described more than a generation ago by Herberg (1960) to raise the question whether the American institutional complex portrayed in this article persists or whether, as the older paradigm would have it, we are witnessing the latest stage of "secularization."

Consider these figures: between one-third and one-half of those responding to polls have changed denominations in their lives, some of them only to switch back to the affiliation of their youth, more to an adjoining denomination, but many to religious disaffiliation (Hadaway and Marler 1991a; Roof and McKinney 1987, 165). One-fifth of those raised Catholic no longer identify with that faith, and they include an estimated one million Hispanics who have gone over to Protestantism within the past fifteen years (Greeley 1990, 120). The proportion of Americans claiming no religious preference (the people sociologists of religion call "nones") has jumped from 2–3 percent a generation ago to 7–9 percent today. Moreover, with the exception of African Americans, nones do not as a whole occupy alienated or marginal statuses in U.S. society (Glenn 1987; Roof and McKinney

1987, 99; Kosmin, Keysar, and Lerer 1991). Probably as radical as switching—and certainly as unsettling to loved ones—are such surprises as the Pentecostal spirit baptism of lifelong devoted Catholics (Neitz 1987), born-again evangelicalism among mainline Protestants (Warner 1988a), and the "return" of nominal Jews to an orthodoxy they had never before embraced (Davidman 1991; Kaufman 1991).

The voluntarism is attitudinal as well. Gallup (1988, 3) reports that 80 percent of Americans agree that the individual "should arrive at his or her religious beliefs independent of any church or synagogue" (see also Roof and McKinney 1987, 57). Roof (1993) and his associates have tracked accounts of spiritual trajectories of "baby boomers" away from and back toward conventional religion and many syncretic alternatives. Phillip Hammond (1988, 5) speaks of a growing shift from "collective-expressive" church membership in the past to "individual-expressive" religious involvement—voluntary and independent of other social ties—today (see also Hammond 1992). Samuel Heilman (1990, 195) writes that "for the contemporary Jew, corporate identity diminishes and ascription gives way to achievement and autonomy as the most powerful determinants of identity." Elsewhere I have written that evangelical Protestantism upholds an ethic of achieved rather than ascribed recruitment (Warner 1988a: 52–53, 72, 292–293). It is true by definition that membership in such a new denomination as the Metropolitan Community Church is an achieved status; this is true as well for the Vineyard, one of several conservative Christian protodenominations emerging out of the late 1960s Jesus movement and appealing primarily to baby boomers (Perrin and Mauss 1991). These are inherently churches of converts.

In other words, both religious disaffiliation and religious conservatism benefit from "achieved" religiosity; the United States has seen both religious revival and apostasy (Chaves 1989; Roozen, McKinney, and Thompson 1990). Taken-for-granted, traditional religion is passé. Born-again, return-to-the-fold neotraditional religion is all the rage.

The authors of *Habits of the Heart* (Bellah et al. 1985) have most eloquently lamented these individualistic trends. Although they recognize that Americans, no matter how individualistic, seek out like-minded others, they fear that the resulting associations are only "lifestyle enclaves," a term they intend to connote shallowness and mutual narcissism. "When we hear such phrases as 'the gay community' or 'the Japanese-American community,' we need to know a great deal before we can decide the degree to which they are genuine communities and the degree to which they are lifestyle enclaves" (74–75). These authors worry about a culture that encourages Americans "to choose the groups with which [they] want to identify" (154), and they propose instead, in the spirit of the older paradigm, that "there is a givenness about the community and the tradition. They are not normally a matter of individual choice" (227).

I do not wish to dismiss the concerns of Bellah and his colleagues, but there is considerable evidence that religious switchers are morally serious. Kristin Luker reports that nearly 20 percent of the pro-life activists in her study of the abortion controversy were "converts to Catholicism, people who have actively chosen to follow a given religious faith, in striking contrast to the pro-choice people, who have actively chosen not to follow any" (Luker 1984, 196). Evidence that FitzGerald's social centrifuge contributes to moral coherence is presented in Roof and McKinney's analysis of 1972–1984 General Social Survey data, which indicates that Protestants' inveterate switching of denominations is increasingly motivated by moral culture instead of socioeconomic status. Those shifting their allegiance to the liberal Protestant denominations like the Episcopal and the Presbyterian churches are more liberal on matters of women's rights and racial justice than those raised in these communities, while those gravitating to conservative bodies like the Southern Baptists and the Nazarenes are accentuating those bodies' conservatism on sexual morality (Roof and McKinney 1987, 218, 220, 222).[10] Switching is decreasingly likely to mirror upward social mobility and to represent instead genuine religious change; "switchers are, in a very real sense, converts" (Hadaway and Marler 1991, 22). Protestant switching is not entropic (Sullins 1992).

Switching includes the disaffiliation of dropouts to be sure, but for those who shift from one faith community to another it also means greater religious involvement—contributing money to the church, frequent prayer and Bible reading, being "born again," being in agreement with the moral culture of their newfound reference group, searching for more meaning in religious participation (Roof and McKinney 1987; Hadaway and Marler 1991a; Mauss and Perrin 1991). Conservative churches that expect high levels of involvement are organizational beneficiaries of such switching patterns (Mauss and Perrin 1991; Roof and McKinney 1987, 177–179), but liberal churches that take strong stands and make strong demands can attract newcomers as well (Matters 1992; Wiltfang and McAdam 1991).

We also know that irreligion in the United States replicates itself across generations less effectively than active religious preference. Though the proportion of "nones" has roughly tripled since the 1950s, nones tend to generate additional nones less efficiently than Protestants, Catholics, and Jews do their own kind (Roof and McKinney 1987, 169). This may be in part because, in a religious society such as ours, nones are surrounded more by religion than by irreligion. Men are more likely to lack religion than women, but religiously indifferent fathers are particularly poor in passing on their indifference to their offspring. Moreover, the *rate* of disaffiliation is declining. Disaffiliation was common in the young adulthood of baby boomers but is less so more recently (Hadaway and Marler 1991a). Religion is still a prime idiom by which Americans identify themselves.

Yet religion need not represent something in which people are primordially rooted. Religious affiliation in the United States is not tribal. The freedom of Americans to choose with whom they will congregate in service of their most basic values is a freedom not to "pass" as biological kin but to partake as full legatees of cultural traditions that add depth and richness to the association. Literate converts to a religion of the book have immediate access to its communal memory. The religious groups that seem to work best in cosmopolitan America are those that recognize the mobility of their members and bring them into contact with great cultural traditions by incessantly and elaborately recounting the founding narrative (Warner 1988a, chap. 9).

It is helpful in this regard to think of religion in the United States as being subject to the decoupling of culture and social structure (Bell 1976). Religiously relevant statuses are increasingly random with respect to the standard categories of social structure (Caplow 1985; Hammond 1992; Hadaway and Marler 1991a). Thus the new paradigm is not surprised by news of people with modern intellectual resources who reject secularity in favor of "Bible-based" Christianity and "observant" Judaism. Susan Rose (1987, 255) tells of women in an upstate New York religious commune who "knowingly and willingly stepped down and relinquished their authority and power" because they valued relationships with men. Nancy Ammerman (1987, 26–31, 72–102) studied a fundamentalist church in New England whose members were demographically and educationally clustered slightly on the more privileged side of the surrounding middle-class suburb but who withdrew morally from what they felt to be an alien world. Lynn Davidman (1991, chap. 5) spent time with converts to Orthodox Judaism in Manhattan— young, educated, well-employed women who found in traditional religion a legitimation for the families they hoped to create. In each of these studies, religious commitments helped these people set and maintain priorities in a time of perceived bewildering choice.

Has American religion become rootless, evanescent, or arbitrary? No. The breakdown of ascription may be welcomed when, like members of the Metropolitan Community Church, its beneficiaries are convinced that they have been freed to acknowledge their true nature. What the new religious voluntarism amounts to is a centrifugal process, sorting elemental qualities on the basis of which identities are constructed. The evangelical Presbyterians I met in Mendocino, California, had in common not their denominational or educational backgrounds but their histories as migrants to an idealized small town. Their pastor's preaching united their ideological neoparochialism with the theology he had learned in seminary so as to give their common narrative deep resonance (Warner 1988a: 86–87, 205–208). In this way, the breakdown of ascriptive ties to religion can enhance, rather than reduce, the elemental nature that believers attribute to their experiences. From this point of view, social ascription that denies one's true being is seen as arbitrary, while a newfound religion is self-affirming.

I do not wish to overestimate either the extent or the appeal of religious mobility, or to ignore the pain that often accompanies it. Once having chosen a religious home, one is supposed to be and likely to be loyal, and it is probably true that someone dissatisfied with her or his church is as likely to turn away from churches altogether as to seek a church more conformable to personal needs, at least in the short run. There is a norm to the effect that shopping for religion is wrong, and talk of a "religious market" is highly offensive to many people, particularly when it suggests an instrumental attitude toward religion, or ecclesiastical social climbing. Such a norm is no doubt functional for the stability of religious organizations.

What facilitates religious mobility despite such a norm and despite investments in religious capital (Iannaccone 1990) are several social facts, including aggressive proselytization; the emphasis on loyalty to God over institutions that is part of the evangelical—and hence mainline Protestant—tradition; members' intermittent involvement, such that some who are formally church members may not feel committed and therefore not disloyal when they leave; life-cycle events such as marriage, particularly religious intermarriage; children, for whom one may want to choose an appropriate Sunday school; and geographic mobility. Geographic mobility requires people to choose a church. Since denominations are not homogeneous, the church of one's former denomination in the new location may not "feel right." Denominations themselves change, and the switcher may well perceive that it is not she or he who left the fold.

More research is needed on the question whether rates of religious mobility have recently increased over those prevalent in the 1950s, as has been argued by Roof and McKinney (1987) among others. Yet it should be borne in mind that religious individualism and denominational switching characterized earlier periods of U.S. history, particularly the "awakenings" that took place around 1800–1830 and 1890–1920.[11] It was in the former period that the numerical dominance of what later came to be called the liberal Protestant denominations was eclipsed by the surge of the evangelical Methodists and Baptists. The latter period saw the rise of the Holiness, Pentecostal, and fundamentalist movements, the recent visibility of which has so greatly altered the profile of late twentieth-century U.S. religion.

Like the present, these were times of massive geographical and social mobility, when individuals could not effectively follow in the footsteps of their parents but had to "start over" for themselves (FitzGerald 1986, 383–414; see Ryan 1981 for the earlier period and Thomas 1989 for the later). Large numbers heeded the messages of religious innovators, and from these times of intense, revivalistic competition new institutions were born, institutions with the potential to solidify into powerful organizations and even rigid bureaucracies (Pritchard 1984; Barfoot and Sheppard 1980; Poloma 1989). Before entertaining the hypothesis that a new religious order prevails in the United States, it is worthwhile to mine the analogies between the present and the American past.

Such an analogy occurred to the anthropologist Riv-Ellen Prell as she looked back on her study of an early 1970s egalitarian Minyan in Los Angeles. Prell (1989, 27) "came to understand the strong parallels between Minyan members and their parents' generation's constructions of Judaism." "I was struck," she writes, "by what these parallels revealed about American religion, namely that religion had been voluntaristic in America ever since immigrants arrived. What appeared, for example, as a counterculture rebellion had its roots deep in immigrants' attempts to maintain their Judaism within American society."

Conclusion: the New Paradigm and the Agenda of the Field

It is conventional to conclude a paper with a call for more research, but this article—both a research review and a proposal—is such a call. I have highlighted recent work of many scholars, interpreting their findings as only loosely bound (if at all) to the older paradigm. My proposal claims that recent work is more compellingly framed in terms of the newer paradigm. The nascent paradigm itself is the self-conscious project of only a few scholars (without anyone's permission having been asked, it is reasonable in this connection to name Theodore Caplow, Roger Finke, Andrew Greeley, Nathan Hatch, Laurence Iannaccone, Mary Jo Neitz, Daniel Olson, and Rodney Stark), and they do not form a solidary group but a loose school of thought with a common focus on the distinctive institutional parameters of the U.S. religious system—particularly the combination of disestablishment and institutional vitality—as the analytic norm for the study of religion.

Some scholars who are aware of the theoretical ambitions of the new paradigm have spoken out in opposition to it (e.g., Lechner 1991; Breault 1989a), but most scholars in the field are uninvolved in the debate. Yet the claim made here is that, because so much recent research focuses in fact on U.S. religious institutions, there is an immanent direction to the research programs even of those not involved in debates over paradigms. Progress in that direction could be facilitated if, in the work of such persons, the presuppositions of the new paradigm were substituted for the old. If that substitution were widespread, several consequences would ensue:

Students of religious communities and subcultures would focus more on the building of religious institutions and the role of religion in social mobilization and relatively less on the erection and maintenance of plausibility structures.

Students of religious organization would focus as much on the rise of new religious organizations (e.g., Perrin and Mauss 1991) as on the decline of old ones (e.g., Hoge and Roozen 1979), even though data would be intrinsically more difficult to find; those who focus on individuals and organizations would analyze entrepreneurial (Kwilecki 1987; Harrell 1985; Stout 1991) as well as bureaucratic (Chaves 1991a) and professional (Charlton 1978; Carroll, Hargrove, and Lummis 1983) religious careers.

Students of social change would investigate the ways in which religion alternatively facilitates and inhibits collective action, but they would extend their time horizon for these processes to the span of a generation and complicate their models to include indirect effects of group solidarity.

Students of the intersection of biography and social history would assume that individual religious affiliation is not an ascriptive identity set for life but something that can be affirmed and later denied, or vice versa.

The paradigm debate does not crucially impinge on all areas of research in the field; in particular, studies of religious cultures and religious social psychology are less centrally implicated in a paradigm shift whose level of analysis is organizational. Nonetheless it is a radical decision to choose to focus on the European experience of religious monopoly or on the American case of religious cacophony as the analytic norm, or paradigmatic situation, of religion.

Researchers in the field agree that sociology of religion should not be sealed off from the rest of sociology. The present article is based on the assumption that the field contributes most when it recognizes that its empirical field constitutes a central institutional sphere of U.S. society. The nonexclusive strategy taken here has been to codify a paradigm adequate to the best-documented case—the United States—both so that researchers on that case can better understand their findings and so that the parameters of the case itself can be identified. Thus there has just begun one critical line of research that attempts to specify the determinants of the American religious system. Is the key to American religious vitality given in Tocqueville's analysis of the historically apolitical stance of most U.S. religious groups, the notion that American religion has largely stayed out of politics (see, e.g., Caplow 1985)? Or is religious pluralism the key, as Finke and Stark (1988) would have it, the sheer variety of religious choices? Or is it deregulation, the lack of either subsidy or state oversight of religious organizations (see Greeley 1989, 126–127; Iannaccone 1991; Chaves and Cann 1992)? Comparative institutional research, unburdened of the secularization expectations of the older paradigm, will serve to demystify the concept of American exceptionalism (Tiryakian 1991). Until that has been accomplished, the exception may well be taken as the rule.

NOTES

Research for this article began when I was a visiting member of the Institute for Advanced Study, Princeton, New Jersey. Earlier formulations were presented to audiences at the Institute in October 1988, Princeton Theological Seminary in February 1989, a joint session of the American Sociological Association and Association for the Sociology of Religion in San Francisco in August 1989, the Humanities Research Forum and Office of Social Science Research of the University of Illinois at Chicago in January 1990, the department of sociology at Northwestern University in October 1991, and Swarthmore College in November 1991. I am indebted to members of these audiences for their reactions, to numerous colleagues for advice and commentary, and to the Institute for Advanced Study, the Rockefeller Foundation, the National Endowment for the Humanities, the University of Illinois at Chicago, and Northwestern University for support. Rather than implicate by name any of the many individuals who have commented on previous drafts and assisted with this one, I wish to express my deep appreciation to all of them, as well as to four referees for the *American Journal of Sociology*.

1. Peter Berger has recently acknowledged (1986, 226–227) that his early work erred in supposing that modernity in the United States must lead to an erosion of communal, including religious, life. But it is his earlier work that is still influential in the field.

2. It is noteworthy that reports of individual respondents (poll data) yield higher rates of church membership than do ecclesiastical reports (roll data) for the high-status liberal Protestant denominations and lower rates for Roman Catholicism. Thus, many (and in the case of Presbyterians, most) of those who claim in sample surveys to be Protestant church members evidently do not comply with the denominations' membership requirements (e.g., regular attendance and contributions) but instead evidently feel a residual or anticipatory identification with the church community as a reference group. Many of those who claim to be church members are thus said to be effectively "unchurched" (Gallup 1988), thereby explaining the 10 percent discrepancy between poll data church membership and the corresponding roll data figure. The implications of these discrepancies represent a research frontier in the field (see Marcum 1990; Roof and McKinney 1987, 177–179; Hadaway and Marler 1991b).

3. In order to account for recent downturns in religion, some analysts seem to posit that modernity arrived in the United States only in the 1960s, which, in effect, abandons the secularization *paradigm* for a *finding* of "secularization" over a two-decade period (cf. Chaves 1991c, 502). Much more promising from the point of view of the new paradigm is to focus on such specific factors as governmental activity (Wuthnow and Nass 1988) and family formation (Chaves 1991c) as variables affecting church membership and attendance. Meanwhile, overall church attendance has been remarkably stable for the last two decades (Hout and Greeley 1987; Greeley 1989; Chaves 1989, 1991c; Firebaugh and Harley 1991) and specifically Protestant church attendance for the last half century.

4. Butler's "book is path-breaking and simply has no competitor in treating the full scope of religious history in early America" (Hatch on the dust jacket of Butler's book); Hatch's "deeply researched, superbly written book goes to the very heart of the American religious and cultural development" (Butler on the dust jacket of Hatch's book).

5. Butler (1990, 297, 345) cites the work of Stark and Finke (1988; Finke and Stark 1986), and Hatch (1989, 298) cites that of Caplow (1985).

6. Nor do all theorists assume religious wants to be exogenous in the manner of pure microeconomics (cf. Friedland and Alford 1991, 232–235). On the contrary, it seems to be a widespread notion among new paradigm exponents that Americans' high level of religious interest is due in part to the historic vigor of religious organizations in this country (Iannaccone 1991, 161–162). A pathbreaking article by Gary Becker and Kevin Murphy (1988, 675) begins with an epigram from Shakespeare, "Use doth breed a habit," and argues that addictions, which are the dependent variable, "require *interaction* between a person and a good" (694; emphasis added).

7. Keeley (1991) has pointed out that large-scale de facto migration of Mexican laborers continued from 1942 to 1964 through the bracero program. Moreover, until 1946, the

Philippines were a U.S. possession, and substantial numbers of Filipinos came as U.S. nationals in the 1920s (Kitano and Daniels 1988, 78–83). The religious institutions of both groups—Mexican Americans and Filipino Americans—have received astonishingly little scholarly attention.

8. The nuclear family with a division of labor into men's and women's spheres is historically "modern," not, despite the rhetoric of both reactionaries and feminists, "traditional" (see Stacey 1990, chap. 1).

9. The concept of "voluntarism," as used here, stands in the tradition of American religious studies rather than sociological theory. Sometimes called "voluntaryism" (Ahlstrom 1972, 382–383), the religious studies concept refers to the *concrete* institutional facts of separation of church and state and religious freedom in the postrevolutionary United States and the consequent need for churches to rely on persuasion rather than coercion for their support (Littel 1962; Mead 1963). Such "voluntarism," strange and remarkable to Europeans, "became a matter of course to Americans" (Rowe 1924, 53), and over time it evolved into the religious system portrayed here. The "voluntarism" of sociological theory, particularly associated with the early work of Talcott Parsons, concerns the *analytic* question of the categories needed for the analysis of individual action (Alexander 1982). Insofar as Parsons, himself raised a liberal Protestant, conceived modern social order to minimize coercion, the two concepts were no doubt related in his mind. Moreover, since the "new voluntarism" complex conceptualizes an additional, perhaps temporary, movement toward individualism in religion (referred to here later as a disjunction of culture and social structure), the phenomena it delimits are closer still (albeit not identical) to the theorists' concerns. The "new voluntarism" has also been called the "third disestablishment" (Roof and McKinney 1987; Hammond 1992).

10. Roof and McKinney (1987) measure mobility of identifiers, not members, across "families" of denominations, not denominations per se. Thus, for their research purposes, Presbyterians are the same as Episcopalians since both are "liberal Protestants," Lutherans and Methodists are alike "moderate Protestants," and Southern Baptists and Pentecostals are "conservative Protestants." The cultural sorting they map, therefore, is ambiguous with respect to the hypothesis of the declining significance of denominational identities, strictly speaking.

11. The dates are from McLoughlin 1978.

REFERENCES

(References to writings of the author are found in a separate listing at the back of the book.)

Ahlstrom, Sydney. 1972. *A Religious History of the American People.* New Haven, Conn.: Yale University Press.

Alexander, Jeffrey C. 1982. *Positivism, Presuppositions, and Current Controversies.* Vol. 1 of *Theoretical Logic in Sociology.* Berkeley and Los Angeles: University of California Press.

Althauser, Robert P. 1990. "Paradox in Popular Religion: The Limits of Instrumental Faith." *Social Forces* 69 (December): 585–602.

Altman, Dennis. 1982. *The Homosexualization of America.* New York: St. Martin's.

Ammerman, Nancy Tatom. 1987. *Bible Believers: Fundamentalists in the Modern World.* New Brunswick, N.J.: Rutgers University Press.

———. 1990. *Baptist Battles: Social Change and Religious Conflict in the Southern Baptist Convention.* New Brunswick, N.J.: Rutgers University Press.

Asian American Handbook. 1991. *Asian American Handbook.* Chicago: National Conference of Christians and Jews and Asian American Journalists Association.

Barfoot, Charles H., and Gerald T. Sheppard. 1980. "Prophetic vs. Priestly Religion: The Changing Role of Women Clergy in Classical Pentecostal Churches." *Review of Religious Research* 22 (September): 2–10.

Becker, Gary S., and Kevin M. Murphy. 1988. "A Theory of Rational Addiction." *Journal of Political Economy* 96 (August): 675–700.

Bell, Daniel. 1976. *The Cultural Contradictions of Capitalism.* New York: Basic.

Bellah, Robert N., Richard Madsen, William M. Sullivan, Ann Swidler, and Steven M. Tipton. 1985. *Habits of the Heart: Individualism and Commitment in American Life.* Berkeley and Los Angeles: University of California Press.

Bender, Courtney Jane. 1991. "A Radical Reformation: Mennonites in the Age of the Spirit." B.A. honors thesis. Department of Sociology and Anthropology, Swarthmore College, Swarthmore, Pennsylvania.

Berger, Peter L. 1961. *The Noise of Solemn Assemblies.* Garden City, N.Y.: Doubleday.

———. 1969. *The Sacred Canopy: Elements of a Sociological Theory of Religion.* Garden City, N.Y.: Anchor.

———. 1970. *A Rumor of Angels: Modern Society and the Rediscovery of the Supernatural.* Garden City, N.Y.: Anchor.

———. 1986. "Epilogue." In *Making Sense of Modern Times: Peter L. Berger and the Vision of Interpretive Sociology,* ed. James Davison Hunter and Stephen C. Ainlay, 221–235. London: Routledge and Kegan Paul.

Bilhartz, Terry D. 1986. *Urban Religion and the Second Great Awakening: Church and Society in Early National Baltimore.* Rutherford, N.J.: Fairleigh Dickinson University Press.

Billings, Dwight B. 1990. "Religion as Opposition: A Gramscian Analysis." *American Journal of Sociology* 96 (July): 1–31.

Blackburn, Anne. 1987. "The Evolution of Sinhalese Buddhist Identity: Reflections on Process." B.A. honors thesis, Department of Religion, Swarthmore College.

Blau, Judith R., Kent Redding, and Kenneth C. Land. 1991. "The Churching of America: Towards an Explanation of the Growth of U.S. Religious Participation, 1850–1930." Paper presented at annual meeting of the American Sociological Association, Cincinnati.

Bozorgmehr, Mehdi, Georges Sabagh, Ivan Light, and Claudia Der-Martirosian. 1990. "Sources of Ethnicity in an Ethnically Diverse Immigrant Group." Paper presented at annual meeting of the American Sociological Association, Washington, D.C.

Breault, Kevin D. 1989a. "New Evidence on Religious Pluralism, Urbanism, and Religious Participation." *American Sociological Review* 54 (December): 1048–1053.

———. 1989b. "Reply to Finke and Stark." *American Sociological Review* 54 (December): 1056–1059.

Brereton, Virginia Lieson. 1989. "United and Slighted: Women as Subordinated Insiders." In *Between the Times: The Travail of the Protestant Establishment in America, 1900–1960,* ed. W. R. Hutchison, 143–167. Cambridge: Cambridge University Press.

———. 1991. *Training God's Army: The American Bible School, 1880–1940.* Bloomington: Indiana University Press.

Brusco, Elizabeth. 1986. "Colombian Evangelicalism as a Strategic Form of Women's Collective Action." *Feminist Issues* 6 (Fall): 3–13.

Bull, Malcolm, and Keith Lockhart. 1989. *Seeking a Sanctuary: Seventh-Day Adventism and the American Dream.* San Francisco: Harper and Row.

Burdick, John. 1990. "Gossip and Secrecy: Women's Articulation of Domestic Conflict in Three Religions of Urban Brazil." *Sociological Analysis* 51 (Summer): 153–170.

Butler, Jon. 1990. *Awash in a Sea of Faith: The Christianization of the American People, 1550–1865.* Cambridge: Harvard University Press.

Caldwell, Thekla J. 1991. "Men, Women, and Revival: Gender in the Third Awakening, 1893–1918." Ph.D. diss., Department of History, University of Illinois at Chicago.

Caplow, Theodore. 1985. "Contrasting Trends in European and American Religion." *Sociological Analysis* 46 (Summer): 101–108.

Caplow, Theodore, Howard M. Bahr, and Bruce A. Chadwick. 1983. *All Faithful People: Change and Continuity in Middletown's Religion.* Minneapolis: University of Minnesota Press.

Carpenter, Joel A. 1980. "Fundamentalist Institutions and the Rise of Evangelical Protestantism, 1929–1940." *Church History* 49 (March): 62–75.

Carroll, Jackson W., Barbara Hargrove, and Adair T. Lummis. 1983. *Women of the Cloth: A New Opportunity for the Churches.* San Francisco: Harper and Row.

Carroll, Jackson W., and David A. Roozen. 1990. "Congregational Identities in the Presbyterian Church." *Review of Religious Research* 31 (June): 351–369.

Charlton, Joy C. 1978. "Women Entering the Ordained Ministry: Contradictions and Dilemmas of Status." Paper presented at annual meeting of the Society for the Scientific Study of Religion, Hartford, Conn.

Chaves, Mark. 1989. "Secularization *and* Religious Revival: Evidence from U.S. Church Attendance Rates, 1972–1986." *Journal for the Scientific Study of Religion* 28 (December): 464–477.

———. 1990. "Holding the Cohort: Reply to Hout and Greeley." *Journal for the Scientific Study of Religion* 29 (December): 525–530.

———. 1991a. "Segmentation in a Religious Labor Market." *Sociological Analysis* 52 (Summer): 143–158.

———. 1991b. "Secularization in the Twentieth Century United States." Ph.D. diss., Department of Sociology, Harvard University.

———. 1991c. "Family Structure and Protestant Church Attendance: The Sociological Basis of Cohort and Age Effects." *Journal for the Scientific Study of Religion* 30 (December): 501–514.

Chaves, Mark, and David E. Cann. 1992. "Regulation, Pluralism, and Religious Market Structure: Explaining Religious Vitality." *Rationality and Society* 4 (July): 272–290.

Chazanov, Mathis. 1991. "Mosque Has a U.S. Flavor." *Los Angeles Times* (January 25).

Christiano, Kevin J. 1987. *Religious Diversity and Social Change: American Cities, 1890–1906.* Cambridge: Cambridge University Press.

———. 1991. "The Church and the New Immigrants." In *Vatican II and U.S. Catholicism: Twenty-Five Years Later,* ed. Helen Rose Ebaugh, 169–186. Greenwich, Conn.: JAI.

Cooper, Lee R. 1974. "'Publish' or Perish: Negro Jehovah's Witness Adaptation in the Ghetto." In *Religious Movements in Contemporary America,* ed. Irving I. Zaretsky and Mark P. Leone, 700–721. Princeton, N.J.: Princeton University Press.

Cott, Nancy F. 1977. *The Bonds of Womanhood: 'Woman's Sphere' in New England, 1780–1835.* New Haven, Conn.: Yale University Press.

———. 1978. "Passionlessness: An Interpretation of Victorian Sexual Ideology, 1790–1850." *Signs* 4 (Winter): 219–236.

———. 1989. "What's in a Name? The Limits of 'Social Feminism'; or, Expanding the Vocabulary of Women's History." *Journal of American History* 76 (December): 809–829.

Curtis, James E., Edward G. Grabb, and Douglas E. Baer. 1992. "Voluntary Association Memberships in Fifteen Countries: A Comparative Analysis." *American Sociological Review* 57 (April): 139–152.

Dart, John. 1969. "A Church for Homosexuals." *Los Angeles Times* (December 8).

———. 1991. "Church for Gays Alters Mainline Religions' Views." *Los Angeles Times* (June 7).

Davidman, Lynn. 1991. *Tradition in a Rootless World: Women Turn to Orthodox Judaism.* Berkeley and Los Angeles: University of California Press.

Davis, James A., and Tom W. Smith. 1991. *General Social Surveys, 1972–1991: Cumulative Codebook.* National Opinion Research Center, Chicago. Distributed by Roper Public Opinion Research Center, Storrs, Conn.

Denny, Frederick. 1987. *Islam and the Muslim Community*. San Francisco: Harper and Row.

Diamond, Sara. 1989. *Spiritual Warfare: The Politics of the Christian Right*. Boston: South End Press.

Dolan, Jay. 1975. *The Immigrant Church: New York's Irish and German Catholics*. Baltimore: Johns Hopkins University Press.

————. 1978. *Catholic Revivalism: The American Experience, 1830–1900*. Notre Dame, Ind.: Notre Dame University Press.

————. 1985. *The American Catholic Experience: A History from Colonial Times to the Present*. Garden City, N.Y.: Doubleday.

————. 1988. "The Immigrants and Their Gods: A New Perspective in American Religious History." *Church History* 57 (March): 61–72.

Ellison, Christopher G. 1991. "Identification and Separatism: Religious Involvement and Racial Orientations among Black Americans." *Sociological Quarterly* 31 (Spring): 477–494.

Epstein, Barbara Leslie. 1981. *The Politics of Domesticity: Women, Evangelism, and Temperance in Nineteenth-Century America*. Middletown, Conn.: Wesleyan University Press.

Evans, Sara M., and Harry C. Boyte. 1986. *Free Spaces: The Sources of Democratic Change in America*. New York: Harper and Row.

Fenton, John Y. 1988. *Transplanting Religious Traditions: Asian Indians in America*. New York: Praeger.

Fields, Karen E. 1982. "Charismatic Religion as Popular Protest: The Ordinary and the Extraordinary in Social Movements." *Theory and Society* 11 (May): 321–361.

Fields, Rick. 1991. "The Changing of the Guard: Western Buddhism in the Eighties." *Tricycle: The Buddhist Review* 1 (Winter): 43–49.

————. 1992. *How the Swans Came to the Lake: A Narrative History of Buddhism in America*. 3d ed. Boston: Shambhala.

Finke, Roger. 1988. "The Coming of the Catholics, 1850–1926." Paper presented at annual meeting of the Society for the Scientific Study of Religion, Chicago.

————. 1989. "Demographics of Religious Participation: An Ecological Approach, 1850–1980." *Journal for the Scientific Study of Religion* 29 (March): 45–58.

————. 1990. "Religious Deregulation: Origins and Consequences." *Journal of Church and State* 32 (Summer): 609–626.

Finke, Roger, and Rodney Stark. 1986. "Turning Pews into People: Estimating nineteenth Century Church Membership." *Journal for the Scientific Study of Religion* 25 (June): 180–192.

————. 1988. "Religious Economies and Sacred Canopies: Religious Mobilization in American Cities." *American Sociological Review* 53 (February): 41–49.

————. 1989a. "How the Upstart Sects Won America: 1776–1850." *Journal for the Scientific Study of Religion* 28 (March): 27–44.

————. 1989b. "Evaluating the Evidence: Religious Economies and Sacred Canopies." *American Sociological Review* 54 (December): 1054–1056.

————. 1992. *The Churching of America, 1776–1990: Winners and Losers in Our Religious Economy*. New Brunswick, N.J.: Rutgers University Press.

Finney, Henry C. 1991. "American Zen's 'Japan Connection': A Critical Case Study of Zen Buddhism's Diffusion to the West." *Sociological Analysis* 52 (Winter): 379–396.

Firebaugh, Glenn, and Brian Harley. 1991. "Trends in U.S. Church Attendance: Secularization and Revival, or Merely Lifecycle Effects?" *Journal for the Scientific Study of Religion* 30 (December): 487–500.

Fischer, Claude S. 1982. *To Dwell among Friends: Personal Networks in Town and City*. Chicago: University of Chicago Press.

FitzGerald, Frances. 1986. *Cities on a Hill: A Journey Through Contemporary American Cultures*. New York: Simon and Schuster.

Fitzpatrick, Joseph, S. J. 1990. "Catholic Responses to Hispanic Newcomers." *Sociological Focus* 23 (August): 155–166.

Frady, Marshall. 1992. "Outsider, II—History Is upon Us." *New Yorker* 67 (February 10): 41–75.

Friedland, Roger, and Robert R. Alford. 1991. "Bringing Society Back In: Symbols, Practices, and Institutional Contradictions." In *The New Institutionalism in Organizational Analysis*, ed. Walter Powell and Paul J. DiMaggio, 232–263. Chicago: University of Chicago Press.

Furman, Frida Kerner. 1987. *Beyond Yiddishkeit: The Struggle for Jewish Identity in a Reform Synagogue.* Albany: State University of New York Press.

Gallup. 1988. *The Unchurched American—Ten Years Later.* Princeton, N.J.: Princeton Religious Research Center.

———. 1990. *Religion in America, 1990—Approaching the Year 2000.* Princeton, N.J.: Princeton Religious Research Center.

Gilkes, Cheryl Townsend. 1985. "'Together and in Harness': Women's Traditions in the Sanctified Church." *Signs* 10 (Summer): 678–699.

Glenn, Norval D. 1987. "The Trend in 'No Religion' Respondents to U.S. National Surveys, Late 1950s to Early 1980s." *Public Opinion Quarterly* 51 (Fall): 293–314.

Gold, Steven J. 1987. "Dealing with Frustration: A Study of Interactions Between Resettlement Staff and Refugees." In *People in Upheaval*, ed. Scott M. Morgan and Elizabeth Colson, 108–128. New York: Center for Migration Studies.

Gorman, E. Michael. 1980. "A New Light on Zion: A Study of Three Homosexual Religious Congregations in Urban America." Ph.D. diss., Department of Anthropology, University of Chicago.

Greeley, Andrew M. 1989. *Religious Change in America.* Cambridge: Harvard University Press.

———. 1990. *The Catholic Myth: The Behavior and Beliefs of America's Catholics.* New York: Scribner's.

Guth, James L. 1983. "Southern Baptist Clergy: Vanguard of the Christian Right?" In *The New Christian Right: Mobilization and Legitimation*, ed. Robert C. Liebman and Robert Wuthnow, 118–130. Hawthorne, N.Y.: Aldine.

Hackett, David G. 1988. "Sociology of Religion and American Religious History: Retrospect and Prospect." *Journal for the Scientific Study of Religion* 27 (December): 461–474.

Hadaway, C. Kirk. 1990. "The Impact of New Church Development on Southern Baptist Growth." *Review of Religious Research* 31 (June): 370–379.

Hadaway, C. Kirk, and Penny Long Marler. 1991a. "All in the Family: Religious Mobility in America." Paper presented at annual meeting of the Society for the Scientific Study of Religion, Pittsburgh.

———. 1991b. "The Unchurching of America: An Exploration and Interpretation of Post-War Religious Identification and Involvement Trends." Photocopy. United Church Board for Homeland Ministries, Cleveland.

Haddad, Yvonne Yazbeck, and Adair T. Lummis. 1987. *Islamic Values in the United States: A Comparative Study.* New York: Oxford University Press.

Hadden, Jeffrey K. 1969. *The Gathering Storm in the Churches.* Garden City, N.Y.: Doubleday.

———. 1987. "Toward Desacralizing Secularization Theory." *Social Forces* 65 (March): 587–611.

Hammond, Phillip E. 1986. "Religion in the Modern World." In *Making Sense of Modern Times: Peter L. Berger and the Vision of Interpretive Sociology*, ed. James Davison Hunter and Stephen C. Ainlay, 143–158. London: Routledge and Kegan Paul.

———. 1988. "Religion and the Persistence of Identity." *Journal for the Scientific Study of Religion* 27 (March): 1–11.

———. 1992. *Religion and Personal Autonomy: The Third Disestablishment in America.* Columbia: University of South Carolina Press.

Hannigan, John A. 1991. "Social Movement Theory and the Sociology of Religion: Toward a New Synthesis." *Sociological Analysis* 52 (Winter): 311–331.

Harrell, David Edwin, Jr. 1985. *Oral Roberts: An American Life*. San Francisco: Harper and Row.

Harris, James Henry. 1990. "Practicing Liberation in the Black Church." *Christian Century* 107 (June 13–20): 599–602.

Hatch, Nathan O. 1989. *The Democratization of American Christianity*. New Haven, Conn.: Yale University Press.

Hathout, Hassan, Fathi Osman, and Maher Hathout. 1989. *In Fraternity: A Message to Muslims in America*. Los Angeles: Minaret.

Heilman, Samuel C. 1990. "The Jews: Schism or Division." In *In Gods We Trust: New Patterns of Religious Pluralism in America*, ed. Thomas Robbins and Dick Anthony, 185–198. New Brunswick, N.J.: Transaction Books.

Herberg, Will. 1960. *Protestant, Catholic, Jew: An Essay in American Religious Sociology*. 2d ed. Garden City, N.Y.: Anchor.

Hill, Samuel S. 1985. "Religion and Region in America." *Annals of the American Academy of Political and Social Science* 480 (July): 132–141.

Hoge, Dean R. 1976. *Division in the Protestant House: The Basic Reasons Behind Intra-Church Conflicts*. Philadelphia: Westminster.

Hoge, Dean R., and David A. Roozen, eds. 1979. *Understanding Church Growth and Decline, 1950–1978*. New York: Pilgrim Press.

Hout, Michael, and Andrew M. Greeley. 1987. "The Center Doesn't Hold: Church Attendance in the United States, 1940–1984." *American Sociological Review* 52 (June): 325–345.

———. 1990. "The Cohort Doesn't Hold: Comment on Chaves." *Journal for the Scientific Study of Religion* 29 (December): 519–524.

Humphreys, Laud. 1972. *Out of the Closets: The Sociology of Homosexual Liberation*. Englewood Cliffs, N.J.: Prentice-Hall.

Hunter, James Davison. 1983. *American Evangelicalism: Conservative Religion and the Quandary of Modernity*. New Brunswick, N.J.: Rutgers University Press.

———. 1987. *Evangelicalism: The Coming Generation*. Chicago: University of Chicago Press.

———. 1991. *Culture Wars: The Struggle to Define America*. New York: Basic Books.

Hunter, James Davison, and Helen V. L. Stehlin. 1987. "Family: Toward Androgyny." In *Evangelicalism: The Coming Generation*, by James Davison Hunter, 76–115. Chicago: University of Chicago Press.

Hurh, Won Moo, and Kwang Chung Kim. 1990. "Religious Participation of Korean Immigrants in the United States." *Journal for the Scientific Study of Religion* 29 (March): 19–34.

Hutchison, William R., ed. 1989. *Between the Times: The Travail of the Protestant Establishment in America, 1900–1960*. Cambridge: Cambridge University Press.

Iannaccone, Laurence R. 1986. "A Formal Model of Church and Sect." *American Journal of Sociology* 94, suppl.: S241–S268.

———. 1990. "Religious Practice: A Human Capital Approach." *Journal for the Scientific Study of Religion* 29 (September): 297–314.

———. 1991. "The Consequences of Religious Market Structure." *Rationality and Society* 3 (April): 156–177.

Iannaccone, Laurence R., and Carrie A. Miles. 1990. "Dealing with Social Change: The Mormon Church's Response to Change in Women's Roles." *Social Forces* 68 (June): 1231–1250.

Jacquet, Constant H., Jr., and Alice M. Jones, eds. 1991. *Yearbook of American and Canadian Churches, 1991*. Nashville: Abingdon.

Jorstad, Erling. 1990. *Holding Fast/Pressing On: Religion in America in the 1980s*. New York: Praeger.

Kandiyoti, Deniz. 1988. "Bargaining with Patriarchy." *Gender and Society* 2 (September): 274–290.

Kashima, Tetsuden. 1977. *Buddhism in America: the Social Organization of an Ethnic Religious Institution*. Westport, Conn.: Greenwood Press.

———. 1990. "The Buddhist Churches of America: Challenges for Change in the 21st Century." *Pacific World*, n.s. 6 (1990): 28–40.

Kaufman, Debra Renée. 1991. *Rachel's Daughters: Newly Orthodox Jewish Women*. New Brunswick, N.J.: Rutgers University Press.

Keeley, Charles B. 1991. "The Political Response to Mass Immigration: United States, 1890–1915 and 1965–1990." Paper presented at annual meeting of the American Sociological Association, Cincinnati.

Kitano, Harry H. L., and Roger Daniels. 1988. *Asian Americans: Emerging Minorities*. Englewood Cliffs, N.J.: Prentice-Hall.

Kivisto, Peter A. 1992. "Religion and the New Immigrants." In *A Future for Religion? Trends in Social Analysis*, ed. William H. Swatos, Jr., 92–107. Newbury Park, Calif.: Sage.

Kosmin, Barry A., Ariela Keysar, and Nava Lerer. 1991. "Secular Education and the Religious Profile of Contemporary Black Americans." Paper presented at annual meeting of the Society for the Scientific Study of Religion, Pittsburgh.

Kosmin, Barry A., and Seymour P. Lachman. 1991. *Research Report: The National Survey of Religious Identification, 1989–1990*. New York: Graduate School and University Center of the City University of New York.

Kwilecki, Susan. 1987. "Contemporary Pentecostal Clergywomen: Female Christian Leadership, Old Style." *Journal of Feminist Studies of Religion* 3 (Fall): 57–75.

Land, Kenneth C., Glenn Deane, and Judith R. Blau. 1991. "Religious Pluralism and Church Membership: A Spatial Diffusion Model." *American Sociological Review* 56 (April): 237–249.

Lawless, Elaine. 1983. "Shouting for the Lord: The Power of Women's Speech in the Pentecostal Religious Service." *Journal of American Folklore* 96 (October–December): 434–459.

———. 1988. *Handmaidens of the Lord: Pentecostal Women Preachers and Traditional Religion*. Philadelphia: University of Pennsylvania Press.

Lechner, Frank J. 1985. "Modernity and Its Discontents." In *Neofunctionalism*, ed. Jeffrey C. Alexander, 157–176. Beverly Hills, Calif.: Sage.

———. 1991. "The Case Against Secularization: A Rebuttal." *Social Forces* 69 (June): 1103–1119.

Lee, Richard R. 1992. "Religious Practice as Social Exchange: An Explanation of the Empirical Findings." *Sociological Analysis* 53 (Spring): 1–35.

Lee, Sang Hyun. 1991. "Korean American Presbyterians: A Need for Ethnic Particularity and the Challenge of Christian Pilgrimage." In *The Diversity of Discipleship: The Presbyterians and Twentieth-Century Christian Witness*, ed. Milton J. Coalter, John M. Mulder, and Louis B. Weeks, 312–330, 400–402. Louisville: Westminster/John Knox.

Liebman, Robert C. 1983. "Mobilizing the Moral Majority." In *The New Christian Right: Mobilization and Legitimation*, ed. Robert C. Liebman and Robert Wuthnow, 50–73. Hawthorne, N.Y.: Aldine.

Liebman, Robert C., and Robert Wuthnow, eds. 1983. *The New Christian Right: Mobilization and Legitimation*. Hawthorne, N.Y.: Aldine.

Lincoln, C. Eric, and Lawrence H. Mamiya. 1990. *The Black Church in the African American Experience*. Durham, N.C.: Duke University Press.

Lipset, Seymour Martin. 1991. "Comments on Luckmann." In *Social Theory for a Changing Society*, ed. Pierre Bourdieu and James S. Coleman, 185–188. Boulder, Colo.: Westview.

Littel, Franklin Hamlin. 1962. *From State Church to Pluralism*. Chicago: Aldine.

Luckmann, Thomas. 1991. "The New and the Old in Religion." In *Social Theory for a Changing Society*, ed. Pierre Bourdieu and James S. Coleman, 167–182. Boulder, Colo.: Westview.

Luker, Kristin. 1984. *Abortion and the Politics of Motherhood*. Berkeley and Los Angeles: University of California Press.

Marcum, John. 1990. "Phantom Presbyterians." *Monday Morning* 55 (November 5): 13–14.

Marler, Penny Long, and C. Kirk Hadaway. 1992. "New Church Development and Denominational Growth (1950–1988): Symptom or Cause?" In *Research in the Scientific Study of Religion*, vol. 4, ed. Monty L. Lynn and David O. Moberg, 29–72. Greenwich, Conn.: JAI.

Marsden, George M. 1987. *Reforming Fundamentalism: Fuller Seminary and the New Evangelicalism.* Grand Rapids, Mich.: Eerdmans.

——. 1990. "Awash in a Sea of Revisionism." *Evangelical Studies Bulletin* 7 (Fall): 1–3.

Mathews, Donald G. 1969. "The Second Great Awakening as an Organizing Process, 1780–1830: An Hypothesis." *American Quarterly* 21 (Spring): 23–43.

Matters, Michael D. 1992. "Some Cultural Correlates of Congregational Participation in the Sanctuary Movement." Paper prepared for annual meeting of the Midwest Sociological Society, Kansas City.

McGuire, Meredith B. 1982. *Pentecostal Catholics: Power, Charisma, and Order in a Religious Movement.* Philadelphia: Temple University Press.

McKinney, William, and Wade Clark Roof. 1990. "Liberal Protestantism's Struggle to Recapture the Heartland." In *In Gods We Trust: New Patterns of Religious Pluralism in America*, ed. Thomas Robbins and Dick Anthony, 167–183. New Brunswick, N.J.: Transaction.

McLoughlin, William G. 1978. *Revivals, Awakenings, and Reform: An Essay on Religion and Social Change in America, 1607–1977.* Chicago: University of Chicago Press.

Mead, Sidney E. 1963. *The Lively Experiment.* New York: Harper and Row.

Melton, J. Gordon. 1989. *The Encyclopedia of American Religions.* 3d ed. Detroit: Gale Research.

Michaelson, Robert S. 1990. "From the Soil–and Soul–of America." *Los Angeles Times Book Review* (January 7).

Mittelberg, David, and Mary C. Waters. 1992. "The Process of Ethnogenesis among Haitian and Israeli Immigrants in the United States." *Ethnic and Racial Studies* 15 (July): 412–435.

Miyakawa, T. Scott. 1964. *Protestants and Pioneers: Individualism and Conformity on the American Frontier.* Chicago: University of Chicago Press.

Montoya, Alex D. 1987. *Hispanic Ministry in North America.* Grand Rapids, Mich.: Zondervan.

Morris, Aldon D. 1984. *The Origins of the Civil Rights Movement: Black Communities Organizing for Change.* New York: Free Press.

Mullins, Mark R. 1988. "The Organizational Dilemmas of Ethnic Churches: A Case Study of Japanese Buddhism in Canada." *Sociological Analysis* 49 (Fall): 217–233.

National Conference of Catholic Bishops. 1984. *The Hispanic Presence, Challenge and Commitment: A Pastoral Letter on Hispanic Ministry.* Washington, D.C.: United States Catholic Conference.

Neitz, Mary Jo. 1987. *Charisma and Community: A Study of Religious Commitment Within the Charismatic Renewal.* New Brunswick, N.J.: Transaction.

——. 1990. "Studying Religion in the Eighties." In *Symbolic Interaction and Cultural Studies*, ed. Howard Becker and Michal McCall, 90–118. Chicago: University of Chicago Press.

Niebuhr, H. Richard. 1929. *The Social Sources of Denominationalism.* New York: Henry Holt.

Numrich, Paul David. 1992. "Americanization in Immigrant Theravada Buddhist Temples." Ph.D. diss., Department of Religion, Northwestern University.

Olson, Daniel V. A. 1989. "Church Friendships: Boon or Barrier to Church Growth?" *Journal for the Scientific Study of Religion* 28 (December): 432–447.

——. 1993. "Fellowship Ties and the Transmission of Religious Identity." In *Beyond Establishment: Protestant Identity in a Post-Protestant Age*, ed. Jackson W. Carroll and W. Clark Roof, 32–53. Louisville: Westminster/John Knox.

Olson, Daniel V. A., and Jackson W. Carroll. 1992. "Religiously Based Politics: Religious Elites and the Public." *Social Forces* 70 (March): 765–786.

Orsi, Robert A. 1991. "'He Keeps Me Going': Women's Devotion to Saint Jude Thaddeus and the Dialectics of Gender in American Catholicism, 1929–1965." In *Belief in History: Innovative*

Approaches to European and American Religion, ed. Thomas Kselman, 137–169. Notre Dame, Ind.: University of Notre Dame Press.

Parsons, Talcott. 1960. "Some Comments on the Pattern of Religious Organization in the United States." In *Structure and Process in Modern Societies*, 295–321. Glencoe, Ill.: Free Press.

———. 1967. "Christianity and Modern Industrial Society." In *Sociological Theory, Values, and Sociocultural Change: Essays in Honor of Pitirim A. Sorokin*, ed. Edward A. Tiryakian, 33–70. New York: Harper Torchbooks.

———. 1969. "On the Concept of Value Commitments." In *Politics and Social Structure*, 439–472. New York: Free Press.

Perrin, Robin D., and Armand L. Mauss. 1991. "Saints and Seekers: Sources of Recruitment to the Vineyard Christian Fellowship." *Review of Religious Research* 33 (December): 97–111.

Perry, Troy D. 1972. *The Lord Is My Shepherd and He Knows I'm Gay*. Los Angeles: Nash.

Perry, Troy D., and Thomas L. P. Swicegood. 1990. *Don't Be Afraid Anymore: The Story of Reverend Troy Perry and the Metropolitan Community Churches*. New York: St. Martin's.

Poloma, Margaret M. 1989. *The Assemblies of God at the Crossroads: Charisma and Institutional Dilemmas*. Knoxville: University of Tennessee Press.

Powell, Walter W., and Paul J. DiMaggio. 1991. *The New Institutionalism in Organizational Analysis*. Chicago: University of Chicago Press.

Pratt, Henry J. 1972. *The Liberalization of American Protestantism. A Case Study in Complex Organization*. Detroit: Wayne State University Press.

Prell, Riv-Ellen. 1989. *Prayer and Community: The Havurah in American Judaism*. Detroit: Wayne State University Press.

Preston, David L. 1988. *The Social Organization of Zen Practice: Constructing Transcultural Reality*. Cambridge: Cambridge University Press.

Pritchard, Linda. 1984. "The Burned-Over District Reconsidered: A Portent of Evolving Religious Pluralism in the United States." *Social Science History* 8 (Summer): 243–265.

Roof, Wade Clark. 1978. *Community and Commitment: Religious Plausibility in a Liberal Protestant Church*. New York: Elsevier.

———. 1993. *A Generation of Seekers: The Spiritual Journeys of the Baby Boom Generation*. San Francisco: Harper.

Roof, Wade Clark, Dean R. Hoge, John E. Dyble, and C. Kirk Hadaway. 1979. "Factors Producing Growth or Decline in United Presbyterian Congregations." In *Understanding Church Growth and Decline, 1950–1978*, ed. Dean R. Hoge and David A. Roozen, 198–223. New York and Philadelphia: Pilgrim Press.

Roof, Wade Clark, and William McKinney. 1987. *American Mainline Religion: Its Changing Shape and Future*. New Brunswick, N.J.: Rutgers University Press.

Roozen, David A., William McKinney, and Wayne Thompson. 1990. "The 'Big Chill' Generation Warms to Worship." *Review of Religious Research* 31 (March): 314–322.

Rose, Susan D. 1987. "Women Warriors: The Negotiation of Gender in a Charismatic Community." *Sociological Analysis* 48 (Fall): 245–258.

Rosenberg, Bruce A. 1988. *Can These Bones Live? The Art of the American Folk Preacher*. Rev. ed. Urbana: University of Illinois Press.

Rowe, Henry K. 1924. *The History of Religion in the United States*. New York: Macmillan.

Rueda, Enrique. 1982. *The Homosexual Network: Private Lives and Public Policy*. Old Greenwich, Conn.: Devin Adair.

Rutledge, Paul James. 1982. "The Role of Religion in Ethnic Self-Identity: The Vietnamese of Oklahoma City, 1975–1982." Ph.D. diss., University of Oklahoma.

———. 1992. *The Vietnamese Experience in America*. Bloomington: Indiana University Press.

Ryan, Mary. 1979. "The Power of Women's Networks: A Case Study of Female Moral Reform in Antebellum America." *Feminist Studies* 5: 66–86.

———. 1981. *Cradle of the Middle Class: The Family in Oneida County, New York, 1790–1865.* Cambridge: Cambridge University Press.

Sarna, Jonathan D. 1987. "The Debate over Mixed Seating in the American Synagogue." In *The American Synagogue: A Sanctuary Transformed*, ed. Jack Wertheimer, 363–394. Cambridge: Cambridge University Press.

Scherer, Ross P. 1988. "A New Typology for Organizations: Market, Bureaucracy, Clan, and Mission, with Application to American Denominations." *Journal for the Scientific Study of Religion* 24 (December): 475–498.

Sharot, Stephen. 1991. "Judaism and the Secularization Debate." *Sociological Analysis* 52 (Fall): 255–275.

Sherkat, Darren E., and Christopher G. Ellison. 1991. "The Politics of Black Religious Change: Disaffiliation from Black Mainline Denominations." *Social Forces* 70 (December): 431–454.

Shin, Eui Hang, and Hyung Park. 1988. "An Analysis of Causes of Schisms in Ethnic Churches: The Case of Korean-American Churches." *Sociological Analysis* 49 (Fall): 234–248.

Shipps, Jan. 1985. *Mormonism: The Story of a New Religious Tradition.* Urbana: University of Illinois Press.

Shupe, Anson, and William Stacey. 1982. *Born-Again Politics and the Moral Majority: What Social Surveys Really Show.* New York: Edwin Mellen.

Silver, Allan. 1990. "The Curious Importance of Small Groups in American Sociology." In *Sociology in America*, ed. Herbert J. Gans, 61–72. Newbury Park, Calif.: Sage.

Smith, Timothy L. 1968. "Congregation, State, and Denomination: The Forming of the American Religious Structure." *William and Mary Quarterly* 25 (April): 155–176.

———. 1971. "Lay Initiative in the Religious Life of American Immigrants." In *Anonymous Americans*, ed. Tamara K. Hareven, 214–249. Englewood Cliffs, N.J.: Prentice-Hall.

———. 1978. "Religion and Ethnicity in America." *American Historical Review* 83 (December): 1155–1185.

Smith-Rosenberg, Carroll. 1985. *Disorderly Conduct: Visions of Gender in Victorian America.* New York: Knopf.

Snow, David A., and Richard Machalek. 1982. "On the Presumed Fragility of Unconventional Beliefs." *Journal for the Scientific Study of Religion* 21 (March): 15–26.

Sollors, Werner, ed. 1988. *The Invention of Ethnicity.* New York: Oxford University Press.

Stacey, Judith. 1990. *Brave New Families: Stories of Domestic Upheaval in Late Twentieth-Century America.* New York: Basic.

Stacey, Judith, and Susan Elizabeth Gerard. 1990. "'We Are Not Doormats': The Influence of Feminism on Contemporary Evangelicals in the United States." In *Uncertain Terms: Negotiating Gender in American Culture*, ed. Faye Ginsburg and Anna Lowenhaupt Tsing, 98–117. Boston: Beacon.

Stark, Rodney, and William Sims Bainbridge. 1985. *The Future of Religion: Secularization, Revival, and Cult Formation.* Berkeley and Los Angeles: University of California Press.

———. 1987. *A Theory of Religion.* New York: Peter Lang.

Stark, Rodney, and Roger Finke. 1988. "American Religion in 1776: A Statistical Portrait." *Sociological Analysis* 49 (Spring): 39–51.

Stout, Harry S. 1991. *The Divine Dramatist: George Whitefield and the Rise of Modern Evangelicalism.* Grand Rapids, Mich.: Eerdmans.

Stump, Roger W. 1984. "Regional Migration and Religious Commitment in the United States." *Journal for the Scientific Study of Religion* 23 (September): 292–303.

Sullins, Donald Paul. 1992. "Switching Close to Home: Volatility or Coherence in Protestant Affiliation Patterns." Paper presented at annual meeting of the Society for the Scientific Study of Religion, Arlington, Va.

Swatos, William H., Jr. 1979. *Into Denominationalism: The Anglican Metamorphosis.* Storrs, Conn.: Society for the Scientific Study of Religion.

Takayama, K. Peter. 1980. "Strains, Conflicts, and Schisms in Protestant Denominations." In *American Denominational Organization: A Sociological View,* ed. Ross P. Scherer, 298–329. Pasadena, Calif.: William Carey.

Thomas, George M. 1989. *Revivalism and Cultural Change: Christianity, Nation Building, and the Market in the Nineteenth-Century United States.* Chicago: University of Chicago Press.

Thumma, Scott. 1991. "Negotiating a Religious Identity: The Case of the Gay Evangelical." *Sociological Analysis* 52 (Winter): 333–347.

Tiryakian, Edward A. 1991. "L'exceptionnelle vitalité religieuse aux Etats–Unis: Une relecture de *Protestant-Catholic-Jew*" (The exceptional religious vitality of the United States: A rereading of *Protestant-Catholic-Jew*). *Social Compass* 38 (September): 215–238.

Tschannen, Olivier. 1991. "The Secularization Paradigm: A Systematization." *Journal for the Scientific Study of Religion* 30 (December): 395–415.

Wacker, Grant. 1984. "Uneasy in Zion: Evangelicals in Postmodern Society." In *Evangelicalism and Modern America,* ed. George Marsden, 17–28. Grand Rapids, Mich.: Eerdmans.

———. 1991. "A Tar Heel Perspective on *The Third Disestablishment.*" *Journal for the Scientific Study of Religion* 30 (December): 519–525.

Wallace, Ruth A. 1992. *They Call Her Pastor: A New Role for Catholic Women.* Albany: State University of New York Press.

Waugh, Earle H. 1994. "Reducing the Distance: A Muslim Congregation in the Canadian North." In *Portraits of Twelve Religious Communities,* 572–611, vol. 1 of *American Congregations,* ed. James P. Wind and James W. Lewis. Chicago: University of Chicago Press.

Wertheimer, Jack. 1989. "Recent Trends in American Judaism." In *American Jewish Yearbook 1989,* ed. David Singer, 63–162. New York and Philadelphia: American Jewish Committee and Jewish Publication Society.

Wilcox, Clyde, and Leopoldo Gomez. 1990. "Religion, Group Identification, and Politics among American Blacks." *Sociological Analysis* (Fall): 271–285.

Williams, Raymond Brady. 1988. *Religions of Immigrants from India and Pakistan: New Threads in the American Tapestry.* Cambridge: Cambridge University Press.

Wills, Garry. 1990. *Under God: Religion and American Politics.* New York: Simon and Schuster.

Wiltfang, Gregory, and Doug McAdam. 1991. "The Costs and Risks of Social Activism: A Study of Sanctuary Movement Activism." *Social Forces* 69 (June): 987–1010.

Wood, James R. 1981. *Leadership in Voluntary Organizations: The Controversy over Social Action in Protestant Churches.* New Brunswick, N.J.: Rutgers University Press.

Wuthnow, Robert. 1986. "Religion as Sacred Canopy." In *Making Sense of Modern Times: Peter L. Berger and the Vision of Interpretive Sociology,* ed. James Davison Hunter and Stephen C. Ainlay, 121–142. London: Routledge and Kegan Paul.

———. 1988. *The Restructuring of American Religion: Society and Faith since World War II.* Princeton, N.J.: Princeton University Press.

———. 1991. *Between States and Markets: The Voluntary Sector in Comparative Perspective.* Princeton, N.J.: Princeton University Press.

Wuthnow, Robert, and Kevin Christiano. 1979. "The Effects of Residential Migration on Church Attendance in the United States." In *The Religious Dimension: New Directions in Quantitative Research,* ed. Robert Wuthnow, 257–276. New York: Academic Press.

Wuthnow, Robert, and William Lehrman. 1990. "Religion: Inhibitor or Facilitator of Political Involvement among Women?" In *Women, Politics, and Change,* ed. Louise A. Tilly and Patricia Gurin, 300–322. New York: Russell Sage.

Wuthnow, Robert, and Clifford Nass. 1988. "Government Activity and Civil Privatism: Evidence from Voluntary Church Membership." *Journal for the Scientific Study of Religion* 27 (June): 157–174.

Yu, Eui-Young. 1988. "The Growth of Korean Buddhism in the United States, with Special Reference to Southern California." *Pacific World: Journal of the Institute of Buddhist Studies*, n.s. 4 (Fall): 82–93.

Zaretsky, Irving I., and Mark P. Leone, eds. 1974. *Religious Movements in Contemporary America*. Princeton, N.J.: Princeton University Press.

Zikmund, Barbara Brown. 1979. "The Feminist Thrust of Sectarian Christianity." In *Women of Spirit: Female Leadership in the Jewish and Christian Traditions*, ed. Rosemary Ruether and Eleanor McLaughlin, 205–224. New York: Simon and Schuster.

3

A Paradigm Is Not a Theory (1997)

Although Lechner raises some worthwhile points, the basic issue between us is simple. I announced a new *paradigm*, but Lechner insists on reading my article as a proposal for a new *theory*. He applies himself to refuting what he imagines the new theory to be (rational choice) and does me the favor, from his point of view, of absolving me from its advocacy. I trust I will not be thought churlish if I decline the favor and protest that he has misread me. I meant what I said about "paradigms."[1]

True, the article is a compressed book, and it has several subtexts, intending (1) to impart a great deal of sheer factual information about an institutional sphere too many sociologists neglect and (2) to showcase the work of a remarkable new cohort of scholars, many of them admittedly (this volume, 21) having no interest in paradigm disputes.

Yet the main text of the article concerns a paradigm shift in the making, and I intended the argument to be prefigured from the outset both by the title and abstract (with their explicit mention of "paradigms") and by the epigram from Joseph Schumpeter that comes right afterward ("In every scientific venture, the thing that comes first is Vision"). The argument is that scholars of U.S. religion are converging on a new way of thinking about their subject, a new way that contrasts decisively with the old way (which is more often referred to as "secularization theory" than "the old paradigm"). The new way of thinking is not a refutation of the old and does not propose a simple reverse of secularization. Proposing that religion in the United States is disestablished, culturally pluralistic, structurally adaptable, and often empowering, it is a fundamentally different idea.[2]

I meant what I said, but I confess that I didn't say all that I meant. For example, I made no explicit reference to the work of Thomas Kuhn (1970), and I left the contrast between the two paradigms to a schematic table (this volume, 24). I welcome the opportunity to elaborate the "paradigm" argument.

A paradigm is a "gestalt" (Kuhn 1970, 112, 122, 204), a way of seeing the world, a representation, picture, or narrative of the fundamental properties of reality. For the purposes at hand, paradigms may be regarded as metanarratives:

The earth can be seen as the stable center of the universe, about which the sun, the moon, the planets, and the stars orbit, or it can be seen as one of several planets that revolve about the sun, the new (albeit astronomically temporary) center of the universe (Kuhn 1957, 229–231).

The earth may be imagined as a once hot, slowly cooling ball, developing a fixed, thickening shell of continents and sea floors as it cools, the shell cracking and fissuring, the continents rising or falling. Or the earth may be imagined to be still hot and churning inside, so that the thin shell is continually renewed and destroyed by convection, hunks of it floating on the surface until they collide and are consumed, edgewise, in its depths (Stewart 1990, 117–118, 153–160).

Evolution by adaptation may be conceived of as a matter of organisms struggling with their environment (in Lamarck's view) or struggling with each other for the best exploitation of their environment (as Darwin saw it) (Himmelfarb 1967, 317).

The Copernican, geoscience, and Darwinian revolutions represent radical changes in point of view. So also does the new paradigm in the sociology of religion in the United States, as I indicated too cryptically in Table 1 (this volume, 24) and the paragraph summarizing section II of the paper (this volume, 29). Here I will unpack the contrast.

The old paradigm metanarrative begins about eight hundred years ago in medieval Europe, when, by state sanction, a monopoly church commanded sacred authority over the whole society. As a protected monopoly, it was assured assent by formal and informal sanction. (Some versions of this story stress that there were no ideological alternatives, and the church's viewpoint was unquestioningly taken for granted.) Thus people followed its rules and had to regard the local parish as the sole authority over what concerned them (from when to take holidays to what to name one's child to what happens after a relative's death) and to accept as the local representative of the sacred order the prebendary appointed by the central bureaucratic system and supported from its lands. This system constituted the religious order. Since the heyday of this system (roughly the thirteenth century), its hegemony has slowly eroded (the process of "secularization"), both because other powers rose to challenge it and because the sacred answers it provided became less plausible. The increasing implausibility of religious ideas is the result of ideological and cultural pluralism—Islam, the discovery of the New World, the success of the Protestants, the Enlightenment—which offered alternatives that had more plausibility or simply, as alternatives, invalidated the claims of the church. In other words, religious ideas are particularly vulnerable because their primary function is to provide meaning, a function on which they no longer command a monopoly. (That monopoly status was their "plausibility structure.") Some of these sources of erosion were exogenous (contact with other cultures) but others were endogenous, particularly modern science, which, as a differentiated offshoot of religion, shares with it the function of the provision of meaning but fills this need more efficiently than can religion. (This metanarrative stands behind Weber's *Protestant Ethic* and Durkheim's *Division of Labor*.) Religious institutions— the remnant of the church—survive today in shadowy form by specializing in general values that legitimate the institutional order of the society.

Lechner denies that his and other old paradigm proponents' work presupposes the paradigmatic status of medieval Europe. It "simply traces historical change" from "earlier times" to "today," the master change being "secularization." New paradigm proponents ask the obvious questions, Whose history? What earlier times? And secularization from what? The answers are Europe and its previously established religions (Casanova 1994, 12–17).[3] Without such a baseline, "secularization" as a concept has no meaning.

The new paradigm metanarrative begins two hundred years ago in the early republican United States. Most people were not involved in churches, and the dominant ideology, including that represented in social theory, was largely secular. At about that time, religion was disestablished, and a majoritarian political system was instituted. Thus religion no longer enjoyed the support of the state, but also the state made no room for the representation of minorities. Some religious bodies found disestablishment a challenge, but others had already been outsiders to the older establishment and quickly adapted to the new circumstances. Eventually no one body could successfully rule another claimant out of the system. People had to be persuaded to give assent, and religious entrepreneurs and operatives crisscrossed the country to save souls, anathematizing each other and offering a great variety of alternatives to their audiences. People made religious choices, joining up with congregations led by one or another of these competitors. The result within a generation was the creation of a huge, popular, quasi-public social space that women, and later racial minorities, could appropriate to their purposes. The society's encounter with other populations, through immigration, capture, and conquest (factors partly exogenous to the religious system) introduced more social diversity and eventually more competition. Groups gathered under religious banners, deriving much of their identity from these symbols. (This is where Durkheim's *Elementary Forms* comes in handy.) Eventually, religious profession became as much an identity marker in the United States as language, accent, and social class were in Europe, so people were located by the "denomination" to which they adhered. (This is where Weber's "Protestant Sects" is useful, inspired as it was by his visit to the United States in 1904.) When, because of cartelization, the identifications provided by these affiliations become less distinct and/or their demands prove too irksome, disaffiliation can occur, but, because potential rewards continue to be high and barriers to entry low, religious entrepreneurs keep trying to recruit the unchurched. Thus cycles of mobilization and demobilization continue.

A paradigm is indeed not a theory (this volume, 26), and a paradigm shift does not alone invalidate findings or render older theories and methods obsolete

(Stewart 1990). Nor are old paradigms necessarily wrong. In the *very* long run, the entropic vision shared by the old paradigms in religion and geoscience is sure to triumph. So it should be no surprise that Lechner, committed to the old paradigm, can find many points of agreement with me, committed to the new. But he cannot successfully appeal to a "scientific norm" (Lechner 1997, 188) to adjudicate paradigm succession, because in the nature of paradigm disputes there is "no neutral algorithm" to make such decisions (Kuhn 1970, 200). I have claimed (Warner 1991a) that the old paradigm appeals to those with a European background and to those who have *individually* undergone the experience of religious erosion the old paradigm attributes to *the whole of society* (this volume, 26).

The affinity between the new paradigm and rational choice theory is obvious. Religious producers and consumers act rationally, and, given the inefficiency of monopoly, religion flourishes the more choice is available. Unlike some sociologists of religion, I have no fear of the taint of rational choice and am happy to embrace such theorists when, as is the case here (especially Finke and Stark 1992 and Iannaccone 1995), they produce brilliant insights.[4] Nonetheless, as I understand the new paradigm, rational choice theories contribute to it but do not define or constitute it. I pointed this out with the observation (this volume, 24) that the key exemplar of the old paradigm, Peter Berger's *Sacred Canopy*, makes use of economic reasoning to understand what the author saw as the degeneracy of U.S. religion.

I also intended the new paradigm to incorporate the work of other scholars who recognize that American religion flourishes in situations of choice and who had abandoned (or never adopted) the old paradigm's privileging of established or "mainline" religions, whether or not they embraced rational choice. Mary Jo Neitz (1990) and Nancy Ammerman (1997) recommend symbolic interactionism for its capacity to articulate the role of agents, to disaggregate macro phenomena, and to encompass the "decentering" of contemporary organizational life. Without presuming their assent, I suggested that feminist and race/ethnic studies scholars should find the new paradigm more compatible than the old paradigm with the social worlds they investigate (e.g., Braude 1997; Yoo 1996). I am disappointed that Lechner neglects that very important aspect of my paper.

I also regret that I did not make clear enough to Lechner and others that while the "new voluntarism" (this volume, 43–48) involves disaffiliation, it also promotes new and renewed solidarities (this volume, 44–46) and is not so new as to be discontinuous with earlier patterns in U.S. religious history (this volume, 47–48).

It would be silly to claim that the paradigm succession I discuss has anything like the significance of the Copernican or Darwinian revolutions, and I intended no such claim. Yet there was a crisis and there has been a succession. In the article, I cited (this volume, 21) several established scholars who expressed public perplexity with the old paradigm. I did not cite the work of many younger scholars whose struggles with the old paradigm frustrated their ongoing research and muddied their reports to the point of making them unpublishable. One reason I set aside the book on which I was working in 1991 to write the article was to let such scholars know that there was an alternative to the old paradigm, an alternative that *expected* "traditional" religions to flourish in modern society, *expected* diversity to invigorate rather than demoralize religious communities, *expected* religious innovation and religious commitment to go hand in hand, and did not suppose that the decline of mainline Protestantism was the decline of religion. If the old paradigm were as open to the dynamic phenomena of American religious life as Lechner claims, fewer scholars would have wasted time and paper on the equivalent of Ptolemaic epicycles.[5] In the years since publication of my article, such scholars, whether or not they embrace rational choice, have become more aware of alternative perspectives. Work continues to be done and progress to be made.

NOTES

Thanks to Nancy Ammerman, Roger Finke, Laurence Iannaccone, Daniel Olson, Darren Sherkat, and Sidney B. Simpson, Jr., for suggestions and to Frank Lechner for his civility and cooperation. This essay was published as a "Reply" to "The 'New Paradigm' in the Sociology of Religion: A Comment on Warner," by Frank Lechner, in the same issue of the *American Journal of Sociology*. As alike intellectual grandchildren of Talcott Parsons, Lechner and I could carry on for pages about our debts to and differences with his work, but space does not permit such indulgence.

1. Some additional misreadings: Lechner (1997, 186) imputes to me the notion of a "genuine" market, but I talk of no such thing. The "open market" of which I speak means that anybody can set up a religion. Barriers to entry are low. Potential niches are many. Awareness of alternatives is high. Choice is possible and fully compatible with commitment. He claims (188) that I posit "that disestablishment leads to pluralism and competition," but I actually say (this volume, 29) that "pluralism has tended in this society to take on a religious expression." He lectures me (in his note 8) on the debate over the effects of pluralism on religion, a matter to which I devoted a long paragraph (this volume, 27–28), citing the same scholars he does plus several more.

2. Lechner calls these "conventional" claims, and I agree that they are conventional to U.S. religious historians, despite the largely negative reception of Finke and Stark's new paradigm history (1992) among historians, who objected to being lectured about what they already knew (Marty 1995). But the claims are by no means conventional to the exemplar of the old paradigm I identified (Berger 1969).

3. Readers can judge for themselves the Eurocentrism of Lechner's version of the secularization metanarrative (which he labels "the conventional wisdom") in Lechner 1991, 1103–1104, 1107–1108, 1116.

4. In Warner 1997a, I outline some differences with rational choice thinkers, particularly Finke and Stark (1992). One difference is that Finke and Stark speak of an "unregulated market," whereas I speak of an "open" market. I also think they overstate the role of "strictness" and understate that of "distinctiveness" in producing strong religious bodies. I differ with Stark (1997) in proceeding inductively by design.

5. For example, the "community" that Lechner (1997, note 6), following Wilson, sees as the base of religion has, according to Wilson (1982, 159–160), suffered as much "collapse" as religion has. Contrary to the new paradigm, neither communities nor their religions are robust.

REFERENCES

(References to writings of the author are found in a separate listing at the back of the book.)

Ammerman, Nancy T. 1997. "Organized Religion in a Voluntaristic Society." *Sociology of Religion* 58 (Summer): 203–216.

Berger, Peter L. 1969. *The Sacred Canopy: Elements of a Sociological Theory of Religion.* Garden City, N.Y.: Anchor

Braude, Ann. 1997. "Women's History *Is* American Religious History." In *Retelling U.S. Religious History,* ed. Thomas A. Tweed, 87–107, 551–555. Berkeley: University of California Press.

Casanova, José. 1994. *Public Religions in the Modern World.* Chicago: University of Chicago Press.

Finke, Roger, and Rodney Stark. 1992. *The Churching of America, 1776–1990: Winners and Losers in Our Religious Economy.* New Brunswick, N.J.: Rutgers University Press.

Himmelfarb, Gertrude. 1967. *Darwin and the Darwinian Revolution.* Gloucester, Mass.: Peter Smith.

Iannaccone, Laurence R. 1995. "Risk, Rationality, and Religious Portfolios." *Economic Inquiry* 33 (April): 285–295.

Kuhn, Thomas S. 1957. *The Copernican Revolution: Planetary Astronomy in the Development of Western Thought.* Cambridge: Harvard University Press.

———. 1970. *The Structure of Scientific Revolutions.* 2d ed. Chicago: University of Chicago Press.

Lechner, Frank J. 1991. "The Case Against Secularization: A Rebuttal." *Social Forces* 69 (June): 1103–1119.

———. 1997. "The 'New Paradigm' in the Sociology of Religion: A Comment on Warner." *American Journal of Sociology* 103, 1 (1997): 182–192.

Marty, Martin E. 1995. Historian's Response to Finke and Stark's *The Churching of America* prepared for discussion at the Cushwa Seminar in American Religion, Notre Dame University, March 18.

Neitz, Mary Jo. 1990. "Studying Religion in the Eighties." In *Symbolic Interaction and Cultural Studies,* ed. Howard S. Becker and Michal M. McCall, 90–118. Chicago: University of Chicago Press.

Stark, Rodney. 1997. "Bringing Theory Back In." In *Rational Choice Theory and Religion: Summary and Assessment,* ed. Lawrence A. Young, 3–23. New York: Routledge.

Stewart, John A. 1990. *Drifting Continents and Colliding Paradigms: Perspectives on the Geoscience Revolution.* Bloomington: Indiana University Press.

Wilson, Bryan. 1982. *Religion in Sociological Perspective.* New York: Oxford University Press.

Yoo, David. 1996. "For Those Who Have Eyes to See: Religious Sightings in Asian America." *Amerasia Journal* 22 (Spring): xiii–xxii.

4

New Paradigm Histories of American Religion

Roger Finke and Rodney Stark on American Religion after Disestablishment: A Review of *The Churching of America, 1776–1990* (1993)

The Churching of America, 1776–1990: Winners and Losers in Our Religious Economy, is a blurb-writer's dream: "long-awaited," it has been listed for years as forthcoming in its authors' bibliographies.[1] "Influential," its findings, reported earlier in this journal and elsewhere, have already been put to use by such notable religious historians as Jon Butler (1990, 297, 345) and Mark Noll (1992, 153). "Controversial," soon after publication it was denounced by the usually unflappable Martin Marty in the *Christian Century* (1993), and the story was covered (by Peter Steinfels) in the *New York Times* (1993). Is the hype justified? Absolutely.

The main title announces the topic, the astonishing, nearly fourfold increase in rates of church affiliation from the time of the American Revolution to the present. The subtitle refers to the authors' theory, which attributes that increase to the efforts of religious organizations, conceived as more or less successful "firms."

However we are to account for it, the churching of America, a mostly nineteenth-century transformation, was an extraordinary accomplishment more familiar to historians than to sociologists of American religion. Thus the authors' dramatic, highly readable narrative and well-chosen, lively graphics will be of greatest urgency for sociologists, whose students will be enlightened to read, for example, that "single women in New England during the colonial period were more likely to be sexually active than to belong to a church" (22). But the details of the book's story of religious mobilization, particularly Finke and Stark's efforts to quantify colonial and antebellum church affiliation archaeologically, "turning pews into people," represent a major contribution to historical scholarship as well. Given the overall upward trajectory the authors document, one surprising finding of the quantitative research is that rates of church affiliation (or "church adherence") at the outset of the authors' period, 1776, were higher, at 17 percent, than many historians have supposed, and they were already on the upswing.

Perhaps the authors give themselves too much credit for such historical revisionism, yet in truth their quantitative findings call for change in many textbooks. Thus, Finke and Stark argue that the years 1739–1742 and 1800–1830 do not stand out in the numerical record as the first and second "great awakenings" they are conventionally called; "awakenings," they claim, represent cycles of journalistic and scholarly attention to successful, planned campaigns of revivalism (88). Catholics became the largest American denomination only by 1890, not 1850 as often thought, because not all immigrants from "Catholic" countries (such as Ireland and France) were Catholic and because, relative to Protestant church counts, Catholic figures have been inflated by the inclusion of baptized children as "members" (110–113). A sociological stereotype is confounded by the finding, earlier reported by the authors in the *American Sociological Review* (1988), that "the growth of cities increased religious participation" (204). Other notions the authors dispute are that "cults" and new religions particularly flourished in the 1960s and that the 1970s stand out as a time of evangelical eruption. Finke and Stark consistently find continuity in American religious patterns. Thus, likening recent trends of evangelical growth and mainline decline to those in the immediate postcolonial years, the authors write that "it is pointless to search the 1960s for the causes of a phenomenon that was far along by the War of 1812" (249).

Controversy surrounds Finke and Stark's explicitly economic theorizing of these patterns, with its talk of "supply" and "demand," "firms" and "customers," "competition," "market shares," "monopolies," and "cartels." Though they know many people shudder at such language, Finke and Stark employ it aggressively. (Marty complains about their "in your face" writing style; Steinfels calls the book "pugnacious.") But the book ought to lay to rest one specious controversy based on the accusation that market-oriented theories of religion are indifferent to the content of religion. For, according to Finke and Stark, it is above all the content of their message that separates the "winners" from the "losers" among religious firms. "The churching of America was accomplished by aggressive churches committed to vivid otherworldliness" (1), whereas failure is attributed to churches' abandonment of their own religious convictions.

Thus the book will confound those who suppose that market theories of religion can have nothing to say about religion and everything to say about consumerism, for Finke and Stark's market theory does not propose that churches passively adapt to consumers' tastes. After a few perfunctory words about consumer preferences, Finke and Stark settle in to a resolutely "supply-side" analysis (Warner 1993a, 1048–1058), where the dynamics of religious economies are due to activities of the churches themselves. Both the strength and weakness of the authors' subsequent analysis is that they focus not on exogenous or contextual factors in religious growth and decline (whether worldly or otherworldly), but on endogenous, institutional, or ecclesiastical ones. Those who protest that market models denigrate the integrity of religious commitment and promote pandering to fickle consumers quite miss the point.

More to the point of the controversy is the authors' unabashed side taking, theologically akin to triumphalism, politically to populism, their cheering winners and reviling losers on the basis of growth in the proportion, or "market share," of the population enrolled in one or another denomination. The Congregationalists are presented as consistent losers, their market share dwindling steadily for two centuries, and the Baptists, especially their southern branch, are consistent winners. Nazarenes and Assemblies of God are recent success stories, groups enrolling increasing proportions of the population. The Methodists and the Catholics are more complicated, instructive cases.

The authors refer to the Baptists and antebellum Methodists as "upstart sects," both to signal the low repute in which they were held by cultured contemporaries and to adumbrate the ingredients of their success: "high octane faith," vigor, zeal, amateurism (i.e., bivocationalism), revivalism, otherworldliness, the common touch, "low overhead" (81), and local autonomy ("Southern Baptist clergy had no hierarchy to shield them from their own local congregations" [184]).

Conversely, failure is the fruit of "theology" and seminary education, the effect of which, from Harvard and Yale in the eighteenth century to Marty's University of Chicago today, is "to replace faith with theology and belief with unbelief" (86). The key to religious failure is unbridled professionalism, particularly when the clergy get a taste for refinement and respectability. "For the clergy, the costs of remaining a high-tension sect are especially high. They often receive less pay and community respect than their counterparts in 'mainline' denominations, even though they face more stringent demands on their beliefs and behavior. The result: the well-educated clergy and affluent membership are often the first to support a lowering of the tension with the surrounding culture" (169–170). Cognate factors in religious decline are the substitution of ethicalism for devotionalism, organizational ecumenism, Unitarianism (200), and sociology (166–167). These factors have been obscured by scholars because of their "very strong preference for a more refined theology" (5), which itself partakes of the very "corrosive effect of scholarship on religion" (45) that undermines church effectiveness.

Today's mainline ecclesiastical and scholarly communities, for example, are appalled at the rough treatment being accorded those professors and agency heads who have found themselves on the losing side in the current struggle for control of the Southern Baptist Convention, but Finke and Stark imply a different evaluation in their analysis of an earlier purge in the same denomination. "We agree that 'rigorous scholarship' is required of those who would claim to be scholars. We do not agree that standards appropriate for evaluating secular academic institutions are necessarily appropriate for judging institutions organized around a confession of faith. . . . Do those who accepted seminary appointments from a denomination, many of whose most cherished beliefs they held in contempt, deserve sympathy?" (185). Those are close to fighting words.

The authors claim that the Baptists and Methodists overtook the Congregationalists, Presbyterians, and Episcopalians in 1776–1850 because "it was the pur-
suit of souls, not material comfort, that drove their clergy forth" (83), whereas "the
Congregationalists could function only in 'civilized areas' " (71). Likewise, later on
in the nineteenth century, the Catholic Church employed the same revivalist techniques as the evangelical Protestants. Moreover, "Catholic clergy were not of gen-
teel social origin, nor did they aspire to a comfortable salary" (115). Their education
was not corrupting, for aspirants were mostly trained by local priests in diocesan
seminaries. "In the final analysis, the Catholic Church succeeded in America
because it too was an upstart sect" (143).

The Methodists are the paradigmatic case, moving from the winners' column
to the losers' between the beginning and the end of the nineteenth century. In
what became known as the Methodist "miracle" (but the authors attribute to sustained organizational effort), the Methodist market share moved from less than 3
percent of U.S. church members in 1776 to more than one-third by 1850; yet their
growth in market share slowed somewhere around 1850 and their absolute numbers started to fall in the 1960s. The Catholic experience provides another case
example of organizational change: rapid growth in the late nineteenth century,
followed, the authors warn, by signs of incipient decline today. The reasons are the
same: "When successful sects are transformed into churches, that is, when their
tension with the surrounding culture is greatly reduced, they soon cease to grow
and eventually begin to decline" (148).

Finke and Stark's supply-side perspective focuses on the maintenance of vigor
in religious organizations, and they argue that vigor is sapped by the devolution of
sect to church. Consistent with this argument, they regularly assert that it is "tension" and "strictness" that make for organizational strength. Thus, they argue that
"in terms of real costs and benefits, the more 'mainline' the church (in the sense
of being regarded as 'respectable' and 'reasonable'), the lower the value of belonging to it, and this eventually results in widespread defection" (238). Finke and
Stark borrow from economist Laurence Iannaccone one explanation for the association (earlier noted by Dean Kelley) between lowered tension and organizational decline. The mechanism is the "free-rider problem" in low-tension congregations
that dilutes the power participants experience from the songs and prayers in their
own gathering. Policies of strictness, interpreted as "sacrifice plus stigma," act as
"nonrefundable registration fees" (254) to keep out spectators and thereby raise
the power of the religious assembly.

Yet it is not at all clear that Finke and Stark's success stories are unambigu-
ously cases of strictness. Camp meetings were an important ingredient in the
antebellum Methodist miracle, but they were social occasions as well as religious
ones, in which "as many souls were conceived as were saved" (96). The present-
day Pentecostal and charismatic movements, comprising lifelong Protestants,
Catholics who have not left the church, and Hispanics who have, may be a matter
less of a high-*tension* faith than of a high "*intensity*" one, as the authors revealingly

put it (273). The authors concede that a good bit of current disaffection from the Catholic Church is due to papal teaching on birth control, which would have imposed higher sacrifices on Catholics than they were willing to bear; in Vatican II reforms, the church abandoned not so much strictness as distinctive identity markers of an undertheorized "Catholic culture."

Thus the authors neglect to explore why a particular religious message appeals to a particular sector of our society, preferring instead to focus theoretically on the powerful appeal of otherworldly rewards to those whom the society scorns. "Although religion may well have been an 'opiate' of the people in some times and places (especially when monopoly religious organizations have put their fate irrevocably in the hands of the ruling elite), in other instances it would be equally apt to describe religion as the 'amphetamines' of the people" (251). Status is all; subculture is, in effect, a residual category. The authors acknowledge that Catholic parishes were ethnically and linguistically homogeneous internally (and hence arguably subcultural), but they neglect the variety across parishes, preferring to see Irish puritan "sectarianism" as characteristic of the whole of Catholic America (136–138). The postbellum South is seen as an "internal colony" (175), but the implications of this recognition are not explored. Thus, Finke and Stark have to insist that Southern Baptist tradition is essentially sectarian (cf. Ammerman 1990, chap. 2). Contrary to Finke and Stark, it could be argued that in both the Catholic and Southern Baptist cases, it is not so much that the religious body is in tension with the secular culture as that a religiosecular subculture is in tension with the dominant (Protestant, Yankee) society.

Finke and Stark explore but ultimately leave unresolved the vexed issue left ambiguous twenty years ago by Dean Kelley (1972): do conservative churches grow because of what they teach or because of how strictly they teach it? Finke and Stark hint that decline may set in particularly when segments of religious organizations go to war with their own traditions, so that it is not liberalism, per se, but liberal currents in constitutively conservative traditions that spell trouble. "Internal factions demanding a return to a more sectlike faith are always a first sign of the secularization of a religious body" (177).

One may well ask where the market theorizing is in all this. Finke and Stark properly acknowledge the work of H. Richard Niebuhr as a mentor of their sect-to-church modeling, but Niebuhr was aware that there was, in economic terms, a huge market niche for theological refinement, professionalism, and ethicalism. A demand-side perspective would stress this point. Thus, Finke and Stark do recognize that not only educated clergy but also affluent members want their religion to be up to date, which may be taken as one lesson of the Methodist experience. For a century after American Methodism relaxed its policy of circuit riding and began its own system of higher education, the Methodist denomination continued to grow enormously (see, e.g., 113). As Iannaccone has argued elsewhere (1986), there is a stable system of preferences for churches as well as for sects. It is doubtful that sects alone could have brought about the churching of America.

Finke and Stark's essential point is that the free market of American religion disciplines organizations that get "lazy" and stop behaving competitively, take constituents for granted, and act as if their commitment did not need to be constantly nurtured through such means as prayer groups (Baptist), "classes" (Methodist), and confraternities (Catholic). Of course, being in a competitive environment is uncomfortable, and organizations routinely seek out protection from the rigors of the market. In chapter 6, which might have been titled "the mainline ethic and the spirit of monopolization," Finke and Stark document the failure of would-be cartels to curtail paid religious broadcasting in the 1940s and to merge small sectarian rural churches into large, professionally led ones in the 1920s. In default of coercive sanctions, neither effort was successful, and more aggressive firms stepped in to provide the religious services the mainline disdained. Had coercive sanctions been available, Finke and Stark argue, the result would have been that of medieval Europe: an overall depressed level of religious activity. Religion is robust in the United States because nobody has a guarantee to make a living off it.

It should be clear that one can use Finke and Stark's book to argue with, as well as extrapolate from, Finke and Stark's theory, and that is because the book is rich in information and ideas. The data are presented in figures, tables, maps, etchings and photographs (cross-eyed George Whitefield [47] and clear-eyed Charles Grandison Finney [91]), quotations and sidebars, as well as in the authors' forceful prose; the data can thus promote purposes not intended by the authors. The theory is stated at the outset, frequently reiterated, and rephrased elliptically and aphoristically; it can thus promote thoughts not entertained by the authors.

As has this reviewer, most readers of this journal have no doubt previously read one or more of the articles and conference papers that are reprised in this book, but they should not suppose that they have read it all. *The Churching of America* contains much that is new, and the whole is far greater than the sum of the pieces. It is a pathbreaking book.

Grant Wacker on the First Generation of Pentecostals: A Review of *Heaven Below* (2003)

Barely a century old, Pentecostalism is one of the world's most dynamic religious movements, spreading from origins in North America to upward of half a billion adherents worldwide.[2] Drawn from Wesleyan holiness, Oberlin perfectionism, dispensational premillenialism, revivalism, faith healing, and other streams, its adherents converged around 1900 on a conviction that true salvation is only possible through the indwelling of the Holy Spirit, for which, in turn, the only valid evidence is the gift of speaking in tongues. Itinerant teachers and small groups of earnest pupils were putting these ideas to work in scattered locales when, in the spring of 1906, one of them, a black evangelist named William Joseph Seymour, set up shop on Azusa Street in Los Angeles, and the movement caught fire. The "Azusa

Street Revival" went on for three full years. Thousands of people—black, white, and Latino—received the gift of tongues through the baptism of the Holy Spirit, and then went out to spread the word. By 1909, Pentecostals had set up missions in fifty countries, many of them soon to become indigenized. By 1920, Pentecostals in the (mostly white) Assemblies of God and the (mostly black) Church of God in Christ and other denominations had become a major new presence in the American denominational order.

In this long-awaited book, Grant Wacker does not so much tell this story as assume it as background for his real project, a historical ethnography of the founding generation, those who shaped and carried the movement from the turn of the century to the 1920s. Himself raised in a thoroughly Pentecostal family but now a self-defined evangelical, Wacker in effect wants to understand the culture of his grandparents' generation. His project is both descriptive (to know what sense they made of their religious experience, how it affected their worship, work, and leisure, and how they took part, if at all, in civic life) and explanatory (to know how their movement survived and prospered). The key to both quests is the discovery that from the very beginning Pentecostalism held "two seemingly incompatible impulses in productive tension," heavenly aspirations and realistic shrewdness, the "primitive" yearning to be guided by God's spirit in all things, and the "pragmatic" determination to mind the store. "In their heart of hearts," Wacker's Pentecostals prayed as if everything depended on God and worked as if nothing did. Pentecostals knew the life beyond in all its fullness, and the life at hand in all its richness. Thus the title, from a 1906 testimony: "It is heaven below."

The book should appeal to social scientists in several respects. Conceptually, Wacker's approach is more that of the ethnographer than of the narrative historian. The chapters are organized thematically, on such topics as "authority," "customs," "leaders," and "women," not chronologically. (Indeed, one needs to know an outline of Pentecostal history before tackling the book.) Wacker presupposes that early Pentecostals shared a culture, and for its portrayal he draws on testimony from activists, some of whom would not qualify as Pentecostals by the criterion of speaking in tongues, testimony spanning three decades, "more or less as a single moment in time." Although he cites Max Weber primarily as the theorist of Protestantism and routinization, it can be said as well that Wacker makes good use of Weber's ideal-type methodology.

Substantively, the book portrays a nascent social movement at the grass roots. Wacker eavesdrops on "conversations that took place around the kitchen table," by reading between the lines of participants' memoirs and scouring obscure contemporaneous periodicals. Such documents, originally intended to spread the news of God's work in one place to fellow believers in another, are now archived for the use of scholars. Wacker and his assistants conducted content analyses of these primary sources to find, for example, how many speakers at meetings were women (nearly half) and how often reporters took note of interracial worship (seldom). (The results are on file at the Assembly of God seminary in Springfield,

Missouri.) Wacker tries to see the movement as it appeared to its rank and file, not solely as its leaders tried to define it.

That program yields what is theoretically most interesting about the book for social scientists: its thesis that "primitive" piety and "pragmatic" common sense coexisted in the heart of the movement. Explicitly breaking with both routinization and secularization theories, Wacker rejects the view that the movement evolved from otherworldly saintliness to this-worldly secularity or from antinomian enthusiasm to orderly procedure. "Believers juggled those forces from the outset, hour by hour, day by day." Wacker's Pentecostals kept many such balls in the air: uninhibited emotionalism and predictable order in their worship, freelance individualism and disciplined communalism in their organization.

Thus, authority resided in both received doctrine and the voice of the spirit, tempered by prudence. Emboldened by the Holy Spirit as well as by their reading of the prophet Joel, many movement women famously flouted social convention to assume public roles. "Almost immediately," however, others, mindful of public opinion and obstructed by movement patriarchs as well as by their reading of the apostle Paul, decided that they belonged behind their men. Too much the historian to be rigidly consistent on this principle, Wacker analyzes the Pentecostal record on race in a way closer to the routinization model. Racially mixed from the earliest days in Los Angeles, Pentecostal fellowships segregated within a decade, accommodating to Jim Crow conventions without any principled theological insistence that segregation offended God's will.

Wise, witty, carefully but not rigidly argued, and prodigiously researched (the reference notes occupy a quarter of the pages), Grant Wacker's *Heaven Below* will be a source of inspiration and entertainment for readers of this journal.

Joel Carpenter on the Second Generation of Fundamentalists: A Review of *Revive Us Again* (1999)

When it was published in 1997, this social history of American fundamentalism in the second quarter of the twentieth century had been long awaited by the author's fellow religious historians, and it has been well received by them.[3] But it will be of interest as well to sociologists of religion and social movements, for it explains how it happened that the fundamentalist movement, seemingly crushed by a series of defeats in the 1920s, reemerged to the astonishment of onlookers as a culturally visible presence in the 1950s and a major social force by the 1970s.

Joel Carpenter vividly narrates a dramatic fall-and-rise trajectory, from the public humiliation of fundamentalist champion William Jennings Bryan in the 1925 Scopes "monkey trial" and the unsuccessful efforts of fundamentalist forces to purge theological modernists from the Presbyterian and northern Baptist churches in the 1920s to the founding of Fuller Theological Seminary and the emergence of Billy Graham as the nation's evangelist (and United Airlines' top civilian flyer) by the late 1940s. Along the way, we see the protagonists licking their wounds, fencing in the flock, and preaching to the choir, but soon developing an infrastructure of local congregations, Bible institutes, and summer conferences, and then coming back to public engagement and reaching for respectability through their radio and print media, and finally prefiguring new forms of organization through parachurch youth movements. Central to Carpenter's analysis is his conviction that "fundamentalism was a popular movement . . . [with] horizontal, web-like, informal lines of leadership and organization, not vertical, pyramid-like ones." "Movements, like patches of dandelions, grow and spread when they are agitated" (16).

Carpenter's "fundamentalists" are strictly defined at the outset as a subset of evangelical Protestants, theological conservatives who went to the mat over correct doctrine. Their denominational heartland was Presbyterian and Baptist, and their geographic heartland was a crescent of northeastern cities: St. Louis and Chicago to Philadelphia and Boston. Only later did revivalism subdue dogmatism to religious experience and emotion, making possible a conservative brand of ecumenism and the huge rallies of Billy Graham. Carpenter acknowledges an alternative "Pentecostal paradigm" for understanding the resurgence of evangelicalism in the second half of the twentieth century, but he insists that in the first half, fundamentalism was the most influential current in American evangelicalism.

Three aspects of Carpenter's argument are especially noteworthy to sociologists.

First is his profound understanding of the internal complexity and ambivalence of fundamentalism. Fundamentalists thought of themselves simultaneously in two ways, as outsiders and insiders, and they wanted two things at once, purity and influence, separation and engagement. Heirs to the Puritans, they thought of themselves as custodians and trustees of a "Christian America"; the contemporary Religious Right has inherited that conviction from them. On the other hand, having suffered "years of ridicule and ostracism" (116), they felt themselves, much like immigrants, uprooted in a "diaspora" (12). Carpenter ties this ambivalence together with the observation that "fundamentalists like to be liked, yearn to be accepted, and dream of regaining a sweeping influence for their faith across the nation" (242). The attribution of a deep-seated desire for approval from those whose standards they are supposed to scorn is Carpenter's key to the irenic temper of postfundamentalist evangelicalism that his story ends with.

Second is that Carpenter applies what I have called a "new paradigm" analysis to the understanding of the American religious system. In one sense this is obvious, because his book is shot through with economic imagery. To take only one example: "In the free religious marketplace of American society, new religious movements have found ways to wrest a significant market share from older, more respectable bodies that have been less responsive to the changing religious economy" (153). Moreover, rather than bemoaning market consciousness as a recent erosion of sacredness, Carpenter traces religious entrepreneurship back to the beginnings of the American Republic and earlier, to George Whitefield and the

Wesley brothers in the eighteenth century and Charles Grandison Finney and Dwight L. Moody in the nineteenth. Thus, in Carpenter's analysis, economic imagery is connected not to a weakening of religion but to its vitality, widespread appeal, provision of social space for popular mobilization, and structural adaptability to changing conditions.

What I call new paradigm analysis is very much a theme here, but since the book is a copiously documented history monograph rather than a conceptually elaborated sociological one, the theme is not made into a general theory and is not referenced in the otherwise extensive, user-friendly index. Since the sources of new paradigm ideas are as much internal to history (in the work, for example, of Nathan Hatch) as imported from sociology, Carpenter cites sociologists, including me, sparingly.

The third noteworthy aspect of Carpenter's analysis is his understanding of the simultaneous modern*ity* and antimodern*ism* of fundamentalism. Without a conceptual apparatus, he implicitly distinguishes between "modernity" as a constitutive property of our society (entailing pluralism, mobility, individualism, and structural differentiation), and "modernism" as a congeries of contingent cultural currents in modern societies (including, but not entailing, evolutionism, antisupernaturalism, Nazi and Soviet totalitarianism, feminism, sexual freedom, and jazz). These cultural currents have nothing in common except for the facts that their proponents—often joined by outside observers—have declared them an unstoppable "wave of the future" and that fundamentalists have opposed them. There is a difference between the modernistic currents that are anathema to fundamentalists and the modern conditions that are their natural matrix.

Since Weber, it has been a stock of the sociological trade that a religious movement may spawn trends that undermine its further viability, and thus it may be no great surprise to hear that fundamentalists claim to speak for the basic values of Western civilization, that nineteenth-century evangelicalism (of which the fundamentalist movement is an heir) was one of the wellsprings of modern American society, and that early twentieth-century fundamentalism prefigured the changes in mainstream Protestant institutions in the last third of the century that Robert Wuthnow has analyzed. It is quite possible that fundamentalism, like so many other movements, is its own gravedigger.

Yet Carpenter cites Martin Marty to argue that evangelicalism "is the characteristic Protestant way of relating to modernity" (235). Fundamentalism's portability suits Americans' kinetic lifestyle; its focus on the spiritual state of individual lives fits modern society's compartmentalization of religion; and its antielitism mirrors the egalitarianism and populism of American religious life. For Carpenter, fundamentalists' beliefs are less a point of vulnerability than a source of courage that "energized them religiously" (244) and enabled an eventual "wave of creativity" (129) and spiritual power. In their congregationalism and interdenominationalism, fundamentalists produced "the most powerful and effective kind of American ecumenism, . . . [which] was ad hoc, local, and task-oriented" (159).

Carpenter does not skirt, though some may feel he underplays, the darker side of the fundamentalist story, including the reactionary macho/misogynist ideology it embraced in the 1920s and some of its leaders' embrace of anti-Semitic conspiracy theories in the 1930s. What Carpenter does is to go a very long way toward explaining to the satisfaction of a sociologist where the late twentieth-century evangelical resurgence came from.

Donald Miller on "New Paradigm Churches": A Review of *Reinventing American Protestantism* (1997)

Drawing theoretically on a network of social scientists that includes Rodney Stark, Roger Finke, Lawrence Iannaccone, and me—but also historian Nathan Hatch—Donald E. Miller, professor of religion at the University of Southern California, applies the "new paradigm" label I have given to this school of thought to a burgeoning group of West Coast–based churches, including the Pentecostally oriented Vineyard, Calvary Chapel, and Hope Chapel, and by extension such "seeker-sensitive" evangelical churches as Willow Creek and Saddleback community churches.[4] What unites these "new paradigm churches" is that they pay attention to their consumer market by tuning their worship and organizational style to today's culture, not to cultures of the past. Miller's thesis is that the evident success of these churches offers lessons and warnings to a declining Protestant mainline.

In sheer organizational terms at least, the Vineyard and Calvary Chapel associations (on which Miller concentrates) would seem to merit the "winner" designation he bestows on them. Founded in 1965 by former Foursquare minister Chuck Smith and still led by him, Calvary Chapel now claims over 600 congregations in the United States and another 100 worldwide, especially in the former Soviet bloc. Emerging in 1982 from two formerly Calvary-affiliated congregations, the Vineyard numbers some 406 congregations in the United States and another 173 abroad, particularly in the anglophone democracies. To judge from the rich quantitative and qualitative data collected by Miller and his research assistants, Brenda Brasher and Paul Kennedy, Calvary churches appeal to a working- and lower-middle-class constituency and lean toward fundamentalism, while the Vineyards promote the public exercise of gifts of the Spirit (especially tongues and healing) and have a slightly more educated and affluent clientele. Both churches share contemporary worship with guitars and overhead projectors (not organs and hymnals) and low-key teachings (not stentorian, theologically learned sermons) relevant to the everyday lives of people who have learned to value their families more than their careers. This recipe, improvised by such men as Vineyard founders Kenn Gulliksen and John Wimber—all senior pastors are men—on the basis of their musical skills and own checkered histories, appeals to baby boomers and even baby busters whose absence from mainline churches marks those churches as "losers."

Based on extensive interviews and vividly reported episodes of participant observation as well as surveys, Miller's portrait of new paradigm churches highlights not only their upbeat Sunday worship but also their intense, midweek house-group meetings, and the physical intimacy, mentoring, "discipling," and leadership training that they promote. A great deal of religious substance lies under the relaxed, youthful style of these congregations. They give direction to previously aimless lives, channel energies into food pantries and prison ministries, and promote home schooling and marital fidelity. To be sure, the religious substance is consistently conservative—new paradigm Christians believe that it will take changed hearts to bring about a changed world—but is nonetheless serious for that. (Miller invites us to await Brasher's forthcoming book to explore the implications of Calvary and the Vineyard for women's roles [see now Brasher 1998].)

Miller's evidence that the new paradigm churches are highly "demanding" if not classically "strict" is one of the instances where he addresses issues raging in his and my academic fields. (Yet it is frustrating for a social scientist not to be given more information about the sampling procedures that produced the thirty-six-page appendix of questionnaire results.) Another issue is whether the members of these new churches are in fact the "new Christians" so many claim to be or are instead cases of what Canadian sociologist Reginald Bibby calls the "circulation of the saints." Miller's interviewees speak of radically changed identities, but his questionnaire data report that 65 percent of members went to church weekly when they were growing up and 36 percent had fundamentalist or evangelical backgrounds, suggestive of a pattern of backsliding and return. (Another 28 percent—38 percent for Calvary rank and file—say they grew up Catholic, a matter Miller might have spent more time on.)

Indeed, Miller consistently underplays the conservative baggage that new paradigm Christians demonstrably bring with them, both from their family backgrounds (especially for members) and their mentoring by seniors in the movement (especially for pastors), preferring instead to highlight the empirical and pragmatic attitude they bring to both their experience and their frequent Bible studies. Giving excessive credence to respondents' protestations of presuppositionless religion—"no creed but the Bible" as affirmed by the Holy Spirit—Miller overlooks particular echoes of restoration theology and California Pentecostalism. In this regard, the most powerful analysis in the book comes when Miller jettisons the subtitle's implicit claim that the movement is unprecedented and instead uses Hatch's work (*The Democratization of American Christianity*) to see it as the latest example of American revivalism, on the model of the early nineteenth-century Second Great Awakening. Such a more modest reading will render the book more useful for church leaders.

As an instance of charismatic revival, the new paradigm movement will eventually be subject to the "routinization" that now enfeebles the mainline. In the meantime, if not the millennium, the mainline can learn from it. Needed first is to overcome modernity's mind-body dualism, which privileges an excessively cognitive approach to religion. Although more doctrinally guided than Miller is willing to admit, new paradigm churches foster bodily and experiential religion, and he suggests that their mainline counterparts should experiment with the spiritual disciplines of Ignatius and the liturgical style of Taizé. (New paradigm sociologists themselves could profit from Miller's use of William James's *Varieties of Religious Experience*.)

Second, mainline churches should study the new paradigm pattern of organizational loosening and flattening. Not truly democratic, the new paradigm churches nonetheless make room for lay participation, encouraging innovation and fostering leadership through functionally diffuse, religiously inspired home meetings in place of the routinized committee meetings of the mainline, 80 percent of which Miller thinks should be abolished. In this regard, I wish Miller had spent more time explaining exactly how Chuck Smith exerts "extremely strong theological leadership" and how John Wimber expelled the Toronto Airport fellowship from the Vineyard association (an event that goes unmentioned). The new paradigm churches do after all have organizational structures.

Overall, Miller wishes that the mainline would follow the new paradigm lead to become less professionalized. Mainline structures—including maintenance-heavy buildings, educational institutions, clergy placement procedures, and denominational bureaucracies—need to be pruned so that less is invested in keeping up the status quo and more in "bringing God to people and conveying the self-transcending and life-changing core of all true religion." Most pointedly, Miller thinks that schools for pastoral training should be attached not to universities but to local congregations, "especially those flagship churches that are demonstrating leadership." One such school is Chuck Smith's original Calvary Chapel, whose leadership recruitment is governed by the aphorism, "God does not call the qualified, he qualifies the called." Thus Vineyard and Calvary plant new churches either by sending off aspiring leaders with a small core from a parent church or by "franchising" them (the figure of speech is Miller's) to new territory. New paradigm methods applied to the mainline would favor sites with demographic potential and clergy with humble backgrounds but entrepreneurial skills.

Although Miller does not directly address the social justice implications of such a distribution of mainline ministries, he might argue that mainline churches planted by such visionary leaders would, like new paradigm ones, better serve the needs of their members. He seems persuaded by the argument that seminary education creates a peer group of seminarians in place of laity, creating "a distance that is difficult to bridge."

Himself a liberal Episcopalian—he is a member of Pasadena's All Saints Church and has published defenses of liberal Christianity in this journal—Miller stereotypes "the mainline" in order to sharpen his portrayal of new paradigm churches. I hope that an understandable annoyance with Miller's too-frequent reliance on the epithet "bureaucratic" to describe mainline patterns (it certainly doesn't match my small Lutheran congregation) will not prevent the thoughtful reading this book deserves. Miller and his new paradigm churches have much to teach us.

82   A CHURCH OF OUR OWN

NOTES

1. Review of *The Churching of America, 1776–1990: Winners and Losers in Our Religious Economy*, by Roger Finke and Rodney Stark, reprinted by permission from the September 1993 issue of the *Journal for the Scientific Study of Religion*.

2. Review of *Heaven Below: Early Pentecostals and American Culture*, by Grant Wacker, reprinted by permission from the March 2003 issue of the *Journal for the Scientific Study of Religion*.

3. Review of *Revive Us Again: The Reawakening of American Fundamentalism*, by Joel A. Carpenter, reprinted by permission from the June 1999 issue of *Social Forces*.

4. Review of *Reinventing American Protestantism: Christianity in the New Millennium*, by Donald E. Miller, copyright 1997 Christian Century. Reprinted by permission from the November 19–26, 1997, issue of the *Christian Century*.

REFERENCES

(References to writings of the author are found in a separate listing at the back of the book.)

Ammerman, Nancy T. 1990. *Baptist Battles: Social Change and Religious Conflict in the Southern Baptist Convention*. New Brunswick, N.J.: Rutgers University Press.

Brasher, Brenda E. 1998. *Godly Women: Fundamentalism and Female Power*. New York: Routledge.

Butler, Jon. 1990. *Awash in a Sea of Faith: The Christianization of the American People*. Cambridge: Harvard University Press.

Finke, Roger, and Rodney Stark. 1988. "Religious Economies and Sacred Canopies: Religious Mobilization in American Cities." *American Sociological Review* 53 (February): 41–49.

Iannaccone, Laurence R. 1986. "A Formal Model of Church and Sect." *American Journal of Sociology* 94, suppl.: S241–S268.

Kelley, Dean M. 1972. *Why Conservative Churches Are Growing*. San Francisco: Harper and Row.

Marty, Martin E. 1993. "Churches as Winners, Losers." *Christian Century* 110 (January 27): 88–89.

Noll, Mark. 1992. *A History of Christianity in the United States and Canada*. Grand Rapids, Mich.: Eerdmans.

Steinfels, Peter. 1993. "Beliefs." *New York Times*, national ed., February 20.

5

Religion, Boundaries, and Bridges
(1997)

For eight years, I have been tracking religious diversity in the United States, concentrating on the assertion of particularism. I have explored religious communities of "elective parochials"—people who adopt small-town values (Warner 1988a, 1991a), deaf Catholics (Warner and Pappas 1993b), postcharismatic baby boomers (Wedam and Warner 1994b), Korean Protestants (Warner 1990b), Hispanic Catholics (Warner 1994c), and gay and lesbian Christians (Warner 1995), and, for the past four years, I have directed the New Ethnic and Immigrant Congregations Project (Warner and Wittner 1998a). I have presented research findings to many audiences in the United States—through university colloquia, scholarly conferences, public lectures, and media interviews—and here I intend to address questions that, whatever my stated topic, are invariably posed to me in these venues. The questions go something like this: What does it mean for our society that there are so many churches whose signs I cannot read and so many temples that aren't Christian? Are these folks American? Are they a threat? More generally, questioners want to know whether religious particularism—the resurgence of religious boundaries—threatens universalism, or at least the quasi-universalism of a nation whose motto is *e pluribus unum*.

My answer, based on my researches—both my on-site observations and my reading of other observers' accounts—is, "I very much doubt it." Worries about fragmentation, I believe, are based on paying relatively too much attention to what self-appointed advocates for particularisms *say* and too little to what the communities in question *do*. This paper is a frankly speculative attempt to theorize my experientially based convictions on this issue. My theoretical search has led me to focus on the crucial role of *embodied ritual* as a key to the capacity religion has to bridge boundaries, both between communities and individuals.[1] A more complete title might be: "Religion, Discursive Boundaries, and Ritual Bridges, with Special Reference to Post-1965 Immigrant and Ethnic Communities in the United States."

The New Ethnic and Immigrant Congregations Project

As I said, my recent tracking of particularisms has been through the New Ethnic and Immigrant Congregations Project (NEICP), which was concluded at the same meetings as this lecture was given (the Association for the Sociology of Religion, August 1996, in New York). I will refer to the NEICP research reports for illustrative material (see the Appendix to References), and I refer the reader to the collection of those reports that my associate Judith Wittner and I have edited for publication (Warner and Wittner 1998a).

In the interests of full disclosure, it must be pointed out that the rubric for the communities under study by the NEICP—"new ethnic and immigrant" communities— is explicitly defined residually, as the set of those residents of the United States whose numbers have grown substantially since 1965 but whose religious institutions have heretofore been overlooked by scholars in social science, history, and religious studies. Hence the "new ethnic and immigrant" rubric includes not only refugees and transnationals but also all Hispanic/Latino[2] communities in the United States, even though some of their number may have resided within the fifty states for generations. Thus also, the "new ethnic and immigrant" rubric *excludes* the religious communities of European Americans and African Americans, which have already received significant scholarly attention. By "congregations," NEICP refers to local, face-to-face religious assemblies, whether authorized or unofficial.

It must be said that the conception of the NEICP itself bridges scholarly boundaries. First, very little of the literature on recent immigration and ethnicity (e.g., Rumbaut and Cornelius 1995) says anything about religion, which from the point of view of the debate on the future of our society[3] represents a huge scholarly blind spot. Those who are concerned about the future of new immigrants— especially the fate of their children—have learned that a "resilient affirmation of collective ethnic identity" (Rumbaut 1995, 65) is often a factor in their healthy adaptation. Yet the role of religion in such identification has largely been ignored, the recent work of Bankston and Zhou (1996) on Vietnamese youth in New Orleans being a rare exception.[4]

This blindness is all the more ironic since the enormous vigor and variety of new immigrant religious institutions—thousands of Catholic parishes with masses in Spanish and other languages; thousands of Korean, Chinese, and Indian Christian congregations and Hispanic Protestant churches; hundreds of synagogues, Islamic centers, and Buddhist temples; scores of Hindu, Jain, Sikh, and Zoroastrian temples and gurdwaras; and an uncounted number of entrepreneurial and house churches of a huge variety of religions, including Vodou and Santeria—might seem grist for the mill of multiculturalists, while the fact that the great majority of new immigrants are Christian, many of them rather conservative Christian at that, might be mobilized for the argumentarium of assimilationists. Yet few on either side of the multiculturalism-assimilation debate have paid any attention to religion.

In turn, very little of the literature in sociology of religion says anything about new immigrants, except as objects of conversionist or social justice missions. There seems to be a disciplinary amnesia in disregard of the fact that most of the religious pluralism in the United States—the firmly established institutions of Presbyterians and Episcopalians, Lutherans and Catholics, Jews and Orthodox Christians—is the result of previous waves of immigration. It is not that sociology of religion ignores difference. Scholars in ethnic and immigrant studies might be interested—and surprised—to learn that there is a substantial literature in sociology of religion on a "culture war" that is said to be imminent within white middle-class society, having very little to do with persons of color (Wuthnow 1988; Hunter 1991; Wheeler 1996).

Theoretical and Empirical Presuppositions

My argument is oriented by some hypotheses and observations, which, in the scope of this discussion, I can here only assert, not defend.

1. In the United States, religion mediates difference (Herberg 1960; Williams 1988; Warner 1993a, 1994a); religion is the institutional area where U.S. culture has best tolerated difference. Meanwhile, religion is one area of difference that, in the United States, is experienced by most communities as authentically expressed rather than illegitimately imposed (e.g., Goizueta 1995, 29). Thus, not all difference is based on invidious privilege (Wolfe 1992); many differences are affirmed by those whose lives are bounded by them.

2. Since the 1960s, the status-conferral function of religion in the United States has faded in significance, and the cultural reproduction function has increased. In the United States today, religion particularly serves parents' interests in cultural reproduction (Warner 1994–1995; Carter 1994; Warner 1999a). Since the 1960s, many Americans across the spectrum have felt like exiles in their own land (Denby 1996) and, with respect to the role of religious institutions, there is a sense in which many feel like Jews, sojourners in Babylon. The sense of exile is shared by new immigrants.

3. Not to deny the privileges conferred by white skin and middle-class education (see Goizueta 1995, chap. 1), if we talk about "culture" we have to deconstruct the notion of "*the* white middle class" (cf. Portes 1995, 72). Sociologists of religion have perhaps gone too far with talk of culture wars, but they have at least made it clear that white America is not culturally monolithic.

4. For this and other reasons, cultural differences are manifold not only between "new immigrants" and the "host society" but also within the host society. Not only differences of race and ethnicity but also identity and moral culture are salient.

5. Hence, to assess the fate of what we may call the multicultural or assimilationist trajectories, we must look at "contexts of reception" (Cornelius 1995,

II–I2) and "proximal hosts" (Mittelberg and Waters 1992) and recognize that assimilation may be "segmented" (Portes 1995, 75) or "additive" (Gibson 1995; Kim and Hurh 1993) and otherwise different from the "canonical model" (Alba and Nee 1995, 40).

The five points just enumerated are merely asserted, not developed in this paper. The theoretical ambitions of the paper are, first, to move beyond cerebral to embodied understandings of religious communities, to go beyond the theorizing—of both discourse analysts and religious ideologues—that puts thought first, and toward a focus on action and feeling; and, second, taking a lead from Virgilio Elizondo's concept of *mestizaje*, to argue for a new theory of particularism, from either/or polarization to both/and inclusion.

Theory of Boundaries and Experiences of Bridges

My theory of religious pluralism in the United States (Warner 1993a) leads me to expect a stress on difference. Hence I claim (Warner 1994a, 67–73) that the prototypical local religious form in the United States is not the (inclusive, geographically delimited) "parish" but the (exclusive, culturally distinct) "congregation." NEICP was premised on this assumption, and our observations show that many "new immigrant" groups are certainly acting consistently with this expectation, developing many forms of "de facto congregation" (Warner 1994a, 73–82), cementing their cultural identities through religious institutions and ideals.

I particularly expect to see religious groups developing around linguistic boundaries, and I also expect that with linguistic acculturation—the acquisition of English dominance by second and later generations—the immigrant congregation will face a crisis.

Yet despite this theory of boundaries, during the course of the project I witnessed many instances of bridging in congregational religion and experienced gestures of inclusion in events where I did not share the religion or the language, sometimes neither (Warner 1994c). There are other witnesses to such bridging (Wheeler 1996).[5]

I experienced many modest examples of inclusion—where I was brought into the proceedings—during my site visits for the NEICP:[6]

- sharing communion (bread and wine) with friends of Susana Gallardo in their San Jose, California, house church called La Comunidad, followed by a lunch of homemade soup and jug wine;
- along with Nancy Wellmeier, accepting an offer of sweet bread and Mountain Dew at the tail end of a Friday night house church meeting with a group of Mayan Indians in South Central Los Angeles, where they also invited me to make music with them on their room-sized marimba;
- sharing in a coffee hour at Karen Chai's Korean Methodist church and a midday meal at Fenggang Yang's Chinese evangelical church;

- drinking rum during an all-night Vodou ceremony, conducted in Kreyol, and breaking fast afterward with boiled fish and yams, in the company of Elizabeth McAlister and some of her Haitian friends in Brooklyn;
- enjoying a home-cooked south Indian dinner with Sheba George at the home of the priest of St. George's Syrian Orthodox Church;
- joining with Prema Kurien to share in another south Indian potluck supper at the end of a two-and-a-half-hour *pooja* and *bhajan* meeting of the Kerala Hindu Organization—during which the smells wafted into the prayer room from the adjacent kitchen;
- sharing in a late Friday night dinner, seated on the floor of a Muslim home in Garden Grove, California, during a break in a home Qur'an study meeting, in the company of Keng Fong Pang.

If too many of these illustrations involve sharing of food, I can also mention joining in a call-and-response-style chant of "Selassi!" to the leader's "Rastafari!" when I joined Randal Hepner and others at a Twelve Tribes of Israel Sunday congregation meeting in the borough of Queens.

I can recount how a man approached me across the sanctuary of a Sephardic Orthodox synagogue in Los Angeles and, with a wordless smile, placed a tallis on my shoulders and showed me how far into the three-hundred-page Hebrew prayer book the services had gone; this is the synagogue where Shoshanah Feher began her researches among Iranian Jews.

I remember that Luis León and I became, willy-nilly, two members of a four-person Spanish-language prayer circle at an Alcance Victoria church service when the young couple directly in front of us followed their pastor's instructions and turned around to face us, offering their hands.

I was invited to join the shoulder-to-shoulder face-to-the-floor *salat* prayer in the Brooklyn mosque that was Rogaia AbuSharaf's research site—only to be vigorously proselytized at the end of the *jum'ah* ceremony.

Notice that all of these memories concern bodily experiences—eating, drinking, imitative chanting, being touched, holding hands, prostrating—no doubt because in many cases I could not understand the language in which the ceremonies took place and concentrated on what I could feel.

I do not want to make too much of these modest, although deeply appreciated, gestures of inclusion. They were extended toward a privileged representative of the dominant society who was usually (not always) visibly accompanied by a person the group had long accepted into their midst. I mention them not to argue for their macroscopic significance but to reflect upon their sheer possibility.

I noticed other, more significant, examples of apparent inclusiveness during NEICP site visits and other boundary-crossing excursions:

- Fenggang Yang's Chinese church has a white American associate pastor;

- there were other non-Asian Americans than me, especially men, at Karen Chai's Korean church coffee hour, which followed a youth-oriented worship service in the style of the Vineyard;
- the corps of drummers at the Haitian Vodou ceremony, with the exception of their leader, Frisner Agustin, were all white men;
- the assembled congregations for Friday jum'ah prayer at mosques in Brooklyn and Santa Ana (and many other mosques and Islamic centers I have visited) were remarkably diverse in racial phenotype, if not in gender.

What are we to make of this?

The Construction of Religious Boundaries and Bridges

It is a guiding principle (but hardly a patented idea) of the NEICP that *congregations provide cultural space for immigrants and other cultural minorities.* Pyong Gap Min (1992), Yvonne Haddad and Adair Lummis (1987), and Raymond Williams (1988) are among the scholars who have analyzed this function of religious institutions for, respectively, Korean Protestants, immigrant Muslims, and immigrants from diverse religious communities of south Asia. The immigrant church is a home away from home, a place where the language of the home country and its codes of honor enjoy a privilege they do not enjoy in most of the host society. As I like to put it, they are remembrances of Zion in the midst of Babylon.

But immigrant churches are not simple transplants (Smith 1971). Communities, religious and otherwise, are not opaque and sealed-off expressions of primordial essences; they are constructed, using available human methods and materials.

What I think we need to look at is how religious communities are put together (not just reinforced once they exist), and I will do just that, with a stress on rituals that involve the body. Although there are some suggestive hints in the literature on religious conversion (I refer to the work of Lewis Rambo [1993]), I have found little on how solidarity is achieved in the great world religions, and therefore little that directly bears on bridging particularisms in the United States. Hence, I have had to range far afield, using works by anthropologists, ethnomusicologists, and military historians, among others.[7]

I shall begin with a visit in 1989 to a Korean Presbyterian church in Princeton, New Jersey.[8]

I was invited by the congregation's acting pastor, the Princeton theologian Sang Hyun Lee, who warned me in advance that the service—the whole in Korean, of course—would be longer than usual and more elaborate because it was an ordination, but that it would be followed by a good dinner. It would be a special event, and Lee knew I liked Korean food.[9]

The service was standard and dignified Presbyterian, but, at two hours and twenty minutes, very long, and I couldn't understand a literal word of it. But it wasn't opaque, since the ritual was familiar. There was a choral introit; a prayer of invocation (when heads were bowed); the Lord's Prayer and Apostles' Creed (which I recognized by their placement in the liturgy and the cadences of their pronunciation); a Gloria Patri (which I knew through its accompanying music); an offertory, accompanied by a duet of two young boys on the violin; a choral anthem; a Bible reading (by a lay person standing at the lectern); a responsive reading (when people recited from their psalters); several hymns, the congregation standing (one, based on the tune of Beethoven's "Ode to Joy," was a Presbyterian favorite I sang along with); and a long pastoral prayer (heads again bowed, done by a clergyman, his status recognizable because of his robes), followed by a unison "amen."

A less routine, but still normatively Presbyterian, part of the service was the long ceremony of ordination and installation, recited from the prayer book, with eight newly elected elders and deacons coming forward to recite their vows and extant elders coming forward to lay hands on them.

The sermon (twenty-five minutes long) was the toughest part for me, and because this was a service of ordination there were two other long speeches—which I later learned were a charge to the new elders and a charge to the congregation, presented by ministers from neighboring Korean churches—which sorely tested my monolingual limits.

All of this ritual language I recognized and understood: we stood to sing, bowed heads for prayer, and sat and tried to look attentive for instruction; the only thing I found unusual was that the newly ordained elders *bowed* to their predecessors, after the latter had laid hands on them, receiving a bow of acknowledgment in return.

The service was concluded, conventionally enough, with a period of announcements and greetings just before the final hymn and benediction. Reverend Lee introduced various visitors, including me, all of whom were applauded. He also, as he'd told me in advance, invited everyone to join in the congregational dinner, ready to be served in the parish hall.

Now I have said that I couldn't understand a literal word, but that is not *quite* true. I could hear my name pronounced, with a Korean inflection, when Reverend Lee introduced me to the congregation; after the polite applause, he said directly to me, in English, "I just said nice things about you." I also overheard a few words in English before the service from the people in the pew behind me. And midway in the service, when the two Korean American boys had finished their violin duet, Reverend Lee turned to them and said, in English, "Thank you." They replied to him with a bow.

As we went in to dinner, I was greeted in English by a young Korean American man who told me that he was a sophomore at Princeton, hailing from Pennsylvania, where he was a member of a Presbyterian church. He had been one of those sitting behind me. I asked him about the sermon, but he apologized that he'd only been able to follow "the gist of it." Many of the conversations over dinner, and not only those I shared in, were in English.

Now there is a great deal more I could report about what went on that day in Princeton, and a lot we could analyze, but I want to draw two lessons from the story

I have told. One is that some bodily actions—I will speak about music and motion—can bridge linguistic and other cultural boundaries. The other is that the first and most systematic category of newcomer to need a bridge into many immigrant congregations is their own children, the new generation in the host society. Because of them, it becomes clear that religion, like other parts of culture, has to be taught, and therefore that outsiders can be brought in.[10]

Reflecting on this story led me to look into the ways that rituals can create—not only express—social solidarity and that led me to David Kertzer's *Ritual, Politics, and Power*, by which I have been especially enlightened. Kertzer (1988) argues that relationships and identities are *produced* (not only expressed) through rituals. Psychologist of religion Lewis Rambo, in his theory of conversion, agrees: "Ritual actions consolidate the community through singing, recitation, and gestures in unison" (Rambo 1993, 115).[11] It is as much the *emotional power of doing things together* as the *compelling logic of ideological agreement* that produces solidarity.

Drawing on Durkheim, Kertzer says: "Socially and politically speaking, we are what we do, not what we think" (Kertzer 1988, 68). According to him, Durkheim's "genius lies in having recognized that ritual builds solidarity without requiring the sharing of beliefs. Solidarity is produced by people acting together, not by people thinking together" (76). Rambo adds that ritual "offers a form of knowledge that is distinctive from, but as important as, cognitive knowledge; one might call it embodied, or holistic knowledge" (Rambo 1993, 114).[12] To give a hint of the analysis to come, Kertzer (1988, 11–12) stresses that the symbols around which ritual centers can and do carry multiple meanings; the more symbols are ambiguous, the more they can produce solidarity in the absence of consensus (Kertzer 1988, 66).[13]

I recognize a risk of this focus on the emotional and bodily aspect of religion.[14] "Emotional" is an adjective often attributed to the religions of sectarian, exotic, marginal, or otherwise disesteemed groups, even an epithet applied to the religious expressions of women and persons of color, precisely as a way of distinguishing their religious expressions from the presumably more intellectualized and refined expressions of higher-status groups, as in the standard contrast between Presbyterians' supposedly "cerebral" worship and the more "emotional" outpourings of the "sects." But emotionalism is not the special property of sectarian worship, nor is cerebral meaning alien to it (Nelson 1996).[15] Let there be no mistake about it, the religious expressions of the white middle class can be as emotional as those in any storefront church, and they must be so if they are to remain vital. As Barbara Wheeler put it in her H. Paul Douglass lecture: "We [Mainline Protestants], like the evangelicals, are bodied beings, and a religious tradition that has little or nothing to look at, listen to, and touch cannot sustain us very long" (Wheeler 1996, 296). Thus, we must not use the expedient of indexing affect by the cues—loud voices, rapid bodily motions, sweaty skin—that stereotypically code "emotion."

Ethnomusicologist John Blacking warns us not to confuse overt motion with felt emotion: "We cannot say that the Kwakiutl are more emotional than the Hopi because their style of dancing looks more ecstatic to our eyes. In some cultures, or in certain types of music and dancing within a culture, emotions may be deliberately internalized, but they are not necessarily less intense" (Blacking 1973, 33). Speaking for my white Anglo-Saxon Protestant self, I am far more affected by singing my bass part in a dress rehearsal of Bach's B-Minor Mass or Brahms's German Requiem than I was by the intense, energetic Vodou drumming of Frisner Agustin and his corps in a Brooklyn basement. Thus, to deal with the emotional significance of bodily religion is emphatically *not* to focus on marginal religion or to exempt churchly religion from analytic scrutiny. Let us first look at music.

The Creative, Bonding Power of Music

I will begin with another story from my cross-boundary excursions. Two years ago, I was invited by Timothy Matovina to join him and a team of observing participants at the Holy Week observance of the Cathedral of San Fernando in San Antonio, Texas, the dominantly Hispanic but downtown Catholic parish where Virgilio Elizondo was at the time serving as pastor. Our assignment from Matovina was to observe as much of the nearly round-the-clock events as we had the stamina for and then to share our reactions with the others on the study team, including himself and Elizondo. One of the other invited observers was Loyola University philosopher Roberto Goizueta, whose published reflections on the events I will be quoting.

I will focus on only one half-hour-long segment of the observance, the Oración en el Huerto, or prayer in the garden, that followed the Holy Thursday liturgy of the Last Supper, when Archbishop Patricio Flores, in the role of Jesus, washed the feet of the disciples, played by young men of the parish. When the mass was ended, members of the congregation, carrying lighted candles, processed out the door to the plaza across the street, intending to accompany their Lord on his lonely vigil of prayer in the garden of Gethsemane. Over a loudspeaker, the church's cantor led a responsory in chant, beginning each verse in Spanish with a recitation of one of the human attributes of Jesus, and the group responding—as we slowly circled the plaza—with the refrain "Caminemos con Jesús," let us walk with Jesus:

> Jesús, amigo de prostitutes (Jesus, friend of prostitutes; Jesus, son of the carpenter; Jesus, who lived among the people; etc.):
>
> Caminemos con Jesús.

Dozens of times. The chant melody is simple, with the first syllables of the verse sung (in solfege) on *mi* and the succeeding four syllables (e.g., *prostitutes*) on *re, mi, fa, re*; in the refrain, *Caminemos* is chanted to *re* and the three final syllables (con Jesús) on *do, re, mi*.[16]

It is significant that I do not remember what the cantor sang, the various human attributes of Jesus; I remember only my part, the part of the congregation: Caminemos con Jesús. Here is what Goizueta remembers: "The people are walking with Jesus to Gethsemane. It is . . . an experience that stirs all one's senses: the hundreds of flickering candles under a darkening sky, the loud horns of impatient drivers, the wide-eyed stares of curious onlookers, the angry insults of fundamentalist hecklers, and the incense-like fragrance of the smoke wafting from the multitude of candles . . . and always: '*Caminemos con Jesús*' " (Goizueta 1995, 33; see also Elizondo 1983, 41–43). Much more happened over those three days, including much more making of music, but so moved by this memory was Goizueta that his new book (1995) on "Hispanic/Latino theology" is entitled *Caminemos Con Jesús*. So moved was I that upon my return to Chicago and to the writing of my report, I recited that chant to an informant on religious music, J. Michael Thompson, director of music at St. Peter's Church, who told me that it was a variation on a Gregorian Psalm Tone. Indeed, as I suspected, I had sung it to other texts with other congregations in Chicago.

In his book, Goizueta analyzes the theology that he sees behind the text of this and other Mexican American rituals, but I want to stress something else, the sheer power of making music together with so many others—some of whom I met that day, none of whom I had known before, only three of whom (Elizondo, Goizueta, and Matovina) I have seen since—and to acknowledge the long-term effect of that experience on my own thinking.

This is by no means the first time I have been moved, in my heart and my mind, by making music together with others. In the past few years, I have become part of the nationwide revival of shape-note singing (Cobb 1989), a form of folk choral music with dominantly evangelical texts that unites Alabama Primitive Baptists with rust-belt secularists, Jews, and, indeed, liberal Christians. In my book on the Presbyterian church of Mendocino, California, I said a lot about the music the people made and how it drew me in (Warner 1988a, 1–6, 38–40, 42, 50, 73–74, 132, 205, 210, 213), but some critics wanted more attention paid to the topic (e.g., Noll 1989, 2). I can now see what they meant, since I have been surprised not to see more mention—let alone analysis—of music making in others' accounts of contemporary religious communities in the United States.[17]

To understand the capacity music has to create solidarity I have drawn on the work of social theorist Alfred Schutz (1964), ethnomusicologist John Blacking (1973, 1992), developmental psychologist Sandra Trehub (Trehub and Schellenberg 1995), psychiatrist Anthony Storr (1992), and hymnologist Linda Clark (1993).

First, the refrain we sang in San Antonio was simple enough and repeated incessantly enough that it soon became very familiar, even for those who hadn't sung it before. Thus with each verse, the group's solidarity, actual (as lived by the people of the cathedral parish) and nascent (as experienced by outsiders Goizueta and me), was built. "Each time a community stands to sing a hymn, it recreates its identity anew, carrying the past forward into the present" (Clark 1993, 103).

Second is the often-remarked elemental character of the sense of sound (as contrasted with sight), whether due to its connection to more primitive parts of the brain or to the salience of sound in our earliest existence in the sightless world of the uterus. Storr writes (1992, 26): "At an emotional level, there is something 'deeper' about hearing than seeing; and something about hearing other people which fosters human relationships even more than seeing them." Blacking (1992, 304) says that "participation in performance . . . can involve the body's sensori-motor system in such a way that people's responses to the music are felt as an expression of the very ground of their being and an intrinsic part of their human nature."

Third is the fact that a melody cannot be tied to a specific linguistic or con-ceptual content. Clark (1993, 101) says that "hymns are not sets of words on a page but events." Schutz writes that the meaning structure of musical interactions is "not capable of being expressed in conceptual terms" (Schutz 1964, 159); making music together is similar in this respect, he says, to marching, dancing, and mak-ing love (162). Storr notes that music arouses—both elicits and creates—emotional states that are nonspecific (Storr 1992, 27, 30). Blacking (1973, 52; see also 1992, 307) writes that because of this multivocal quality, "the same piece of music may move different people in the same sort of way, but for different reasons. You can enjoy a piece of plain chant because you are a Roman Catholic or because you like the sound of the music: you need not have a 'good ear' to enjoy it as a Catholic, nor need you be a believer to enjoy it as music." Because of its fundamental ambigu-ity, making music together is one of those ritual acts that Kertzer talks about that can produce solidarity without consensus.[18]

That may be why music's power has often excited the suspicions of religious leaders. Here is Saint Augustine (from the *Confessions*), as quoted by Anthony Storr (1992, 22): "I waver between the danger that lies in gratifying the sense [sic] and the benefits which, as I know, can accrue from singing. Without committing myself to an irrevocable opinion, I am inclined to approve of the custom of singing in church, in order that by indulging the ears weaker spirits may be inspired with feelings of devotion. Yet when I find the singing itself more moving than the truth which it conveys, I confess that this is a grievous sin, and at those times I would prefer not to hear the singer."

Finally, music allows us to transcend the dilemma of the individual and the communal. I can sing bass passably well, but there are few bass parts—short of solo arias beyond my capacity—that sound good alone. I need the sopranos, not to mention the altos and tenors. The same principle goes for the violist, the bas-soonist, and the tuba player; and even instruments that sound good alone—the violin, the flute, and the soprano voice—have an immeasurably enriched reper-toire of personal expression when yoked to others. Beyond these perhaps too instrumental considerations is the fact that music allows us to experience the being of the other not as a limitation on but as a fulfillment of our own being. As Schutz puts it, making music together involves a "tuning-in relationship," which is "established by the reciprocal sharing of the Other's flux of experiences in inner time, by living through a vivid present together, by experiencing this togetherness as a 'We'" (Schutz 1964, 177; see also Neitz and Spickard 1990). And Blacking writes:

"To feel with the body is probably as close as anyone can ever get to resonating with another person" (Blacking 1973, 111, also 51). Psychologist of religion Rambo concludes that "a person enacting this kind of ritual [he specifies singing as one type] transcends the self and becomes a part of the larger community, empowered by a sense of connection with others" (Rambo 1993, 118).

The Case of Ritual Motion in Common

One of the NEICP reports, that of Elizabeth McAlister, contains an account of Haitians and Italians occupying the same ritual space in the elaborate, highly physical festival of Our Lady of Mount Carmel in east Harlem. Attaching different—now overlapping, now mutually incomprehensible—meanings to their joint activity, these two groups forge a kind of symbiosis that unites them in a tenuous solidarity (at the expense, alas, of their neighboring Puerto Ricans). I will use the work of William McNeill to reflect on this kind of bonding, but first I will recount another story from my recent travels with the New Ethnic and Immigrant Congregations Project.[19]

On an autumn Friday afternoon in 1994, I accompanied Dr. Rogaia AbuSharaf to the Brooklyn brownstone mosque she was researching for her NEICP project. Awaiting the midday prayer, Dr. AbuSharaf and I were guests of the imam, in his upstairs suite, where we were served tea, and we conversed there with her Sudanese friend, Osman, while the imam prepared his *khutbah*, or sermon.

As the time approached for jum'ah prayer, Osman and I went to the prayer room (as a woman, Dr. AbuSharaf was not welcome there), and we were early enough to get an advantageous spot on the floor and see the room fill to overflowing with hundreds of men: Arab, Indian, African, African American, and Caucasian. (Among them was a man who looked just like me: a big man with a coat and tie, pink skin, gray hair, and a beard, no doubt a professor.) We all listened to two khutbahs, one in English by an Indian immigrant from Yemen named Haj Ali, the other in Arabic by the imam, a scholar from Egypt. As the call went out for prayer, I whispered to Osman to excuse myself, intending to leave the now very crowded room to make room for a Muslim to pray, but Haj Ali, who had joined us, invited me to pray with them.

From previous visits to mosques, I knew how one makes the motions of salat, standing, gesturing with hands to the ears and abdomen, bowing, kneeling, and prostrating. The angle of rugs on the floor tells one which way to face, and the men line up shoulder to shoulder with just enough space between ranks to allow, during prostration, a few inches between the top of one's head and the toes of the next rank. But I had never been in a room more packed. There was literally no extra room, no onlooker's space. It was a case of leave the room or join the ritual.

For the first time, I went through the motions of the salat—about five minutes—and I have to report that the exercise felt good; it felt brotherly, in fact.[20] When it was over, as most people left the room to return to their workplaces, Osman, Haj Ali, the imam, and some others joined me in discussion, and some of them politely challenged their idea of my social science perspective. (I directed them to Dr. AbuSharaf, who by then had come down to the prayer room from the imam's suite; this was after all her research site.) Some of the men went to speak with her, but Haj Ali and a few others stayed with me and tried to convince me that I was a Muslim. It was the first time that I had ever been proselytized by a Muslim, and, although one might say that I had asked for it, I was a bit taken aback. I said that while I respected the Prophet Mohammed, as a Christian I had trouble with his claim to be the seal of the prophets. At length, Haj Ali relented, but I realized that his pressure represented a desire to expand the boundaries of his community, not simply to protect its ethnic purity, and to that extent I was both flattered by his attentions and encouraged for the future of our society.[21]

For some time I had been entertaining the idea, based on class field trips to my students' Islamic centers in Chicago and research-related site visits to mosques in New York and Los Angeles, that the power of praying together, the fraternity of what I have called "perfect unison" (Warner 1994a, 64), must be part of the remarkable appeal of Islam for American converts, particularly African American men.[22] The act of prayer is egalitarian and shoulder to shoulder, uniting men across ethnic, status, and generational boundaries; a man may pray in this fraternal way with his own son. The unison voices responding to the imam—*amin, amin*—are low and suggestive of willfully restrained power.

My personal involvement in the physical act of salat reinforced that hunch, but only in the last year have I found a theorist willing to explain the phenomenon. He is historian William McNeill, author of *The Rise of the West* and *Plagues and Peoples*, and his latest Book, *Keeping Together in Time*, is a long reflection on the historical significance of what he calls "emotional bonding through rhythmic muscular movement" (McNeill 1995, 52). McNeill begins with his own experience of marching on a Texas drill field as an army draftee in 1941: "A sense of pervasive movement in unison is what I recall; more specifically, a strange sense of personal enlargement; a sort of swelling out, becoming bigger than life, thanks to participation in collective ritual" (2).

Halfway through McNeill's book (1995, 90), I ran into his speculation on the role of the "muscular side [of] Moslem worship, . . . the prescribed ritual of prayer which required assembled believers to bow before God," in the rapid spread of the new faith of Islam across old cultural and linguistic boundaries in the Middle East in the first decades of its history: "Performed together five times a day, in a rhythm defined by the summons and example of the prayer leader . . . and lasting for several minutes each time, this sort of prayer obviously required Moslems to move rhythmically and in unison. It is possible . . . that public demonstration of membership in the Community of the Faithful in this fashion may have had the incidental effect of arousing emotional warmth and solidarity. . . . This is an attractive hypothesis, because what made the Moslems so surprisingly successful in the first decades of their history was the extraordinary way the new faith proved capable of transcending ancient tribal rivalries."[23] For those of us who study religion in a highly mobile society, an especially compelling aspect of McNeill's analysis of "emotional bonding through rhythmic muscular movement" is his stress on the emergent character of the resulting solidarities.[24] Thus the emotion he speaks of "affects those who take part in it more or less independently of how they may have been connected (or divided) by prior experience." Hence, keeping together in time "could and did become a way in which all sorts of new groups could define themselves, both by differentiation from within existing communities and by allowing marginalized persons or complete outsiders to coalesce into new, more or less coherent groups" (52).

In common with Kertzer, McNeill speaks of the multiple meanings that such ritualized mutual motion can carry. "The excitement aroused by rhythmic movement with others is inherently diffuse. Heightened emotion can find various and even contradictory expressions, depending on the expectations participants bring to the exercise. . . . [Thus] identical (or almost identical) motions of arms and legs may induce love or hate, exorcise danger, or invite possession of the spirits" (McNeill 1995, 64; see also 155). Charismatic leaders may channel the resulting solidarities in brutal or humane, secular or religious, directions.[25]

On Embodied Ritual

I would like to say more about the place of food, especially communal meals, in the production of religious solidarity, but the bulk of the literature I have found on the topic (Dodson and Gilkes 1995; Kostarelos 1995; Williams 1974) focuses specifically and descriptively on the black church, where sharing food is undoubtedly of central importance.[26] Yet sharing food, commensality, clearly is a widespread and emotionally significant practice in many other religious bodies as well.[27]

So I shall conclude this section of my remarks with some principles of the contributions of bodily ritual to the production of solidarity: they allow repetitive action and thus enhanced synchronization; the multivocality and diffuseness of the symbols they are directed toward or through which actions are coordinated do not require propositional consensus to promote solidarity; they employ common human capacities—motion, sound, taste—and are hence capable of crossing cultural boundaries; they can promote consciousness of kind, awareness of our species-being; they can therefore bond persons to one another and create new communities.

Now I do not intend to deny that there are many other sources than mutual bodily actions of bridging—mixing and permeability—both within religion and across society (popular culture, economic structures, etc.) as well as extrareligious sources of division and invidious discrimination. Many of them—especially an economy that seems to be eliminating decent, entry-level jobs—are no doubt more powerful than the religious factor. But I am asked, given my expertise, to focus on religion, and that I have done. And I have concentrated on a theme—the capacity of bodily ritual to create communities—that I think has been largely neglected in the literature. (The presidential address given by Nancy Ammerman [1997b] the day before this lecture is a welcome exception.)

Beyond Assimilation and Multiculturalism to Mestizaje

I will conclude by pointing to a new theory (I neither can nor need to develop one here) capable of dealing with the two-sided reality I have described: a society with a multitude of particular communities but also with multiple bridges between them. To fathom this reality, we need to go beyond the alternatives of "assimilation" (which denies the reality of difference) and "multiculturalism" (which denies the reality of inclusion) to what Virgilio Elizondo has called mestizaje. The standard U.S. theory of assimilation is based on an *osmotic* image of one-way pressure and absorption. Anglo-Americans need to learn from the Hispanic experience of *mixing* or mestizaje, to comprehend bridging. "It is the traditionally dominant group that will have to have the greater humility to face itself openly and admit that it has much to receive, much to learn, from the groups that it has previously considered inferior" (Elizondo 1983, 27).

U.S. society and its culture have changed greatly over our history, but we have not wanted to admit it. From early colonial days, we have been a people who worry over boundaries, borders, and stockades. Protestant Europeans arrived in North America with the intention to settle what they imagined was a wilderness, and eventually they came across the Atlantic in sufficient numbers to realize that goal, pushing the native inhabitants out of the way as a nuisance. The colonists were proud of maintaining their European purity, and the national conceit was that everyone, with the exception of the imported Africans, had maintained that purity. So the United States could have a dichotomous racial system—white or "colored," later "black"—with a residual category left over for the natives on their reservations.

By contrast, Catholic Europeans came to Central and South America with the intention to subdue and plunder what they soon recognized were advanced civilizations, and they came at first in amazingly small numbers, given the task at hand.[28] Maybe fewer of them were eager to leave their Iberian homeland for the unknown West. Be that as it may, they conquered a continent, but they did not so nearly eradicate its inhabitants. So while on the southern front as well as on the northern, Europeans killed many natives, many natives in the south were also left to absorb them—their blood, their language, and their religion. A new people was born, and racial classification in Latin America, though no less invidious than in the United States, is more finely graded. Thus in much of Latin America, mixture is part of the social consciousness instead of just its subconscious, whereas we in the United States still think publicly in categorical terms, no matter how ambiguous our nightmares. So we tend to be suspicious of cultural difference and to insist on assimilation to a preexisting ideal.[29]

There is a similar obsession with ideal purity on the part of some of those who care and speak for the interests and rights of racial and ethnic minorities in the United States, an unwillingness to countenance mixing, assimilation, and permeability of cultures. I submit that we have to go beyond (1) essentialist advocates for multiculturalism who insist, despite evidence to the contrary, that there is *no way* that newcomers will assimilate to the corrupt culture of the United States, (2) fearful advocates of English-only monoculturalism, who insist, despite the evidence, that newcomers will not assimilate, and (3) theorists of "culture wars," who ignore the enormous cultural complexity of U.S. society that stands outside of or athwart the left/right cultural divide between Protestant evangelicals and post-Protestant liberals.

Bridges are constructed. But so is difference. And we can learn better how to construct difference in less alienating ways. The point is that our constructions of difference are too categorical, and this under the influence of theorists who, while they themselves may not be religious, operate under U.S. Protestant notions of purity and difference.

The fact is that our culture is gloriously impure, even at its Protestant core:

- There is a new sacramentalism in American Protestantism, developed partly under non-Protestant, Roman Catholic, and Eastern Orthodox inspiration, including the inspiration of the Spanish-origin Cursillo movement (Warner 1988a, 258–260), which, as Susana Gallardo (in her NEICP report) and Ana-María Díaz-Stevens (1993) have pointed out, was brought to the United States by Puerto Ricans and Chicano/as.
- The modern Pentecostal movement, whose rapid worldwide spread is testimony to its transcultural appeal, began under the inspiration of a black preacher in Los Angeles, galvanizing a congregation of blacks, Hispanics, and whites.[30]

Speaking of racial bridges and boundaries in the United States, Michael Eric Dyson writes that blacks and whites "are intimately joined, forged into a sometimes reluctant symbiosis that mocks the rigid lines of language and identity that set them apart. *American culture is inconceivable without African American life*" (Dyson 1996, 124; emphasis added).[31]

I could go on with more examples of what Luis León, in his NEICP report, ironically dubs "cultural oxymorons," allegedly impossible mixtures like "Pentecostal mariachi." They include feminist-influenced evangelicals (Stacey 1990), Pentecostally inspired gays and lesbians (Warner 1995), and Episcopalians whose favorite hymn is "Amazing Grace" (Clark 1993). These are not instances of one-way assimilation, where a monolithic society simply forces the newcomer, the marginalized, and the outsider into its preexisting mold, but a two-way process where a new mixture is constantly being created.

This is the reality, produced *in part* by what I have spoken of as embodied rituals and what Nancy Ammerman (1997b) calls "practices," that needs better theorizing.[32] As Elizondo says: "It is in the fiesta that a new common 'we' begins to be experienced. We belong together because we have experienced a new unity and universality. Eventually the words will be found to explain it, but in the meantime the new reality has begun to emerge" (Elizondo 1983, 124).[33]

Reprinted by permission from *Sociology of Religion*, vol. 58 (Fall 1997). © Association for the Sociology of Religion. Delivered as the 1996 Paul Hanly Furfey Lecture.

NOTES

The influence of Anne Heider on my life (and necessarily on this paper) is incalculable, and the boundary between my thinking and that of Nancy Ammerman has become increasingly indistinct. A discussion with Mary Jo Neitz on the occasion of the 1979 visit of Pope John Paul II to Chicago reverberated in my mind as I wrote, and Sang Hyun Lee and Timothy Matovina provided more recent food for thought. Nancy Eiesland, Gary Laderman, and members of their Candler School of Theology seminar commented on an earlier draft. I have also bene- fited from conversations with and suggestions from José Casanova, Joy Charlton, Luis León, Omar McRoberts, Joan H. Smith, Julius Solomon, James Spickard, Anthony Stevens-Arroyo, J. Michael Thompson, Sandra Trehub, Elfriede Wedam, and Judith Wittner, and from my ongoing involvement with the fellows of the New Ethnic and Immigrant Congregations Project. None of the persons or groups mentioned bears any responsibility for the views expressed here.

1. I have developed a complementary argument on the nature of the new religious partic- ularism itself in Warner 1999a.

2. Neither of these terms is fully satisfactory (see Goizueta 1995, 12–14). In this paper, I will use them equally to refer to U.S. residents of Mexican, Puerto Rican, and Cuban origin, as well as to U.S. residents with origins in other Spanish-speaking countries of the West- ern Hemisphere and to descendants of those Mexicans whose homelands were incorpo- rated into the United States by the 1848 treaty of Guadalupe-Hidalgo.

3. Not to mention the present and future of the communities themselves (e.g., Yoo 1996).

4. Also seen as a key to the life chances of the second generation is a "private school sys- tem" that "insulates children from contact with [the "adversarial subculture" of] native minority youth while reinforcing the authority of parental views and plans" (Portes 1995, 73, 74), but the preponderant role of religious communities in the provision of such sys- tems is ignored.

5. A dramatic recent example of bridging was the sustained field research of Samuel Freed- man, a Jewish journalist, with St. Paul Community Baptist Church, an African American and, of course, Christian congregation in Brooklyn pastored by Rev. Johnny Ray Young- blood. The research is reported in Freedman 1993 and the bridging effort in Freedman 1996.

6. The following references are to research projects reported at the 1996 A.S.R. meetings (see Appendix to References here and Warner and Wittner 1998a). Oral presentations based on those reports were presented in the hours before and after the Furfey lecture in the same hotel conference room.

7. There is a growing literature on the body in ritual (e.g., McGuire 1990), but it strikes me as focusing more on the cultural meanings ritual imposes on the body (i.e., how the body is displayed in ritual or how meanings are inscribed upon the body) than on how the body shapes the experience of ritual, which is my particular interest in this paper.

8. The following account is based on field notes dated March 5, 1989.

9. For Lee's own contribution to the topic of this paper, see Lee 1991.

10. I do not mean to claim that the way to bring children into the religious community is through nonverbal ritual. The NEICP report of Prema Kurien argues otherwise, but that of Sheba George suggests that parents' failure to include their children in musical ritual is devastating for intergenerational transfer of religion.

11. "Ritual helps people to learn to act differently[, f]rom the details of when to bow, kneel, and stand, to how to carry a Bible or address the minister, priest, rabbi, to more profound truths and teachings" (Rambo 1993, 115). Other scholars (e.g., Roberts 1993, 88) have looked at the sensual aspect of *settled* communities: "Any ethnographic analysis of ritual . . . would need to pay attention to which senses are employed to transmit the culture and to sacralize it."

12. To my intuition, this theory sheds light on the commonplace observation in sociology of religion of the robustness of the behavioral measure of frequency of church attendance. For example, Bankston and Zhou (1996) find that how often an inner-city Vietnamese American boy goes to church predicts how well he will do in school and how likely he is to stay off drugs.

13. Citing the Catholic philosopher Bernard Lonergan, Roberto Goizueta writes: "Because the symbol communicates primarily through affect rather than through logic, it 'has the power of recognizing and expressing what logical discourse abhors: the existence of internal tensions, incompatibilities, conflicts, struggles, destructions.' " Thus symbols "effect [human] relationships" and can transcend the either/or mentality of discourse (Goizueta 1995, 27).

14. Many theorists employ the word "danger" rather than "risk" in this context, but I am mindful of the risks of calling ideas "dangerous."

15. "Academic observers have often treated the presence of the 'emotional' service among the lower class as the phenomenon to be explained, instead of examining the *variation* of ritual style across all socioeconomic status groups. Thus, scholars have used the 'nonemotional' worship of the middle and upper classes as an implicit normative benchmark, and treated 'emotional' worship as a deviant form of ritual, explicable only by reference to unique psychic needs endemic to life at the bottom of society" (Nelson 1996, 395).

16. On the occasion of the Furfey lecture (August 16, 1996), this chant was sung, with the G below middle C as *do*. On a piano, it could most easily be played on "white keys" as EEEEE . . . . DEFD, and DDDDD . . . . CDE.

17. Clark 1993 is an exception.

18. Blacking (1973, 104) writes: "Music is not a language that describes the way society seems to be, but a metaphorical expression of feelings associated with the way society really is." Hence, music can promote relationships across linguistic barriers (Storr 1992, 9, 20; Blacking 1973, 115.)

19. The following account is based on field notes dated October 14, 1994. The pseudonyms are the invention of Dr. Rogaia AbuSharaf.

20. I suspect, on the basis of dynamics articulated far more profoundly by Nancy Jay (1992) than I could, that cultural production through muscular bonding is more intentional for men than is it for women; it may indeed be a particular obsession of men. Not that women are less susceptible to bodily ritual: "Moving together rhythmically for hours on end can be counted on to strengthen emotional bonds among those who take part— women as much as men" (McNeill 1995, 27). But it seems plausible that women are less likely than men to be needful of seeking out a group of strangers with whom to develop a wholly new solidarity.

21. Many who heard me say this expressed surprise, interpreting proselytization as a violation of the norms of civility. Having marched in Berkeley's Sproul Plaza in the 1960s and

done field research among evangelicals in the 1970s, I am used to proselytization, political and religious. As uncomfortable as it can be, the alternative—when groups take their identities as primordial and unbridgeable—worries me more.

22. Let me reiterate that emotional power in religion is not the exclusive property of nonmainstream religion.

23. Speaking of ancient urban societies in the Middle East, McNeill writes that marginalized persons "often responded to unhappy circumstances by inventing new communities for themselves. Such communities were tied together partly by ideas about future redress of grievances (often by supernatural agency), and partly by practical mutual support. And, as innumerable such groups discovered, at the practical level, keeping together in time was the most efficacious way to establish warm emotional bonds" (McNeill 1995, 57).

24. "In big, anonymous cities, the need [for community] is acute. It follows that in an age when more and more persons find themselves adrift in such cities, muscular bonding is likely to become more rather than less important in defining and redefining who we are and with whom we share a common identity" (ibid., 150).

25. McNeill observes (1995, 65) that Western society has tended to identify dance with sexuality since the Renaissance, but this is a historical blindness on our part. Dance can carry fervent religious meanings as well as sexual ones.

26. Some highlights in this literature: Eating together is one of "the actual sites and mechanisms . . . through which community is gathered and actualized in the Black Church" (Dodson and Gilkes 1995, 520). Food is "sung about. It is worried over. It is prayed over" (521). "The love ethic that pervades the ideology of African American churches is constantly underscored and reaffirmed in the exchanges of food and the celebration of church events with grand meals" (535). Preparing meals (which can take days), eating and serving, and cleaning up are all occasions for "lively social intercourse" and "catalysts for interaction among the members" (Williams 1974, 84–88). "The kitchen is 'the crossroads of the state.' All are seen here at one time or another" (86). First Corinthians Missionary Baptist Church has a free weekly supper, accommodating some three hundred persons, which invariably features fried chicken (Kostarelos 1995, 90–94), what Dodson and Gilkes (1995) call "gospel bird." The First Corinthians meal is open to all, not just members.

27. For some further considerations, see Ammerman 1997a, chapter 8.

28. Among them were those who came to convert and care for the souls of the indigenous inhabitants. If *all* Catholic Europeans had had the intention to plunder, we would know far less today about their depredations, chronicled by the men of the cloth, than we in fact do.

29. "One achieves full citizenship in the nation-state by becoming a culturally blank slate" (Rosaldo 1993, 201).

30. "Unlike most Christian fundamentalists, Pentecostalists invite the Spirit more than they invoke Scripture, with all the anarchic, innovative possibilities that this implies" (McNeill 1995, 86).

31. Dyson (1996) goes on to mention the indelible contributions to American culture of Martin Luther King, Jr., and Malcolm X, Toni Morrison and Alice Walker, Duke Ellington and John Coltrane, Ralph Ellison and James Baldwin.

32. Another strength of Elizondo's and Goizueta's theorizing, based at it is on Hispanic/Latino popular Catholicism, is a philosophic anthropology that rejects individual-versus-society dualism. "The assertion that personal identity is intrinsically relational, or given by others from 'outside,' is . . . the corollary of a sacramental worldview" (Goizueta 1995, 50; see also Elizondo 1983, 30).

33.   "It is through . . . foundational celebrations that the core knowledge of the group func-
      tions and is passed on as living tradition and the fundamental myths of the group take
      shape and are articulated. . . . In this way, celebrations are not just the effects of what
      has been; they are likewise the cause of what is yet to come" (Elizondo 1983, 121).

REFERENCES

(References to writings of the author are found in a separate listing at the back of the book.)

Alba, Richard, and Victor Nee. 1995. "The Relevance of Assimilation for Post-1965 Immigrant
      Groups." New York: Report to the Social Science Research Council.

Ammerman, Nancy Tatom. 1997a. *Congregation and Community.* New Brunswick, N.J.: Rutgers
      University Press.

———. 1997b. "Organized Religion in a Voluntaristic Society." *Sociology of Religion* 58: 203–216.

Bankston, Carl L., III, and Min Zhou. 1996. "The Ethnic Church, Ethnic Identification, and the
      Social Adjustment of Vietnamese Adolescents." *Review of Religious Research* 38: 18–37.

Blacking, John. 1973. *How Musical Is Man?* Seattle: University of Washington Press.

———. 1992. "The Biology of Music-making." In *Ethnomusicology: An Introduction*, ed. H. Myers,
      301–314. New York: W. W. Norton.

Carter, Stephen L. 1993. *The Culture of Disbelief: How American Law and Politics Trivialize Religious
      Devotion.* New York: Basic Books.

Clark, Linda J. 1993. "Songs My Mother Taught Me: Hymns as Transmitters of Faith." In *Beyond
      Establishment: Protestant Identity in a Post-Protestant Age*, ed. J. W. Carroll and W. C. Roof,
      99–115. Louisville, Ky.: Westminster/John Knox.

Cobb, Buell E., Jr. 1989. *The Sacred Harp: A Tradition and Its Music.* Athens: University of Georgia
      Press.

Cornelius, Wayne A. 1995. "Educating California's Immigrant Children: Introduction and
      Overview." In *California's Immigrant Children: Theory, Research, and Implications for Educa-
      tional Policy*, ed. R. G. Rumbaut and W. A. Cornelius, 1–16. San Diego: UCSD Center for
      U.S.-Mexican Studies.

Denby, David. 1996. "Buried Alive: Our Children and the Avalanche of Crud." *New Yorker* 72
      (19): 48–58.

Díaz-Stevens, Ana-Maria. 1993. *Oxcart Catholicism on Fifth Avenue: The Impact of the Puerto Rican
      Migration upon the Archdiocese of New York.* Notre Dame, Ind.: University of Notre Dame
      Press.

Dodson, Jualynne E., and Cheryl Townsend Gilkes. 1995. " 'There's Nothing Like Church
      Food'—Food and the U.S. Afro-Christian Tradition: Re-membering Community and Feed-
      ing the Embodied S/spirit(s)." *Journal of the American Academy of Religion* 63: 519–538.

Dyson, Michael E. 1996. *Between God and Gangsta Rap: Bearing Witness to Black Culture.* New
      York: Oxford University Press.

Elizondo, Virgilio. 1983. *Galilean Journey: The Mexican-American Promise.* Marynoll, N.Y.: Orbis
      Books.

Freedman, Samuel G. 1993. *Upon This Rock: The Miracles of a Black Church.* New York: Harper
      Collins.

———. 1996. "Crossing the Border." *CommonQuest* 1 (Spring): 12–21.

Gibson, Margaret A. 1995. "Additive Acculturation as a Strategy for School Improvement." In *Cal-
      ifornia's Immigrant Children: Theory, Research, and Implications for Educational Policy*, ed. R. G.
      Rumbaut and W. A. Cornelius, 77–105. San Diego: UCSD Center for U.S.-Mexican Studies.

Goizueta, Roberto S. 1995. *Caminemos Con Jesús: Toward a Hispanic/Latino Theology of Accompa-
      niment.* Maryknoll, N.Y.: Orbis Books.

Haddad, Yvonne Yazbeck, and Adair T. Lummis. 1987. *Islamic Values in the United States: A Com-
      parative Study.* New York: Oxford University Press.

Herberg, Will. 1960. *Protestant, Catholic, Jew: An Essay in American Religious Sociology.* 2d ed. Garden City, N.Y.: Doubleday.

Hunter, James Davison. 1991. *Culture Wars: The Struggle to Define America.* New York: Basic Books.

Jay, Nancy. 1992. *Throughout Your Generations Forever: Sacrifice, Religion, and Paternity.* Chicago: University of Chicago Press.

Kertzer, David L. 1988. *Ritual, Politics, and Power.* New Haven, Conn.: Yale University Press.

Kim, Kwang Chung, and Won Moo Hurh. 1993. "Beyond Assimilation and Pluralism: Syncretic Socio-cultural Adaptation of Korean Immigrants." *Ethnic and Racial Studies* 16 (October): 696–713.

Kostarelos, Frances. 1995. *Feeling the Spirit: Faith and Hope in an Evangelical Black Storefront Church.* Columbia: University of South Carolina Press.

Lee, Sang Hyun. 1991. "Korean American Presbyterians: A Need for Ethnic Particularity and the Challenge of Christian Pilgrimage." In *The Diversity of Discipleship: The Presbyterians and Twentieth-century Christian Witness*, ed. M. J. Coalter, J. M. Mulder, and L. B. Weeks, 312–330 and 400–402. Louisville, Ky: Westminster/John Knox.

McGuire, Meredith B. 1990. "Religion and the Body: Rematerializing the Human Body in the Social Sciences of Religion." *Journal for the Scientific Study of Religion* 29: 283–296.

McNeill, William H. 1995. *Keeping Together in Time: Dance and Drill in Human History.* Cambridge: Harvard University Press.

Min, Pyong Gap. 1992. "The Structure and Social Functions of Korean Immigrant Churches in the United States." *International Migration Review* 26: 1370–1394.

Mittelberg, David, and Mary C. Waters. 1992. "The Process of Ethnogenesis among Haitian and Israeli Immigrants in the United States." *Racial and Ethnic Studies* 15: 412–435.

Neitz, Mary Jo, and James V. Spickard. 1990. "Steps Toward a Sociology of Religious Experience: The Theories of Mihaly Csikszentmihalyi and Alfred Schutz." *Sociological Analysis* 51: 15–33.

Nelson, Timothy J. 1996. "Sacrifice of Praise: Emotion and Collective Participation in an African American Worship Service." *Sociology of Religion* 57: 379–396.

Noll, Mark A. 1989. "The Historical Maturity of the Sociology of Religion." *Evangelical Studies Bulletin* 6: 1–5.

Portes, Alejandro. 1995. "Segmented Assimilation among New Immigrant Youth: A Conceptual Framework." In *California's Immigrant Children: Theory, Research, and Implications for Educational Policy*, ed. R. G. Rumbaut and W. A. Cornelius, 71–76. San Diego: UCSD Center for U.S.-Mexican Studies.

Rambo, Lewis. R. 1993. *Understanding Religious Conversion.* New Haven, Conn.: Yale University Press.

Roberts, Keith A. 1993. "Ritual and the Transmission of a Cultural Tradition: An Ethnographic Perspective." In *Beyond Establishment: Protestant Identity in a Post-Protestant Age*, ed. J. W. Carroll and W. C. Roof, 74–98. Louisville, Ky.: Westminster/John Knox.

Rosaldo, Renato. 1993. "Border Crossings." In *Culture and Truth: The Remaking of Social Analysis*, 196–217. Boston: Beacon Press.

Rumbaut, Rubén. 1995. "The New Californians: Comparative Research Findings on the Educational Progress of Immigrant Children." In *California's Immigrant Children: Theory, Research, and Implications for Educational Policy*, ed. R. G. Rumbaut and W. A. Cornelius, 17–69. San Diego: UCSD Center for U.S.-Mexican Studies.

Rumbaut, Rubén, and Wayne A. Cornelius. 1995. *California's Immigrant Children: Theory, Research, and Implications for Educational Policy.* San Diego: UCSD Center for U.S.-Mexican Studies.

Schutz, Alfred. 1964. "Making Music Together: A Study in Social Relationship." In *Studies in Social Theory*, vol. 2 of *Collected Papers*, 159–178. The Hague: Martinus Nijhoff.

Smith, Timothy L. 1971. "Lay Initiative in the Religious Life of American Immigrants." In *Anonymous Americans*, ed. T. K. Hareven, 214–249. Englewood Cliffs, N.J.: Prentice-Hall.

Stacey, Judith. 1990. *Brave New Families: Stories of Domestic Upheaval in Late Twentieth-century America*. New York: Basic Books.

Storr, Anthony. 1992. *Music and the Mind*. New York: Free Press.

Trehub, Sandra E., and E. Glenn Schellenberg. 1995. "Music: Its Relevance to Infants." *Annals of Child Development* 11: 1–24.

Wheeler, Barbara G. 1996. "You Who Were Far Off: Religious Divisions and the Role of Religious Research." *Review of Religious Research* 37: 289–301.

Williams, Melvin D. 1974. *Community in a Black Pentecostal Church: An Anthropological Study*. Pittsburgh, Pa.: University of Pittsburgh Press.

Williams, Raymond Brady. 1988. *Religions of Immigrants from India and Pakistan: New Threads in the American Tapestry*. Cambridge: Cambridge University Press.

Wolfe, Alan. 1992. "Democracy Versus Sociology: Boundaries and Their Political Consequences." In *Cultivating Differences: Symbolic Boundaries and the Making of Inequality*, ed. M. Lamont and M. Fournier, 309–325. Chicago: University of Chicago Press.

Wuthnow, Robert. 1988. *The Restructuring of American Religion: Society and Faith since World War II*. Princeton, N.J.: Princeton University Press.

Yoo, David. 1996. "For Those Who Have Eyes to See: Religious Sightings in Asian America." *Amerasia Journal* 22 (Spring): xiii–xxii.

APPENDIX TO REFERENCES: NEICP REPORTS PRESENTED AT 1996 A.S.R. MEETINGS

Abusharaf, Rogaia M. Structural Adaptations in an Immigrant Muslim Congregation in New York.*

Chai, Karen. Competing for the Second Generation: English-language Ministry in a Korean Protestant Church.*

Feher, Shoshanah. From the Rivers of Babylon to the Valleys of Los Angeles: The Exodus and Adaptation of Iranian Jews.*

Gallardo, Susana L. "Sal Si Puedes": Reform and Resistance in a Chicano Catholic Parish.

George, Sheba M. Caroling with the Keralites: The Negotiation of Gendered Space in an Indian Immigrant Church.*

Hepner, Randal L. The House That Rasta Built: Church-building among New York Rastafari.*

Kurien, Prema. Becoming American by Becoming Hindu: Indian Americans Take Their Place at the Multi-cultural Table.*

León, Luis D. Born Again in East Los Angeles: The Congregation as Border Space.*

McAlister, Elizabeth. Haitian Vodou Meets Italian Catholicism in East Harlem: The Madonna of 115th Street Revisited.*

Pang, KengFong. Who Are the Chams? Maintaining Dual Congregations as an Adaptive Strategy in Cultural Identity Management among Vietnamese/Cambodian Muslim Refugees in America.

Wellmeier, Nancy J. Santa Eulalia's People in Exile: Maya Religion, Culture, and Identity in Los Angeles.*

Yang, Fenggang. Tenacious Unity in a Contentious Community: Cultural and Religious Dynamics in a Chinese Protestant Church.*

*See R. Stephen Warner and Judith G. Wittner, eds., Gatherings in Diaspora: Religious Communities and the New Immigration (Philadelphia: Temple University Press, 1988), for revised, complete report.

6

Enlisting Smelser's Theory of Ambivalence to Maintain Progress in Sociology of Religion's New Paradigm (2004)

Sociology of religion is in the midst of a theoretical shift that I identified (and tried to accelerate) in a widely cited article now over a decade old (Warner 1993a). Exactly what the new approach—variously called "the new paradigm," the "religious markets" perspective, and "the economic approach to religion"—entails, whether it is properly called a "paradigm" or "theory" shift, and how far its scope extends are issues I return to here later. Yet there can be no doubt that a fundamental divide exists between the new sociological understanding of religious vitality, especially in the United States, and the older wisdom that expected European-style secularization to be the fate of religion across the modern world. This divide pits the new view—broadly shared by Rodney Stark, Roger Finke, Laurence Iannaccone, and me, among others who, to my mind, include Nancy Ammerman and Mary Jo Neitz—against such "old-paradigm" figures as Steve Bruce, Karel Dobbelaere, Frank Lechner, and Bryan Wilson.[1] My primary disciplinary goal in this chapter is to encourage fence-sitters to line up with the new paradigm by recognizing that it does not entail the rational choice postulates articulated within it by Finke, Iannaccone, and Stark but is open to other social-psychological perspectives.

Neil Smelser, whom I first encountered as my theory professor when I was a Berkeley undergraduate in 1962, figures in this chapter as my mentor over the long term of my career. Especially since his 1997 American Sociological Association presidential address (1998), he has been my stimulus in thinking through why the "new paradigm," as I have defined it, does not rest on a rational choice theory of human motivation and can be strengthened by recognizing the applicability of ambivalence.

This chapter has four parts. First, I briefly trace the development of the new paradigm in the sociology of religion. Second, I cite what would be anomalies in the new paradigm if its foundation were to be taken as rational choice theory. Third, I draw on Smelser's work on ambivalence to help explain those anomalies without abandoning the fundamental insight of the new paradigm. Finally, I briefly outline some theoretical implications.

Background to the "New Paradigm"

About the time that the flurry of interest in 1960s-era "new religious movements" was about to fade, the resurgence of fundamentalism and other forms of conservative religion in the 1970s and 1980s led to renewed interest in religion among sociologists and to a growing awareness that conventional theoretical expectations were not working. Having been led to expect that religion would survive in modern society only in otherworldly forms among the underprivileged in society's backwaters or in harmless mysticism among the idle elite, sociological researchers, often dissertation students, kept coming back from the field with challenges to the reigning perspective. These researchers encountered thriving, not merely surviving, religious movements that they found among educated and affluent people, not the disinherited, at society's crossroads instead of its margins. Many of these movements were making a difference, whatever we might think of it, in their communities, challenging school boards and boycotting places of entertainment. And instead of being solitary practitioners, the people in these movements came together to celebrate their faith, not only expressing preexisting solidarities but often creating new ones.

The religious movement I first studied, in 1976, was that of an evangelical revival in the Presbyterian church of Mendocino, California. Many of my informants were newcomers both to their religion, being what they called "new Christians," and to their small-town place of residence, being what I called "elective parochials" (1988, chap. 3). My study originally had been intended to address issues in political sociology: I wanted to understand how a respectable old institution, which happened to be one of the oldest Protestant churches in California, could flourish after having been taken over by a radical movement of young people of dubious reputation, who happened to be late 1960s-style "hippie Christians." The political sociology frame failed (because the conflicts in the church did not occur at the places the theory expected between the straight and the hip). But having invested heavily in the ethnographic fieldwork, I was not about to give up. I realized that the study could make a major contribution to sociology of religion, but that was a field in which, despite having done my graduate work at Berkeley, one of its major centers, I had no training. My theory training at Berkeley, much of it with Smelser (see Smelser and Warner 1976), was the grounds not only of my employability (teaching sociological theory has been my bread and butter for over thirty years) but also of my confidence that I could teach myself a new field to salvage my project.

So, using techniques honed under Smelser's tutelage—he always insisted that you could not claim to understand a theory until you had paid attention not only to its concepts and propositions but also to the way these ideas were connected to the empirical phenomena they were supposed to explain—I read the literature bearing proximately and remotely on evangelicalism and religious institutions. I focused both on what was asserted explicitly and on what was assumed implicitly. At length, I found much that was of value, but probably in ways that the authors of the various books and articles I read did not intend (Warner 1979). Teaching sociology of religion by then at the University of Illinois at Chicago (UIC), I also began to explore Chicago-area religious institutions with the students in my classes, going with them to their churches, synagogues, mosques, and temples, some of which seemed to be languishing while others flourished. The generalization dawned on me that churches and other religious institutions flourish when they reflect, as well as engage, the cultures of the people who are their local constituents. Such religiocultural localism is possible, in turn, because religion in the United States is disestablished, or, as I put it in the conclusion to the book that came out of the Mendocino study, "for Americans, religion and community autonomy go hand in hand." The local congregation is where "the laity have historically had their way" (Warner 1988a, 290–291). But as I read the extant sociology of religion—a field founded in the 1900s by Europeans for whom the demise of a once-powerful established church loomed large in the background, and presided over in the 1960s by Americans who saw in the imminent collapse of the self-appointed WASP establishment the long-expected end of the road for conventional religion in the United States—I found that field ill prepared to recognize the local and popular roots of American religious vitality. The surprisingly novel idea that *the disestablishment of U.S. religion was the key to its robust appeal*, and thereby to its vitality, was the germ of my next project, which eventuated in the formulation of what I came to call the new paradigm.

I worked on the disestablishment-vitality idea during a year's fellowship at the Institute for Advanced Study made possible by the reception of the book on the evangelicals of Mendocino. It was then that I realized that others were coming to conclusions about American religion similar to mine, including Mary Jo Neitz (1987) and Nancy Ammerman (1987), who had discovered instances of vital but not modernized religion in the midst of the modern world; Roger Finke and Rodney Stark (1988, 1989; see now also Finke and Stark 1992), sociologists who spoke of "religious economies"; and the economist Laurence Iannaccone (1991), who spoke of "religious market structures." I saw that still others, especially historians (Littel 1962; Mead 1963), had long recognized that the genius of American religion lay in its disestablishment, and they also used economic imagery to understand it (Bilhartz 1986; Butler 1989; Hatch 1989; Stout 1991; Carpenter 1997). This view was diametrically opposed to the one according to which disestablishment eroded the "taken-for-granted" quality of religion that shored up its "plausibility," a view central to the sociology of religion inspired by the European founders of the discipline and the (European) religious history they took for granted (Berger 1969).

My sociological colleagues and the American religious historians we consulted agreed that the secret of American religious vitality is what some of us called the "open market" for religion in the United States, a condition that has prevailed for two hundred years, since the early Republican period. Under disestablishment, there is no state subsidy for religion, but there is also no state licensing of religion. When religion is disestablished, it is not the property or the prerogative only of the privileged. Disestablishment serves to stimulate the energies of entrepreneurs, because anyone can hang out a shingle and set up a church. Because that is so, it often makes good sense for ordinary people to embrace their religions, and religion is therefore more often an arena of agency than a setting of victimization. Accordingly, I proposed that corollaries to the disestablishment of (or open market for) American religion are that orthodoxy, whether in doctrine or structure, is not privileged, that religion is a space available for subcultures, and that religion can be an area of empowerment for minorities (Warner 1993a). I gathered materials on such nonhegemonic religious institutions and movements as the black church, immigrant churches, gay churches, women's involvement in American religion, and twelve-step groups. Such was the outline of what by 1991 I was calling a new paradigm for the study of American religion. Much progress has been made on the new paradigm in the past decade (Warner 2002).

As much as I felt (and still feel) that Stark, Finke, and Iannaccone, who explicitly embraced rational choice theory, were saying things broadly similar to what I was saying, I had several reasons for not thinking of the new paradigm as a general application of economic or rational choice theory. First and most important, some of those who regarded America's religious disestablishment as a deviant state or degenerate condition for religion (and thereby adhered to what I called the Eurocentric old paradigm) themselves employed economic models to analyze what they saw as the system's tenuousness and shallowness (Berger 1969, chap. 9; Moore 1994; cf. Warner 1993a, 1053). If economic theory was central to the construction of their old paradigm, it could not be what defined the new paradigm. Second, the idea of economists that I (as well as historians Terry Bilhartz [1986] and Nathan Hatch [1989]) found most congenial for understanding American religion was "supply-side" imagery, the openness of the system to the efforts of would-be religious entrepreneurs. I passed this image on to Finke (1997), but I was less taken by "demand-side" imagery, the idea that people's orientation to the religions offered them is analytically identical to their orientation to goods on the consumer market, an approach taken by Stark, Iannaccone, and their colleagues (Stark and Bainbridge 1987; Stark and Finke 2000; Iannaccone 1990; cf. Warner 1993a, 1057). Third, I was most confident of what we knew about religion in the United States, which is, after all, the site of the populations and institutions on which most contemporary sociology of religion has been done, as well as the field of expertise of the historians from whom many of us have learned so much. Thus the new paradigm as I understood and clearly labeled it was a model specifically for "the sociological study of religion in the United States," an institutionally distinct system where religion was constitutively disestablished (Warner 1993a, 1046, 1055, 1080), not a theory of religion in general. Because I was not proposing a new

theory of religion but a new, or better yet, newly asserted, vision of the fundamental properties of American religion, as distinct from the European religion
that had originally inspired the founders of sociology of religion, I properly called
my construction a "paradigm," not a "theory" (Warner 1993a, 1044; 1997a; 1997b).

As one steeped in the tradition of sociological theory, I had more general reasons to be leery of rational choice as a general theory. First, as Talcott Parsons
argues, sociology entailed the foundational idea that social action is structured;
accordingly it had to reject the economists' competing idea that wants are exogenous (or as Parsons said, "random" [1949, 59–60]). As I perceive this particular
case, religion enjoys diffuse support in the American value system; the needs met
by religion in the United States may be met through other institutional channels
in other societies (e.g., political movements in much of modern Europe). Second,
sociologists of the economy are suspicious of the idea that a market can be "unregulated," a formulation that Stark and Finke seem drawn to (2000; Finke and Stark
1992). As I said in a 1994 conference devoted to internal discussion: "What we new
paradigm scholars had hit upon was not so much an economic theory of an unregulated religious market as the institutional secret of American religion as an open
religious market, where barriers to entry were low but religion was a respected,
popular, and, to a great extent, protected, idiom" (Warner 1997a, 95). Third, at the
Institute for Advanced Study in 1988, Susan Harding helped me see that rational
choice formulations are usually oblivious to power, assuming the availability of
choice to all; as a result of her prodding, I saw in particular that women's chances
of finding empowerment in religion depended on there being a differentiation
between family and religious institutions (Warner 1993a, 1072). Religious disestablishment does not empower women or youth under a system of household
monopolies (Collins 1975, chap. 5); minorities generally are not empowered when
the religious system is one of *cuius regio, eius religio* (Chaves and Gorski 2001). If it
is the case that religion in the United States empowers minorities, as it is, part of
the reason has to do with the particularities of social structures in the United
States—for example, that the black church is not simply the church of plantation
owners that black people attend, and that women's place in the church is not
simply a function of their status as particular men's wives (see Heyrman 1998).

Nonetheless, just because I did not conceive the new paradigm to be a general
theory of religion, I would not have felt compelled to theorize my uneasiness about
rational choice were it not for three additional stimuli. First is the fact that,
despite my intention, my 1993 article is often glossed in the literature (most
recently by Christiano, Swatos, and Kivisto 2002, 42) as one of the "seminal" contributions to "the rational choice theory" of religion. I want to set the record
straight. Second is the research that I am currently directing in the Youth and Religion Project at UIC, where, in interviews and focus groups with college students
and depth studies of their religious institutions and those in which they were
raised, we keep encountering cases of enthusiastic embrace and equally vehement
rejection of religious identity that are hard to account for in terms of rationality.

Third, I now teach Smelser's presidential address to the American Sociological Association, "The Rational and the Ambivalent in the Social Sciences" (1998), in my contemporary theory course to show the continuity in functionalism's response to rational choice theory (cf. Parsons 1954), and I have found it a fount of wisdom for my studies of religion in general. Smelser has helped me see my way around the limitations of rational choice theory as applied to religion (Warner, Martel, and Dugan 2001e).

(What Would Be) Anomalies in American Religion (If We Were to Adopt a Rational Choice Theory)

It would be a mistake to reject out of hand the application of rational choice theory to religious phenomena, especially in the hands of such insightful scholars as Stark, Iannaccone, and their associates. Their applications are not crude. In particular, the implication that many American church leaders seem both drawn to and repelled by—that churches flourish when they pander to popular taste—is almost directly opposite the implication drawn by these theorists themselves (Warner 2002). They say instead that churches flourish when they are "strict" and impose "gratuitous costs" on their members (Iannaccone 1994). Moreover, rational choice assumptions do not yield unambiguous predictions, which, if it were true, might render the perspective a straitjacket, a theoretical iron cage that left no room for theoretical creativity or individual agency. To the contrary, one who uses a rational choice theory of religion can enrich our understanding, as does Stark in his explanation of the rise of Christianity (1996). Anti–rational choice crusading is uncalled for.

In conceptualizing rational choice, I follow the formulations of Iannaccone (1997) and Stark and Finke (2000). Rational choice theory explains choice of action as a means of maximizing utilities given the constraints imposed by circumstances, where (1) the utilities actors care about tend not to vary across actors and situations; (2) as a consequence, the *explanans*, or independent variable, is the set of circumstances facing actors, including both expected benefits and costs of contemplated actions and the religious alternatives offered; and (3) the benefits and costs of religious participation are in large measure a function of the ideas about the supernatural taught by the particular religious alternative chosen. Accordingly, the rational choice perspective views actors as generic, not idiosyncratic; indeed for theoretical purposes, actors are interchangeable. The outlook of such generic actors is not clouded by ignorance, and they can fairly well judge what is in their enlightened self-interest. Although this perspective may appear to diminish individuality, it rests at bottom on the same humane instinct as the admonition that we should not judge one of our fellows until we have walked a mile in her or his shoes.

I find rational choice theory most helpful to understand the "supply side" of choices made by religious organizations and entrepreneurs, but less so when what we are trying to understand is the "demand side" of people's motivations for being religious or irreligious (cf. Pizzorno 1986). What I see in American religion suggests that we need to take into account much besides circumstances, or objective realities, including inclinations that vary from group to group, from person to person, and, most critically, within persons. Consider:

Of the one third or so of Americans who are not affiliated with a religious institution (the "unchurched"), most are believers in religious ideas. In other words, defection from or refusal to participate in religion is *not* accounted for primarily by unbelief (Smith et al. 1998, 154–173; Stark and Finke 2000, 76–77). With the literally hundreds of denominations and other religious communities available to Americans and our system of open communications, one would think that people could find a church to accord with their beliefs. Something else must be keeping them away.

Many who are affiliated with a religious institution (the "churched") do not personally subscribe to the doctrines their religious communities teach (Ammerman 1997). Something else must be keeping them there.

Some of the unchurched believers are those people who say that they are "spiritual, but not religious." The meaning of religious affiliation seems to differ from person to person.

When Protestants have differences with their churches, they tend to switch to denominations where they fit in. When Catholics part company with their churches, they tend to stay away altogether (Sherkat 2001). The meaning of religious affiliation seems to differ from group to group.

Evangelism—or proselytization—often makes nonevangelicals angry; it does not merely leave them indifferent, as product advertising would. Having one's religious affiliation questioned is different from being invited to buy a new car. Correlatively, leaving one's religion is a cause of great pain for people who would seem to have many reasons to get out (Warner 1993a, 1079; Warner, Martel, and Dugan 2001e). Religious affiliation is not affectively neutral.

Protestant fundamentalists rail against the godless secular society, but frequently, as in the energy they put into educating their offspring, they aspire to achieve the prestige conferred by the standards of that society. They seem to have mixed motives (Carpenter 1997).

Instrumental motivation, *do ut des*, does not work well in religious affairs. Such is the wisdom of social science (Warner 1993a, 1070–1071; cf. Smilde 2003), as well as of religion itself. ("Those who want to save their life will lose it, and those who lose their life for my sake will find it" is one of the rare sayings attributed to Jesus in all four Gospels.) Many of the purported benefits of religion, including the well-being of individuals and the realization of their communities' aspirations, come only as a byproduct of religious commitment and do not serve as its goal. So although religion does good things for people individually and collectively, it cannot be explained by motivation to seek those good things. This stricture seems particularly salient for the understanding of the black church. It is difficult to see where in the motivational structure of the hypothesized economic actor might reside the wellspring of the passion, and especially the courage, that religion has historically engendered among African Americans (Chappell 2002).

In the Youth and Religion Project particularly, we have come across orientations to religion that are puzzling if one assumes that religious involvement is simply rational. For example, in a focus group of Latina college students, mainly Mexican American women of Catholic heritage, most of the participants expressed anger with the church of their upbringing and said they had abandoned its practice; yet two of them had recently baptized their children in the Catholic Church and only one had taken the step of actually leaving the church for the Protestant alternative. In a focus group of college men defined as "Christian," those who were the children of immigrants (they were Asian Americans) insisted that they had much to learn from their (also Christian) parents religiously, whereas several of those who were European Americans dismissed the idea that they had anything to learn from their parents—this despite the distinct probability that the Asian American immigrant youth could correct their parents' English, while the latter had learned their English, as well as their religion, from their parents. On the other hand, Muslim women in another focus group, most of them children of immigrants from India and Pakistan, spoke of the enthusiasm with which, as students new to college, they adopted the religiously mandated *hijab*, or head covering, that their mothers had shunned. Some of them reported with pride (there is no other word for it) that their sisters and even their mothers were following suit. The Youth and Religion Project learned that the most active, popular religious group on the UIC campus (where Catholics, mainline Protestants, and Jews can gather in buildings they own under the tutelage of religious professionals of their own persuasion) is the student-run Muslim Student Association, which meets for weekly prayer in whatever room of the student union is available on Friday afternoon. Off campus, we have studied the successful youth program of a "seeker church" that goes to great lengths to reduce any "religious" trappings from their services in order to attract hundreds of twenty-something singles (Kovacs 2000). Analyzing these services, where one seldom sees a cross and never a hymnal, we nonetheless could not believe that those who flock to them are uninterested in religious things (God, sin, and salvation). Meanwhile, for years my sociology of religion class has regularly enrolled students who claim to be spiritual but not religious and those (sometimes the same people) who were raised in a church (usually Catholic) and claim not to have been back since they moved out of their parents' home. These students are bewildered to find that the church today, with women serving as "lectors," "commentators," and "Eucharistic ministers," is not the same as the one they left.

How Smelser Helps

The focus-group component of the Youth and Religion Project was intended to help us begin to understand what college students, most of them newly emancipated from their parents' homes, felt about their religion—what they found positive in it and what negative (Warner, Martel, and Dugan 2001e). They told us plenty, and, from earlier acquaintance with UIC students, we were not surprised to hear that the Mexican American women had almost nothing good to say about the Catholic Church, and that the second-generation Indo-Pakistani women had nothing bad to say about Islam and the Prophet Mohammed. All complaints that we might have expected these high-achieving, Americanized Muslim women to lodge against their religion were lodged instead against the *cultures* of the countries from which their parents had immigrated. In fact, the extemporaneous conversations we elicited from these eighteen- to twenty-two-year-old young women neatly replicated discourse we had read in ethnographic accounts of their religioethnic communities.

What we were not prepared for was the admission on the part of two of the Mexican American women, late into the discussion, that for all their differences with the Church, they had been married there and had their sons baptized there. One said: "For me it's kind of funny, when I started questioning the Catholic Church. When I got married, where was I going to get married? My husband was Catholic. And how was I going to raise my child? . . . I can't really get married in the Catholic Church, because I'd be a hypocrite because I disagree with most of the things. I haven't gone to church in, like, years. Only once in a big while. Finally, I ended up getting married in the Catholic Church because that's what I grew up with. I baptized my son into the Catholic Church, although I don't agree completely with the Catholic Church, but that's all I know." She actually did know of an alternative—the Protestant missions that line the side streets in Chicago's Mexican neighborhoods and that had converted one of the other focus-group participants—but to judge from the rest of the discussion, she likely shared the disdain for Protestant proselytizers expressed by Spanish-language front-door stickers made available to Mexican families by the Catholic archdiocese. The stickers say that the family that dwells herein is Catholic, thank you.

The other young mother in the focus group explained that her warmly embraced Mexican culture was inextricable from her reluctant Catholicism: "It's, like, synonymous with Catholicism. A lot of the traditions are viewed as Catholic. . . . So I want my child to grow up with those traditions. They're synonymous with the Catholic religion. . . . I don't agree with the ideology, but I agree with the tradition. I want to instill in him those morals, those values, those traditions."[2]

The Youth and Religion Project had intended the focus groups to elicit from students the good and bad news about religion. We did not really expect to hear people say both that they did and did not want to be part of the Catholic Church.[3] We had not expected that their feelings would be so mixed, so ambivalent.

Rational choice theory presupposes rationality, which is another way of saying that people know what they value and can weigh the things they value against one another. One objection many scholars of religion raise against such a presupposition stems from their conviction that people value religion differently from other things, such that worship services and, say, secular entertainment are incommensurable for many of the people who participate in both. Yet pastors as much as rational choice theorists know that at least some members of their congregations experience trade-offs between church and the Super Bowl. Ambivalence is something else, something that defies the very foundation of rationality, because it means that people both want and do not want the same thing, or, more typically, both hate and love the same object. Having encountered such an explicit instance of ambivalence, we decided to consider what might be the general place of ambivalence in religious social psychology. For that purpose we turned to "The Rational and the Ambivalent in the Social Sciences" (1998), Neil Smelser's presidential address to the American Sociological Association.[4]

Smelser argues that intrapsychic ambivalence—"the simultaneous existence of attraction and repulsion, of love and hate" toward the same object (5)—is an emotional state the existence of which can be expected under certain circumstances, and that in such circumstances it vitiates the assumption of actors' rationality. To that extent and in such circumstances, theorists must entertain the postulate of ambivalence as an alternative to that of rational choice. Following Freud, Smelser thinks that the circumstances that generate ambivalence are especially found in relationships that are inescapable, those on which the actor is dependent, those from which she is not free to leave. Smelser's "general proposition is that dependent situations breed ambivalence, and correspondingly, models of behavior based on the postulate of ambivalence are the most applicable" in situations of dependence (8). Parent-child relationships are relationships of dependence and the locus classicus of ambivalence. Another prime setting for ambivalence is found in "those groups, organizations, and social movements that demand commitment, adherence and faithfulness from their members." This category includes "churches, ethnic and racial identity groups" (6, 9). Following this reasoning, the Youth and Religion Project, focused as it is on the intersection of these two settings, should have expected to encounter expressions of ambivalence all along and should from the outset have entertained the postulate of ambivalence as a presupposition in designing the research.

As much as sociology of religion rightly regards U.S. religion ever since disestablishment as a key element of the U.S. "voluntary sector" and an aspect of civil society standing between the state and the economy, religion is ordinarily not experienced by children—at least not those who grow up in religiously affiliated families—as a realm of their own free choice. Many of Youth and Religion Project's youthful informants, indeed, recall that they were "forced" to go to Sunday school. Those students who are disappointed to learn that the church they left as soon as they could has moved in the direction of values they profess (e.g., inclusion of women) seem almost to embrace ambivalence, as if the church they love to hate has no right to change. Whatever the attitude of grownups toward their religion, dependent minors for the most part do not experience it as something they are free to take or leave.

Dependence is itself a variable. Thinking back on the difference between the Asian American and European American college men on how much they felt they had to learn from their parents, we supposed that the former might be objectively less dependent on their parents than the latter.[5] To be sure, the Asian students' expression of respect for their parents may testify to the cultural power of Confucian filial piety (and their white counterparts' disdain for their parents' knowledge may similarly stem from the culturally approved American discourse of generational rebellion). Yet it seems equally likely that the Asian students were *in fact* less dependent on their immigrant parents and more likely to have learned their own way in American society while the white students *in fact* learned the rudiments of their culture from their parents and might well expect to make their first down payments on the security of their parents' highly appreciated bungalows.

If dependent relationships breed ambivalence, those relationships from which individuals are free to withdraw, or those in which they know that they will live only temporarily, are settings wherein individuals can indulge impulses toward emotional involvement with psychological impunity. Referring to such relationships as "odyssey" situations, Smelser includes ocean voyages, summer camps, the college years, and scholars' temporary residence at his own Center for Advanced Study in the Behavioral Sciences (9). "People, sometimes strangers, are thrown together in physical proximity, but they know this close contact will end in time." Such situations are "typically lived and remembered with unalloyed sentimentality and nostalgia." In such settings, we should expect to find less ambivalence generated; indeed, about them we should expect to find an exhilarating experience of freedom expressed. More generally, as Smelser quotes Edward Lawler, "positive emotion generated by choice processes strengthens affective ties to groups credited with making choice opportunities available" (9, citing Lawler 1997).

Here, we thought Smelser had unlocked a secret of the collective enthusiasm of Muslims on the UIC campus, given a strategic particularity of their religious practice. Whereas the obligatory day of Christian worship is Sunday, the corresponding day for Muslims is Friday. Since most UIC students commute to school from home, many Christian students are no doubt pressured to accompany their parents to church, whereas Muslims' communal prayer occurs at school on a school day. Insofar as the primary religious venues for our Muslim women are on campus rather than the mosques they may have attended with their parents as children, religious involvement for the UIC Muslims may partake of the "odyssey" experience, something associated with the college years, not with their families of origin. By contrast, the Mexican American women, living at home and no doubt subject to Sunday-morning nagging, experience their religion not as a campus-based activity—they seem unaware of the Newman Center—but in the context of their parents' and grandparents' parishes. Thus for many UIC Mexican American students, religion is something imposed on them, whereas for their Muslim peers, religious activity is freed from parentally imposed obligations and associated instead with the new friends they have made in the university. Evangelical Christianity, the second most visible student religious community on the UIC campus—and the religiosity of the most popular off-campus college-age groups we studied—defines itself by a ritual, being "born again," in which individuals publicly take charge of their religious lives by "turning around" from the past and declaring themselves to be new persons.

To speak of variations in ambivalence brings up another contribution of Smelser's paper. Having essayed an explanation of the *generation* of ambivalence in relationships of dependence, he also, although less systematically, considers the various *expressions* of ambivalence, the ways it is manifested, taking a lead once again from Freud. Being a "*powerful, persistent, unresolvable, volatile, generalizable*, and *anxiety-provoking* feature of the human condition" (6, emphasis in the original), ambivalence is something we try to avoid experiencing, seldom successfully. "Ambivalence tends to be unstable, expressing itself in different and sometimes contradictory ways as actors attempt to cope with it" (5). Originating in one relationship, ambivalence may find expression in another, as mixed feelings about one's father are projected onto one's analyst or one's God. Ambivalence may be repressed, reversed (where the negative emotion is given a positive expression, as in "love thine enemy"), displaced (appearing in seemingly unrelated thoughts and actions), projected, or split.

An example of "splitting ambivalence" is where the positive side of the ambivalence is transferred into "an unqualified love of one person or object and the negative side into an unqualified hatred of another" (6). With less extreme expressions, what the UIC Muslim women say about religion and culture is an excellent example of such splitting: everything admirable and conducive to their aspirations is attributed to Islam (Williams and Vashi 2001); everything suspect and deleterious is attributed to Indian, Pakistani, or Palestinian culture (Warner, Martel, and Dugan 2001e). Convinced that the Mexican culture they feel to be central to their own identities is inextricable from the Catholicism they disdain, our Mexican American women did not have such a luxury.

Another common example of splitting that Smelser cites is the expression of in-group solidarity and out-group hostility, where the actually complex world of social relations is viewed "dichotomously—as friends or enemies, believers or non-believers, good or evil" (10). Mexican Americans who do, despite the risk of disinheritance, convert to Protestantism dichotomize their religious trajectory— although once again, their way of expressing themselves is less extreme than Smelser puts it.[6] Such converts speak, both in our focus groups and in my sociology of religion class, of their preconversion affiliation in highly pejorative terms: "I used to be Catholic, but now I'm Christian." Of such either/or thinking, Smelser comments: "We do not understand the full significance of this categorization, but one of its apparent functions is to diminish the internal ambivalence bred by commitment by splitting it between inside and outside. I know of no mechanism that better protects the fragile solidarity of these intense groups" (10). Being a Protestant does not come easily to Chicago Mexican Americans; it is not a simple rational choice.

We think it reasonable to hypothesize that the legions of baby boomers and GenXers who report that they are "spiritual but not religious" (Roof 1993, 76–79; Beaudoin 1998, 23–26) find in that expression a way of splitting the ambivalence they feel about religious institutions, especially those whose Sunday schools and masses they felt forced to attend. Interest in religious things—prayer, relationship with God, ultimate meaning, help in times of distress—remains high with members of these cohorts even as many have dropped out of church (or never went in the first place); it is not helpful to regard them as simple unbelievers. God is good; church is bad. Some prefer to go it alone in their spiritual quest (Bellah et al. 1985). But many wish to reach out to others, like those who flock to "seeker churches" that radically minimize any churchlike appearance, meeting in "auditoriums" instead of sanctuaries and offering "teachings" instead of "sermons" in rooms furnished with folding chairs and overhead projectors instead of pews and hymnals. The designers of such churches, like the one studied by the Youth and Religion Project that attracts so many college- and post-college-age singles, evidently think of young people's attitude toward religion in terms similar to those suggested by Smelser's ambivalence theory. If it reminds them of church, out it goes. If it appears to be something you'd never see in church, give it a try.

One youth program we studied—we call it "Soul Station"—applies this principle, as it were, in reverse. Sponsored by a highly modernized church in the Reformed tradition, which itself traditionally scorns "religious" things like statues and stained glass in favor of Bible stories and transparent preaching, Soul Station's Saturday-night college-age worship features candles, icons, low lighting, and long periods of silent meditation (Cravens and Warner 2001d). Previous generations already threw out the mystical religious trappings; as members of what has been called the "Millennial Generation," Soul Station youth may reintroduce them (Howe and Strauss 2000, 234–237).

Some Implications

I have argued that the attribution of rationality, in its technical sense, to the relationship of individuals to their religion, or irreligion, is misleading insofar as such relationships may symbolize relationships of dependence, particularly the universal, though variably intense, dependence of minors on their caretakers. Dependence generates ambivalence, and, at a minimum, ambivalence compromises rationality. Ambivalent persons may irrationally reject what they really want and may irrationally embrace things that are not good for them.

I have not argued that religion is a particular arena for the free play of the irrational. Maturity means emancipation from juvenile dependence. For purposes of sociological theory, we assume that adults are free to make informed choices, subject, of course, to their own conceptions of right and wrong as well as a myriad of objective constraints (Rubinstein 2001). In particular, the argument of this chapter should not be confused with a competing theory that attributes irrationality to religious commitment itself, so-called plausibility theory (Berger 1969). According to this theory, religious beliefs are maintained to the extent that believers are shielded from awareness of potentially disconfirming alternatives, especially competing religions and modern science. Theorists of European secularization have adduced this theory to explain what they see as the fatal consequences for religion of "modernity," particularly the Enlightenment and the encounter with cultures outside of Christendom. According to this theory, religion, especially conservative religion, persists in the modern world only when its objective implausibility is shored up by "plausibility structures," devices whereby the community of believers isolates itself from engagement with the outside world.

It will be clear that plausibility theory, the theoretical heart of the old paradigm, is precisely what I set out to overturn in formulating the new paradigm. Beyond the sociological commonplace that people like to surround themselves with like-minded others, there is no evidence for the claims of plausibility theory (Stark and Finke 2000), whose advocates may fairly be accused of projecting their own cognitive insecurity onto the rest of society. Conservative religion is not especially vulnerable in contemporary America (Smith et al. 1998), and scientific rationality is not popularly hegemonic. In contrast to European religion, which secularization theorists perceive to have reached its apogee five hundred years ago under conditions of establishment, American religion developed in the crucible of modernity and disestablishment (Warner 1991a), enlisting a vast population during a century of rapid urbanization and cultural diversification.

Thus we need not return analytically to the dependent minor's view of U.S. religion—in the past or the present—as anything less than voluntary.[7] A decade ago, I wrote that the old-paradigm view of U.S. religion, which contrasts an imagined past where religion was a given with a present where religion is optional, "narrates the psychological experience of intellectuals who emerge from religiously conservative families to the religiously indifferent world of the academy." Thus it appeals to those who "have undergone psychologically" the process "that the old paradigm attributes sociologically to Western society as a whole" (Warner 1993a, 1054).[8]

There is another respect in which this chapter, along with its theoretical catalyst, does not reject rationality as a working assumption. Like Smelser, I have as my goal not to supplant rationality but to supplement it. The attentive reader will have recognized that the logic I attribute to "seeker churches," which lower perceived "religious" barriers to participation in actually religious communities, is a rational one: they do what is in their power to meet their goals, which most grandly are to save souls and most immediately to fill seats. Although both rational choice and ambivalence can be usefully employed as *postulates*, or presuppositions of theorizing (which we do when we *assume* that children who inherit their religion from their parents will be ambivalent about it and when we *assume* that religious leaders will respond to what they see as the needs of their constituents and organizations), neither is, or ought to be, an ideology that demands consistency. Moreover, we have also treated ambivalence, and could treat rationality, as an *explanandum*, a dependent variable, specifically a sentiment whose variable intensity can be explained. This paper is in part a recommendation to sociologists of religion that they consider the applicability of the logic of ambivalence to the understanding of religious activity and religious feelings.

NOTES

1. Peter Berger, whom I identified in 1993 as the leading champion of the "old paradigm," seems to have switched sides. He now acknowledges that the proposition underlying his early work—that modernity inevitably leads to secularization—was mistaken when applied to the United States, and that the European experience, which served as the model for his early work, is itself exceptional, not a promising base on which to generalize (1969, 2001).

2. "In classical Catholicism, exit was virtually impossible" (Smelser 1998, 12).

3. One of our focus-group participants expressed the hope that she "can still consider myself Catholic and kind of not."

4. References to this article hereafter are by page number only.

5. "[M]ore than other family systems, the American makes the child highly dependent emotionally on its parents, particularly the mother." For boys especially, this situation is highly conducive to the development of a "deep ambivalence toward moral values" (Parsons 1954, 344–345).

6. The Youth and Religion Project's focus-group participants and sociology of religion students of Mexican background report that their families warn that their becoming Protestant would mean renouncing their cultural heritage; some families threaten to throw them out of the house.

7. The past since about 1800. Before then, religion was indeed established in some of the American colonies and, to varying degrees, obligatory.

8. In the interest of full disclosure, I should acknowledge that I myself did not grow up in a religious family and was in fact baptized (in the Presbyterian Church, U.S.A.) at my own initiative at age fifteen.

REFERENCES

(References to writings of the author are found in a separate listing at the back of the book.)

Ammerman, Nancy. 1987. *Bible Believers: Fundamentalists in the Modern World.* New Brunswick, N.J.: Rutgers University Press.

———. 1997. "Golden Rule Christianity: Lived Religion in the American Mainstream." In *Lived Religion in America*, ed. David Hall, 196–216. Princeton, N.J.: Princeton University Press.

Beaudoin, Tom. 1998. *Virtual Faith: The Irreverent Spiritual Quest of Generation X.* San Francisco: Jossey-Bass.

Bellah, Robert N., Richard Madsen, William M. Sullivan, Ann Swidler, and Steven M. Tipton. 1985. *Habits of the Heart: Individualism and Commitment in American Life.* Berkeley and Los Angeles: University of California Press.

Berger, Peter L. 1969. *The Sacred Canopy: Elements of a Sociological Theory of Religion.* Garden City, N.Y.: Anchor.

———. 2001. "Reflections on the Sociology of Religion Today." *Sociology of Religion* 62 (Winter): 443–454.

Bilhartz, Terry D. 1986. *Urban Religion and the Second Great Awakening: Church and Society in Early National Baltimore.* Rutherford, N.J.: Fairleigh Dickinson University Press.

Butler, Jon. 1989. *Awash in a Sea of Faith: The Christianization of the American People, 1550–1865.* Cambridge: Harvard University Press.

Carpenter, Joel A. 1997. *Revive Us Again: The Reawakening of American Fundamentalism.* New York: Oxford University Press.

Chappell, David. L. 2002. "Religious Revivalism in the Civil Rights Movement." *African American Review* 36 (Winter): 581–595.

Chaves, Mark, and Philip S. Gorski. 2001. "Religious Pluralism and Religious Participation." *Annual Review of Sociology* 27: 261–281.

Christiano, Kevin J., William H. Swatos, Jr., and Peter Kivisto. 2002. *Sociology of Religion: Contemporary Developments.* Walnut Creek, Calif.: Alta Mira.

Collins, Randall. 1975. *Conflict Sociology: Toward an Explanatory Science.* New York: Academic Press.

Finke, Roger. 1997. "The Consequences of Religious Competition: Supply-Side Explanations for Religious Change." In *Rational Choice Theory and Religion: Summary and Assessment*, ed. Lawrence A. Young, 46–65. New York: Routledge.

Finke, Roger, and Rodney Stark. 1988. "Religious Economies and Sacred Canopies: Religious Mobilization in American Cities." *American Sociological Review* 53 (February): 41–49.

———. 1989. "How the Upstart Sects Won America: 1776–1850." *Journal for the Scientific Study of Religion* 28 (March): 27–44.

———. 1992. *The Churching of America, 1776–1990: Winners and Losers in Our Religious Economy.* New Brunswick, N.J.: Rutgers University Press.

Hatch, Nathan O. 1989. *The Democratization of American Christianity.* New Haven: Yale University Press.

Heyrman, Christine Leigh. 1998. *Southern Cross: The Beginnings of the Bible Belt.* Chapel Hill: University of North Carolina Press.

Howe, Neil, and William Strauss. 2000. *Millennials Rising: The Next Great Generation.* New York: Vintage.

Iannaccone, Laurence R. 1990. "Religious Practice: A Human Capital Approach." *Journal for the Scientific Study of Religion* 29 (September): 297–314.

——. 1991. "The Consequences of Religious Market Structure." *Rationality and Society* 3 (April): 156–177.

——. 1994. "Why Strict Churches Are Strong." *American Journal of Sociology* 99 (March): 1180–1211.

——. 1997. "Rational Choice: Framework for the Scientific Study of Religion." In *Rational Choice Theory and Religion: Summary and Assessment*, ed. Lawrence A. Young, 25–45. New York: Routledge.

Kovacs, Daniel. 2000. "Social Class and Youth Ministries." Senior honors thesis, Department of Sociology, University of Illinois at Chicago.

Lawler, Edward J. 1997. "Affective Attachments to Nested Groups: The Role of Rational Choice Processes." In *Status, Networks, and Structures: Theory Development in Group Processes*, ed. J. Skvoretz, J. Szmatka, and J. Berger, 387–403. Stanford, Calif.: Stanford University Press.

Lechner, Frank J. 1991. "The Case Against Secularization: A Rebuttal." *Social Forces* 69 (June): 1103–1119.

Littel, Franklin Hamlin. 1962. *From State Church to Pluralism*. Chicago: Aldine.

Mead, Sidney E. 1963. *The Lively Experiment*. New York: Harper and Row.

Moore, R. Laurence. 1994. *Selling God: American Religion in the Marketplace of Culture*. New York: Oxford University Press.

Neitz, Mary Jo. 1987. *Charisma and Community: A Study of Religious Commitment Within the Charismatic Renewal*. New Brunswick, N.J.: Transaction Books.

Parsons, Talcott. 1949. *The Structure of Social Action: A Study in Social Theory with Special Reference to a Group of Recent European Writers*. Glencoe, Ill.: Free Press.

——. 1954. "Psychoanalysis and the Social Structure." In *Essays in Sociological Theory*, 336–347. Rev. ed. Glencoe, Ill.: Free Press.

Pizzorno, Alessando. 1986. "Some Other Kinds of Otherness: A Critique of 'Rational Choice' Theories." In *Development, Democracy, and the Art of Trespassing: Essays in Honor of Albert O. Hirschman*, ed. A. Foxley et al., 355–373. Notre Dame, Ind.: Notre Dame University Press.

Roof, Wade Clark. 1993. *A Generation of Seekers: The Spiritual Journeys of the Baby Boom Generation*. San Francisco: HarperSan Francisco.

Rubinstein, David M. 2001. *Culture, Structure, and Agency: Toward a Truly Multidimensional Sociology*. Thousand Oaks, Calif.: Sage.

Sherkat, Darren E. 2001. "Tracking the Restructuring of American Religion: Religious Affiliation and Patterns of Religious Mobility, 1973–1998." *Social Forces* 79 (June): 1459–1493.

Smelser, Neil J. 1998. "The Rational and the Ambivalent in the Social Sciences." *American Sociological Review* 63 (February): 1–15.

Smilde, David. 2003. "Skirting the Instrumental Paradox: Intentional Belief Through Narrative in Latin American Pentecostalism." *Qualitative Sociology* 26 (Fall): 313–329.

Smith, Christian, with Michael Emerson, Sally Gallagher, Paul Kennedy, and David Sikkink. 1998. *American Evangelicalism: Embattled and Thriving*. Chicago: University of Chicago Press.

Stark, Rodney. 1996. *The Rise of Christianity: How the Obscure, Marginal Jesus Movement Became the Dominant Religious Force in the Western World in a Few Centuries*. Princeton, N.J.: Princeton University Press.

——. 1997. "Bringing Theory Back In." In *Rational Choice Theory and Religion: Summary and Assessment*, ed. Lawrence A. Young, 3–24. New York: Routledge.

Stark, Rodney, and William Sims Bainbridge. 1987. *A Theory of Religion*. New York and Bern: Peter Lang.

Stark, Rodney, and Roger Finke. 2000. *Acts of Faith: Explaining the Human Side of Religion*. Berkeley and Los Angeles: University of California Press.

Stout, Harry S. 1991. *The Divine Dramatist: George Whitefield and the Rise of Modern Evangelicalism.* Grand Rapids, Mich.: Eerdmans

Williams, Rhys H., and Gira Vashi. 2001. "Hijab and American Muslim Women: Creating the Space for Autonomous Selves." Paper presented at annual meeting of the Midwest Sociological Society, St. Louis, April 4.

PART TWO

Close-ups and Overviews of Diverse Congregations

7

Mirror for American Protestantism

Mendocino Presbyterian Church in the Sixties and Seventies (1990)

In 1975, I began a sociological study of the Presbyterian church of Mendocino, California, a small rural community on the coast north of San Francisco, and I have followed the fortunes of the congregation over the past fourteen years. After overcoming some initial preconceptions of what could be gained from the study, I realized that the church's social history in the 1960s and 1970s mirrors the changes undergone by white American Protestantism in the same years, and my recent book, *New Wine in Old Wineskins*, recounts that representative social history in concrete detail.[1] After a discussion of the combination of sociological and historical methods employed, this chapter presents a brief theoretical scheme for tracing the post—World War II trajectory of American Protestantism and an outline of the history of Mendocino Presbyterian Church, both the theory and the history drawn from *New Wine*. Then, on the basis of new research done specifically for this volume, the story is brought up to the mid-1980s. The chapter concludes with some tentative lessons to be derived from the Mendocino experience.[2]

Research Methods: Sociology and History

I began the research in Mendocino with a social scientific orientation, less interested in the religious identity of the congregation than in its presumed sociological significance. Personal contacts indicated that the pastorate of the church had recently undergone an abrupt change toward evangelicalism and that the membership was growing rapidly. Therefore, I thought the congregation would be an ideal natural laboratory for investigating firsthand some generic social processes of theoretical concern, namely the forging of consensus (as indexed by the pattern of growth) out of conflict (that presumably accompanied the change in pastorate). Other sociologists emulated in this work have studied social processes in such sites as World War II internment camps,[3] hospital operating rooms,[4] soccer clubs,[5] mining towns,[6] rural communes,[7] and urban neighborhoods.[8] I happened to choose a church.

Accordingly, the project employed field research methods, also called ethnographic and qualitative methods. Among sociologists and anthropologists this process ordinarily involves three components: observing, interviewing, and gathering information from preexisting sources.[9] I lived in Mendocino from May through December 1976 and regularly attended Sunday worship services, played the role of an acknowledged participant-observer in a Friday-night charismatic praise-and-teaching meeting, participated in a weekly prayer meeting in the manse from July through October, sat in as an observer on one meeting of the trustees and another of the session, went to monthly public hearings of the Mendocino Historical Review Board, and accepted invitations to Rotary luncheons, progressive dinners, and ice cream socials. I took extensive notes on all of these events and many others, including work parties, campouts, picnics, potlucks, and parades. These observations in 1976 were supplemented by others made on brief visits of two days to one week in years prior and subsequent to my residence in the community, spanning the years from 1975 to 1986. In the end, field notes on over four hundred hours of events relevant to the life of the congregation had been amassed.

I conducted formal interviews with about sixty persons in Mendocino, lasting anywhere from one-and-a-half hours to the better part of two working days, and I maintained informal ongoing conversations with another two dozen informants, who shared confidentially their experiences and perspectives on matters pertaining to the church and the community. Some of these persons were members of the congregation, some were regular attenders, some were former members, some were affiliated with the charismatic group that used the church social hall on Friday nights, and some, like the Catholic priest and a newspaper columnist, were knowledgeable outsiders.

Many sources of preexisting information were consulted. These included local newspapers, the telephone book, the county register of voters, friends' souvenirs, various newsletters, and, of course, the church itself. From the beginning I had access to the church's current membership roster, its monthly newsletters, and tape recordings of Sunday services begun in 1974. Later, the pastor loaned me documents from his personal files and attendance records for the church dating back to 1959. Eventually the session granted access to its book of minutes, which I read for the years 1957 through 1982. I have in my files copies of the formal annual reports to the congregation for 1960 through 1989.

As more materials were gathered pertaining to the past—or, put another way, as the sociological "data" more closely approximated gleanings from archives and oral histories—I realized I was doing a form of history. Moreover, as more was learned about the congregation, it became evident that the conflict did not exist where I had first expected it. The evangelical turn taken by the church in 1973 was immensely popular with every segment of the congregation. A serious, sustained conflict did exist, but it was among evangelicals, not between them and their predecessors in the congregation. To understand the evangelicals required framing the study in terms of a literature specifically devoted to religion, not conflict and consensus. Moreover, since the analysis eventually extended backward (and forward) in time from the period of this field research, the report became a narrative of change in a particular Presbyterian congregation rather than a dissection of processes in a generic social laboratory. So it was that a sociologist, trained in a field whose norm is to label research sites with pseudonyms,[10] came to write a congregational social history that the Library of Congress catalogued by a real town name.[11] Yet in keeping with sociological tradition, all personal names of Mendocino people have been replaced with pseudonyms.[12]

New Wine in Old Wineskins was well received by my social science colleagues as well as well as by historians. I believe that this reaction is attributable both to its interdisciplinary approach and, more important, to the intrinsic significance of the history of Mendocino Presbyterian Church.

Theoretical Considerations on Recent Church History

As Figure 7.1 shows, the membership curve of Mendocino Presbyterian Church approximates that of the United Presbyterian Church in the 1950s and 1960s, impressive growth followed by slow decline.[13] In the 1970s, however, the congregation's fortunes took an abrupt turn for the better, and its growth curve in that decade resembles that of the Assemblies of God rather than the Presbyterian Church. What makes these statistics remarkable is that the theological stance of the church took corresponding turns in the early 1960s toward social justice and, in

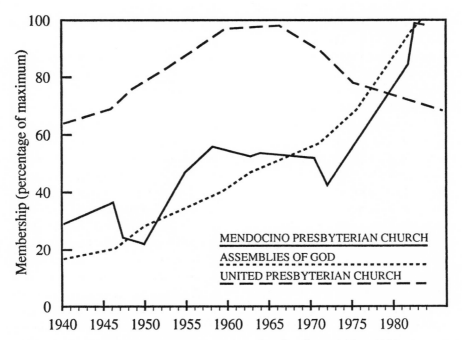

FIGURE 7-1 Memberships in three Protestant churches from 1939 to 1982 measured in percentage of maximum membership

the early 1970s from liberalism to evangelicalism. In effect, Mendocino Presbyterian went from being the kind of "sociable" church theologian Will Herberg described in the 1950s, through a period of activism under two of sociologist Jeffrey Hadden's "new breed" clergymen in the 1960s, to the growth under conservative auspices that ecumenical executive Dean Kelley made famous in the 1970s.[14]

In the late 1970s, when this history was being prepared for publication, the reigning concepts in the sociology of religion were inadequate to the task.[15] Scholars who talked about choices faced by Protestant churches tended to collapse the alternatives to only two. Churches, it was said, could provide either comfort or challenge to their congregations, playing the part of the priest or the prophet, preaching in the language of either private or public Protestantism. Though this dichotomy is not wholly absurd, it could not map the path the Mendocino church had traveled. It was necessary to develop a two-dimensional scheme to analyze the currents within contemporary Protestantism.

The first dimension deals with the theological debate that has organized and divided American Protestantism for a century, the debate between the emphasis on social change and that on individual salvation. With some misgivings I call the alternatives "liberalism" and "evangelicalism," and I follow church historian Martin Marty in arguing that the two poles are best conceived sociologically as parties—informal but persisting social networks—rather than sets of attitudes or articulate theologies.[16]

The other dimension respects a more abstract but also more ancient tension, endemic to Christianity, between the charismatic experience of the religious movement and the settled routine of the church, and I call the poles those of nascent versus institutional religion.[17] Nascent religion mobilizes people to 100 percent–plus commitment, but institutional religion presupposes that its adherents have rewarding and demanding lives outside the religious sphere. Despite the prejudices of partisans, the two dimensions are independent, and four recognizable types emerge.[18] Mendocino knew them all in the 1960s and 1970s.

Nascent liberalism caught the public eye in the 1960s in the radicalism of the Berrigan brothers and Presbyterian John Fry of Chicago; it came to the Mendocino church in the person of Pastor Peter Hsu, fresh out of seminary in 1962. Nascent evangelicalism characterized the Jesus movement of the end of that decade, which came to northern California in the form of revivals and missions to the hippies and to Mendocino Presbyterian in 1964 when Larry Redford, veteran of the Navigators and alumnus of Fuller Theological Seminary, joined the church and was soon elected an elder. Institutional liberalism can be encountered in many Presbyterian (and a few Baptist) congregations, at some denominational headquarters, and in many university chapels; Mendocino had a taste of it in the late 1960s under Pastor Mark Kimmerly. Institutional evangelicalism is the leaning of the journal *Christianity Today* and of hundreds of Baptist (and some Presbyterian) congregations in the United States; from the mid-1970s onward institutional evangelicalism fairly describes the church in Mendocino, with Pastor Eric Underwood, also a Fuller alumnus, in its pulpit.

Sketch of Church History, 1959–1982

Mendocino Presbyterian Church betrayed little sign of its remarkable future when the congregation celebrated its centennial in 1959.[19] A period of rapid membership growth during the 1950s had peaked the year before at 160 after bringing the appearance of new prosperity to the physical plant and conviviality to the many group activities. Veterans recall that the church had as much an ethnic as a religious profile, being the place of worship of the descendants of the town's New England founders, in distinction from the later-arriving Portuguese, whose progeny went to the Catholic church. Aside from occupying California's oldest Presbyterian church building in continuous use, the Mendocino church was typical and undistinguished.

The changes felt in the 1960s had particular sources in Mendocino, but ones commensurate with what happened to other American churches in that decade. The region's economy, based for a century in lumber, fishing, and agriculture, was too weak in the 1960s to make room for all the graduates of the high school, but those indigenous youth were being replaced by exurbanite artists and bohemians, foreshadowing a new period of prosperity and fame for Mendocino as a tourist mecca, on-location film center, and retirement community. The Presbyterian church's beloved and influential pastor emeritus, Frederick Althorpe, who had led the congregation from 1931 to 1935 and again from 1952 to 1957, was disappointed with the response of his successor to these changes, and Althorpe thought, upon that man's retirement, that the church ought to seek out a young pastor with new ideas.[20] The nearby denominational training center, San Francisco Theological Seminary, was in the midst of an exciting liberal phase. The Presbyterian Church in California had a historic mission to the Chinese American community.

So it happened when the pulpit became vacant in 1962 that the best candidate for pastor in the salary range the small church could afford was Peter Hsu, a twenty-seven-year-old Chinese American from San Francisco with distinguished credentials and great personal charm.[21] Not only would Hsu become the first non-white pastor of a white Presbyterian church in California, but he and his wife would be only the second Chinese family in a community not known for its cosmopolitanism. Nonetheless, with courage on all sides and a fair amount of politicking, the search committee selected him, the congregation voted the call, and Hsu accepted. A jazz buff, tennis player, and all-around quick study, Hsu made many fast friends in Mendocino, and he and his wife began raising children. Among the few bitter memories he harbors of his Mendocino years is one that concerns not his parishioners but the Hollywood producers of *The Russians Are Coming, the Russians Are Coming*, who, filming on location, wanted to employ his clerical robe for a character in the movie but not Hsu himself as an extra. Small-town American churches don't have Chinese pastors, they told him. When he left for a denominational staff position after serving Mendocino for four years, the congregation had learned firsthand of the superficiality of race as a social criterion and knew that the church had the resilience to meet unforeseen challenges.

But Peter Hsu disturbed more than the racial profile of the church. The California legislature had just passed the Rumford Fair Housing Act, and a ballot referendum in 1964 mobilized thousands of liberal activists to save Rumford and defeat Proposition 14, which called for its repeal. In forums up and down the coast, Hsu spoke out vigorously for fair housing. At the same time, he did what he could locally in support of the efforts of desegregationists in the South, and by his last year in Mendocino he preached against the war in Vietnam. These activities made many Mendocino Presbyterians retrospectively proud of themselves in the 1970s and attracted a few members into the church from the growing artists' community in the 1960s, but Hsu's activities also antagonized some politically conservative members of the congregation. Other members asked portentously where the pastor found the time to do all his political work. The result, along with Mendocino's demographic decline in the 1960s and other contingencies to which churches are subject, was that attendance suffered and money was tight (see Table 7.1).

The congregational meeting to elect a search committee for Hsu's successor gave evidence that Hsu had left a divided congregation behind, but Hsu's supporters won out over his antagonists in the balloting.[22] The successor was to be a man of similar conviction, also one with recent experience at San Francisco Theological Seminary. Mark Kimmerly, thirty-four years old and the veteran of one pastorate, was also sympathetic to the civil rights and peace movements. But by theological conviction (neoorthodox) and personal character (reflective), his preferred mode of pastoral leadership was more that of moderator than point man.

TABLE 7-1

Mendocino Presbyterian Church Membership and Attendance, 1959–1988

Pastorate	Year	Attendance[a]	Membership[b]	Percentage[c]
Higginson	1959	76	154	50
Higginson	1960	66	152	45
Higginson	1961	74	146	51
Higginson	1962 (to May)	77	143	54
(interim)	1962 (May-July)	71		49
Hsu	1962 (July on)	77		53
Hsu	1963	72	145	50
Hsu	1964	68	147	46

(Continued)

TABLE 7-1. (*Continued*)

Hsu	1965	68	151	45
Hsu	1966 (to October)	59	152	39
(interim)	1966–1967 (2 mos.)	50	154	32
Kimmerly	1967 (Feb. on)	72		49
Kimmerly	1968	66	142	46
Kimmerly	1969	65	148	44
Kimmerly	1970	67	148	49
Kimmerly	1971	78	124	60
Kimmerly	1972 (to June)	79	136	58
(interim)	1972–1973 (9 mos.)	74	138	54
Underwood	1973 (March on)	116		79
Underwood	1974	160	154	95
Underwood	1975	172	181	93
Underwood	1976	186	186	91
Underwood	1977	176	223	78
Underwood	1978	170	228	70
UnderDoug[d]	1979	191	256	73
UnderDoug	1980	200	264	72
UnderDoug	1981	196	295	67
UnderDoug	1982	201	293	68
UnderDoug	1983 (to Sept.)	202	297	68
(interim)	1983 (Sept. on)	169		57
(interim)	1984	169	295	57
(interim)	1985 (to Sept.)	173	296	58
Koch	1985 (Sept. on)	204		68
Koch	1986	199	300	70
Koch	1987	189	271	72
Koch	1988	174	255	69
Koch	1989		252	

[a]Attendance: arithmetic average of recorded Sunday worship attendance for period indicated, excluding Easter and other special services.

[b]Membership: recorded by session and reported to General Assembly at beginning of calendar year indicated.

[c]Percentage: attendance divided by average membership for period indicated; a rough index of mobilization.

[d]Bruce Douglas added to staff as associate pastor.

He looked for programs calculated to unite the congregation and found an ideal one in the building centennial soon to be celebrated when he arrived in 1967. The impeccable appearance of the church plant today is thus due more to Kimmerly than to any other person. He had relatively more concern for the particular traditions of the Mendocino church than did his immediate predecessor, so, without turning his back on higher judicatories or the ethics he had learned in seminary, his pastorate put more of the church's resources into local priorities.[23]

Among local concerns was the increasing appearance in Mendocino of emigrants from the urban counterculture, back-to-the-land hippies and refugees from the draft. During Kimmerly's first summer (1967), San Francisco's notorious Summer of Love, Kimmerly proposed to Larry Redford, a local schoolteacher and church elder, that Redford turn his underutilized rural ranch into a religious retreat center for those seeking escape from the drug culture. Redford, an evangelical convert of the 1950s who with his wife had been introduced to the charismatic movement in Los Angeles in the early 1960s, first viewed the idea cautiously, then with wholehearted commitment. His decision seemed to be confirmed by the subsequent mass conversion of a nearby hippie commune in 1971–1972, whose newly charismatic members became an additional constituency for his ministry.[24]

Though Redford and his new converts did not share Kimmerly's particular religiosity, the people of Mendocino Presbyterian Church had been liberalized by Kimmerly and Hsu to a broader conception of Christian fellowship, and the church welcomed the ex-hippie charismatic Christians who began to show up sporadically at Sunday worship, pouring into the old church by the score from their painted buses. Meanwhile, other newcomers began to swell the church's membership rolls, the first of what in the 1970s would become a flood of relatively young and affluent retirees drawn by the picturesque lure of Mendocino. The numerical decline of the 1960s, caused more by demographics than by Hsu's or Kimmerly's ideologies, ended when membership bottomed out at 124 at the end of 1970.

When Kimmerly left in 1972 to accept another call, the church organization was thus in a healthy, if lean, state. But his and Hsu's actual theological teaching had left little articulate legacy. The liberal political movements each pastor had embraced were in disarray, and religious enthusiasm—what I call the nascent state—seemed for the time to be monopolized by the new charismatic Christians. Three evangelicals, led by Redford, were elected to a seven-person pastor search committee, and their determination and confidence easily overcame fitful attempts from the committee's fragmented majority to enunciate a nonevangelical vision of the church. The committee turned aside from the denominational seminary, which Redford thought was the source of erroneous teachings on the Bible, in favor of a graduate of Fuller Theological Seminary, which Redford himself had attended. In effect, they opted for a brand of Presbyterianism that had its origins in the fundamentalist wing of the denomination prior to its defeat by the forces of modernism early in the century.[25] The committee chose Eric Underwood, who had seven years' experience as associate pastor of a large, conservative Presbyterian church two hundred miles to the south, and he was called to the Mendocino pulpit early in 1973.

By any standard measure, Underwood's pastorate was an immediate and sustained success (see Table 7.1). Sunday-morning attendance soon doubled, and membership grew rapidly in its wake, reaching 295 in 1981. Giving increased, too, so that the church's budget at the end of the decade was ten times larger (four times larger in constant dollars in those years of severe inflation) than when Underwood came to Mendocino. A higher proportion of that larger budget went to the denomination's judicatories and missions than was the case in the liberal 1960s, even as the congregation doubled its ministerial staff with the addition of a youth pastor, sponsored a refugee family from Southeast Asia, and, in default of municipal authority (Mendocino being unincorporated), acted as steward for a parcel of valuable land given by a private benefactor for the enjoyment of the community. But witness for structural change of society was muted, as much because of the discouragement of its youthful advocates in Mendocino and the rest of the country as to Underwood's evangelicalism.

One of the causes of the vigor of the church in the 1970s was the population growth of Mendocino County, part of a nationwide trend for rural counties in that decade. But other northern California Presbyterian churches did not capitalize on the opportunity the way the Mendocino church did. (This is shown in a brief quantitative analysis in *New Wine*, 183–189, 310–311.) It is necessary then, to look to Underwood's preaching in order to understand his success. His message contained two deeply intertwined themes, the evangelical theology he had learned at Fuller and the kind of parochial social ethic Martin Luther had developed in rejecting the rule of the cosmopolitan Roman church.[26]

Neither a charismatic nor a fundamentalist, Underwood was an evangelical who held that the Bible is authoritative on matters of faith and doctrine. Unlike Harold Lindsell, champion of biblical inerrancy and vice-president of Fuller during Underwood's years as a student, Underwood was not given to polemics.[27] Instead, he assumed for his congregation the prosaic truth of New Testament salvation and miracle stories, explicating in detail the background understandings likely held by the original audiences of those stories, always suggesting the humanity common to the first and twentieth centuries. Underwood taught his congregation to pray to the living, listening God for their own and their loved ones' humble personal needs. He offered on their behalf each week a long pastoral prayer—intimate and extemporaneous but also stately and carefully structured—and he fostered the growth in the church of home prayer meetings and telephone prayer chains. He concluded every sermon with a subdued but unmistakable echo of the Baptist altar call, inviting hearers to dedicate their lives to Jesus, and he thus reminded the congregation each week that the core of his theology was justification by faith.[28] A succession of spirited elders ran the evangelism committee to follow up on Underwood's repeated invitations and brought scores of newcomers into the fellowship. One heard often in those days of miraculous changes wrought by the Lord in the lives of Mendocino Presbyterians.

Underwood's parochialism came down to the teaching that there is nothing on earth more real than the other persons we encounter and no obligations more salient than faithfulness to one's family. In a sermon on prayer Underwood said: "Our prayers are not impersonal. We pray specifically and name those who are in need of God's hand. We have only one reason to suppose that God will answer our prayers for those whom we love. Jesus answers prayer when it arises from a total relationship of loving concern on our behalf."[29] He provided a model of such concern for his congregation by his involvement as a town pastor, making daily rounds to the grocery store and post office that functioned as informal community centers and keeping detailed mental notes on the progress of the people of Mendocino, inside and outside his congregation. What he learned about Mendocino and its idiosyncrasies appeared in his sermons and prayers by way of object lessons and vivid illustrations.

As a matter of principle, he pressed for the congregation's financial generosity to the denomination, but his insistent localism tended to disregard denominational affairs; after 1979, he allocated involvement in presbytery and its social issues to his associate, the new youth pastor, Bruce Douglas, who was a graduate of McCormick Seminary, and to one elder whose pattern of ecclesiastical involvement derived from his pre-Mendocino church. Unlike Peter Hsu, who regularly suggested that the church he pastored lacked cosmopolitan awareness, Underwood adroitly suggested that Mendocino Presbyterian Church was precisely the place that the living God was working. What made this a particularly compelling message was that the majority of the church's members had chosen as adults to move to Mendocino as the ideal small town. Underwood's philosophical parochialism matched their elective parochialism.

Underwood's orthodox theology exalted God's three persons, and his social teaching dignified the local congregation gathered in the Lord's name. He attracted evangelicals and elective parochials, and their enthusiasm attracted others. Membership more than doubled by the end of the decade, contributions multiplied exponentially, and the programs of the church enlisted whole new corps of volunteers. Veterans of Redford's Antioch Fellowship, a quarter of whom were professional schoolteachers, infused the Sunday school with new blood. Evangelical artists—painters, woodworkers, needleworkers, sculptors, potters, and musicians—lent their talents to worship and church decor. The women's auxiliary—officially the United Presbyterian Women's Association, unofficially the Ladies' Aid, and by many years the longest-lived club within the church—expanded to two groups, one composed mostly of the elderly, widowed women who had long predominated in it, the other bringing together spirit-filled mothers with school-age children living at home. The church had a noticeably younger age profile in the Underwood years.

The church became a busier place. Proportionately more men were available to serve on the session, the governing board, whose activities seemed to become more consequential, and particularly on the Board of Deacons, the designated body of servers, which had before been overwhelmingly a women's preserve. The Board of Trustees, legally responsible for church property and finances, which had been merged with the session under Hsu's pastorate, continued as a male bastion regardless of pastorate until it was structurally abolished during Underwood's last year and its functions assumed by a subcommittee of the session. In the long run, the spiritual side of church activities assumed greater power and came to predominate over the secular, with no diminution of lay energies.

This augmentation of lay leadership is not wholly attributable to Underwood's pastorate. Indeed, lay leaders prepared the way for him in the first place. Members of Larry Redford's fellowship were the core of Underwood's enthusiastic new recruits, and members who joined during Mark Kimmerly's tenure had reinvigorated the music program before Underwood's arrival. What they prepared, Underwood consolidated, and, despite the long pastorless period that followed his pastorate, the level of mobilization after him was permanently higher than before (see Table 7.1). We shall return to the post-Underwood story later.

Underwood's church thought of itself as a melting pot for new Christians from diverse geographical, occupational, educational, ethnic, and religious backgrounds. A liberal Presbyterian might expect that the legatees of Hsu and Kimmerly would chafe at Underwood's evangelical regime, but his preaching united the congregation. For one thing, the stress on "biblically based teaching" that the search committee saw on his résumé turned out to be an educational strong point, appreciated by liberals and evangelicals alike. For another, a lay veteran of Redford's Antioch Fellowship became a local sponsor of the Roman Catholic–inspired Cursillo movement, bringing scores of church members, including most of the session, in contact with a mystical and aesthetic spiritualism that sat astride the Protestant theological party system.

There was conflict in the congregation in the 1970s, not between evangelicals and liberals but among the evangelicals themselves, between the institutional actor Underwood and the movement leader Redford, the man who had engineered his call. They differed over public, secular education as opposed to private, sectarian education and over the proper handling of backsliders from the conventional ethic of chastity and sobriety they shared. Most of all they fought for the allegiance of the new Christians converted by the Jesus movement. These issues kept the two men locked in struggle for five years before Underwood and his church eventually, in 1978, triumphed over Redford and the remnant of his fellowship.[30] The cost of their struggle was loss of some of the spiritual fervor that had made the church enticing to veterans of the counterculture (see Table 7.1). Then, too, Mendocino was not in fact isolated from cosmopolitan economic currents, and the local cost of living became too steep for many ex-hippies, who had to emigrate. Growing marijuana degenerated from a recreation in Mendocino County to an industry, and Underwood became an outspoken critic of the drug culture. In the early 1980s Mendocino Presbyterian still prospered but felt more conventional and less heterogeneous than it had in the heady days of mid-'70s revival.

Population turnover is one constant in the experience of Mendocino and its Presbyterian church. "Mendocino is a tube," Mark Kimmerly thought in 1969, and in 1988 the church regularly celebrated a "litany for the scattering of the saints." As much as it has gained from immigration, the church is always losing members to emigration, but it leaves its mark on their lives.[31] Peter Hsu has been a prominent church executive, author, and seminary professor since his years in Mendocino, and he tells his students that they can do politics if they take care of their pastoral base. Mark Kimmerly had sixteen years as pastor of a solidly founded, growing church on California's central coast before his recent move to a church in the Pacific Northwest. He cautions that those who join the church out of concern for particular issues are seldom as reliable church members as those who are drawn to the church's theological traditions, and he is increasingly inclined to stress biblical literacy as an educational priority for his congregation. Bruce Douglas has been solo pastor of a Pacific Northwest Presbyterian church for five years, and to his long-standing political liberalism he has added some of Eric Underwood's theological conservatism. He was part of the campaign to cleanse his local community of the tarnish of a neo-Nazi group quartered there, but he now also serves on the steering committee of the local Walk to Emmaus center (a Protestant version of Cursillo). Larry Redford joined a militant charismatic parachurch organization when he left Mendocino Presbyterian, and he worked for that ministry for ten years as a school administrator. He and his wife continue to be full-time workers for Christ, always trying to push the church away from humanism and toward God. Eric Underwood himself grew bitter about the effect of Mendocino's secular culture on his children, and he finally tired of the pressures of pastoring the church. He accepted a new call in 1983 to a large church in a more socially conservative Southern California community but was dismayed to find his new congregation overwhelmingly Republican.

Another Story: Mendocino Presbyterian, 1983–1985

When Eric Underwood left, Mendocino Presbyterian was suddenly without the leader who had been at its helm for ten years, the longest pastoral tenure in the church's history.[32] Tired of Mendocino though he was when he resigned, his preaching still carried power and conviction, and a succession crisis was to be expected. The lines of the ensuing protracted conflict were just those that I had expected to encounter when I began the study in 1975, liberal versus evangelical. But as was the case in 1972, the issues and protagonists were not merely holdovers from the previous shift in church direction. Those who had fought each other in 1972 were not rehearsing the issues in Peter Hsu's call of 1962 but instead bringing conflicting visions of the future to bear. Similarly in 1983, at issue was not the relative value of Underwood's legacy as opposed to Hsu's or Kimmerly's, but the direction in which new leaders wanted to take the church. The reason was the same:

most of the contenders were new to the church and had experiences with it of no greater duration than the recently concluded pastorate.

A pastor-nominating committee was elected in October 1983. Its members began their work by dividing into two subcommittees, one to produce a survey of the state of the church, its membership, and the community (the "church information form" or CIF), and the other to compose a statement of the goals of the congregation (a "mission study"). But it soon became evident that the nominating committee was deeply divided along theological party lines that coincided roughly with the subcommittees—liberals on the CIF group and evangelicals on the mission group—and the weekly meetings became unpleasant. Participants report that when they recessed for lunch, half the members would sit at one table and the other half at another, and members of the one faction would refer to those of the other as "they" and "them." Behind their backs, they reviled each other respectively as "churchmen" and "cultists."

The nominating committee persevered long enough to hear a candidating sermon from one prospect, but they were so deeply divided on the ensuing evaluation of that person that a delegation went from the committee to the presbytery, then to the session, asking that they be disbanded. With due procedures, the committee was discharged in December 1984, after fourteen months of acrimony. With safeguards against emotional spillover from the first committee, a second committee was elected at the annual congregational meeting in February. Four months later, the required information and mission reports already having been produced by the first committee, they found their candidate. Forrest Koch was elected in July and formally installed in October 1985. The new pastor was, like Underwood, an alumnus of Fuller Theological Seminary, and his call can therefore be interpreted as a victory for the congregation's moderate conservatives. But the victory was a costly one, and Koch enjoyed no honeymoon with his new congregation. The hiatus lasted more than two years, and memories of the controversy were fresh and bitter when I visited Mendocino in 1988.

The failure of the first nominating committee had many sources. The presbytery, members of which were aware that the congregation's organizational vitality had been accompanied by a relative neglect of the priorities of higher judicatories, appointed as liaison to the committee the pastor of a church in a nearby town, from which town the Mendocino church had drawn significant membership during Underwood's years. The committee itself included a number of individuals with strong personalities and determined agendas. Two interim pastors in 1983–1985, neither of them eligible for the permanent position, represented the liberal and evangelical poles of theological partisanship in the Presbyterian Church and thus heightened ideological awareness. The first, who served during 1984, was an able, outspoken liberal, a "scholar" to his admirers, a "Unitarian" to his theological critics, and had recently retired from a long, highly successful pastorate. The second, in the pulpit early in 1985, was an equally outspoken evangelical, formerly with the

Billy Graham Evangelistic Association, and was characterized alternately as "bombastic" and "inspiring." The first man fueled Mendocino evangelicals' suspicions of the denomination's leanings. The second man, though he arrived after the first nominating committee had disbanded, served liberals as a highly salient symbol of the kind of minister they had hoped the pastor search would screen out; his presence thus retrospectively increased consciousness of what had been at stake in the 1984 struggle.

But the deeper cause of the ideological polarization on the first nominating committee was Underwood's very success in drawing to the church a cross-section of the diverse immigrants that the town of Mendocino attracted from the wider world. Among these immigrants were newly retired but affluent and still vigorous lay alumni of other California Presbyterian churches, and they brought to Mendocino profound ecclesiastical loyalties. The church in California is theologically divided (since well before the PCUSA-UPCNA merger of 1958), and congregations have long identified themselves with one or the other side of the divide. St. John's in Berkeley and First Church in Palo Alto were carriers of the liberal tradition. Berkeley First and Walnut Creek were equally identified with the evangelical.

Articulate and informed laypersons from churches like these brought their contrasting orientations to Underwood's Mendocino Presbyterian during its period of rapid growth in the 1970s. With Underwood's departure, their already conflicting expectations were placed on the agenda. "This time, we want a Presbyterian," one of the liberals is reported to have said at the time the first nominating committee was constituted, whereas the conservatives responsible for the mission study wanted the congregation to be described officially as "an evangelical church." The two sides split on their opinions of the tutelage of the presbytery, liberals upholding it as a source of procedural legitimacy, evangelicals seeing it as meddlesome.

It had been part of Underwood's genius as a social engineer to minimize theological differences in his congregation by accentuating cultural ones. Rather than address evangelicals and liberals, he celebrated the coexistence of the hip and the straight.[33] He wanted Christianity to be a unifying force in his congregation. But the first interim pastor recognized Mendocino's theological diversity, and he evidently felt it his obligation to help the members confront their differences. A liberal himself, he held frank talks with those to his right until they lost trust in him, and he helped fellow liberals understand the ways they differed from their evangelical brethren. Although he preached, in effect, that people in his heterogeneous congregation must learn to be tolerant of each other, his leadership thus aroused mutual suspicion in the minds of the attentive and constitutionally combative liberal and evangelical laypersons who took leading roles in the first nominating committee. Liberals felt they had a model in the first interim pastor, whereas the embattled evangelicals looked to Underwood, whom they called for advice. Eventually both the first interim pastor and Underwood were admonished by officers of the presbytery to keep out of the deliberations.

The meeting to constitute the second nominating committee was preceded by intense mobilization, and when it was called to order people could see that the evangelicals would win. Disproportionately younger than the liberals with fewer resources and more young children, these evangelicals had not been dominant on the session in Underwood's last years, nor on the first nominating committee, but they were still church members. "Now we'll get our church back," one of them is reported to have said as the meeting convened, and the prophecy was borne out by the result four months later. Members of the first nominating committee and their kin, including some of the most determined partisans in the church, were declared ineligible to serve on the second nominating committee. Those who were elected (including two Antioch Fellowship veterans) were marginally younger, of marginally longer tenure in the Mendocino church, and considerably more likely to be both theologically conservative and politically liberal than those on the first committee, who, in turn, were polarized between those liberal and those conservative on *both* dimensions.[34]

The second committee's deliberations were relatively simple, but their choice, a youthful Fuller-educated political liberal who would rather call himself a "trinitarian" than wave the red flag "evangelical," could not satisfy the embittered partisans of the first nominating committee. To judge from membership and attendance records (see Table 7.1), as well as from my interviews, discontent persists in the church, and Pastor Koch has some tough sledding. As new recruits replace those who leave (whether or not for reasons pertinent to their experience in the church), Koch hopes to enjoy a constituency harboring no resentment from earlier struggles.

Yet there is still deep commitment from the lay people and a solid financial base; the church recently hired another full-time youth worker to continue Bruce Douglas's work. Partisan differences within the congregation and between Underwood and Douglas aside, the youth program of the church in the last decade seems to have borne fruit. The activism and idealism of the generation who grew up in Mendocino's Christian community as the offspring of parents influenced by the charismatic movement is impressive: the eighteen-year-old leader of the local campaign to prohibit offshore oil drilling in Mendocino County, the young man joining the missionary effort to translate the Bible into as yet unwritten languages, the feminist poet in her junior year at college, the two musicians in a social protest rock band, and the young men and women helping out both sides in Central America's civil wars. What is so impressive about these individuals is their evident sense of values, of who they are and what they stand for, their selflessness and idealism, and their ease in a variety of circumstances. Collectively, they are a tribute to the church in Mendocino.

Lessons from Mendocino

The epilogue to *New Wine* begins with the words of William Cowper, "God moves in a mysterious way," for two reasons. One reason is that these words have been set to simple and stirring music from the Scottish Psalter to create a great hymn that should be sung in more Presbyterian churches. The other is to express the humbling recognition that must impress any student of church history: human labor seldom produces exactly what is designed.

1. *Churches, being social organizations, so refract our actions that what we intend is seldom what we accomplish.* We cannot foresee or control all the factors that intervene in the course of our projects. The disproportion between our intentions and our effects is the greater the more ambitious our schemes; thus it is particularly those in the nascent state whose ideals are frustrated by social realities. Individuals and families arrive in the community, and others leave, for reasons that are far beyond the congregation's power to influence. Students in seminary prepare to become pastors without knowing what sort of churches will call them; nonwhites and women can wind up in odd places, as Peter Hsu found. Those to whom the church reaches out may accept ecclesiastical aid but not the theology behind it, as Mark Kimmerly learned from the hippies. Radical aspirations may be tempered by the natural conservatism of the congregation, as both Peter Hsu and Larry Redford found to their chagrin. Yet for all the sources of uncertainty and confutation, one must stand in awe at the daily perseverance of those who faithfully discharge their pastoral responsibilities, for the institutional state requires as much effort, if not vision, as the nascent. Mendocino has been favored for a quarter century by those hard workers who have been called to its pulpit.

   Pastors do not labor alone, a point that *New Wine* addresses at great length. The way for Eric Underwood was paved (with ironic results indeed) by Larry Redford, a lay leader. The membership growth over which Underwood presided depended on the work of lay evangelicals.[35] The church survived the hiatus of 1983–1985 because elders and deacons continued to be elected and to serve. Peter Hsu enjoyed the fellowship of the retired Frederick Althorpe, a member of his congregation, as well as the fellowship of the presbytery. After leaving Mendocino, Mark Kimmerly saw his new congregation grow to a membership of 350, for whom he could be the sole ordained minister because he fostered lay leadership.

2. *Demographic change offers opportunity but does not define destiny.* Unlike most small-town Presbyterian churches in northern California, the Mendocino church during Underwood's pastorate benefited from the influx of population to rural America in the 1970s. To do so, the church had to be open and attractive to newcomers. The requisite flexibility for such change was a legacy of Hsu's and Kimmerly's years, when the dominantly indigenous population of Mendocino and its church was largely replaced by immigrants of differing culture. Those *born* in the small town were succeeded by those *drawn* to the small town. A powerful outreach to such persons was the work of evangelicals like Larry Redford, but Hsu and Kimmerly intuited from the outset that those to whom the church's outreach must be directed are not defined as "others" solely

on the basis of racial or ethnic identification. The church has a mission to cultural others as well. The continuing turnover in the church's membership rolls—a reflection of Mendocino's appealing culture, unstable economy, and consequent geographic immigration and emigration—made room for new leadership and new programs, even as it played havoc with long-range planning.

3. *Lay involvement is not particularly motivated by liberal or conservative political agendas.* Putting the affairs of the church in the hands of local laity is a risk inherent to the Protestant tradition. Local laity may diverge from what seminary-trained ministers see as the calling of the church or the will of God. They almost inevitably differ among themselves, and their interpretations may be in thrall to culture, as the people of Mendocino idealized their local community. But the divisions within the Mendocino church were religious ones, not political or based on social privilege. Those who turned toward evangelicalism in the 1970s did not feel that their class privileges had been jeopardized by Peter Hsu; they were not motivated by a conservative political agenda (the few true reactionaries having left the church in the 1960s) but by a religious one. In the 1980s, collective mobilization on issues of the Right (pro-life) and the Left (sanctuary for Central American refugees) is shunned by the session with an even hand because the issues are controversial. The church today is divided not politically but ecclesiastically. Church observers to whom political issues are uppermost should not assume that rank-and-file church members define the world accordingly. The political and theological divides do not coincide.

4. *The polarization now emerging in the church threatens to divide evangelicals from denominational loyalists.* In recent interviews with past and present members of Mendocino Presbyterian, I was struck by a recurring theme of self-conscious, intradenominational contentiousness. Laypersons and ministers both spoke of the need to return to traditional Presbyterian emphases, but with significantly different meanings. This traditionalist refrain was used to encompass such different criteria as fiscal accountability, the authority of scripture, and speaking in tongues. In particular, liberals defended the importance of listening to the presbytery while evangelicals questioned the presbytery's authority. This pattern may be specific to Presbyterians in California and especially to the presbytery of the Redwoods, but a related pattern has been found among members of the Reformed Church in America. Donald Luidens and Roger Nemeth found in that denomination that Martin Marty's "public Protestantism" was weak and "private Protestantism" was robust; they also discovered another party, institutional loyalists, whose theology was privatistic but whose loyalties were toward the denomination more than toward any theological party.[36] A popular, theologically liberal party does not, for all practical purposes, exist.

5. *Liberals should not feel threatened by popular theological conservatism; indeed, they depend on it.* The Mendocino experience in the 1970s shows that a congregation with an evangelical identity and parochial concentration can nonetheless be a faithful partner in a predominantly liberal and cosmopolitan denomination.

Underwood himself spent little time with the presbytery, but he encouraged certain elders and his pastoral associate to do so. Furthermore, he coaxed his trustees to allocate generous sums to the denomination, about 11 percent of a vastly increased church budget, a proportion higher than any of the previous pastorates since 1955.[37] The personalism of his theology generated not individualism but vital collective activity.[38] A similar division between parochial piety and denominational social vision is characteristic of the Roman Catholic church in the United States. It seems that the career of one of the most outstanding figures of "public Protestantism"—Reinhold Niebuhr—presupposed that his mother kept the parochial fires burning.[39] For such a division of labor to work, evangelicals need to learn from Eric Underwood not to see apostasy in social action, while liberals need to learn from Bruce Douglas not to see cowardice in conservative theology.

Despite the polemics that followed Underwood's leaving Mendocino, those who took their Mendocino experiences with them elsewhere—the scattered saints—have come to appreciate the broader unity of the church. Notwithstanding their theological identities, they have come to recognize that the theological party system is a barrier to communion. Peter Hsu calls himself an evangelical but thinks that his books on youth ministry would not be used in an evangelical church because of his association with the distrusted national bureaucracy. Mark Kimmerly remains close to the ecclesiastical center, shying away from both "issue-oriented" and "spirit-filled" as ecclesiastical slogans. Eric Underwood says that the difference between the 1960s and 1970s, rather than that between liberals and evangelicals, distinguishes his pastorate from those of his predecessors. He adds that his, Hsu's, and Kimmerly's responses to a multiple-choice theological quiz would be indistinguishable to a seminary grader. Bruce Douglas, Peace Corps veteran, now heads his presbytery's evangelism committee. To judge from the experience of Mendocino Presbyterian under Forrest Koch's pastorate, the leadership of younger, family-oriented, theologically conservative, but social-justice-concerned people may be an augur of things to come in the Presbyterian Church. Even the contentious issues of women's rights and feminism may move toward resolution—as modeled by Peter Hsu's pastorate—by the appointment of newly ordained women ministers to small, traditional churches. These are some possibilities from which one can take fresh courage.

From *The Mainstream Protestant "Decline": The Presbyterian Pattern.* Used by permission of Westminster John Knox Press.

NOTES

1. R. Stephen Warner, *New Wine in Old Wineskins: Evangelicals and Liberals in a Small-Town Church* (Berkeley: University of California Press, 1988).
2. The present chapter was drafted while the author was a Visiting Member of the School of Social Science, Institute for Advanced Study, Princeton, New Jersey, and completed at the University of Illinois at Chicago. I am grateful to these institutions for their support. For their comments on an earlier draft, I thank Anne Heider, John Mulder, Louis Weeks,

and several present and former affiliates of Mendocino Presbyterian Church. These acknowledgments may be added to those recorded in *New Wine*, 341–344.

3. See Rosalie Wax, *Doing Fieldwork: Warnings and Advice* (Chicago: University of Chicago Press, 1971).

4. See Marcia Millman, *The Unkindest Cut: Life in the Backrooms of Medicine* (New York: Morrow, 1976).

5. See Janet Lever, *Soccer Madness* (Chicago: University of Chicago Press, 1983).

6. See Kai T. Erikson, *Everything in Its Path* (New York: Simon and Schuster, 1976).

7. See Bennett M. Berger, *The Survival of a Counterculture: Ideological Work and Everyday Life among Rural Communards* (Berkeley: University of California Press, 1981).

8. See Jonathan Rieder, *Canarsie: The Jews and Italians of Brooklyn Against Liberalism* (Cambridge: Harvard University Press, 1985). Although the books by Millman, Lever, Erikson, Berger, and Rieder were published after my research began, the authors had previously given me valuable suggestions based on these ongoing research projects.

9. Standard treatises include John Lofland and Lyn Lofland, *Analyzing Social Settings: Qualitative Observation and Analysis*, 2d ed. (Belmont, Calif.: Wadsworth, 1984) on participant observation and interviewing; and Eugene J. Webb et al., *Non-Reactive Measures in the Social Sciences*, 2d ed. (Boston: Houghton Mifflin, 1981), on preexisting data.

10. For the most famous example, see Theodore Caplow, Howard M. Bahr, and Bruce A. Chadwick, *All Faithful People: Change and Continuity in Middletown's Religion* (Minneapolis: University of Minnesota Press, 1983).

11. The Library of Congress cataloged *New Wine* under "Mendocino Presbyterian Church" as BX9211.M4145W37. Nancy Ammerman's *Bible Believers: Fundamentalists in the Modern World* (New Brunswick, N.J.: Rutgers University Press, 1987) is in many ways similar to *New Wine* and was reviewed along with it in a sociological symposium on congregational studies (*Sociological Analysis* 50 [1989]: 419–427). But Ammerman abides by convention and gives her site a pseudonym ("Southside Gospel Church"). The Library of Congress cataloged *Bible Believers* under "fundamentalist churches" as BX7800.F864A45.

12. For further details of methods employed in the original study, see *New Wine*, chap. 3, and R. S. Warner, "Oenology: The Making of *New Wine*," in *A Case for the Case Study*, ed. Joe Feagin, Anthony Orum, and Gideon Sjoberg (Chapel Hill: University of North Carolina Press, 1991).

13. This section of the essay is based on *New Wine*, chap. 2. Table 1 is reprinted from *New Wine*, 175. The data are detailed in *New Wine*, 24–25.

14. Will Herberg, *Protestant, Catholic, Jew: An Essay in American Religious Sociology*, 2d ed. (Garden City, N.Y.: Doubleday, 1960); Jeffrey K. Hadden, *The Gathering Storm in the Churches* (Garden City, N.Y.: Doubleday, 1969); Dean M. Kelley, *Why Conservative Churches Are Growing*, 2d ed. (San Francisco: Harper and Row, 1977).

15. See R. Stephen Warner, "Theoretical Barriers to the Understanding of Evangelical Christianity," *Sociological Analysis* 40 (Spring, 1979): 1–9; and R. Stephen Warner, "Monistic and Dualistic Religion," in *Religious Movements: Genesis, Exodus, and Numbers*, ed. Rodney Stark (New York: Paragon House, 1985), 199–220.

16. Martin E. Marty, *Righteous Empire: The Protestant Experience in America* (New York: Dial Press, 1970), chap. 17.

17. These terms are borrowed from Francesco Alberoni, *Movement and Institution*, trans. Patricia C. Arden Delmoro (New York: Columbia University Press, 1984).

18. *New Wine*, 60–64; for a similar typology, see David A. Roozen, William M. McKinney, and Jackson W. Carroll, *Varieties of Religious Presence: Mission in Public Life* (New York: Pilgrim Press, 1984).

19. This section of the essay is based on *New Wine*, chaps. 4–12.

20. *New Wine*, 93.

21. This is an opportunity to correct a mistake in *New Wine* (93), where Hsu's age at the time he came to Mendocino is recorded as thirty-four, which was, in fact, the age of his successor, Mark Kimmerly, at the time of the latter's call.

22. *New Wine*, 100–101.

23. *New Wine*, 102–106, 156–158.

24. The organization Redford founded, known eventually as the Antioch Fellowship, is analyzed in detail in *New Wine*, chaps. 5, 10, and 11, as a case of the *ecclesiola in ecclesia*.

25. See George M. Marsden, *Reforming Fundamentalism: Fuller Seminary and the New Evangelicalism* (Grand Rapids, Mich.: Eerdmans, 1987).

26. Martin Luther, "An Appeal to the Ruling Class of German Nationality as to the Amelioration of the State of Christendom," in *Martin Luther: Selections from His Writings*, ed. John Dillenberger (Garden City, N.Y.: Doubleday Anchor, 1961), 403–485.

27. Marsden, *Reforming Fundamentalism*, chaps. 11–12. Underwood was well aware of the inerrancy issue at Fuller, and it was he who first introduced me to Harold Lindsell, *The Battle for the Bible* (Grand Rapids, Mich.: Zondervan, 1976).

28. *New Wine*, 197–198.

29. *New Wine*, 201.

30. This conflict is analyzed in detail in *New Wine*, chaps. 10–11.

31. This paragraph is based on *New Wine*, 302–304, and on interviews and observations conducted in 1988; see note 32.

32. This section of the essay is based on new research conducted in the summers of 1988 and 1989, supported by the Presbyterian Church in the Twentieth Century project, which is funded by a grant from the Lilly Endowment to Louisville Presbyterian Theological Seminary. I am indebted to these institutions for support, but neither they nor the officers and members of Mendocino Presbyterian Church, present or past, bear any responsibility for the findings reported here; that responsibility is the author's. In the 1988–1989 project, approximately twenty individual participants were interviewed, many of them in new addresses away from Mendocino; documents from the church office pertaining to the years 1982–1989 were examined; and several services of worship were observed. The present chapter represents the sole publication based on that research; original notes remain in the author's files.

33. See *New Wine*, 7, 86–87, 134–135, 207, 219–220.

34. Using the statistic called Yule's Q, the correlation between political and theological conservatism on the first pastor-nominating committee was +1.0; on the second, −.85. Mendocino Presbyterian Church was *not* polarized over politics in the 1980s, and the pro-Sanctuary, anti-Contra study group included strong evangelicals as well as liberals.

35. See *New Wine*, 209–211, 260–263.

36. Donald A. Luidens and Roger J. Nemeth, " 'Public' and 'Private' Protestantism Reconsidered: Introducing the 'Loyalists,' " *Journal for the Scientific Study of Religion* 26 (December 1987): 450–464.

37. See *New Wine*, 277–281.

38. I prefer not to use the terminology of Martin Marty's *Righteous Empire*. Theological "privatism" is conducive to "public" life *within the congregation*; see *New Wine*, 51, 289–296.

39. Richard Wightman Fox, *Reinhold Niebuhr: A Biography* (New York: Pantheon, 1985), 69.

8

The Place of the Congregation in the Contemporary American Religious Configuration (1994)

After a period of neglect by scholars and denominational leaders, the *congregation*—a term this chapter uses to speak of local religious assemblies in general—has returned to the spotlight. Despite neglect, the congregation remains the bedrock of the American religious system. It is in congregations that religious commitment is nurtured and through them that most voluntary religious activity is channeled. Indeed, with due respect for pluralism and caution about overgeneralization, I would maintain that the significance of congregations is *increasing*. In the United States today, we are seeing convergence across religious traditions toward de facto congregationalism, more or less on the model of the reformed Protestant tradition of the congregation as a voluntary gathered community.

This convergence toward de facto congregationalism is happening despite, indeed partly because of, the increasing divergence of religious cultures in the United States; it constitutes both assimilation to a deep-seated interdenominational American religious model and selective adaptation of normative elements contained in the various religious traditions that make up our pluralist mosaic. Purists within few, if any, of these traditions can wholly embrace the congregational model; yet neither is it totally foreign to any of these traditions. The model is at variance with the official ideals of some of the most Americanized of U.S. religious traditions—for example, the Presbyterian Church (U.S.A.) and the U.S. Roman Catholic church—but aspects of it suit the needs of some more recent, and more exotic, arrivals to this country—for example, Pakistani Muslims and Thai Buddhists. Although culturally specific, the growing convergence toward the American congregational model is not therefore a simple case of cultural imperialism or morphological fundamentalism, and those religious educators with an ecumenical calling need not shun it in the name of multiculturalism.

No mere book chapter could fully substantiate such a far-ranging thesis, and the evidence submitted in this chapter varies in quality and quantity, in depth and breadth. The chapter's best established but least extensive evidentiary base is *New*

Wine in Old Wineskins, my ethnographic social history of Mendocino Presbyterian Church in the 1960s and 1970s, a California church whose pastors traversed the same trajectory from social justice to evangelicalism that much of American Protestantism followed in those turbulent years.[1] More extensive but less intensive are observations based on field trips to metropolitan Chicago places of worship that I have taken with my students since 1978 as exercises in the sociology of religion.[2] Building on these field trips, I have carried out more intensive research on Christian congregations within two radically different communities, Korean Americans and gays and lesbians, materials from which appear later in the chapter.[3] Scholarly interest in congregational studies has been rapidly growing, and I therefore also draw upon recent literature on contemporary developments in the form of monographs, articles, conference papers, dissertations, theses, and the first volume of *American Congregations.*[4] Some developments, however, most notably the burgeoning of Latino Protestant congregations, are still seriously underresearched, and I have had to make use of stories in local newspapers and popular journals to document them. Throughout, my emphasis is on contemporary congregations.

Ecclesiastical Arithmetic

By various estimates, there are over three hundred thousand local religious assemblies in the United States today, about one for every four hundred Americans claimed as members of religious bodies. Research done in 1988 for Independent Sector, a Washington, D.C., clearinghouse for nonprofit organizations, counted 294,271 congregations (churches, synagogues, temples, and mosques) in the United States outside of Hawaii and Alaska.[5] The National Council of Churches (NCC) 1991 *Yearbook* reports on the basis of "current" (1989 and 1990) and "noncurrent" statistics provided by denominations that there are 350,337 congregations of Christians, Jews, Buddhists, and "miscellaneous" groups (mostly Unitarians) in the United States.[6] Based as it is on Yellow Pages listings for the contiguous forty-eight states, the Independent Sector figure is clearly too low. The NCC count, however, includes some data over thirty years old and does not correct for some congregations' multiple denominational affiliations; it is probably too high.

The majority of these congregations go by familiar Judeo-Christian labels of European origin. As frequenters of country byways will suspect, the United Methodist Church and the Southern Baptist Convention are the largest groupings, each claiming over thirty-six thousand congregations. The Evangelical Lutheran Church in America, the Presbyterian Church (U.S.A.), and the Assemblies of God each claim over eleven thousand. Seven historically African American Christian denominations (the African Methodist Episcopal Church, the A. M. E. Zion Church, the Christian Methodist Episcopal Church, the Church of God in Christ, the National Baptist Convention of America, the National Baptist Convention,

U.S.A., Inc., and the Progressive National Baptist Convention, Inc.) together claim over sixty-six thousand congregations. In 1991, after some deep cutbacks, there remained 19,971 Roman Catholic parishes in the United States, and, in 1990, 3,416 Jewish synagogues were reported. All of these figures are reported in the *Yearbook* of the National Council of Churches, whose communications office takes pains regularly to assemble denominational statistics.[7]

The profile of American congregations has changed in two remarkable ways since the watershed year of 1965 identified by Martin Marty in his chapter in *American Congregations*, the year Watts exploded and the Vietnam War escalated, when the reforms of the Voting Rights Act of 1965 and Immigration Act of 1965 were made law, the year when Vatican II concluded and decades of sustained growth in mainline Protestant church membership reversed. The first change in American congregations is apparent to the byways traveler (and is duly recorded in the *Yearbook*): the mushrooming of conservative Protestant congregations and the disappearance of mainline ones. According to recent figures reported by the NCC, nearly thirteen thousand fewer congregations of six mainline Protestant denominations (American Baptist, Episcopal, Lutheran, Methodist, Presbyterian, and United Church of Church) existed in 1987 than had existed in 1965. Their numbers were replaced by more than thirteen thousand additional congregations of six conservative denominations (Assemblies of God, Church of God [Cleveland, Tennessee], Jehovah's Witnesses, Latter-day Saints, Nazarenes, and Seventh-Day Adventist).[8] This shift is obvious in small towns all across America, whose outskirts are strewn with brand-new wood-frame houses of worship and adjoining parking lots for the local Assemblies, Kingdom Halls, and Mormon wards, and whose stately brick downtown Presbyterian and Congregational churches have been merged or recycled as community museums and professional office buildings.[9]

The *Yearbook* data tell only part of the story of the shift in congregational presence. For example, they do not report the 350 congregations of Calvary Chapel, or the 250 of the Vineyard, or the 210 of the Fellowship of Inner-City Word of Faith Ministries, three new Southern California–based protodenominations of charismatic Christian congregations, whose affiliates are now scattered all over the country.[10] The Independent Sector's study of congregations provides further insight into the conservative congregational shift. Of congregations existing at the time of the study (1987), the more recent the founding, the more likely they were to characterize themselves as conservative. Forty-seven percent of the congregations founded before 1900 called themselves "liberal" or "moderate," whereas 68 percent of those founded since 1970 labeled themselves "conservative" or "very conservative."[11]

The second recent change in the profile of congregations—especially noticeable in metropolitan America—is the flowering of immigrant religious centers. The abolition of country-of-origin quotas in the immigration law of 1965 has made it possible for very different, and often non-European, religious communities to get a toehold in the United States, and many of these groups are sufficiently new and scattered to have escaped the purview of the NCC. The *Yearbook*, for example, includes data from only one Buddhist body, the century-old Japanese-origin Buddhist Churches of America (who report 19,441 members in sixty-seven congregations for 1989). From other sources, we hear of sixty-seven Korean Buddhist centers less than twenty years old, sixty Japanese Buddhist temples, over one hundred Southeast Asian Theravada "wats," and in all over five hundred Buddhist meditation centers. At last report, there were forty-some ecumenical Hindu temples and thirty-seven centers of the mostly Gujarati Swaminarayan sect. Estimates of Muslim centers, some of them designated mosques, range from three hundred to two thousand.[12]

In addition, about two thousand of the Protestant congregations listed by the NCC *Yearbook* are Korean ethnic congregations among the Southern Baptist, United Methodist, Presbyterian (U.S.A.), Assemblies of God, and other denominations. A new Korean Presbyterian denomination, the Korean Presbyterian Church in America, has more than two hundred local congregations nationwide. Another fast-growing category of Protestant congregations is that of the various Hispanic peoples in the United States, now about 9 percent of the U.S. population (or 22.5 million), according to the surely undercounted 1990 census. The Gallup organization estimates that 20 percent of U.S. Hispanics claim a Protestant affiliation, and Hispanic Protestant congregations abound in cities such as New York, Chicago, and Los Angeles. Yet I know of no national enumeration or even an estimate of their numbers in the United States or their denominational affiliations.[13] The Church of God in Christ, the black Pentecostal denomination, claims 15,300 congregations, more than the Evangelical Lutheran, Episcopal, or Presbyterian (U.S.A.) churches. In short, the mix of American congregations, definitely including those of Protestants, is becoming at once more conservative and more multicultural.

When we speak of increasing pluralism in American religion, we usually have in mind the proliferation of denominations and religious movements. Nearly sixteen hundred different denominations are reported to exist in the United States and Canada, from tiny schismatic groups to the huge Roman Catholic church, and eight hundred nationally organized religious special-purpose groups, from the Fellowship of Christian Athletes to the Ecumenical and Evangelical Women's Caucus.[14] But when we speak of the grassroots religious participation that visitors to the United States have always remarked on, we speak of people all over the country regularly gathering to worship together, at appointed times and places, in congregations by the hundreds of thousands.

Such ecclesiastical arithmetic tells us that the fortunes of congregations must be more uneven than those of the denominations with which most of them are affiliated. We know that denominations come and go—arising by schism and disappearing by merger[15]—and wax and wane,[16] but of necessity these vicissitudes will be visited upon the population of congregations with much greater frequency.

The smooth growth-and-decline curves we can draw from the membership statistics of Protestant denominations obscure the ragged plots of the ups and downs of their constituent congregations.[17] When a major denomination reports the loss of a substantial proportion of its members, thousands of its constituent congregations may have ceased entirely to exist. Denominational decline means contraction at the national level—lower budgets and loss of jobs—but decimation—widespread congregational demise—at the local.

Moreover, denominational and congregational fortunes need not mesh. One conclusion of the Notre Dame Study of Catholic Parish Life conducted in the 1980s was that "relative to the life of the rest of the church, parishes seem to have a life of their own."[18] When a denomination is growing, planting new congregations and recruiting new members, some individual congregations will nevertheless be dying. When a denomination is declining, some congregations will be burgeoning. Sociologist Samuel Kincheloe's classic analysis of "the behavior sequence of a dying church" concerns an inner-city Chicago parish suffering from neighborhood change in the 1920s, when its parent denomination was thriving. My own history of Mendocino Presbyterian Church chronicles the similarly countercyclical phenomenon of rapid congregational growth at a time of sustained denominational decline.[19] As a matter of sheer statistics, then, the congregation is not the denomination writ small.

The Congregation in the Context of Other Religious Bodies

While both may be called "the Presbyterian church" and while they are organizationally linked, a world of difference lies between Mendocino Presbyterian Church and the Presbyterian Church (U.S.A.). That the first is a local assembly of persons and the second a national network of assemblies is the beginning of the matter, but that they go by the same name is equally important. Congregation and denomination are and do different things, but they are historically intertwined. The denomination owns rights to the logo that points the traveler to the local congregation a couple of blocks to the right or left off the state highway through town. Some other local congregation was the school that bred into the traveler the desire to seek out like-minded worshipers while on the road. Ideally and minimally, the denomination is an organization for the furtherance of religious commitments, whereas the congregation is a community for the nurturance of those commitments.

To the extent that the *denomination* exists—a reality that various primitivist Protestant groups have long fought and that some new immigrant groups are just starting to cope with—it serves several functions. It plants congregations (and accepts other self-started groups into its fold, which is how organized Presbyterianism first came to Mendocino in 1859). It trains, certifies, disciplines, nurtures, and pensions members of the clergy (more broadly, religious professionals). It provides leadership for congregations between pastors and financial support during lean times. It defines doctrine and carries out nonlocal mission.

The *congregation* is where members are recruited, baptized, catechized, confirmed, absolved, administered the sacraments, registered, received by letter, counted, asked weekly for their substance, mobilized for service, disciplined, and buried. As the local branch of the people of God, it is the organizer of worship, religious instruction, community service, stewardship, and fellowship.

In comparison to religiously oriented or quasi-religious small groups like Alcoholics Anonymous chapters and home prayer meetings (which likely involve at least a fifth of the adult American population),[20] congregations and the denominations to which the majority of them belong have in common that they are relatively stable and institutionalized. Congregations and denominations alike may be chartered, commissioned, consecrated, dedicated, franchised, or incorporated, and they typically have addresses, offices, and phone numbers. But unlike religious special-purpose groups like Americans United for Separation of Church and State or Moral Majority, which also have offices and telephones, congregations and denominations typically provide for extensive participation. They are not segmental associations whose "memberships" are little more than lists of names in a computer. In contrast to religiously inspired social movements like the Women's Christian Temperance Union, the American Anti-Slavery Society, Operation Rescue, and Sanctuary, which also involve members deeply, congregations and denominations do not define themselves in terms of a single issue of public policy; they have multiple purposes.

Congregations and denominations differ in the chances that their members will encounter one another face to face. A substantial fraction, sometimes a majority, of the members of a congregation will see each other every week, whereas a tiny proportion of the members of a denomination (as many as three-tenths of a percent for the highly mobilized Southern Baptists) are in each other's presence at conventions held once a year or less, with members of regional judicatories falling somewhere between. Yet this does not mean that denominations therefore lack the personal element that gives congregations their rich, many-layered, and emotion-laden texture. To the contrary: the work of denominations is carried out by people who see each other often and are often intimately known to one another. Denominational organs—agencies, lobbies, seminaries, publishing houses—bring people together in ways that, if anything, accentuate the effect of congregating. Task-force meetings, seminars and workshops, cafeteria conversations, summer institutes, and travel to conferences are some of the ways that bonds of solidarity and common outlooks are inculcated at the denominational level.[21]

Sociologically, the most important contrast between denominations and congregations (as well as between, on the one hand, religious special-purpose groups and seminaries and, on the other, religious small groups and social movements) is that the former are staffed by religious professionals—those who earn their living in the field of religion—and the latter are constituted by religious amateurs who spend their time, and some of their money, in the name of religion. The Bakkers and the Rajneeshes aside, religion is not a sure way to get rich, and religious professionals must be in it for more than the money, as a true vocation. Parishioners, for their part, have typically mixed motives, some of which can be quite venal. The professional-amateur distinction is not a contrast in religious purity, but it is fundamental.

Congregations are by definition local assemblies, whereas denominations are regional, national, or international organizations, and each of the two levels is suited for different activities. Sociologist Phillip Hammond has proposed a general rule for appropriate allocation of ministry activities to ecclesiastical levels. He classified activities from an "expressive" pole to an "instrumental" one and ecclesiastical levels from that of the congregation to that of the national board. Hammond placed worship at the expressive end and legislative lobbying at the instrumental, with home visitation, help with welfare agencies, and building retirement homes arrayed between. Hammond's rule was this: "The more instrumental the orientations required by the activity, the more effectively can it be carried out by a regional, national, or specialized ministry; but the more expressive the orientations required, the more effectively can the activity be carried out by a local parish ministry."[22] We can expect, therefore, that congregations are typically groups of amateurs spending disproportionate time on activities that are hard to define, whereas denominations will have professionals devoted to articulate goals.

Accordingly, when we look at the congregation from the point of view of the denomination, and vice versa, we can appreciate the misgivings each body seems to have about the other, even as they depend on each other. The congregation, from whose tithes and offerings the denomination derives the bulk of its income, too often appears from above to be a social club whose members neglect the calling of their faith in favor of the pleasure of one another's company. The denomination, from which the congregation typically derives its leadership, its hymnody, and its confessional identity, too often appears from below to be a bureaucracy serving officials' career interests and heterodox agendas. At worst, congregations and denominations regard each other as means and themselves as ends.

Scholars of religion have tended to share these one-way points of view, as participants in the Congregational History Project have documented. The chapters by Langdon Gilkey and Martin Marty in *American Congregations* shed light on the historiography of recent American Protestant thought and its appreciation of the congregation. It seems that the dominant voices in American Protestantism at midcentury, influenced by both prewar social gospel and postwar existentialism, took for granted the local religious nurture on which their praxis depended and relegated congregational life to the discredited private sphere. Mainline Protestant congregations were cajoled by theologians and judicatories to look outward for missions to carry out, and they were held up for praise when and if they tried to make a difference in the lives of precisely those who were not their own members.[23] Concentration on the life of the congregation itself was attributed to "the sin of 'morphological fundamentalism.' "[24]

Even Donald Metz, in one of the few sociological books of the 1960s concerned with congregational life, shared this systematic externalist bias. Writing about six newly founded congregations in suburban California communities, he cautioned: "Aside from such *privatized* family troubles as juvenile lawlessness or marital difficulties, there is not much that could be termed social problems in the community. The congregation in this situation may have to look hard for an *outlet* for such intentions of service as it might have. . . . [T]here is a distinct *danger* that the new congregation will be satisfied to *internalize* its activities" (emphasis added).[25] In such an intellectual climate, it is no surprise that many clergy of serious purpose felt they could be prophetic in direct proportion to their distance from the local congregation.[26]

Recently, the pendulum has swung away from the denomination's point of view. The statistical decline of the mainline denominations that set in after 1965 caused introspection at headquarters. Feminists questioned the good faith of formal organizations in general and clerical hierarchies in particular. Journalists turned their attention to such cross-denominational newsmakers as the electronic church. Laity got involved with such paradenominational movements as evangelicalism, charismatic renewal, Cursillo de Cristiandad (a spiritual renewal movement of lay Roman Catholics) and Walk to Emmaus (its Protestant analog), Marriage Encounter, liturgical renewal, *havurot* (home-based Jewish prayer and study groups), and Sanctuary.

For the time being, many observers agree that the congregation is worthy of attention and respect. In the Mendocino Presbyterian Church, the social-activist pastor Peter Hsu had told his elders in 1963 that, "basically, our church exists for mission," leaving no doubt that mission meant international peace and racial justice. A decade later, Larry Redford, the evangelical chairperson of the church's pastor-search committee, insisted that "the mission of the church is the church," meaning the Mendocino congregation; and the vitality and faithfulness of the congregation under the pastor the committee chose made his redefinition of mission itself seem prophetic.[27]

The Congregation as a Voluntary Community

The typical American congregation is a voluntary religious community. To say that the congregation is a *religious* community is to say that it is ordinarily a face-to-face assembly of persons who together engage in many activities, all of them somehow understood as having "religious" meaning, few of them lacking emotional significance. To say that the congregation is a *voluntary* community is to say that mobilization of members must rely on idealism or personal persuasion rather than coercion or material incentives, but *voluntary* also signifies, particularly in the United States, that the congregation cannot assume the loyal adherence of its members as if they were all part of the same tribe; it must actively recruit them.

Using the terms of Talcott Parsons's sociological theory, the American congregation is a collectivity-oriented, functionally diffuse, affective, and particularistic social grouping but essentially an "achieved" rather than "ascribed" one. *Collectivity-orientation* means that members are enjoined to concern themselves with the welfare of the group, not only with their own interests (which is *self-orientation*). When an interpersonal relationship or social institution is *functionally diffuse*, as opposed to *functionally specific*, the burden of proof rests with those who would exclude a potential activity as illegitimate, and the relationship or institution will tend to absorb activities that are feasible given available resources and the default of alternative agencies. *Affective* relations are those that are in themselves emotionally satisfying; the opposite—typically the "businesslike" orientation—is *affective neutrality*. Expectations that parties to a relationship should be bound by their common membership in a particular category (for example, religion, place of residence, ethnicity, family) are *particularistic*; expectations that persons should transcend such categories in their dealings with others are *universalistic*. Statuses into which we are born (sex, race, national origin) are *ascribed*; those we have discretion over (which have come in modern society to include occupation and education) are *achieved*.[28] The communalism and voluntarism of the American religious system chronically frustrate efforts to make congregations over into finely tuned instruments of divine mission, and they persistently require congregations to look inward to the sources of their sustenance. We can see the significance of this when we consider some widely recognized and approved activities of congregations—worship, education, mission, and stewardship—before turning to what may be the master function of congregations in such a pluralistic society as the United States: fellowship.

Worship

To congregate is, as Martin Marty points out, to meet, and this is particularly salient in worship. Indeed, for many believers and traditions, collective expression is normatively essential to religious experience.[29] Protestant hymns generally have parts for four voices. Catholics pass the peace through the hands of those around them. Jews need a minyan of ten for certain prayers and two *gabbaiim* to oversee the reading of the Torah. Muslims join in prayer every Friday and are expected once in a lifetime to come together (now by the millions) in Mecca.

Moreover, worship is sensual. One's faculties and senses are mobilized to attend to the light streaming though stained glass (and a shadow across the soloist's face), the sound of the choir (and of a crying child), the grip of the greeter's hand (and the hardness of the pews), the scent of incense (and of someone's aftershave), and the taste of communion wine. Islam tries to avoid sensuality in worship, but its very ethic of plainness is itself a high aesthetic, bringing its own pleasure in the contemplation of Islamic architecture, Arabic calligraphy, nonrepresentational decoration, and hand-loomed rugs. Moreover, one cannot fail to be moved by the sound of communal prayer, when, in response to the imam's Arabic chant, masses of bodies accomplish sacred calisthenics in perfect unison.

With the richness of the human surroundings and the sensory input, worship always carries as much in the way of diffuse connotation as in doctrinally pure denotation. No matter how high-toned the worship, worship itself is affective and diffuse, and worship is only the beginning of congregational life.

Religious Education

In our highly mobile society, a good deal of attention is paid to religious education, as the structure of denominations and paradenominational agencies attests. Seminaries offer degrees, and congregations hire specialists in Christian education. Sunday-school curricula are constantly reworked and competitively advertised. Adult-education materials are available in bewildering variety from denominational agencies and mail-order catalogs. Yet effective education requires the translation of standardized materials into the idiom of the student body. In the world of churches, therefore, educators, including preachers and teachers, must learn the local culture, as the evangelical pastor Eric Underwood did in Mendocino in the 1970s.[30] Drawing on the work of James Hopewell, a pioneer in congregational studies, religious educator Barbara Wheeler writes: "The task of the leader . . . is to harvest the local knowledge that the congregation cannot express or judges to be unimportant, to bring it to consciousness and give it shape."[31] The religious educator can be truly effective only by bearing in mind the unique body of stories that members of a congregation tell about their common experience.

Hopewell worked with Anglo-Saxon Protestant congregations in relatively traditional American settings. How much greater is the need for the teacher to be fluent both in religion and in the setting of the congregation (Christian theologians might say "in both Christ and culture") when the congregation is one of immigrants! Effective education is inescapably particularistic.

Mission

From the congregation's point of view, mission can mean little more than collecting and sending financial contributions to denominational agencies, but most likely it involves one or more of a bewildering array of activities undertaken by members of the congregation—visiting, cooking, driving, cleaning, tutoring, building, studying, debating, leafleting, letter writing, picketing—where sharing the activity is part of its meaning. Because of the diverse human resources of those serving any given mission project (as well as other sources of unpredictability), a committee set up for one purpose easily develops new ones. In some churches, women's rights groups find themselves taking up the issue of homosexuality within a few meetings. A support group for an overseas orphanage becomes as well a study group on the issue of transracial adoption. The Church and Community Project at McCormick Seminary in Chicago documented how congregational mission projects, even under professional guidance that is oriented to articulate social theory, often have results unintended by their initiators.[32] Mission, which we often think of as purposive, goes off in many directions and is thus another source of functional diffuseness in congregations.

Stewardship

Every religious organization in a formally voluntary religious system must have some way of acquiring and allocating material resources. For most congregations, this is done by volunteers who (at worst) get saddled with the job or who (at best) are called to it by reason of their skill and inclination. Professional religious critics suspect that such volunteers carry out their tasks to the detriment of prophetic values, and professional religious managers that they do so by complying with small-town, small-business norms of logrolling and back-scratching. But volunteers' particularistic skills (or local knowledge) are evidently effective, for local congregations garner $40 billion in individual gifts each year and an average of ten hours per month of volunteer time on the part of ten million of their laity, as estimated by the Independent Sector survey.[33] Without this money and time, not only local congregations but also denominations and seminaries would be out of business.

The inherent functions of the congregation are carried out, in short, in a largely unbureaucratic, noninstrumental manner, which is remarkable when we consider the immense size of our society's religious sector and the increasingly bureaucratic character of most of our organizational lives. It is likely that their communal character, along with their public nature, is part of the attraction that congregations hold for their members. In the congregation, one can feel at home as a member of a large family in a huge living room. Of course, not only sweetness and light pertain in congregations, any more than in families. But congregations and families fight over many things, not just questions of public policy. A study of local church conflicts in even such a politically aware community as the neighborhood of the University of Chicago shows that only a minority of conflicts take place along a liberal-conservative axis; congregational conflict, too, is diffuse and particularistic.[34]

Fellowship

The United States is a nation of joiners with a puritanical, individualistic ethos, and its intellectuals talk of sociability most often with a bad conscience, a fact that inhibits the study of religion. Social scientists have mapped the profound link between religion and social integration, but this is a link that is suspect to theologians. Peter Berger, a sociologist as well as a Protestant existentialist theologian, articulated the suspicion a generation ago in *The Noise of Solemn Assemblies*. All religions serve to socialize individuals to the norms of their group, however narrow these may be, and endow them with a good conscience about their limitations, however little justified that conscience may be, and this is particularly true when religion occupies the conspicuous place that it does in the United States. "Suffice it to say here that a religious establishment such as ours is highly conducive to 'bad faith,'" wrote Berger.[35] In the pluralist society that is the United States, fellowship is both the most typical and the most problematic function of congregations.

Yet fellowship is inherent to congregating. The contemporary meaning of *congregation* is contained in the word's Latin derivation, an "assembling" (flocking, herding, gathering) together of people. It is appropriate that the volume in which this chapter first appeared and the Congregational History Project that sponsored it use the term *congregation* for the local religious unit, for it is meeting with other men and women that is the heart of the American congregational experience. *Parish*, on the other hand, has Greek roots referring first to the neighbor (the *oikos*, or household nearby) and second, with further spatial reference, to the district under the supervision of an elder. Parish has valuable connotations, particularly in reminding us that a common residence often means a common fate, which the congregational spirit too readily obscures. But it is a different concept.[36]

Thomas Day, satirizing Protestantization in Roman Catholic church music, invidiously contrasts the Catholic parish ideal to the Protestant congregational one. He likens the congregation to a chartered bus returning from a hobbyists' convention, filled with contented, like-minded people, whereas the parish is like a city bus crawling through crowded streets, open to anyone who has the modest fare. The congregation may be made up entirely of people who subscribe to the same selection of highbrow magazines, whereas the parish has to deal with the "whole magazine rack." The congregation is an exclusive "private club," whereas the parish is a "human zoo," made available as a "public utility for everybody." "Four thousand people who call themselves Protestant and live in the same area will take themselves to a variety of places on Sunday morning: the fundamentalist Baptist church, the Quaker meeting house, the High Church Episcopalian establishment, the Salvation Army, and so on. Four thousand people who call themselves Roman Catholic and live in the same neighborhood will find themselves in the same parish. Seated in the same pew will be the union leader, the union-busting employer, the nun with a degree in theology, and the saintly man who puts a dollar underneath the statue of the Infant of Prague for good luck."[37] Day's vision is an appealing one, but he knows that it historically depended for its realization on government support, financial endowment, or noblesse oblige. If the proletarian, the capitalist, the woman theologian, and the superstitious man occupy the same pew today in the United States, it is because they are somehow *drawn* to be there together. They do not *have* to be.

The practices of congregation and parish briefly converged in the experience of the early New England Puritans. Those who had come together across the Atlantic, and even further into the wilderness to places like New Haven, did so to escape religious decadence and to found a new order. They established parishes on these shores that were in the first generation also congregations, because the territory they encompassed was coextensive with the white population that had migrated together. Thus *congregation* and *parish* are conflated in the usage of the American Congregational tradition, and many a New England town still has its "First Church" on the green with "United Church of Christ" in small print within parentheses underneath.

But the New England "parishes" ceased to carry binding obligations early in our national history, and the use of the term by Protestants has been an archaism ever since, as both the Baptist and Roman Catholic traditions recognize. For Catholics a congregation is a collegium, as it is for Protestants, but a worldwide one with its meeting place in the Vatican. For strict Baptists (and they abound), congregational autonomy requires that territorial bodies can be only "conventions" and those who deliberate in them only "messengers." In this view, the denomination is emphatically a social network, not an authority. For better or worse, the American Protestant congregation (and increasingly the Catholic parish, as I argue later) is an assembly of people who choose to be together.

Sociological theorist Allan Silver traces the prominence of fellowship in American public life to congregationalism, which constituted, he claims, "the core religious culture in America during its formative period . . . , the most influential religious 'deep structure'" in our heritage. "In congregational doctrine, there is something sacred and irreducibly ultimate about the moral texture of face-to-face relationships organized as local congregations. . . . On this view, the church is composed of compacts made among freely choosing persons." In contrast to European ecclesiology and sociology, which stress the role of hierarchy and territoriality in the constitution of the parish, the American ideal is that "the congregation is created by the consent of individuals not merely to join it, but to create it continuously by their continuous consent."[38] Historian Timothy Smith goes further to argue that the congregational ideal of a "worshiping brotherhood" rooted in souls, not soil, was developed in all of the colonial Protestant communions regardless of their previous theories of church polity.[39] The gathered congregation has an ancient, ecumenical heritage as a social form in the United States.

Contemporary sociologists of religion have determined that denominations grow when they found new congregations and decline when they do not. It may be that new church development itself causes denominational growth or that robust denominations have the confidence to plant congregations whereas dispirited ones think they cannot or should not.[40] Whatever the direction of causation, it is plausible that one reason for the correlation is the dynamic of friend seeking among religious Americans. Mobile Americans implicitly recognize that new congregations are places where new friends can effectively be sought out. Research by sociologist Daniel Olson has shown that when a congregation is settled, its members tend to have all the friends they have room for, and they have less incentive to seek out new recruits. New and growing congregations make more room for those who seek fellowship.[41] This is probably why suburban churches have grown faster since World War II than urban or rural ones. As Phillip Hammond proposes: "(a) people in fractionated society need centers of community, and (b) local parishes may provide such centers."[42]

In a society of immigrants, it was perhaps inevitable that religious gatherings would serve as places of fellowship. In the religious assembly, immigrants gathered at least in part to speak the language of the old country and to celebrate its festivals. The congregation was a gemeinschaft in the midst of the alien gesellschaft. There, immigrants did not have to contend with the demands of the new society but could relax in an atmosphere of relative familiarity. The post-1965 surge in immigration has extended the ecumenical reach of the fellowship functions of religion. In his survey of religious adaptations of immigrants from South Asia, religion scholar Raymond Williams observes: "In the United States, religion is the social category with clearest meaning and acceptance in the host society, so the emphasis on religious affiliation and identity is one of the strategies that allows the immigrant to maintain self-identity while simultaneously acquiring community acceptance."[43]

Korean Americans, who number around eight hundred thousand, avail themselves of the congregational form as a Korean world within the American world. In a recent major study of Chicago-area Korean Americans, sociologists Won Moo Hurh and Kwang Chung Kim found that an astonishing 77 percent are involved in churches. Church affiliation itself was found to be conducive to the mental health of women; holding a church office, which 23 percent of church affiliates did, was similarly healthy for the men. "The Korean ethnic church seems to play an important role in satisfying the needs for social status, prestige, power, and recognition within the immigrant community," Hurh and Kim observed. "These needs would be particularly strong for those male immigrants who are expected to 'succeed' in the new country but cannot penetrate into the mainstream of the dominant group's social structure."[44]

Immigrant Muslims seem to derive similar benefits from their religious participation. According to historian Yvonne Yazbeck Haddad and sociologist Adair Lummis: "There is no question that for a considerable number of Muslims today the mosque plays an important role in social integration. This is particularly true for women whose lives may be isolated and lonely and for whom events at the mosque provide a welcome opportunity to interact with others of the community."[45]

But it is not only immigrant newcomers who enjoy the benefits of American religion as a private-public space, a meeting ground whose virtual owners are privileged to define the terms of discourse. The decline of the historic mainline denominations has prompted reflection on the extent to which they long served to enshrine values that we now recognize as those of an elite minority. Only a generation ago, observes sociologist William McKinney, such congregations nurtured a "belief in an innate hierarchy in which social values, values of taste, moral values and intellectual values all combine in a self-evident pattern," a "feeling of being right and open-minded at the same time, of being at once well-bred and progressive."[46] Whether we regret or welcome the demise of such a confident belief system, the perspective of time and fortune makes clear both its partiality and the role of mainline congregations in its former dominance.

Because religious affiliation is presumptively legitimate in American society (if no longer socially obligatory for the metropolitan upper middle class) and religious pluralism taken for granted, the local congregation has long served as a site for many activities that are not necessarily religious, from English-language instruction for immigrants to wholesome entertainment for teens. The imperative for such ancillary activities typically being prescribed not by the broader religious tradition but by the situation of the local congregation, congregations within the same denomination are as greatly varied as the localities within which they exist. As Barbara Wheeler has noted: "More than seminaries or denominational structures, which play a part in constructing traditions but which have privileges that insulate them from some of the consequences of doing that, congregations are the places . . . where the struggle to find religious meaning in a chaotic world occurs in the most complete and complicated way."[47]

The sociocultural aspect of congregational life, the extent to which congregationalism permits groups to celebrate their culture, should not be disdained. The congregation is not only a place where suburbanites can make friends and foreigners can avoid speaking English. It is not only a place where one's parochial prejudices can be affirmed out of earshot of unwelcome strangers (or a demanding ethic can be proclaimed to a faithful remnant). It is also one of the few places in our society where the oppressed can predictably expect to find encouragement. One of the most powerful expressions of American congregationalism is found in African American churches, and it was African American churches in the South that formed the organizational nucleus of the civil rights movement. In the black congregation, ingredients for a successful challenge to segregationist society were assembled: respected leaders, membership rosters, meeting spaces, financial systems, and the presence of a powerful God.[48]

Religious associations encourage the weak by invoking powers that outsiders respect, give lip service to, or merely tolerate. Thus church is one of the few places in rural America where girls from patriarchal households can go on their own without prompting suspicion of their intentions.[49] Members of black churches are serious about the power of the same God white society claims to revere, expecting God "to help them cope with joblessness, poverty and discrimination by transforming their despair into hope," in the words of pastor James Henry Harris.[50]

Besides being an acceptable form of association, religious gatherings are also relatively free from scrutiny. As sociologist Aldon Morris describes the atmosphere of Southern black churches: "Behind the church doors was a friendly and warm environment where black people could be temporarily at peace with themselves while displaying their talents and aspirations before an empathetic audience."[51]

Religious association is "private" in the sense that church is like family: just as passersby don't ordinarily drop in for dinner, they don't ordinarily walk into your church. That means that confidences can be shared, confidences like the need to overcome both internal temptation and external oppression. Thus lower-class black churchgoers are told by their pastors to avoid some temptations in their environment—partying, drinking, and drugs—even as they celebrate other aspects of their culture—gospel music, chanted sermons, and colorful dress—and chastise their oppressors.[52]

Congregations can function as protected enclaves in a hostile world. Middle-class white parents have a good chance of protecting their children from harm by their freedom to choose desirable neighborhoods, but black families are more likely to be segregated into neighborhoods with high rates of pathology. Religious communities can help them to guide their children. A feminist student on my campus, an American black woman raised as a Muslim, had this to say about her seemingly paradoxical commitment to a patriarchal religion: "In the MSA [Muslim Students' Association], no one *expects* me to fail. . . . Blacks give lip service to the importance of education, but if you are black and a good student while growing up, you do not get encouragement, at least not from anyone besides your parents. 'There she is with that book again,' they'd say. But Muslims expect me to be educated and to question things, so that I can use my education to live and spread Islam."[53] Congregations of the Metropolitan Community Church are also enclaves: here gay men and lesbians can meet and pray for each other, hold their partner's hand at the communion rail, mend bad habits, heal psychic wounds, volunteer home care for persons with AIDS, meet political candidates, and organize demonstrations.[54] In this way, church can be a place for people to develop a morale with the power to transform not only the world outside but also themselves inside, without risking the attention of the dominant society, which would be ready to use what the oppressed tell each other as an excuse to blame the victim.

Insofar as all Americans are minorities today—I emphatically include religious liberals of the old mainline—the congregation, with its diffuse, affective, and particularistic nurturing capacity, can help them resist their own particular temptations of the surrounding culture and nourish their higher aspirations.

De Facto Congregationalism and the Declining
Significance of Denominationalism

The congregational form of local organization is the sanctioned, official norm among only a few of America's religious communities, notably Baptists and Jews (see the chapters by Wayne Flynt and Karla Goldman and Jonathan Sarna in the first volume of *American Congregations*), as well as the unmerged Congregationalists, the Christian Churches, Friends, and Brethren. Formal congregationalism is doctrinally foreign to most of the prominent American denominational traditions—the Catholic, Episcopal, Presbyterian, and Lutheran lineages as well as the

Methodists and their many offshoots. Nonetheless, the congregational mentality has great practical force as an unofficial norm in American religious life.[55]

To be sure, formal polity matters. Religious organizations, more or less by definition, are ideological organizations, and organizational forms are typically prescribed by ideology. Organizational ideals (for example, "apostolic succession" and "the priesthood of all believers") do count for some purposes.[56] In particular, the less congregational the constitution of a denomination, the more likely it is that church pastors can take controversial stances on local issues, because they cannot formally be fired by their congregations.[57] This does not mean that congregationalism always conduces to conservatism, however. A recent controversial example is that of providing "sanctuary" from U.S. Immigration authorities for Central American refugees. The chances that a local religious assembly will declare itself a sanctuary are greatly enhanced by formal congregational polity, perhaps because only independent congregations have the freedom to risk government seizure of their property.[58]

Yet regardless of formal polity, the history and current situation of religious communities in the United States have a communal and congregationalist bias at the local level and an organizational and bureaucratic one at the national. George Papaiouannou's study in the first volume of *American Congregations* of a Greek Orthodox parish reminds us that the highly episcopal Greek Orthodox Archdiocese of North and South America was begun at the local level by congregations of self-made businessmen.[59] On the other hand, the formally congregational Baptists have spawned great national bureaucracies.[60] Over the past generation, Protestant denominations have experienced the waxing and waning of hierarchy—of effective presbyterianism and episcopalianism—but the end result, as Donald Metz intuited over twenty years ago and sociologist Robert Wuthnow has recently analyzed, has been the "declining significance of denominationalism" for church members, for congregations, and for the society at large.[61]

Throughout the 1950s and 1960s, mainline Protestant denominations buried old differences through mergers and federations in order better to carry on what they saw as God's work. The northern Presbyterians merged with the more conservative United Presbyterians, the old New England Congregationalists with midwestern German Calvinists, and the Anglo-Saxon-origin Methodists with the German-origin Evangelical United Brethren. Lutheran bodies with German, Norwegian, and Swedish roots came together, and they began to talk of reuniting with the Catholics. Mainline denominations formed the National Council of Churches, and several of them shared its headquarters building on Riverside Drive in New York. Eventually, it became easier to recognize mainline Protestant leaders by their opinion on public affairs than by their theology, and it became difficult to discern what, other than a common label, connected the various leadership cadres to the grass roots.[62]

The concept of the "declining significance of denominationalism" has several aspects. Denomination as a sociological variable has decreasing explanatory power in sociological research on beliefs and behavior of the laity, no doubt in part because so many Americans switch denominational affiliation during their lives.[63] Denominations that were historic antagonists have increasingly similar policies and structures. Congregations within the same denomination vary wildly in theology, liturgy, and social values. Amidst the clamor over centralized bureaucracy, mainline Protestant denominational agencies as well as the professional staff of the National Council of Churches have been cut back, and the denominational structures are internally divided between bureaucrats and judicatories (what sociologists call "staff" and "line").[64] Wuthnow argues that the impact of religion on public affairs is increasingly mediated not by denominations (or federations of denominations like the National Council of Churches) but by "special-purpose groups," whose members are typically individuals who share some focused concern.[65]

One reaction to denominational and interdenominational liberal ecumenism was the growth of a cross-denominational conservative reaction that further blurred historic identities.[66] Each of the mainline denominations has at least one outspoken theologically or politically conservative pressure group within, groups that seem to be in contact with each other through paradenominational conferences and publications.

A kind of local ecumenism also links the grassroots conservatives, but it is cultural more than policy oriented, and it bypasses the denominations. Anthropologist Melinda Wagner, in her recent study of nine Christian grade schools located near each other in an Appalachian valley, found that the schools preached a generic conservative Christian faith and required group prayer but did not stress finer points of doctrine or ritual, despite the fact that the schools were sponsored by congregations affiliated with denominations of very different stripes, from new charismatic, evangelical, and fundamentalist to old Holiness and Pentecostal. School administrators played down their denominations' particularities, and many teachers looked forward to the establishment of an "all-Christian" high school in the central town, for which they would collectively serve as feeders.[67]

At the present time, in seeming response to unrest at the local, regional, and paradenominational levels, mainline Protestant denominations are decentralizing. The United Church of Christ and the Presbyterian church have moved their headquarters from New York closer to their heartlands. As conservative opinion within their communions has been mobilized, liberal Episcopal and Presbyterian church leaders have tried to preserve room for maneuver as well as to avoid schism by accepting permissive rather than mandatory resolutions on such controversial issues as gay rights and consecration of women bishops. Much the same dynamic seems to be operating within the Reform and Conservative branches of American Judaism.[68] When liberal policies were hegemonic, liberal church leaders took advantage of episcopal and presbyterian structure. In a conservative time, decentralization is a fallback position for liberals, but it gives headquarters less leverage to enforce uniformity—on whatever issue—across congregations.[69] On matters of "lifestyle," congregations increasingly go their own way, so there are diametrically opposed "Bible-believing" congregations and "reconciled" ones (those who are accepting of gays) in all the mainline churches. "Walk-in closets," parishes widely known but not officially acknowledged to welcome homosexual men, are a widespread feature of the Anglo-Catholic wing of the Episcopal Church, whatever the current policy of that denomination on the legitimacy of homosexual expression.[70]

De facto congregationalism implies that congregations can chart their own religious course despite their denominational ties. For example, many Presbyterian congregations use the popular evangelical hymnal *Hymns for the Living Church* instead of one of the denominational hymnals. Although they must comply with denominational pastor-search procedures, many have chosen ministers trained at the independent evangelical Fuller Theological Seminary rather than at one of the denominational seminaries. The label *Presbyterian* on the door no longer conveys a great deal of information to the first-time visitor to a local church.[71]

De facto congregationalism also means that the local church is effectively constituted by its members, not by geography. In a city like Chicago, the mobility of congregations and the stability of edifices are often evident in building cornerstones and carved inscriptions. A former synagogue in Greek revival style is now owned by a Puerto Rican Pentecostal church. Another synagogue is now a Greek Orthodox church. A German Lutheran church built at the turn of the century is now owned by Hispanic Seventh-Day Adventists. What was built as an Anglo-Saxon Presbyterian church and was later sold to a Korean congregation now houses an Orthodox church for Arab Christians, many of whom came from a town where their families had been settled for a dozen generations.[72]

De facto congregationalism is seen across the American religious spectrum. Despite the conservative ascendancy in the Southern Baptist Convention, which may mean that nonconforming seminary faculty stand to lose their jobs, "local church autonomy was not just a symbol"[73] and congregationalism is robust in the SBC. Lay involvement is strong, and the gathered-church ideal encourages local group homogeneity. The average tenure of Southern Baptist pastors is thirty months, and the denomination is increasingly multicultural, with ethnically distinct congregations worshiping in eighty-seven different languages and dialects.[74] Southern Baptist churches have structural similarities with Orthodox Jewish synagogues, which place the greatest emphasis on rabbinical authority but at the same time need rabbis least, because the laity are so active.[75]

Korean Presbyterians provide an instructive example of the declining significance of denominationalism among Protestants and the increasing pressures toward de facto congregationalism.[76] There are approximately three hundred ethnic Korean congregations in the Presbyterian Church (U.S.A.), and they represent the fastest-growing sector of that denomination. One of these congregations, in fact the oldest Korean American church, recently succeeded in withdrawing from the denomination and legally taking along its property, for which it had paid. The judge held that the congregation, the Korean United Presbyterian Church of Los Angeles, clearly never meant to comply with the denomination's rule that the congregation holds property only in trust for the denomination. "We are pleased that the issue of whether the Presbytery has the ability to determine who is the rightful congregation has finally been addressed by the court," said the congregation's lawyer as the judge's decision in the four-year lawsuit was announced. "We hope that the Presbytery will not carry the case any further and will allow the Korean church to worship as it pleases."[77] Here the liberal secular American language of rights was invoked to argue for the religious autonomy of a largely immigrant congregation.

Presbyterians constitute a plurality of Christians in Korea, and they were accustomed in their homeland to practices that contravene PCUSA rules and customs, including life terms for ruling elders, exclusion of women from ordination, and a relatively literal reading of the Bible. The fact that 200 congregations have joined the Korean Presbyterian Church in America (as well as about 1,500 congregations enrolled in other American denominations) represents an option for Korean immigrants of which American Presbyterian leaders are very much aware. One response has been the establishment of a nongeographical, ethnic judicatory within the PCUSA, Han Mi Presbytery, expressly for Korean Americans. The denomination wants to hold on to its congregations, but the result is that Presbyterianism becomes structurally more diverse.

A form of de facto congregationalism seems to be rising among American Catholics. Two congregational processes, both likely related to the rising social status of American Catholic laity, seem to be taking place. One is the greater role for laity and women religious in the ritual and administration of the parish, a development that can claim both the virtue of Vatican II sanction and the necessity of addressing the priest shortage. There are many studies of this process.[78] The other process—the "floating" of laity from parish to parish in search of a spiritual home—is widely acknowledged by clergy and laypeople, but I know of no large-scale systematic studies of it.

It is no secret that many lay Catholics have a proprietary attitude toward their parishes to which they are not canonically entitled.[79] It seems plausible that the history of national ethnic parishes and changing neighborhoods in American cities combines with lay Catholics' transportation resources to create among them a sense of entitlement to parishes suited to their own liking. Meanwhile, since midcentury, Catholics have been secure in their Americanness and middle-class standing. No longer does the parish have to be a refuge from a hostile world; it can now be more a vehicle for expression.[80]

I see impressionistic evidence of de facto congregationalism in widely varied sources. Journalist Andrew Sullivan observes that Catholic laity are aware of "the shifting emphasis from parish to parish and priest to priest on the fundamentals of the faith: the balance of fact and metaphor in scriptural interpretation, the shift from the sacrament of confession to the dominant role of the Eucharist, notions of social responsibility, of community-based worship, of scriptural rather than theo-logical catechism, of obligation to the poor, witness to the unborn, the old, and the emergence of both charismatic and old-style devotional traditions."[81] Sociolo-gist Melissa Ray studied a midwestern parish whose members "identified them-selves and their faith in terms of the specific parish of St. Alicia first and only then in terms of the larger institutional church." She calls their attitude one of "partial alienation," but it is part of what I mean by de facto congregationalism.[82]

In a study of a Catholic diocese in the upper Midwest, Donald LaMagdeleine and John Glesser report that the present bishop "has not hindered the develop-ment" of "ideologically homogeneous parishes" to meet the needs of diverse con-stituencies.[83] As one of my Catholic neighbors told me about the attitude of the hierarchy in the Chicago archdiocese, "They'd *like* you to go to the parish where you're registered, but they would rather you went to some other Catholic church than none at all." Father Thomas Propocki, vice-chancellor of the Archdiocese of Chicago and a canon lawyer, had this to say on the matter in an interview: "Because of the social mobility of our current society it makes sense to let people choose parishes."[84]

Such church officials may be relying on a liberal interpretation of a revision of Catholic canon law effective since 1983. Canon 518 provides: "As a general rule a parish is to be territorial, that is it embraces all the Christian faithful within a certain territory; whenever it is judged useful, however, personal parishes are to be established based upon rite, language, the nationality of the Christian faithful within some territory or even upon some other determining factor." Thus canon law says that the norm is that parishes are to be territorial, with boundaries determined by the bishop, but that exceptions are now formally permissible.

The official comment on the change is this: "Following Vatican II, the First Synod of Bishops (1967) recognized the need to constitute personal jurisdictions although it confirmed the principle of territoriality in church organization. This meant that territory no longer is considered a constitutive element but only a determining element of the community of the faithful." Four exceptions were rec-ognized by the bishops: Eastern rite parishes; common-language parishes; national-origin parishes (which may now be established by the bishop—a change from the 1917 law, which required permission from the Vatican for such parishes); and the fourth: "Various other groups could include college and university personnel, mil-itary forces, charismatic groups, etc. Following Vatican II a number of bishops . . . allowed certain experimental parishes to develop under their supervision. They did this to meet the spiritual needs of various groups. . . . Some hold that strictly territorial groupings of the faithful are frequently artificial and deadening as the territorial principle as a norm for parish affiliation becomes increasingly obsoles-cent. . . . Although the territorial principle makes for good order, the needs of modern Christians have become so varied and their styles of commitment have expanded so much that a new approach today is important."[85]

In the spring of 1991, sociology student Carol Biesadecki interviewed a cross-section of twenty-five Chicago-area Catholics who identified themselves in response to her advertisements as those who attend mass at a parish other than the one they live in. She called them "floaters," and they gave many reasons for venturing from their home parish. Some went for a particular priest and his homilies, or for the cultural style they perceived among the parishioners. Some went to experience intimacy, others majesty. Some wanted an elaborate liturgy, others an abbreviated one. Some wanted a more convenient time, while others were sorely inconvenienced by the miles and hours that their floating took. Some who had moved to the suburbs returned to the urban parish of their youth. No single reason for floating dominated, yet there were some patterns: women and younger persons were slightly more likely to cite the particular priest, younger people to be drawn to the cultural style of fellow parishioners, and older people to be drawn by nostalgia for the past and a sense of intimacy in their chosen parish. In other words, floating does not mean that Catholics agree on one liturgical, musical, architectural, theological, or political style, but rather that they feel increasingly free to find the style that does suit them. As Biesadecki put it: "If the parish environment does not provide an atmosphere for a productive spiritual life, it makes sense to find one that does."[86]

The experience of a new African American parish in the Chicago archdiocese seems to be a tacit concession to the concept of the local church as a gathered community. Saint Benedict the African, in the South Side neighborhood of Englewood, represents a consolidation of five preexisting parishes into a new building. The consolidation was necessary because Englewood had lost most of its white (particularly Irish American) population in the last generation, the people whose ancestors built many of these churches. "Where Englewood residents were once Catholic in large proportions, they are now maybe 2 percent Catholic," observes reporter Grant Pick, and the rest, he says, are predominantly Baptists, Methodists, and Pentecostals. The heritage of St. Benedict's parishioners shows in the design of the building, whose main architectural focus is a stone baptistry pool twenty-four feet in diameter and three-and-a-half feet deep, which, says Pick, is "reminiscent of the Baptist tradition in which countless Englewood Catholics were raised." In the words of one parishioner: "This church was built for us, in our time. Our old churches were built for other people, who abandoned those churches. Now we have a feeling of ownership."[87]

Structural convergence toward the American model of congregational life seems to be taking place also among Muslims in America, as Earle Waugh observes in the first volume of *American Congregations* and as other students of the Muslim experience in America agree.[88] The mosque, established in Islam as a place for prayer, has become in Alberta an educational and service center to meet the needs of the Muslim community, a kind of church, with adult classes, potlucks, and coffee hours. The imam, who according to Islamic practice should be expected only to lead prayers, is asked on this side of the Atlantic to celebrate marriages, counsel families, visit the sick, conduct funerals, and represent his people among the local clergy, modeling himself in the process on priests, pastors, and rabbis. This might be called a form of assimilation, but it is done not only to meet immigrants' secular needs but also to help them perpetuate their religion. At the same time that old-country traditions weaken, the religious significance of the mosque increases.[89]

Muslims in Toledo, Ohio, have developed organizational patterns on the con-gregational model, according to the research of Islamicist Frederick Denny. They have instituted membership, with annual dues, and they hire their imam as an employee of the corporation. They have a council of elders comparable to those of Presbyterians, but the council "has supreme authority over the affairs of the cen-ter. At this point the analogy with Presbyterian polity breaks down, for in the case of the Toledo Islamic Center there is no official transcendent authority like Pres-byterianism's synod and general assembly."[90]

Similar processes are going on among Asian-origin Buddhists. The Korean Buddhist Kwan Um Sa temple in Los Angeles occupies the opulent second story of a former Masonic temple catercorner from the headquarters of Han Mi Presbytery, and the Buddhist leaders are well aware of the Christian model and competition. The temple's abbot told an interviewer that "church membership increased rap-idly after he initiated several social service and family counseling programs, including marriage and youth counseling, hospital arrangement, hospital visits, arrangement for Social Security benefits, etc. The church's van provides trans-portation for elderly members."[91] Japanese American Jodo Shinshu Buddhists use the word *church* for their places of worship, which also are used to stage elaborate American-style weddings and to host ethnic food bazaars. To judge from appear-ances, these Buddhists do not sit on mats but on pews purchased from American church-supply houses.[92]

At the Sri Lankan Buddhist *viharas* of New York and Washington, lay involve-ment centers on scheduled events, festivals, and special occasions, with most of the observances occurring on Sundays. "This scheduling is a concession to the demands of American society, which has traditionally reserved Sundays for reli-gious observances," observes religious historian Anne Blackburn. Those who live at long distances from the viharas are able to come only for such events as Sin-halese New Year, in April, and Vesakha, commemorating the Buddha's birth, enlightenment, and death, in May. At such times, congregants can enjoy the rare pleasures of speaking Sinhalese with nonfamily members and sharing others' home-cooked traditional foods. Instead of being immersed in a taken-for-granted Buddhist environment, these Sri Lankans must organize to enjoy the benefits of religious ritual, devotions, and instruction for their children.[93]

Sociologists Paul DiMaggio and Walter Powell have invented the term *institu-tional isomorphism* to label the general process of modeling that produces the particular convergence I call de facto congregationalism. They argue that "organi-zations that copy other organizations" have a "competitive advantage" and contend that "in most situations, reliance on established legitimated procedures enhances organizational legitimacy and survival characteristics."[94]

Because of post-1965 immigration, Los Angeles is reported to have the greatest variety of Buddhisms in the 2,500-year history of that faith, and Buddhist leaders there are confronting unprecedented challenges and opportunities for institution building and ecumenical cooperation. The Dalai Lama recently gave this advice to the Buddhist Sangha Council of Southern California, which comprises members of a dozen ethnic groups: "Another thing we should consider is that our Christian brothers and sisters, and also some Jewish and Hindu organizations, take a very active role in social work, in social welfare, in education, in health. But Buddhist monks, Buddhist traditions, are somewhat lacking in that. . . . We could have more activity in these areas of social service."[95] As Los Angeles becomes more culturally diverse, more religious organizations that take the form of American congregations are likely to grow within it.

Beyond Tribalism to Voluntarism:
From Ascription to Achievement in Religion

Not all denominations are declining in significance, nor are all congregations going their own separate ways. Mormon wards resemble each other closely, as we are informed by the research reported by Cheryll May, Dean May, and Jan Shipps in the first volume of *American Congregations*, and the parent denomination, the Church of Jesus Christ of Latter-day Saints, is formidable. Moreover, sociologists know that the category "Mormon" carries predictive power in social surveys. But this should remind us that denominationalism, when denominations were communities more than organizations, historically helped people to understand who they were, to forge their cultural identity.[96] In other words, there is no intrinsic religious contradiction between *denomination* and *congregation*. The contradiction, when it exists, is organizational.

Under what circumstances can Americans' insistence on having their own churches be reconciled with the churches' being something more than flattering cultural mirrors for their members? Or, to put the question another way, how can the commitments of religious traditions be made the commitments of the local laity?

It needs to be said that there are costs to congregationalism, de facto and otherwise. The local group can go off on its own idiosyncratic way, which in the case of Jim Jones's People's Temple was well off the deep end.[97] Years before Jones's trek to Guyana and the subsequent mass suicide, the People's Temple ranch near Ukiah, California, was already a negative symbol of "Lone Ranger Christianity" for a post-hippie charismatic Christian fellowship I studied in 1976, whose leaders fitfully sought out "spiritual covering" in lieu of affiliation with one of the mainline denominations they scorned as temples of "churchianity." They eventually aligned with the "spiritual shepherding" movement of Bob Mumford and Dennis Peacocke, the guiding principle of which was that "everyone should know who is over you and who is under you in the Body."[98]

More likely than spiritual idiosyncrasy, however, is the opposite pattern, where the congregation conforms excessively to its local environment, becoming a spiritualized replica of secular parochialism. The more congregational the local church, the more responsive and vulnerable it is to its local environment. Not only does narrow parochialism offend transcendent religious values, it also religiously disadvantages those who are socially disadvantaged in the parochial environment, for example, those women and youth whose religious involvement is entailed by the patriarchal families in which they are bound.

Denominations can help otherwise subordinated voices be heard. For example, denominational (and otherwise cross-congregational) ties have helped African American women achieve practical influence in the affairs of such officially male-dominated churches as the Church of God in Christ, as sociologist Cheryl Townsend Gilkes has shown.[99] The Camp Ramah movement, a youth-oriented network in the United States and Canada closely connected to Conservative Judaism and the Jewish Theological Seminary, has provided an atmosphere where classical Jewish texts "could spring to life without the obtrusiveness of either familial background or urban distractions." On the basis of intense camp experiences, Ramah alumni later became catalysts for change in Conservative synagogues, particularly in participatory and feminist directions.[100] It should be noted that such conferences and summer camps derive part of their power from an even more radical application of the gathered-community principle than the one exemplified by the local congregation: they bring women and young people together across, rather than within, circumscribed geographic locales.

Denominational bonds can transcend congregational cultures. Early in its career as a denomination, the Universal Fellowship of Metropolitan Community Churches, whose founding congregations were overwhelmingly composed of gay males, made a conscious commitment to sexual equality. The UFMCC now claims the highest proportion of female clergy in any Protestant denomination.[101] Some Korean American Presbyterian church leaders argue that staying within the mainline American denominational fold is essential to maintain the commitment of second-generation youth. An autonomous Korean American denomination, they fear, would be utterly dominated by the first-generation patriarchal culture that American-reared young people often want to flee.[102] Leaders of the fledgling interethnic American Buddhist Congress were treated to the following observation made at Wat Dhammaram, a Chicago-area Thai Buddhist temple, by one of their number. He complained that Wat Dhammaram's leaders are so obsessed with maintaining old-country customs and language that they failed to notice their own children speaking English among themselves during a special ceremony—conducted in Thai—in the children's honor! In effect, the ABC is applying the principles of the American-style church federation in order to overcome cultural captivity.[103]

We should be careful, however, not to phrase the cultural conflict between the presumably cosmopolitan denomination and the equally parochial congregation in stark terms of sexism, ageism, or racism. Even if we assume that the denomination represents less compromised religious teachings than the congregation represents, it does not follow that religious leaders face the choice of either abject capitulation to, or radical conversion of, a presumed primordial local culture. The local cultures that congregationalism builds upon are not simple givens to which the craven church-growth specialist merely accommodates.[104] Local cultures are more protean than that, and they can be turned to religious purposes.

The pastorate of Eric Underwood in Mendocino is an example. Educated in business administration at UCLA and in Bible and homiletics at Fuller Theological Seminary, Underwood was a first-rate evangelical preacher who instantly appealed to one sector of the congregation he came to pastor in 1973: the born-again ex-hippie Christians that Jesus movement evangelists had left in the wake of their revivals on the Mendocino coast. But Underwood intuited another, albeit inchoate, cultural ideal more widely shared in his congregation than the vocabulary of southern-style revivalism, an intuition that began with the simple observation that Mendocino's population swarmed with newcomers from very diverse backgrounds. Listening to their elaborate life stories and overhearing their casual conversations, Underwood discovered how far they had come to get to Mendocino and how much their decision to take up residence in a small town cost them. Because his own ethical principles stressed the virtues of face-to-face relationships ("structural sin" was a concept foreign to him), he could identify with his parishioners' stories. In his sermons, he reframed these stories in biblical terms and helped even the near secularists in his congregation understand the relevance of Christianity for their lives, even as he prodded them to acts of humility, decency, and generosity. In the end, his congregation prospered materially and spiritually and contributed heavily to its parent denomination.[105]

The Universal Fellowship of Metropolitan Community Churches provides another example. This two-hundred-congregation denomination began with a gathering of twelve persons in Troy Perry's living room in 1968. Perry felt called to share with other gay men (and eventually lesbians) a conviction that he later used as the title to his first autobiography: "The Lord is my shepherd and He knows I'm gay." From his own experience, including a five-year immersion in Los Angeles's gay underground and a lifesaving vision of having been created gay by a benevolent God, Perry knew how profound were feelings of unworthiness among his acquaintances but also how surely evangelical faith could overcome these feelings. On such grounds he founded his church. His first followers were a mixed lot—former Roman Catholics and former Baptists predominated—but Perry preached from the outset a message that spoke to their need for redemption in the face of social stigma. Over time Perry arrived at an eclectic liturgy that suited the group; his first sermon, for example, was on Job's dispute with his interlocutors. The Metropolitan Community Church communion offers a choice of Catholic wine or Baptist—and teetotaler—grape juice. When the AIDS crisis hit, death did not spare the UFMCC, but congregations pulled together as places of help and hope.[106]

Mendocino Presbyterian Church and the congregations of the Metropolitan Community Church that I know of are genuine communities: they are characterized by diffuse, affective, particularistic, and collectivity-oriented relations. But they are not communities into which one is born. Few people in the Mendocino church in the mid-1970s had grown up there, and in 1968 no one had been brought up in the UFMCC.[107] These churches, in other words, are not communities by social ascription but by choice. Moreover, such choices are not necessarily conservative. The members of Unitarian-Universalist churches are predominantly so by reason of adult conversion, not upbringing. Unitarianism is an achieved faith.[108] For this reason, the church-growth movement's "homogeneous unit principle" is not equivalent to tribalism. The identities and experiences on the basis of which religiously relevant cultural communities form are not necessarily those with which we are born: they are as likely to be matters of "lifestyle" (more typically an orientation to hearth and home than to homoerotic relationships) as of race.[109] Or, like deafness, they may crosscut (rather than mirror) social structural divisions.[110] Contingent or not, they are given meaning in the name of religious ideals that themselves are understood as perennial.

I used to be wryly amused when my contemporaries complained that stagnation had settled in after the social changes we tried to introduce in the 1960s. Didn't they realize, I wondered, how rapidly our world continued to change after the protests died down? Didn't they see that whole ways of life were disappearing? that the American industrial working class had reproduced its last generation? that the "family wage" was gone? that each child was being raised by more different people? that the WASP was becoming a minority? that there was a greater variety of persons of color in the United States than ever before? that organizations we used to take for granted—"the phone company," Pan-American World Airways, Pacific Stereo—had vanished? that it was getting steadily more difficult to become a home owner or a college graduate?[111] Without even thinking of changes in the Amazon Basin, Southeast Asia, the Middle East, and Eastern Europe, were not these changes plenty to confront?

We live in "interesting times." Few of us can carry out plans our parents made, nor can our children afford to heed our detailed worldly advice.[112] That with which we were born is seldom that with which we will die. To assume that religious identity is not problematic in these circumstances—that church members do not need to be convinced to be church members—has been the basic error of mainline Protestant planning over the past generation. Somehow, it was thought to be beneath the dignity of the Presbyterian Church to tell people they ought to be

Presbyterians. It seemed enough to tell them, given their Presbyterianism, what their societal obligations were. Today, even Jews, whose identity tends to be far more ascribed than is that of Protestants, have to be told what it means to be Jewish; at least many of their leaders think so. Older recipes have lost their relevance, and older identities their draw.

But not everything that is sacred has melted away. We are not yet a nation of monads. Americans are still religiously minded, and the congregational form of organization is robust. When Americans need the support of others to become better persons, they form congregations, places where people recognize each other and pay attention to each other in the sight of whatever they take to be ultimate. Some de facto congregations are found in and around seminaries: whatever the theory of congregation, students as well as the people back home feel the need for the interpersonal affirmation that congregations provide.[113] Post-sixties Jewish youth began another kind of congregation, *havurot*, "small intimate fellowships for study, prayer, and friendship . . . [which] allowed for individual participation and spontaneity."[114] Many large local churches make use of weekly "house-church" meetings to give their otherwise anonymous members the benefit of true congregational life. The new denomination called the Vineyard does this, as do, my informants tell me, Korean megachurches. (The Korean Methodists call their smaller meetings Sok Hoe, or "classes.") Another extensive category of de facto congregations are the thousands of twelve-step groups that have sprung up to help people cope with everything from alcoholism to their own propensity to violence, with the support and criticism of like-minded others in the sight of God as she or he is imaged.[115]

A FEW YEARS AGO, I went with my sociology of religion class to the regular weekly meeting of Dignity-Chicago, the local chapter of the national organization for gay Catholics. The meeting—really an unauthorized mass—took place on Sunday evening at Second Unitarian Church on the North Side, where the group took refuge after being expelled under Vatican pressure from the parish hall where their meetings had been held for fifteen years. I assumed it was not an oversight that the name of the priest celebrant was not announced, but everything else about the mass was in order. There was a procession, a six-person choir accompanied by guitar, a psalm and epistle read by lay lectors, the alleluia, the Gospel reading and a ten-minute homily by the priest, plenty of lay eucharistic ministers, and the dismissal, all in just under an hour. The sex ratio was highly skewed—indeed four of the five women present were members of my class—and the Lord's Prayer was recited using inclusive language, but the most unusual thing about the mass, my class agreed, was how enthusiastically the whole group of about eighty sang the hymns. We weren't used to that among Catholics.[116]

Afterward, we were greeted by one of the officers, and when we remarked on their singing, he had a ready answer. "We have chosen to be here," he said. "We are a congregation."

NOTES

I owe all of the stimulus for this paper, and many of the observations in it, to the Congregational History Project and my fellow seminar participants, some of whose work is cited herein. I am also deeply indebted to my students for their research and their initiative on field trips. The writing was supported by my home institution, the University of Illinois at Chicago, by the courtesy of the Department of Sociology at Northwestern University, and by a fellowship from the National Endowment for the Humanities. Fred Kniss and Daniel Olson commented on an earlier draft when it was presented to the fall 1991 meeting of the Chicago-Area Group for the Study of Religious Communities, and Allan Silver and James Wind provided written critiques of the same draft. Their comments were of great help in the process of revision.

1. R. Stephen Warner, *New Wine in Old Wineskins: Evangelicals and Liberals in a Small-Town Church* (Berkeley and Los Angeles: University of California Press, 1988); see also R. Stephen Warner, "Mirror for American Protestantism: Mendocino Presbyterian Church in the Sixties and Seventies," in *The Mainstream Protestant "Decline": The Presbyterian Pattern*, ed. Milton J. Coalter, John M. Mulder, and Louis B. Weeks, 198–223, 250–253 (Louisville: John Knox, 1990); and R. Stephen Warner, "Oenology: The Making of *New Wine*," in *A Case for the Case Study*, ed. Joe Feagin, Anthony Orum, and Gideon Sjoberg, 174–199 (Chapel Hill: University of North Carolina Press, 1991).

2. For example, see R. Stephen Warner and James S. Pappas, "Seeing the Word," *Christian Century* 110, 20 (June 30–July 7 1993): 663–665.

3. R. Stephen Warner, "The Metropolitan Community Church as a Case Study of Religious Change in the U.S.A." (paper presented at annual meeting of the Society for the Scientific Study of Religion, Salt Lake City, 1989); R. Stephen Warner, "The Korean Immigrant Church in Comparative Perspective" (paper presented at colloquium "The Korean Immigrant Church: A Comparative Perspective," Princeton Theological Seminary, Princeton, N.J., February 16–18, 1990).

4. For a survey of this literature, see R. Stephen Warner, "Work in Progress Toward a New Paradigm for the Sociological Study of Religion in the United States," *American Journal of Sociology* 98 (March 1993): 1044–1093.

5. Virginia A. Hodgkinson, Murray S. Weitzman, and Arthur D. Kirsch, *From Belief to Commitment: The Activities and Finances of Religious Congregations in the United States* (Washington, D.C.: Independent Sector, 1988).

6. Constant H. Jacquet, Jr., and Alice M. Jones, eds., *Yearbook of American and Canadian Churches, 1991* (Nashville: Abingdon Press, 1991), 265.

7. Kenneth B. Bedell, ed., *Yearbook of American and Canadian Churches, 1993* (Nashville: Abingdon Press, 1993). The count of congregations for the African Methodist Episcopal Church is taken from the 1991 *Yearbook*.

8. Lauris B. Whitman, ed., *Yearbook of American Churches, 1967* and *1968* (New York: National Council of Churches, 1967 and 1968); Constant H. Jacquet, Jr., ed., *Yearbook of American and Canadian Churches, 1989* (Nashville: Abingdon Press, 1989).

9. I have received this impression during travels all over the United States. The pattern was documented for Oswego, New York, by W. Seward Salisbury in "Continuity and Change in the Organization and Practice of Religion in a Small City in One Generation,

1951–1984" (paper presented at annual meeting of the Society for the Scientific Study of Religion, Louisville, 1987).

10. James T. Richardson, "Calvary Chapel: A New Denomination?" (paper presented at the conference "Evangelicals, Voluntary Associations, and American Public Life," Wheaton [Ill.] College, June 14, 1991); Randall Balmer, *Mine Eyes Have Seen the Glory: A Journey into the Evangelical Subculture in America* (New York: Oxford University Press, 1989), 12–30; Robin Dale Perrin, "Signs and Wonders: The Growth of the Vineyard Christian Fellowship" (Ph.D. diss., Department of Sociology, Washington State University, 1989); Les Parrott III and Robin D. Perrin, "The New Denominations," *Christianity Today* 34 (March 11, 1991): 29–33; John Dart, "Themes of Bigness, Success Attract Independent Churches," *Los Angeles Times* (July 20, 1991); "First FICWFM Convention a Huge Success," *Ever Increasing Faith Messenger* 12 (Fall 1991): 4.

11. Hodgkinson et al., *From Belief*, 10.

12. Tetsuden Kashima, *Buddhism in America: The Social Organization of an Ethnic Religious Institution* (Westport, Conn.: Greenwood Press, 1977); Tetsuden Kashima, "The Buddhist Churches of America: Challenges for Change in the 21st Century," *Pacific World: Journal of the Institute of Buddhist Studies*, n.s. 6 (1990): 28–40; Eui–Young Yu, "The Growth of Korean Buddhism in the United States, with Special Reference to Southern California," *Pacific World: Journal of the Institute of Buddhist Studies*, n. s. 4 (1988): 82–93; Donald K. Swearer, "Expatriate and Refugee: Theravada Buddhism in America" (paper presented at conference "Minority Religious Experience in America," Connecticut College, New London, Conn., 1989); Don Morreale, ed., *Buddhist America: Centers, Retreats, Practices* (Santa Fe: John Muir Publications, 1988); Raymond Brady Williams, *Religions of Immigrants from India and Pakistan: New Threads in the American Tapestry* (Cambridge: Cambridge University Press, 1988), 56, 179; John Y. Fenton, *Transplanting Religious Traditions: Asian Indians in America* (New York: Praeger, 1988), 178; Yvonne Yazbeck Haddad and Adair T. Lummis, *Islamic Values in the United States: A Comparative Study* (New York: Oxford University Press, 1987), 4; M. Arif Ghayur, "Muslims in the United States: Settlers and Visitors," *Annals of the American Academy of Political and Social Science* 454 (March, 1981): 150–163; Yvonne Yazbeck Haddad, Introduction to *The Muslims of America* (New York: Oxford University Press), 3.

13. Robert Suro, "Switch by Hispanic Catholics Changes Face of U.S. Religion," *New York Times* (May 14, 1989); Jorge Casuso and Michael Hirsley, "Wrestling for Souls," *Chicago Tribune* (January 7–9, 1990); Lynn Smith and Russell Chandler, "Catholics, Evangelical Christians Battle for Latino Souls," *Los Angeles Times* (December 2, 1989); Lawrence A. Young, "Hispanic Disaffiliation from the U.S. Roman Catholic Church" (paper presented at annual meeting of the Association for the Sociology of Religion, Cincinnati, 1991); Kevin J. Christiano, "The Church and the New Immigrants," in *Vatican II and American Catholicism: Twenty-Five Years Later*, ed. Helen Rose Ebaugh (Greenwich, Conn.: JAI Press, 1991), 169–186; Alex D. Montoya, *Hispanic Ministry in North America* (Grand Rapids, Mich.: Zondervan, 1987); *Religion in America—1990* (Princeton, N.J.: Princeton Religious Research Center), 30, 79. One source gives a figure of 687 Hispanic Protestant congregations for Los Angeles County in 1987 (Justo L. González, *The Theological Education of Hispanics* [New York: Fund for Theological Education, 1988], 3), and another reports 157 Hispanic Protestant churches in the San Francisco Bay Area (Stewart Stout, *Las Historias: A Guide to Hispanic Protestant Churches in the San Francisco Bay Area* [Pasadena, Calif.: IDEA, 1988], 10). Given the census and Gallup figures and assuming further that only half of U.S. Hispanic Protestants are members of ethnic congregations serving as many as one thousand persons each, we could make the extremely conservative guess that there are some two thousand Hispanic Protestant congregations in the United States, many of them affiliated

with such historically Anglo denominations as the Southern Baptists, Disciples of Christ, Assemblies of God, Seventh-Day Adventists, and Mormons, many of them outposts of Latin American–based denominations, and many independent. I know of no monographic case study of any such congregation, however.

14. J. Gordon Melton, *The Encyclopedia of American Religions*, 3d ed. (Detroit: Gale Research, 1989); Robert Wuthnow, *The Restructuring of American Religion: Society and Faith since World War II* (Princeton, N.J.: Princeton University Press, 1988), 107–112.

15. Robert C. Liebman, John R. Sutton, and Robert Wuthnow, "Exploring the Social Sources of Denominationalism: Schisms in American Protestant Denominations, 1890–1980," *American Sociological Review* 53 (June 1988): 343–352.

16. Dean R. Hoge and David A. Roozen, eds., *Understanding Church Growth and Decline, 1950–1978* (New York: Pilgrim Press, 1979).

17. Compare Dean M. Kelley, *Why Conservative Churches Are Growing*, 2d ed. (San Francisco: Harper and Row, 1977), chaps. 1–2, with Warner, *New Wine*, 26, fig. 5.

18. Joseph Gremillion and Jim Castelli, *The Emerging Parish: The Notre Dame Study of Catholic Life since Vatican II* (San Francisco: Harper and Row, 1987), 47.

19. Samuel C. Kincheloe, *The Church in the City: Samuel C. Kincheloe and the Sociology of the City Church*, ed. Yoshio Fukuyama (Chicago: Exploration Press, 1989), chap. 3; Warner, *New Wine*.

20. In a 1990 Gallup survey 29 percent of a representative sample of adult Americans said they were currently involved in small support groups that met regularly, and 60 percent of those reported that their group was linked to a church or synagogue; other reports estimate that there exist some 150,000 "twelve-step" groups currently meeting in the United States. Robert Wuthnow, "Small Group—Key to Spiritual Renewal?" (Princeton, N.J.: George H. Gallup International Institute, 1990); Randolph G. Atkins, Jr., "Twelve-Step Groups as Modern Forms of Religious Life" (paper presented at annual meeting of the Society for the Scientific Study of Religion, Pittsburgh,1991).

21. The social life of the religious agencies seems to be an underresearched topic. The preceding sentences draw upon Nancy Ammerman, *Baptist Battles: Social Change and Religious Conflict in the Southern Baptist Convention* (New Brunswick, N.J.: Rutgers University Press, 1990); Jeffrey K. Hadden, *The Gathering Storm in the Churches* (Garden City, N.Y.: Doubleday, 1969); Paul M. Harrison, *Authority and Power in the Free Church Tradition* (Princeton, N.J.: Princeton University Press, 1959); Sherryl Kleinman, *Equals before God: Seminarians as Humanistic Professionals* (Chicago: University of Chicago Press, 1984); George Marsden, *Reforming Fundamentalism: Fuller Seminary and the New Evangelicalism* (Grand Rapids, Mich.: Eerdmans, 1987); and Henry J. Pratt, *The Liberalization of American Protestantism: A Case Study in Complex Organization* (Detroit: Wayne State University Press, 1972); as well as on my own observations at 475 Riverside Drive and other religious sites.

22. Phillip E. Hammond, "Aging and the Ministry," in *Aging and Society*, ed. Matilda White Riley, John W. Riley, Jr., and Marilyn E. Johnson, vol. 2, *Aging and the Professions* (New York: Russell Sage Foundation, 1969), 293–323, quotation at 315.

23. Warner, *New Wine*, 97.

24. George W. Webber, *The Congregation in Mission: Emerging Structures for the Church in an Urban Society* (Nashville: Abingdon Press, 1964), 13.

25. Donald L. Metz, *New Congregations: Security and Mission in Conflict* (Philadelphia: Westminster Press, 1967), 36.

26. "Certainly, most denominational officials regard the growth of bureaucracy and increasing social distance as benefits. The officials are allowed to posit and pursue new programs

with a minimum of traditional interference. They are more protected from sticky confrontations with nonprofessional church members. They are able to recruit innovative staff members who are more anxious to serve the denomination's 'Southeast Asia desk' or its 'campus ministry' than a suburban pulpit." N. J. Demerath III and Phillip E. Hammond, *Religion in Social Context: Tradition and Transition* (New York: Random House, 1969), 187.

27. Warner, *New Wine*, 97, 164, 274–281. Liberal sociologist Wade Clark Roof articulates the mood of ecclesiastical reevaluation: "It was not until the 1950s that liberal intellectuals decided that the laity's preoccupation with personal faith encouraged self-absorption at the expense of theological and social issues. Perhaps it is time for a more balanced perspective. . . . Our preoccupation with universals often blinds us to sources of strength found in the particular. . . . Universality arises out of the particular, not the other way around." Wade Clark Roof, "The Church in the Centrifuge," *Christian Century* 106 (November 8, 1989): 1013–1014.

28. Adapted from Talcott Parsons, *The Social System* (Glencoe, Ill.: Free Press, 1951), chap. 2; see also Warner, *New Wine*, 52–53.

29. Emile Durkheim, *The Elementary Forms of the Religious Life* (New York: Free Press, 1965), 62.

30. Warner, *New Wine*, 86–87, 170, 204–208.

31. Barbara G. Wheeler, "Uncharted Territory: Congregational Identity and Mainline Protestantism," in *The Presbyterian Predicament: Six Perspectives*, ed. Milton J. Coalter, John M. Mulder, and Louis B. Weeks (Louisville, Ky.: John Knox, 1990), 87; James F. Hopewell, *Congregation: Stories and Structures* (Philadelphia: Fortress Press, 1987), esp. chap. 7.

32. Carl S. Dudley, "From Typical Church to Social Ministry: A Study of the Elements Which Mobilize Congregations," *Review of Religious Research* 32 (March 1991): 195–212.

33. Hodgkinson et al., *From Belief*, chap. 4. The 1993 *Yearbook* (258) gives the figure of $17.2 billion in total 1991 or 1992 contributions for thirty-six reporting denominations comprising 44.7 million members (which amounts to $384 per capita). These reports include most of the old "mainline" churches but, unfortunately, do not include any of the historic African American churches, the Churches of Christ, the major Pentecostal churches, the Mormon churches, the Roman Catholic church, most Eastern Orthodox churches, or any non-Christian bodies; in other words, the recent *Yearbook* figures exclude approximately two-thirds of U.S. church members.

34. Penny Edgell Becker, Stephen J. Ellingson, Richard W. Flory, Wendy Griswold, Fred Kniss, and Timothy Nelson, "Straining at the Tie that Binds: Congregational Conflict in the 1980s," *Review of Religious Research* 34 (March 1993): 193–209.

35. Peter L. Berger, *The Noise of Solemn Assemblies* (Garden City, N.Y.: Doubleday, 1961), 102.

36. Based on *The Compact Edition of the Oxford English Dictionary* (New York: Oxford University Press, 1971), 516–517, 2079.

37. Thomas Day, *Why Catholics Can't Sing: The Culture of Catholicism and the Triumph of Bad Taste* (New York: Crossroad, 1991), 103; also 79, 122, 87.

38. Allan Silver, "The Curious Importance of Small Groups in American Sociology," in *Sociology in America*, ed. Herbert J. Gans (Newbury Park, Calif.: Sage, 1990), 61–72; quotations from 61–63.

39. "Denominations" were later brought into being by such congregations to strengthen and support them, according to Timothy L. Smith in "Congregation, State, and Denomination: The Forming of the American Religious Structure," *William and Mary Quarterly* 25 (April, 1968): 155–176; see also Donald G. Mathews, "The Second Great Awakening as an

Organizing Process, 1780–1830: An Hypothesis," *American Quarterly* 21 (Spring 1969): 23–43.

40. Penny Long Marler and C. Kirk Hadaway, "New Church Development and Denominational Growth (1950–1988): Symptom or Cause," in *Research in the Scientific Study of Religion*, ed. Monty L. Lynn and David O. Moberg (Greenwich, Conn.: JAI Press, 1992) 4: 29–72.

41. Daniel V. A. Olson, "Networks of Religious Belonging in Five Baptist Congregations" (Ph.D. diss., Department of Sociology, University of Chicago, 1987); see also Phillip Barron Jones, "An Examination of the Statistical Growth of the Southern Baptist Convention," in *Understanding Church Growth and Decline*, ed. Dean R. Hoge and David A. Roozen, 170–172; and Wade Clark Roof, Dean R. Hoge, John E. Dyble, and C. Kirk Hadaway, "Factors Producing Growth or Decline in United Presbyterian Congregations," in ibid., 202.

42. Hammond, "Aging," 319n.

43. Williams, *Religions of Immigrants*, 11.

44. Won Moo Hurh and Kwang Chung Kim, "Religious Participation of Korean Immigrants in the United States," *Journal for the Scientific Study of Religion* 29 (March 1990): 19–34, at 31; see also Sang Hyun Lee, "Korean American Presbyterians: A Need for Ethnic Particularity and the Challenge of Christian Pilgrimage," in *The Diversity of Discipleship: The Presbyterians and Twentieth-Century Christian Witness*, ed. Milton J. Coalter, John M. Mulder, and Louis B. Weeks (Louisville, Ky.: Westminster/John Knox, 1991).

45. Haddad and Lummis, *Islamic Values*, 55; see also the study of Lac La Biche by Earle Waugh in *American Congregations*, ed. James P. Wind and James W. Lewis, vol. 1 (Chicago: University of Chicago Press, 1994), chap. 10.

46. William McKinney, "Revisioning the Future of Oldline Protestantism," *Christian Century* 106 (November 8, 1989): 1015.

47. Wheeler, "Uncharted Territory," 87.

48. Aldon D. Morris, *The Origins of the Civil Rights Movement: Black Communities Organizing for Change* (New York: Free Press, 1984).

49. Elaine Lawless, *Handmaidens of the Lord: Pentecostal Women Preachers and Traditional Religion* (Philadelphia: University of Pennsylvania Press, 1988), 72, 86.

50. James Henry Harris, "Practicing Liberation in the Black Church," *Christian Century* 107 (June 13–20, 1990): 599.

51. Morris, *Origins*, 6.

52. Frances Kostarelos, "First Corinthians Missionary Baptist Church: An Ethnography of an Evangelical Storefront Church in a Black Ghetto" (Ph.D. diss., Department of Anthropology, University of Chicago, 1990).

53. From an interview by Brook E. Lake, student at the University of Illinois at Chicago. Reported in a sociology of religion term paper, fall quarter, 1989.

54. Warner, "The Metropolitan Community Church."

55. Silver, "Curious Importance."

56. Gary P. Burkart, "Patterns of Protestant Organization," in *American Denominational Organization: A Sociological View*, ed. Ross P. Scherer (Pasadena, Calif.: William Carey Library, 1980), 36–83.

57. James R. Wood, *Leadership in Voluntary Organizations: The Controversy over Social Action in Protestant Churches* (New Brunswick, N.J.: Rutgers University Press, 1981), 59–83. See also N. J. Demerath III and Rhys H. Williams, *A Bridging of Faiths: Religion and Politics in a New England City* (Princeton, N.J.: Princeton University Press, 1992), 182.

58. Michael D. Matters, "Some Structural Correlates of Congregational Participation in the Sanctuary Movement: Research in Progress" (paper presented at annual meeting of the Association for the Sociology of Religion, Cincinnati, 1991).

59. Theodore Saloutos writes, in *The Greeks in the United States* (Cambridge: Harvard University Press, 1964): "Each church community was a democracy unto itself. It was governed by a board of trustees or directors, many of whose members were small independent businessmen, marked by that commanding proprietary air so often found in the self-made man. Authority was vested in these laymen; and many a clergyman discovered, much to his astonishment, that if democracy was diverting or rewarding for his parishioners, it was not exactly so for him. Despite the shortage of qualified priests, laymen remained in unquestioned control of church administration. They displayed a zeal for detail that confounded the clerics. There was little danger of clerical domination in the Greek church communities of the United States" (129).

60. Ammerman, *Baptist Battles*; Harrison, *Authority and Power*.

61. Wuthnow, *Restructuring*, chap. 5. "[D]ifferences in denominational activity are most visible in the structure of ecclesiastical government. At the congregational level there appears to be a minimal difference between denominations in what are considered to be appropriate activities" (Metz, *New Congregations*, 22).

62. Daniel V. A. Olson and Jackson W. Carroll, "Religiously Based Politics: Religious Elites and the Public," *Social Forces* 70 (March 1992): 765–786; Hadden, *Gathering Storm*; Douglas W. Johnson, "Program Dissensus Between Denominational Grass Roots and Leadership and Its Consequences," in *American Denominational Organization*, ed. Scherer, 330–345; K. Peter Takayama, "Strains, Conflicts, and Schisms in Protestant Denominations," in ibid., 298–329; Mark Chaves, "The Intradenominational Power Struggle: Declining Religious Control of Protestant Denominational Organization" (paper presented at annual meeting of the Association for the Sociology of Religion, Cincinnati, 1991).

63. Wade Clark Roof and William McKinney, *American Mainline Religion: Its Changing Shape and Future* (New Brunswick, N.J.: Rutgers University Press, 1987), chaps. 2, 5. As a variable, denomination still has predictive power for the attitudes of religious professionals (see Daniel V. A. Olson, "Restructuring among Protestant Denominational Leaders: The Great Divide and the Great Middle" [paper presented at annual meeting of the Association for the Sociology of Religion, Cincinnati, 1991]), which I suspect is due to the role of denominations in clergy careers.

64. Mark Chaves has made a similar distinction between the "agency structure" and the "religious authority structure." See his "Segmentation in a Religious Labor Market," *Sociological Analysis* 52 (Summer 1991): 143–158.

65. Wuthnow, *Restructuring*, chap. 6.

66. Mark A. Noll, "The Eclipse of Old Hostilities Between and the Potential for New Strife among Catholics and Protestants since Vatican II," in *Uncivil Religion: Religious Hostility in America*, ed. R. N. Bellah and F. E. Greenspahn (New York: Crossroad, 1987), 86–109.

67. Melinda Bollar Wagner, *God's Schools: Choice and Compromise in American Society* (New Brunswick, N.J.: Rutgers University Press, 1990); idem., "The Demise of Denominationalism and the Rise of Ecumenism Inside Christian Schools" (paper presented to the Institute for the Study of American Evangelicals, Wheaton, Ill., June 1991).

68. David Heim, "Sexual Congress: The Presbyterian Debate," *Christian Century* 108 (June 26–July 3, 1991): 643–644; Julia Duin, "Episcopalians Fail to Resolve Sexuality Issues," *Christianity Today* 35 (August 19, 1991): 46–47; Jack Wertheimer, "Recent Trends in American Judaism," in *American Jewish Yearbook 1989*, ed. David Singer (New York and Philadelphia: American Jewish Committee and Jewish Publication Society, 1989), 63–162, at 124–139.

69. Similarly, denominational rigidity can become a resource for temporarily triumphant conservatives, as the Southern Baptist Convention is now finding; see Ammerman, *Baptist Battles*, chap. 7. Similarly out of character, it might seem, Orthodox Jewish leaders used civil courts to enforce the use of the *mehitza* to segregate men's and women's seating; see Wertheimer, "Recent Trends," 72; and Lawrence J. Schiffman, "When Women and Men Sat Together in American Orthodox Synagogues," *Moment* 14 (December 1989): 40–49.

70. Although I have visited such churches and informants have told me of others, I know of no scholarly studies of them. On the affinity of Anglo-Catholicism and aspects of gay culture, however, see David Hilliard, "UnEnglish and Unmanly: Anglo-Catholicism and Homosexuality," *Victorian Studies* 25 (Winter 1982): 181–210; and John Shelton Reed, "'Giddy Young Men': A Counter-Cultural Aspect of Victorian Anglo-Catholicism," *Comparative Social Research* 11 (1989): 209–236.

71. Morgan F. Simmons, "Hymnody: Its Place in Twentieth-Century Presbyterianism," in *The Confessional Mosaic: Presbyterians and Twentieth-Century Theology*, ed. Milton J. Coalter, John M. Mulder, and Louis B. Weeks (Louisville, Ky.: Westminister/John Knox, 1990), 162–186 and 293–295, at 181–182; Marsden, *Reforming Fundamentalism*, 265–266; Warner, *New Wine*, passim; Warner, "Mirror"; R. Stephen Warner, "Visits to a Growing Evangelical and Declining Liberal Church in 1978," *Sociological Analysis* 44 (Fall 1983): 243–253.

72. R. Stephen Warner, "Starting Over: Reflections on American Religion," *Christian Century* 108 (September 4–11, 1991): 811–813.

73. Ammerman, *Baptist Battles*, 271.

74. Ellen M. Rosenberg, *The Southern Baptists: A Subculture in Transition* (Knoxville: University of Tennessee Press, 1989), 103, 112.

75. Wertheimer, "Recent Trends," 109.

76. Lee, "Korean American Presbyterians."

77. John H. Lee, "Judge Rules Korean Church, Not Presbytery, Owns Property," *Los Angeles Times* (January 11, 1990); see also John H. Lee, "Koreans Sue Presbytery, Allege Bias, Deceit, Theft," *Los Angeles Times* (February 5, 1989).

78. Dean Hoge, *The Future of Catholic Leadership: Responses to the Priest Shortage* (Kansas City, Mo.: Sheed and Ward, 1987); Gremillion and Castelli, *The Emerging Parish*, chap. 6; William D'Antonio, James Davidson, Dean Hoge, and Ruth Wallace, *American Catholic Laity in a Changing Church* (Kansas City, Mo.: Sheed and Ward, 1989), chap. 5; Ruth A. Wallace, *They Call Her Pastor: A New Role for Catholic Women* (Albany: State University of New York Press, 1992).

79. Timothy L. Smith, "Lay Initiative in the Religious Life of American Immigrants," in *Anonymous Americans*, ed. Tamara K. Hareven (Englewood Cliffs, N.J.: Prentice-Hall, 1971), 214–249; Jay P. Dolan, *The American Catholic Experience: A History from Colonial Times to the Present* (Garden City, N.Y.: Doubleday, 1985), chap. 6.

80. Gremillion and Castelli, *Emerging Parish*, chap. 2; Eugene Kennedy, *Tomorrow's Catholics, Today's Church* (San Francisco: Harper and Row, 1988), chap. 4.

81. Andrew Sullivan, "Incense and Sensibility: The Spiritual Confusions of American Catholicism," *New Republic* 203 (September 24, 1990): 33–38, at 34.

82. From "Religious Organizations, Organization Theory, and Social Theory" (paper presented at annual meeting of the Association for the Sociology of Religion, Cincinnati, 1991), 9; based on Melissa Ray, "Blest Be the Ties that Bind: Interpretive Appropriation of External Mandates in an Organizational Culture" (Ph.D. diss., Department of Sociology, University of Wisconsin–Madison, 1991).

83. "Crumbling Pillars: Diocesan Leaders' Perceptions of Catholic Institutional Change" (paper presented at annual meeting of the Association for the Sociology of Religion, Washington, D.C., 1990), 14.

84. From an interview conducted by Carol Biesadecki and reported in her "Why Do Catholics Float?" (B.A. honors thesis, Department of Sociology, University of Illinois at Chicago, 1991).

85. Canon law citation and commentary from Joseph A. Janicki, "Parishes, Pastors, and Parochial Vicars (cc: 515–552)," in *The Code of Canon Law: A Text and Commentary*, ed. James A. Coriden, Thomas J. Green, and Donald E. Heintschel (Commissioned by the Canon Law Society of America, New York, N.Y., and Mahwah, N.J.: Paulist Press, 1985), chap. 6, at 418–419. I am indebted to Carol Biesadecki for this reference.

86. Biesadecki, "Why Do Catholics Float?" 45.

87. Grant Pick, "Resurrection," *Chicago Reader*, August 9, 1991, 1, 20–28.

88. Haddad and Lummis, *Islamic Values*, 54–59.

89. Waugh, "Reducing the Distance: A Muslim Congregation in the Canadian North," in *American* Congregations, vol. 1, *Portraits of Twelve Religious Communities*, ed. Wind and Lewis, chap. 10.

90. Frederick Denny, *Islam and the Muslim Community* (San Francisco: Harper and Row, 1987), 113. In a later paper, Denny observes that "Muslim legists are having to demonstrate, to themselves and their co-religionists, that such developments are Islamically acceptable." Frederick M. Denny, "Church/Sect Theory and Emerging North American Muslim Communities: Issues and Trends" (paper presented at annual meeting of the Society for the Scientific Study of Religion, Virginia Beach, Virginia, 1990), 2.

91. Yu, "The Growth of Korean Buddhism in the United States," 90; author's field notes, December 4, 1989.

92. Kashima, *Buddhism in America*, 184–189, 130, 135–137; author's field notes, September 4, 1991.

93. Anne Blackburn, "The Evolution of Sinhalese Buddhist Identity: Reflections on Process" (bachelor's thesis, Swarthmore College, 1987), quotation from 71. John Fenton notes that "in America, Hindu temples tend to become like other American voluntary associations, and in time they will begin to resemble American synagogues and churches" (*Transplanting Religious Traditions*, 179). My own observations as well as those of my students suggest that Sunday is becoming the busiest day at Muslim centers in the United States

94. Paul J. DiMaggio and Walter W. Powell, "The Iron Cage Revisited: Institutional Isomorphism and Collective Rationality in Organizational Fields," *American Sociological Review* 48 (April 1983): 147–160, at 155.

95. *Changing Faces of Buddhism in America: The Dalai Lama Meets the Buddhist Sangha Council of Southern California, July 5, 1989* (Los Angeles: Buddhist Sangha Council of Southern California, 1989), 19.

96. William H. Swatos, Jr., "Beyond Denominationalism? Community and Culture in American Religion," *Journal for the Scientific Study of Religion* 20 (September 1981): 217–227.

97. John R. Hall, *Gone from the Promised Land: Jonestown in American Cultural History* (New Brunswick, N.J.: TransAction Books, 1987); David Chidester, *Salvation and Suicide: An Interpretation of Jim Jones, the People's Temple, and Jonestown* (Bloomington: Indiana University Press, 1988).

98. Warner, *New Wine*, chaps. 5, 6, 10, 11, and epilogue, quotation at 240; Peacocke appears under the pseudonym "Gary Armstrong." See also Sara Diamond, *Spiritual Warfare: The Politics of the Christian Right* (Boston: South End Press, 1989), chap. 4.

99. Cheryl Townsend Gilkes, "'Together and in Harness': Women's Traditions in the Sancti-fied Church," *Signs* 10 (Summer 1985): 678–699.

100. David Wolf Silverman, "A Word from the Editor" [introducing four articles on Ramah], *Conservative Judaism* 40 (Fall 1987): 3–66, at 3; Wertheimer, "Recent Trends," 127–130.

101. Troy D. Perry with Thomas L. P. Swicegood, *Don't Be Afraid Anymore: The Story of the Reverend Troy Perry and the Metropolitan Community Churches* (New York: St. Martin's Press, 1990), chap. 7; author's interviews in Los Angeles with Rev. Elder Donald Eastman (August 15, 1989) and Rev. Elder Nancy Wilson (December 3, 1989). The UFMCC has an increasing proportion of women among its members, estimated by Reverend Eastman as 30 percent, and a number of congregations with lesbian majorities.

102. Sang Hyun Lee, "Called to Be Pilgrims: Toward an Asian-American Theology from the Korean Immigrant Perspective," in *Korean American Ministry: A Resourcebook*, ed. S. H. Lee (Princeton, N.J.: Princeton Theological Seminary, 1987), 90–120; Young Pai, Deloras Pemberton, and John Worley, *Findings on Korean-American Early Adolescents and Adolescents* (Kansas City: University of Missouri School of Education, 1987); Warner, "Korean Immigrant Church"; see also Mark R. Mullins, "The Organizational Dilemmas of Ethnic Churches: A Case Study of Japanese Buddhism in Canada," *Sociological Analysis* 49 (Fall 1988): 217–233.

103. William K. Bartels in the registrants' booklet for the American Buddhist Congress convocation (November 17–19, 1989), held at Wat Dhammaram in Bridgeview, Illinois; author's interviews with American Buddhist Congress leaders, Los Angeles, December 4, 1989, and August 29, 1991.

104. This is evidently the view of Ellen Rosenberg in her book *Southern Baptists*: "There is a marketing philosophy behind it [Southern Baptist Convention growth]: find out who the congregation really is, not what you think it is or would like it to be, and set about meeting its needs" (108). James H. Smylie finds such a church-growth strategy "troublesome biblically, theologically, and ethically, . . . because it fails to deal seriously with the identity of the Christian community as a community that is inclusive and that transcends the prejudices of race" ("Church Growth and Decline in Historical Perspective," in *Understanding Church Growth and Decline*, ed. Hoge and Roozen, 69–93, at 82).

105. Warner, *New Wine*, esp. chaps. 7–9 and 12.

106. Troy D. Perry, *The Lord Is My Shepherd and He Knows I'm Gay* (Los Angeles: Nash, 1972); Perry and Swicegood, *Don't Be Afraid Anymore*; Kittredge Cherry and James Mitulski, "We Are the Church Alive, the Church with AIDS," *Christian Century* 105 (January 27, 1988): 85–88; Warner, "The Metropolitan Community Church."

107. Gay activists argue, indeed, that no one is raised to be gay; they differ mightily on whether people are born gay, with gay Christians for the most part affirming that they are (see Warner, "The Metropolitan Community Church"). A recent analysis of the controversy is found in Andrew Sullivan, "The Politics of Homosexuality," *New Republic* 208 (May 10, 1993): 24–37.

108. Robert B. Tapp, *Religion among the Unitarian Universalists: Converts in the Stepfather's House* (New York: Seminar Press, 1973).

109. See R. Stephen Warner, "Congregating: Walk Humbly at Rock Church," *Christian Century* 109 (October 28, 1992): 957–958.

110. Warner and Pappas, "Seeing the Word."

111. In *Brave New Families: Stories of Domestic Upheaval in Late Twentieth Century America* (New York: Basic Books, 1990), Judith Stacey analyzes the impact of such changes in the lives of Silicon Valley women of the working class and the role of their religious involvements

in helping them reorganize their lives. See also Dan Morgan, *Rising in the West: The True Story of an 'Okie' Family from the Great Depression Through the Reagan Years* (New York: Alfred A. Knopf, 1992).

112. These ideas were stimulated by Deborah Sherman, "Becoming Workers: From High School to Work among Black and White Workers" (Ph.D. diss., Department of Sociology, University of Illinois at Chicago, 1991).

113. I have in mind Rosemary Radford Ruether, *Women-Church: Theology and Practice of Feminist Liturgical Communities* (San Francisco: Harper and Row, 1988).

114. Wertheimer, "Recent Trends," 150; Riv-Ellen Prell, *Prayer and Community: The Havurah in American Judaism* (Detroit: Wayne State University Press, 1989); Shirah W. Hecht, "Religious Congregation in a New Mode: Tradition, Social Change, and the Public Expression of Diversity" (paper presented at annual meeting of the Society for the Scientific Study of Religion, Virginia Beach, Virginia, 1990).

115. William Madsen, "A.A.: Birds of a Feather," chap. 9 in *The American Alcoholic* (Springfield, Ill.: Charles C. Thomas, 1974).

116. Thomas Day remarks, in *Why Catholics Can't Sing*, "I have heard a congregation of fifty elderly Episcopalians produce more volume than three hundred Roman Catholics" (1).

9

The Metropolitan Community Churches and the Gay Agenda

The Power of Pentecostalism and Essentialism (1995)

Beginning with the claim—more asserted than documented—that the gay church in general and the Metropolitan Community Churches in particular are major actors in the movement for gay rights, it is the thesis of this chapter that the source of MCC's effectiveness is that it is an American church. The MCC was founded with a conservative theology and anthropology and an evangelical message, and organized on conventional lines first as a congregation and later as a denomination (the Universal Fellowship of Metropolitan Community Churches). Occupying the legitimate social space accorded to religion in the United States and flourishing in locales (such as California, Texas, and Florida) characterized by both religious vitality and social tolerance, the MCC is a church of, by, and for gay men and increasingly lesbians which mobilizes the resources and engenders the courage needed to challenge societal and internalized homophobia.

Based on memoirs, primary documents, secondary literature, and the author's observations and interviews, and informed by the author's comprehensive theory of religion in the United States, the chapter—more an analysis than a history—narrates the early development of the MCC. In the uprooted but demographically concentrated gay population of Los Angeles, Troy Perry found a ready market for his heartfelt message that homosexuality is innate and God's gift. A lifelong Pentecostal, he conceived of God in personal, not legalistic, terms that informed his biblical hermeneutic. A vigorous religious entrepreneur, he was both palpably committed to his message and willing to package it in liturgical styles suited to the deep-seated but varied religious backgrounds of his new constituents. Well aware of his own limitations as a high school dropout, Perry early welcomed into MCC leadership circles men (and soon women) of substantial educational and ecclesiastical accomplishment, and together they established a presbyterian structure for the new denomination. Within little more than a decade, the UFMCC had applied for membership in the National Council of Churches. Although Perry led a public demonstration against job discrimination within six months of the founding of the MCC and has continued his political activism, the MCC was and is first of all a religious community.

A note on terminology is in order. I intend "homosexual" to refer to those who define their sexuality by their erotic attraction to members of their own sex. "Gays," for the most part, refers to male homosexuals who are socially open about their sexual orientation, "lesbians" to females analogously oriented. I follow convention on "homophobic," which has come to mean inordinate fear or hatred of homosexuals, not of one's own sex. Analogously, "homophile" refers not to homosexuals per se, but to those who support the rights of homosexuals. In this sense, the present paper may be regarded as, in part, a homophile treatise.

Entrepreneurial and Pastoral Beginnings

In October 1968, eight months before Stonewall, when the patrons of a gay bar in New York rose in protest of a vice squad raid, Troy Perry did something equally audacious in Los Angeles. He met with twelve people in his living room in the first worship service of a homosexual-affirming religious group which he called the "Metropolitan Community Church." He deliberately chose the form of the American religious congregation to bring a gospel of God-given homosexuality to the gay community. In 1990, the denomination he founded and still heads, the Universal Fellowship of Metropolitan Community Churches, claimed some 12,576 communicant members in 195 congregations in the United States (Bedell 1993, 253), and nearly 100 congregations in fifteen other countries worldwide.

Already in 1970, Perry was the top vote getter in balloting for the Conference Committee of the North American Conference of Homophile Organizations (Duberman 1993, 312). By the early 1980s, according to Altman's survey of homosexual rights movements, the Metropolitan Community Churches were "perhaps the closest there is to a grass-roots national organization" for gay rights. "The network provided by [gay] religious groups, in particular the MCC, . . . [is] the largest organized sector of the gay community, and like other religious groups they can draw on strong reserves of commitment and dedication. . . . In many places the church is the only form of the gay movement that exists" (Altman 1982, 123). The Metropolitan Community Church has put the issue of rights for sexual minorities permanently on the agenda of the mainline churches (and in such forums as *Christian Century*) and has fought numerous public battles for gay rights, in particular the successful campaign against the 1978 Briggs initiative in California (Dart 1991).

The background of the MCC could hardly have seemed less auspicious, however. In 1963, Troy Perry was a twenty-three-year-old high school dropout with a wife and two children who had been preaching for nearly ten years in Georgia, Florida, Alabama, Illinois, and California, when he decided once and for all that he was homosexual. He confessed his orientation to his superior in the Pentecostal Church of God of Prophecy in Santa Ana, California, and was immediately defrocked.

His wife left for home in Alabama with the boys (whom he did not see again for nineteen years), and he left the parsonage in order to learn how to be a gay man in Southern California.

For five years Perry kept mostly away from church, moving between his mother's home in suburban Los Angeles, gay bars and coffee shops in West Hollywood, a sales job with Sears, Roebuck, and a two-year hitch in the army, until a crisis precipitated the reconciliation of his early Christian and latter-day homosexual selves. In despair over the breakup of what he calls his first intense love affair, he attempted suicide by slashing his wrists, but in a hospital emergency room he felt God's love in the voice of a friendly stranger. He confessed in his heart that he had made an idol of his erstwhile lover, putting that man in the rightful place of God. With this act of repentance, Perry recalls: "I knew that I had passed the major crisis of my life. . . . I knew that God cared about me and that He was with me, all the way—wherever that would lead me" (Perry 1972, III; for another version of this memoir, see Perry and Swicegood 1990, 30).

Shortly thereafter, still in the glow of his own epiphany, Perry tried unsuccessfully to bring God's comfort to another former lover, called Carlos, who had been arrested in a vice raid on a gay bar. Carlos knew that his carefully closeted life had been ruined, and he laughed in derision when Perry told him that God loved him nonetheless. Perry was moved: "I felt the weight of his disaster upon me. I had made my way back to God enough, and I was still Pentecostal enough that I knew I could talk to God. So I knelt down and said, 'All right, God, if it's Your will, if You want to see a church started as an outreach into our community, You just let me know when.' And that still small voice in the mind's ear just let me know—now!" (Perry 1972, 8). With that, Perry placed an ad with his own picture in the new gay paper in Los Angeles, the *Advocate*, and he spread the word in his favorite bar, The Patch. The ad said that the Metropolitan Community Church, himself preaching, was holding religious services every Sunday at a Huntington Park address (which happened to be Perry's own home). The first Sunday after the ad appeared, October 6, 1968, there were twelve people to greet Perry as he walked into his specially decorated living room carrying a Bible and wearing a borrowed ecclesiastical robe. Most of them were friends like his housemate Willie Smith, and only three were strangers attracted by the ad. The next week, there were thirteen in the congregation. Then fifteen. But the fourth Sunday, only eight people came, and Perry thanked God for preparing him in advance for disappointment with a sermon on the topic "Despise Not the Day of Small Things." The week after, however, there were more than twenty, and the congregation reached three hundred within a year, meeting by then in the theater building where Willie Smith worked as projectionist.

Within four years, Perry's MCC congregation numbered some eight hundred members and became a force to be reckoned with among Los Angeles churches. In the spring of 1969, Perry went on a salary of $150 per week and was able to quit his outside job to become a full-time pastor (Enroth and Jamison 1974, 36; Swicegood

1974, 219–220). For Perry, the success of the church "meant, among other blessings, a steady income and hot meals on the dining room table" (Perry and Swicegood 1990, 48). Thus did Perry reconcile his early ministerial vocation with his gay life.

In so doing, he trod ironically familiar ground. Alongside George Whitefield in the eighteenth century, Charles Grandison Finney in the nineteenth, and his older contemporary Oral Roberts, Perry was a religious entrepreneur (Warner 1993a, 1051, 1057, 1081). As Perry recalls it: "The only way I knew to begin a church was the way I had been taught in the South, and I still do not know any other—that is, to tell people openly who you are and where they can find you" (Perry and Swicegood 1990, 37).

To be successful, Perry's strategy required that there be a cultural market for his ideas, and his life as a gay man between 1963 and 1968 had introduced him to it. A distinctive gay male urban subculture had developed in the years after World War II in the United States, and Los Angeles was one of the cities—San Francisco, San Diego, Houston, Chicago, Miami, and New York were others—to which gay men migrated in search of its bars and tearooms. In the culturally open atmosphere of the 1960s, gay newspapers began to appear (Adam 1987a; D'Emilio 1983; Epstein 1987; FitzGerald 1986; Godfrey 1988). So the word about Troy Perry's new church got around town quickly.

Indeed, Perry's own relatively untroubled state of mind owed much to that subculture. *The Homosexual in America*, by the pseudonymous Donald Webster Cory (1951), which Perry found in a bookstore's gay magazine section early in the 1960s, convinced him that he belonged to the category of homosexuals and precipitated his initial decision to give up his family and his church. He had been able to come out of his closet with relative ease because in Los Angeles he could readily find gay meeting places like Pagola's and The Patch, and models of openness like Willie Smith. Convinced as a boy by Christian preachers that God loved him, he was convinced as an adult by a gay network that his homosexuality was not to be borne alone. Troy Perry thus built his church on the grounds of both a Christian heritage and a nascent homosexual community.

Many of the MCC's first communicants had deep-seated but long-frustrated religious yearnings. As part of a study of homosexual identity, sociologist Barry Dank surveyed the Los Angeles membership two years after the founding and discovered that more than half of those responding had previously been members of the clergy or had seriously considered a ministerial career (Dank 1973, 84–86, 243). One of Perry's first recruits was the Reverend Richard Ploen, a minister and college teacher with a solid Presbyterian background, who helped Perry with the church's evolving doctrine and liturgy. Another recruit was "Papa" John Hose, a former minister, who organized the first MCC satellite church in San Diego. It seemed that there were many gay men eager to hear the gospel of God's unconditional love, and some of them wanted to go to work for the new church (Enroth and Jamison 1974, 65; Perry 1972, 129, 135, 192; Dart 1969).

Perry's first MCC sermon told the story of Job, a good man upon whom devastation had been visited but who stubbornly defied the patronizing assurances of his peers that he must have done something to incur the wrath of God. Job stood by his righteousness and faith—"I know that my Redeemer liveth" (Job 19:25)—and was ultimately vindicated by a vision of God himself. Everyone in the room was moved to tears by Perry's evangelical message, and he was inspired to begin his second Sunday service with the Pentecostal refrain that has since become his trademark: "If you love the Lord this morning, would you say 'amen'!"

As his congregation grew over the months, so did his confidence. "Here before his congregation stood a showman out of the same mold as the pulpit greats of the past such as Aimee Semple McPherson and Billy Sunday. Energy flowed from Troy Perry and ignited his entire congregation." Those are the words of Perry's ghostwriter, Charles Lucas, three years after the founding, but Dennis Altman, radical theoretician of the gay movement and no partisan of religion, concurs, calling Perry "perhaps the most charismatic leader yet produced by the American gay movement" (Altman 1982, 27; Lucas 1972, 230). Perry also had a sense of humor. Early in the MCC years, Laud Humphreys suggested to Perry that he was the Martin Luther King of the gay movement, but Perry countered that Martin Luther Queen would be more like it (Humphreys 1972, 151). On the sole occasion I have heard him preach (in June 1988), Perry radiated vitality and cheer and never seemed to pause for breath. At the door after the service, he gave parishioners a powerful embrace and the visitor a piercing gaze. Although I recognized then what I later read freely acknowledged in his two autobiographies—that he is not a scholar, an intellectual, or even an eloquent speaker—I did not wonder that people were willing to follow him (see also Glaser 1988, 38–39; Dank 1973, 25; Swicegood 1974; Tobin and Wicker 1972, 229; cf. Perry 1972, Perry and Swicegood 1990).

Perry's teaching developed from the revelation that one can be both gay and Christian. Theologically, Perry would say, God comes first. With his Pentecostal background and off-and-on Bible college training, Perry is at home with the language and symbols of conservative Protestantism. He thinks of God in personal and supernatural, New Testament terms. He always insists that the MCC is first of all a Christian church, a church universal enough to reach out to all God's children. From the outset, some of his strongest supporters, including his mother, have been members of the straight world. In that sense, the MCC resists being called "the gay church."

Yet Perry also teaches that in the life of the individual, sexual orientation comes first. He rather fancifully claims a sensual memory of the joining of sperm and ovum in his own conception as a homosexual, and he knows as a matter of faith that homosexuality is "preordained" (Perry 1972, 10; see also Perry and Swicegood 1990, 235). Indeed, if there is one article of faith that unites Christian gay men today it is that their sexual orientation is indelible. It is something over which they can and ought to have no control. For Troy Perry, the combination of that conviction with the evangelical image of a benevolent and powerful God produces a surpassing affirmation of gay identity. So it is that the first and most significant gay church should be theologically conservative, not liberal. "For the MCC member the conversion experience takes the form: Jesus loves *all* men; He loves even gay people; ergo gay is good" (Bauer 1976, 125; see also Sullivan 1994).

But Perry had ideological work to do with the Bible. At the coffee hour following the first MCC service, he had been unprepared for the plea of one young gay man, torn between the good news of Perry's message and dread from his own fundamentalist background, that he contend with God's word on homosexuality as found in scripture. Perry asked for two weeks' study time. More consequential for the fundamentalists he had to address than the widespread but shallow use of the Sodom story as a rebuke to sexual perversity (many scholars think the sin of Sodom was lack of hospitality to strangers) were the outright condemnation of homosexual acts in the Mosaic Law (e.g., Leviticus 20:13) and the "due penalty" of God pronounced by the apostle Paul upon men inflamed with lust for one another (Romans 1:27) (Swicegood 1974, 143ff).

Perry brought determination to his task along with knowledge gained in several courses of formal Bible study. Most important for his hermeneutic efforts, his love of the Lord antedated his knowledge of the Bible. In early adolescence, he had come under the influence of his aunt Bea, pastor of a Pentecostal assembly in rural Georgia, who spoke before her congregation the prophecy that Troy was called to be a preacher. It was in Aunt Bea's church that, barely out of childhood, Perry gave his first, four-minute sermon. For Troy Perry, religion had always been a matter of love, not law.[1]

His solution to the apologetic problem was twofold. He first assimilated the Levitical prohibition of homosexual relations to the Old Testament law from which Jesus freed the faithful: rules and regulations concerning diet, dress, slaveholding, and a myriad of other matters (see also Sullivan 1994, 52). He then elevated above Paul's evident homophobia three other lessons from the New Testament: Jesus' message of love, the silence of the Gospels themselves on the subject of homosexuality, and Jesus' own personal life as an unmarried peripatetic who kept company with twelve men. A good deal more Bible work has been done in the twenty years since Perry's initial problem-driven study (e.g., Arthur 1982), and positive models for same-sex relationships have been found in the stories of Ruth and Naomi, David and Jonathan, and Jesus and the disciple John. But the outlines of Perry's first solution stand today in the teaching of the MCC and other gay religious groups. Gay Christians like Troy Perry have not forgotten the evangelical tradition; they have found in its Pentecostal variant a vision of grace with which to subdue a judgment of law.[2]

On the basis of his army service, Perry had a model of a heterogeneous but same-sex organization recruiting without regard to race, color, or creed, and he expected a religiously heterogeneous—albeit homosexual—assembly to appear in response to his advertisements. So he determined in advance to be pragmatically eclectic on the matter of ritual forms. For the first service, he took the advice and borrowed the robe of a minister friend who insisted that the modest circumstances of Perry's living room had to be set off by the dignity of clerical attire. Perry now wears a white cassock and black stole for services and a clerical collar and black shirt for his daily routine. Another friend advised Perry that Hollywood sophisticates would expect wine for communion, not the evangelical's grape juice, and that a weekly communion called for a sermon of no more than twenty minutes. MCC services now offer a choice of juice or wine.

Two other liturgical features developed to become characteristic of the MCC. Perry's one-time roommate, Willie Smith, who was raised a Seventh-Day Adventist, inaugurated the "Singspiration," a preservice hymn fest, during the first year, and many congregations now celebrate it. Even more entrenched in the MCC is an extended, emotionally and physically touching communion, where individual congregants or (more often) couples are enveloped in a lengthy embrace by the server, who whispers a personalized prayer into their ears (for a description, see Riley 1991, 18–22).

Thus, MCC services have come to feel like an eclectic mix of Catholic, Episcopal, and Lutheran liturgical forms with the preaching style, gospel hymns, and democratic prayer circle of twentieth-century charismatic fellowships. In his survey of pioneering MCC members, Dank found that those originally Roman Catholic were a plurality among the respondents, about a quarter, while those of Baptist background accounted for 14 percent (Dank 1973, 35–37; see also Enroth and Jamison 1974), proportions close to the makeup of the general religious population (Roof and McKinney 1987). The liturgical mix evidently worked, and a great variety of observers over the years have found the MCC service "a powerful statement of unity" (Gorman 1980, 70–72), "impressive and moving" (Coleman 1971, 117), and "the most grateful celebration of Christ I had ever attended" (Mollenkott 1979; see also Enroth and Jamison 1974, 31–34; Lyles 1983; Swicegood 1974, 186; and Glaser 1988, 38–39).

Yet the MCC is not for everyone, what with systematically varying religious tastes. One group in Atlanta was inspired by Troy Perry's vision but put off by high-church elements in the local MCC service, and they formed their own, more traditionally evangelical, congregation in 1977 (Thumma 1987, 123–125). On the other end of the spectrum, Laud Humphreys—gay man, ordained Episcopal priest, and sociology professor—told me that he could not stomach even the faint echo of biblical fundamentalism in Perry's preaching (interview with Laud Humphreys, Los Angeles, June 29, 1988). The MCC has, in other words, a denominational culture.

Like conventional religious organizations, MCCs are social as well as religious centers. This is an observation made by those friendly as well as those hostile to the enterprise. Barry Dank, an admirer of Perry's work, said of the MCC in 1970 that "the church has members who vary in religiosity from fundamentalist Protestant to agnostic and atheist. Two of the most active members, and the most socially committed, have been an agnostic and a Jew. Socially one can find the homosexually 'married couple' seeking friends, to the persons who come to church to find 'one-night stands'" (Dank 1973, 33–34). Bauer reports, on the basis of participant observation in the Denver parish of the MCC, that the congregation welcomed the cruiser. "The attitude is that 'They are here, as opposed to a gay bar, and are listening to the word of God'" (Bauer 1976, 121). Evangelical critics Enroth and Jamison (1974) have a less charitable view of the same phenomenon.

The upshot is that Perry and his early followers had the audacity to claim for homosexuals the social space given over to subcultural groups through American churches. The claim was not automatically honored. Soon after the founding, the church was visited by a contingent from the police vice squad seemingly bent on entrapment (Perry 1972, 137–138; Dank 1973, 29), and the congregation's early rental agreement with the Huntington Park Women's Club was abrogated when the club found out what kind of "church" their tenants were. The Los Angeles church was burned in 1973 and other MCC churches—in San Francisco, Nashville, New Orleans, and Atlanta—have been the target of arsonists over the years (Perry and Swicegood 1990, 71–72, 76). Yet, "church" has legitimating and mobilizing power in our society, and the MCC has taken advantage of it. Laud Humphreys (1972, 152) observed: "There are several advantages to such gay religious organizations. Due to the nation's tradition of religious freedom, gay churches enjoy some protection from legal and social stigma. This form of stigma redemption enables gays to deduct contributions to their cause from income taxes, as well as to profit from the tax-exempt status of their parsonages and meeting places. They can sponsor dances with little likelihood of police interference and provide an umbrella for a wide range of social, publishing, and service activities." A church was the ideal vehicle to address the twin needs of people like Carlos, Perry's friend under arrest: to stop persecution of gays by straight society and to heal gays' internal wounds. The solidarity provided by congregational religious life was the key to both ends.

Congregational and Denominational Development

The MCC became a recognizable church swiftly but not neatly. One step leapfrogged ahead of another: first a need-oriented program, then a formal structure, then vice versa. As people came forward to volunteer, Perry appointed assistant ministers, a board of directors, and deacons, but only later were procedures established to elect officers. A round-the-clock volunteer hotline known as the Crisis Intervention Committee assumed much of the traffic from Perry's home phone, which, even before he was on salary, rang incessantly with calls for information, counseling, and emergency aid. Legal incorporation of the congregation came one year after it was a going concern.

The denomination, the Universal Fellowship of Metropolitan Community Churches, was formed after another six months, by which time MCC outposts had already been established in San Diego and San Francisco and the Los Angeles congregation had been dubbed the "Mother Church." After a revival-style fundraising campaign, the Mother Church moved into its own remodeled home (a church built in 1906 but long since vacated) in March 1971. Perry stepped down as pastor in Los Angeles five years after the founding to become formal head (chief elder, or "Moderator") of the denomination, a full-time prophet and troubleshooter. Twenty-five years after the founding, a framed document on the wall of the current location of the Mother Church (just outside Los Angeles, in Culver City) testified anachronistically that the congregation had been chartered by the denomination on October 6, 1968. (These paragraphs are based on Swicegood 1974; Perry 1972; Enroth and Jamison 1974; Birchard 1977; and the author's field notes.)

Current Elder-Clerk Don Eastman recounts a decisive encounter between Perry and one of his ex-clergy coworkers, "Papa" John Hose, in the early days of the MCC. According to Eastman, Hose said that he drove Perry to Echo Park to take a look at Aimee Semple McPherson's Angelus Temple. Years after Sister Aimee's heyday in the 1920s and death in 1944, the Temple she founded seemed a mausoleum of dimly remembered charisma. "Do I have to tell you why I brought you here?" Hose reportedly said to Perry. The point was to warn the young leader what can happen to a church that is too closely built around the personality of one leader. Eastman said that, as influential as he is, Perry tries not to swing his weight too heavily in the MCC. Thus the church has institutionalized as an organized and democratic, not charismatic and authoritarian, body (interview with Donald Eastman, Los Angeles, August 15, 1989).

Today, the UFMCC has a presbyterian-style formal polity and an elaborate structure. It is governed by decisions made at biennial General Conferences, consisting of delegates from individual churches and regions; it is overseen by a seven-member board of elders (chaired by Perry from the outset), who are elected by the General Conference;[3] and it is administered by a staff under the direction of an elder-clerk, who, like Perry, is headquartered in Los Angeles. There are district coordinators in the United States, Canada, Australia, and England, a national AIDS ministry, a system of commissions charged with questions of clergy credentials and doctrine, a board of pensions, and a monthly two-color newsletter (Bedell 1993, 104; UFMCC 1991).

Social action has been on Perry's agenda for the UFMCC from the beginning. It was, after all, a police raid and the subsequent arrest of his friend Carlos that was Perry's catalyst for founding the church. The first extraparochial action came in April 1969. The Los Angeles congregation was asked to picket the local headquarters of a San Francisco shipping firm that had fired an employee when his picture appeared with his gay lover in the Berkeley Barb. The demonstration went on for days and drew abundant publicity, hostile as well as friendly. The man did not get his job back, but the demonstrators learned that they "weren't afraid of anything or anybody. . . . We had lost a battle, but our line was drawn" (Perry 1972, 149, 154).

A month later Perry endorsed a political candidate from the pulpit, a challenger to the Hollywood-area city councilman who had boasted of his support of

LAPD raids on gay bars. The incumbent lost and blamed "about three thousand homosexuals" and "slimy newspapers" for his defeat (Swicegood 1974, 233–234). In June 1970, Perry and the MCC were instrumental in overcoming police resistance to a permit for the first annual gay pride parade commemorating the Stonewall Riot. The permit granted, Willie Smith and Troy Perry were conspicuous in the parade (Perry 1972; Swicegood 1974).

Perry's clergy peers in the Mother Church, his board of directors, and the congregation were not unanimously in favor of these activities. Some felt they endangered the fragile life of the church; some did not want to be associated with the stylistic and political militants who could be expected to show up at parades; some said that the church paid Perry to be a pastor and preacher, not an activist; some complained of inadequate prior consultation with colleagues and members. A full congregational meeting was called by the board in July 1970, and Perry handily survived the vote of confidence only after hearing the remonstrations of some longtime allies.[4] But in subsequent years, Perry has testified before the California state legislature and helped pass a 1975 sexual privacy law, and the MCC helped defeat the 1978 Briggs initiative, a statewide plebiscite which would, among other measures, have denied the rights of gay persons to be schoolteachers (Perry and Swicegood 1990).

Yet the very possibility of activism rested on the fact that the MCC was first of all a church. The biggest MCC turnouts came for weekly worship services, where gay people could assemble in a benign setting to greet one another, sing, pray, hear inspired preaching, and take communion. Religion had to be at least part of the solution to gays' concerns, because it was so clearly a large part of their problem of guilt and isolation. Although Christianity is not inherently homophobic (Boswell 1980), most of its branches have been so for hundreds of years. Prejudice against gays pervades churches in the United States, and religiosity is the strongest single predictor of the widespread view that homosexuality is immoral (Greenberg 1988, 468). If it is true that many gay men are nonetheless deeply implicated in religion, there must be—alongside a natural chariness and suspicion of religious institutions—a huge built-in demand among gays for a religious message that would speak genuinely and positively to such needs by overturning religious condemnations. That is what the MCC provided.

In the view of Nancy Wilson, a member of the UFMCC clergy since 1972, former elder-clerk of the denomination, and currently pastor of the Mother Church, most people come to the MCC to find a "safe place," not to shake up society. Although Wilson herself has insisted since 1974 on bringing the UFMCC's cause before the National Council of Churches, she knows on the basis of her pastoring experience that "challenging" *a congregation* is a very middle-class religious idea. As the MCC expanded its constituency into the working class, she told me, the early emphasis on activism tended to fade. So when in her preaching she gets too far way from "God loves you" themes, she hears about it from her congregation (interview with Nancy Wilson, Culver City, December 3, 1989). Fundamentally, the MCC is a church, not a pressure group.

The MCC has been most successful in organizing new congregations in locales where two conditions obtain, a sufficient level of tolerance to have attracted a population of self-identified homosexuals and a social climate hospitable to religion. In pure form, these conditions would seem to be logical opposites, and we would not expect to find MCC congregations in Bible Belt hamlets or in North Korea. But cities in California and Florida combine the requisite social space with the religious ferment that MCC depends upon. The MCC is an urban church. But not all cities are fertile recruiting ground, and the MCC has been relatively more successful in religious locales like Dallas than in secularized venues like New York. For example, during 1993, the ten congregations of the UFMCC most often listed in their denomination's monthly roster of big givers ("Top Twenty Tithes") were located, from top down, in Houston, Jacksonville, Washington (D.C.), San Francisco, Fort Lauderdale, Toronto, Dallas, Long Beach (California), Culver City (the Los Angeles Mother Church), and St. Petersburg. The also-rans were in Sarasota, Kansas City, Denton (Texas), Tampa, and Sacramento. Conspicuously absent from this dominantly Sunbelt and heartland list were Boston and New York.[5]

The example of the MCC spurred the emergence of other groups directed to concerns of gays, for example Dignity, the association for gay and lesbian Catholics, founded in San Diego in 1969 by a former priest who had heard about Perry's work in Los Angeles. Upwards of twenty gay/lesbian Jewish synagogues have been formed in the United States since 1972, when Congregation Beth Chayim Chadashim began meeting at MCC–Los Angeles (Cooper 1989–1990). Between 1972 and 1976, parallel associations for gay and lesbian concerns were established in many mainline Christian groups, some of them "de-facto congregations" (Warner 1994a, 73–82), others "special purpose groups" (Wuthnow 1988, 100–131; see also Warner 1993a, 1064–1068).

The various religious groups—congregations and caucuses—for gay and lesbian concerns constitute a growing and relatively unified presence in the churches. The advent of Dignity, in particular, augmented the intellectual depth of the movement by bringing into play the tradition of Catholic scholarship. John McNeill, expelled from the Jesuit order because of his refusal to abandon his homophile ministry, is now the unofficial theorist of the movement, something that Troy Perry, whose own autobiographies had to be pieced together by professional writers out of snatches of interviews, legislative hearings, official letters, and extemporaneous sermons, would not claim for himself. Activists in these groups are often well connected to the national staffs of their respective denominations, and a nationwide network of gay Christian activists has been in place for fifteen years. (This paragraph based on Coleman 1987; McNeill 1987; and Rueda 1982, who is hostile to the movement but useful nonetheless.)

In the early 1970s, progress in the denominations for gay and lesbian concerns seemed to be rapid. Homophile groups were organized in most denominations. Two large Lutheran denominations and the Episcopal, United Methodist, southern Presbyterian, and Unitarian-Universalist churches as well as the United

Church of Christ went on record in support of civil rights for homosexuals. A self-affirming gay man was ordained in the UCC in 1972 and a lesbian in the Episcopal Church in 1977. In 1978 another gay man was retained as pastor of a Methodist congregation in New York City. The Catholic Church seemed in 1975 to have decided that homosexual orientation is morally neutral. A task force in the (northern) Presbyterian church appointed in 1976 was hopeful that its recommendation for ordination rights for gays would be approved at the 1978 national denominational assembly (Hewitt 1983). Sentiment was expressed in the MCC itself that they soon might be able to go out of business when the other churches caught up with them (Cleath 1970; Coleman 1971; Gorman 1980, 74–75).

The apogee of official reform may have come with the highly publicized application of the UFMCC for membership in the National Council of Churches in 1981. Although there was considerable sentiment in favor of the MCC among NCC staff and liberal delegates and although the MCC had been granted observer status in the ecumenical body, the question of membership raised for friends of the NCC the specter of conservative departures (particularly of the Eastern Orthodox bodies) that would further weaken the organization. The MCC application was first sent out for study, then postponed, then tabled (Lyles 1982, 1983). Yet the MCC will not leave the NCC alone, and in June 1991, the two groups convened a Dialogue Committee, with Revs. Kittredge Cherry and Nancy Wilson representing the UFMCC (Cherry 1991).

A backlash in the straight denominations slowed progress at the end of the 1970s, and to some extent, early progress was illusory. The various ordinations were actions of regional judicatories and did not set precedents for denominational policy. Conservative groups counter-mobilized when they heard of gay rights activities within their denominations, and motions to extend ordination rights to gays were crushed in the Presbyterian and Methodist churches. The Southern Baptist Convention hardened its already conservative stance.

Denominational pronouncements are the most overtly political of church activities. Churches are formally dedicated to ideology, and the more one moves to the higher organizational reaches, the more ideologies of all sorts are the primary agenda, untempered by personality (Warner 1994a, 60–61). As long as a morally conservative majority of American Protestantism is mobilized for a fight in denominational assemblies, formal recognition of the legitimacy of "gay Christians" in mainline Protestantism is unlikely. Conservatives will have to be outmaneuvered or persuaded; they are not outnumbered.

Adam traces the relative progress and regress to the contrast between "liberal Protestant congregations where policy is determined democratically" and "conservative Protestant, orthodox, and Roman Catholic churches, with authoritarian structures" (Adam 1987a, 136), but this formula is seriously misleading. The Presbyterian and Methodist backlashes were grassroots mobilizations against caucus-based liberal proposals, and aside from the MCC, the most vigorous discussion of gay rights in religion goes on in the Catholic Church. "Ironically, the most freedom to disagree with the 'official' position was found in the Roman Catholic Church, the most doctrinaire and hierarchical of all the denominations" (Hewitt 1983, 351; also 271–275, 307–308, 349).

Adam suffers from the common conflation of religious democracy with religious liberalism. Yet he has a point in stating that progress can be expected in some "congregations," for it is in congregations that gays can come together to define their own religious truth, as they did in the first MCC in 1968. In straight congregations, gays might expect the hard shell of received doctrine to be vulnerable to quiet, respectably uttered claims of humanity (Carrington 1990). Thus, many gay Christian activists have concluded that the struggle for recognition must move to the congregational level. Networks of local churches welcoming gays have come together among Presbyterians ("More Light" congregations), Methodists, and Lutherans ("Reconciled" congregations). Scores of Catholic and Episcopal parishes offer a home to gays. Some, whose advertisements can be found in gay newspapers, are overtly welcoming; others, known by word of mouth in gay and lesbian circles as "walk-in closets," keep a lower official profile.

However radical the eventual end point may be, the movement for gay and lesbian rights within the churches has proceeded by old-fashioned, often slow and protracted, religious means. This is true both for "open and affirming" congregations within straight denominations (Carrington 1990) and for the rise of an open and affirming denomination, the UFMCC, within the American religious system. In an obvious bid for normalization and respectability, Perry increasingly speaks of the UFMCC as "our denomination" (compare Perry 1972 with Perry and Swicegood 1990, especially 49–53), as if he and his followers are part of the American religious system for the long haul.

Evangelical Theology and Essentialist Anthropology

The ideology of the homophile movement was contested during the first years of the MCC, and gay Christians made a fateful contribution to the debate. Just when liberationists proclaimed the end of fixed sexual categories, Troy Perry preached that homosexuality was innate. Until recently, the former position was received wisdom among intellectuals, but the latter has become the party line within the gay community itself.[6]

Perry drew on lessons from the reformist stage of the movement for black civil rights (see Bloom 1987, 120–154). Gays, in this view, were a persecuted minority, but their first step to emancipation was to overcome their own fear. Only then could they stand together, face their oppressors, and demand the rights due to all persons. This much Perry learned from reading *The Homosexual in America* (Cory 1951). "When I finished the book I knew without the shadow of a doubt that I was a homosexual; I was gay. And there was just nothing for me to be afraid of any longer. This was it. I could honestly look at myself in the mirror, and say to myself, 'You know something, you're a homosexual.' And it didn't upset me" (Perry 1972, 78). Perry's 1972 autobiography opens with these words (Perry 1972, 3): "One thing is sure. We homosexuals must all learn to rid ourselves of the sense of shame that we have been conditioned to accept from the heterosexual world. Such shame is no longer acceptable to any of us. How could we go on being ashamed of something that God created? Yes, God created homosexuals and homosexuality. It exists throughout history, and all over the world." Coming out together would banish fear and conquer shame, which "comes, I think, through a sense of being alone. I'm sure that all homosexuals feel alone—often desperately alone—for long stretches of time. I know I did. And, being alone, being lonely, gives anyone a sense of solitary isolation. That is what has made us vulnerable to the oppressive nature of the heterosexual world."

In effect, Perry set out to build a positive identity on the basis of a given, previously devalued, category, "homosexuality." It was an audacious strategy, similar to Foucault's "reverse affirmation," wherein the members of a stigmatized group rally around the label applied to them and assert their pride in that identity (Epstein 1987, 17–18, citing Foucault 1980, 101).[7] Yet it was crucial to Perry's achievement that the basis of identity, "homosexuality," was a gift of God, not an arbitrary social imposition.

At the same time that Perry was drawing hundreds of recruits to his church, a more thoroughgoing assault on prejudice closer to Foucault's ideal was under way from people who wanted to overturn socially imposed gender categories themselves. At Catholic University in Washington, D.C., in 1970, a polite conference on religion and homosexuality heard an impolite proclamation from the D.C. Gay Liberation Front that began: "We demand that you stop examining our homosexuality and become homosexual yourselves" (Rueda 1982, 325). Stemming more from the cultural politics of the late 1960s than from the militant reformism of the early 1960s, radical gay liberation proposed to free all people from the dichotomized social shackles of homosexual versus heterosexual roles and masculine versus feminine identities. Drawing on the theories of Herbert Marcuse (that sexual repression is the foundation of social oppression) and the empirical findings of Alfred Kinsey and his associates (that there is a continuum rather than a dichotomy of heterosexual to homosexual experience), liberationists sought to unleash the bisexual and androgynous potential in everyone. *Homosexual: Oppression and Liberation* (Altman 1973) is usually cited as a theoretical manifesto of this phase of the movement.

By now, there is an immense academic literature on these matters, and the poles represented by Perry and Altman reflect positions now known as "essentialism" and "constructionism." The issues are complex, and they include debates on the etiology of same-sex attraction (see Ruse 1988; Gagnon 1987; Bell, Weinberg, and Hammersmith 1981; Whitam and Mathy 1986; Burr 1993). But the prior question is whether it makes sense to speak of homosexuality as a thing at all, as a state or condition which does or does not characterize the sexuality of a given individual, or whether homosexuality is not better understood as a concept that has been contingently applied to label (and stigmatize) a part of the infinite and plastic range of human behavior (Boswell 1982–1983). Such a simple matter as the indefinite article ("I am a homosexual" versus "I am homosexual") signals a philosophic gulf. The former idea, homosexuality as an essence, is the older and more conventional modern view, both in commonsense language and in social scientific and medical literature until the 1960s. The latter, homosexuality as a construct, is newer, postmodern, and more intellectually daring.

For our purposes, it is remarkable that, after an initial flirtation with the constructionist position around 1969 to 1972, the gay community in the United States hewed to the essentialist alternative.[8] At first, there was no consensus on the etiological question of what "causes homosexuality," and in fact many gay men evinced some hostility to the very question. But they did agree on the reality of homosexuality. The shoe fit, and they wore it (FitzGerald 1986, 57–58; Epstein 1987, 11–12; Adam 1987b, 747; Risman and Schwartz 1988, 129; Fierstein 1988, 52).[9]

The arguments for essentialism are many. Historian John Boswell studies the continuity of gay culture, which would disappear if the category were arbitrarily and externally imposed. Philosopher Michael Ruse adjudicates etiological theories, which would be nonsense if there were not something to explain. Sociologist Frederick Whitam wants to secure civil rights for homosexuals, and he believes that society is willing in principle to recognize rights for ascriptively defined groups, who are not responsible for their condition. "If the categories 'homosexual/heterosexual' and 'gay/straight' are the inventions of particular societies rather than real aspects of the human psyche, there is no gay history" (Boswell, 1982–1983, 93; see also Ruse 1988; Whitam and Mathy 1986; Grahn 1984).

The counterarguments are also many. For some, essentialism raises the specter of genocide, an ideology convenient for those who would as soon do away with homosexuals altogether. The innate homosexuality theory also justifies a policy of neglect with respect to AIDS as an essentially "gay disease" that straight society need not worry about. Essentialism divides gays from those who, by reason of their social stigma, are natural political allies. Essentialism reifies gender categories that disadvantage women in general and thereby tends to divide gay men from lesbians and feminists (Van Gelder 1991). Essentialism violates what many sociologists believe to be true about human personality (see Epstein 1987; Richardson 1983–1984; Thumma 1987).

But constructionists have, from the grassroots gay point of view, some unsavory allies themselves. They include therapists who trade on "curing" homosexuality, and cultural conservatives who maintain the childhood seduction theory in order to deny schoolteaching jobs to gays. Above all, there are the religious conservatives who insist that homosexuality is a "choice" subject to moral condemnation. Evangelical theologian Carl Henry, for example, says: "What the gay world needs is redemption, not reinforcement" (cited approvingly in Enroth and Jamison 1974, 133; see also Pattison and Pattison 1980; Dallas 1992; for surveys of the issues as they bear on religion see Thumma 1987; and Hewitt 1983).

To these threats, homophile Christians respond with endless variations on the essentialist theme:

Troy Perry:
> I caught the brass ring. And, I'm sure that homosexuality was in my genes, and in my soul, from the very beginning (Perry 1972, 10).

Chris Glaser, rejected candidate for ordination in the Presbyterian Church:
> Homosexuality is not a philosophy. It's what God made me (Glaser 1989).

Virginia Ramey Mollenkott, Plymouth Brethren scholar:
> One of the things I did was sit in front of a mirror, look myself in the eye, and say over and over again, "Virginia, you're a lesbian. God knew you were a lesbian from the foundation of the world, and God loved you, just as you are" (Mollenkott 1986).

"Thomas," member of a gay evangelical church in Atlanta, quoting a translation of Psalm 100, verse 3:
> It is He that hath made us and not we ourselves (cited in Thumma 1987, 133).

Malcolm Boyd, Episcopal priest:
> Gays have a "natural God-given sexual orientation" since they are "human beings created in God's image." "In time I offered thanks to God for the gift of being gay" (Boyd 1986, 74, 76, 2).

John McNeill, ex-Jesuit:
> God so created humans that they develop with a great variety of both gender identities and sexual-object choices. . . . Always and everywhere a certain percentage of men and women develop as homosexuals or lesbians. They should be considered as part of God's creative plan. Their sexual orientation has no necessary connection with sin, sickness, or failure; rather, it is a gift from God to be accepted and lived out with gratitude. God does not despise anything that God has created (McNeill 1987, 243).

Andrew Sullivan, Roman Catholic layman and editor of the *New Republic:*
> Like faith, one's sexuality is not simply a choice; it informs whole ways of being. . . . And like faith, it points toward something other and more powerful than the self (Sullivan 1994, 47).

Rev. Elder Nancy Wilson, MCC clergywoman since 1972:

> The first time Wilson went into a lesbian bar it was as if she had spent all her life to that point in Wonderland and had now walked through the looking glass back into the real world. It was a place where she could be all of who she was. "These are my people," she thought, and she used the Greek word, *ethne*, to express this. Through them, she felt linked to other of her people in every culture and in every epoch (interview with Nancy Wilson, 1989).[10]

John Shelby Spong, Episcopal Bishop of Newark, New Jersey:

> Research consistently seems to support the assertion that sexual orientation is not a matter of choice; that it is not related to any environmental influence; that it is not the result of an overbearing mother or absent father or a seductive sexual encounter (Spong 1988, 71–72).

Thomas Hanks, reviewing Greenberg (1988) in the UFMCC newsletter:

> If homosexuality is a social construct then conceivably a homosexual public school teacher might seduce a student and socially "construct/recruit" a homosexual out of an innocent heterosexual adolescent (Hanks 1990).

Mary Borhek, whose son is gay, formerly a member of an independent Pentecostal church, now an Episcopalian:

> I would point out that no one *chooses* his or her sexual orientation; it is a "given" with which each person has to learn to live (Borhek 1982, 462).

A group of parents of lesbians and gays, associated with Dignity:

> We "lean toward a biological cause" in part so as to put "an end to the blame game" (Griffin et al. 1986, 29–30).

The power of gay Christian essentialism is that it (1) invokes a powerful and benevolent God to proclaim the issue of homosexuality to be beyond human control, thereby concentrating the energy of gays themselves on changing their circumstances; (2) frees parents from doubt; (3) denies that homosexuality is in any way contagious; (4) expresses solidarity with grassroots gay culture; and (5) demands, as a matter of simple justice, inclusion of gays as simply another tile in the American mosaic. The strategy is pluralist, not revolutionary, since gays are presented to be the same as the rest of Americans by virtue of being trivially different: "We go to bed with members of our own sex" (D'Emilio 1983; Altman 1982, 123).[11]

It seems likely that grassroots essentialism stands behind what Randy Shilts called "the marked lack of hysteria among most Americans" toward the AIDS epidemic and what critic Susan Sontag conceded were "checks on the impulse to stigmatize people with the disease," even as it may have detracted from the urgency with which the medical crisis was addressed. Increased incidents of "gay bashing" cannot be denied, but neither can the political victories homophiles have won in most legislative referenda and the increased civil tolerance shown in public opinion polls in the 1980s (Shilts 1987, 353, 284, 519, 570; Sontag 1988, 97–99). If gay people are *essentially* different, the mass of society can feel the safer behind their symbolic boundary (see Douglas 1966). At the same time, essentialism seems to promote reconciliation with parents, since they are freed from self-recriminations and from anger over their children's willful rejection of their values. Outspoken parents, as represented in the nationwide organization Parents and Friends of Lesbians and Gays (PFLAG), pull essentialism in a pluralist rather than separatist direction (Griffin et al. 1986).

Always a pluralist reform movement rather than a radical reconstruction movement, the MCC was a repository of traditionalism available to gays gravitating toward moral conservatism in sexual relationships as knowledge of AIDS spread in the late 1980s and romance, dating, coupling, and family values came in style in the gay community (FitzGerald 1986, 119; Risman and Schwartz 1988, 142; Fierstein 1988, 48). From the beginning, the MCC has celebrated "holy unions" for committed couples who have lived together half a year and wish to proclaim public vows. In the same spirit, Nancy Wilson, current pastor of the MCC Mother Church and elected UFMCC elder, refuses to concede "family values" to the straight world: "I am a daughter, a sister, an aunt and a niece; a spouse in a committed relationship for ten years; a godmother; and a pastor to a local congregation (and to a worldwide MCC family)" (Wilson 1987, 845).

Above all, MCC congregations provide a setting for emotionally supportive interaction. The touching that has always characterized MCC services—the hand-to-hand prayer circle, the communion embrace—has acquired new sacramental meaning in the era of AIDS for those deemed untouchable elsewhere. The implicit trust inherent to a group known to each other first of all by their common stigma is deepened in testimony and prayer sessions by the disclosure of symptoms and test results. The heavy burden of giving care to the sick is borne more readily by those who know they are not alone and fear that they may need care next (see Cherry and Mitulski 1988; Riley 1991).

The theological wellspring of the MCC is the spirituality of Troy Perry, a life-long Pentecostal, who has prophesied in tongues from the MCC pulpit and gone into the desert to seek God's guidance (Perry and Swicegood 1990, 161, 307). Unlike many theological liberals and feminist theologians, Perry adheres to a concept of God as a personal and majestic transcendent being with the power to create homosexuals as well as heterosexuals and to demand that he, Perry, defy convention and establish a church for those of God's children left out by those who misunderstand this. Perry is empowered by that experience of God, and he founded the MCC on it. According to its by-laws, the UFMCC explicitly "moves in the mainstream of Christianity" and is officially committed to the historic creeds' affirmations of the trinity, the authority of scriptures, and salvation by faith (UFMCC 1991).[12] Perry has struggled to defend the MCC's theological and liturgical conservatism against assaults from what he calls "unitarian and less evangelical" pastors in the denomination, and he seems genuinely convinced that "all would be well" for the MCC only so long as "our church continued to follow Jesus" (Perry and Swicegood 1990, 307).

Toward the Future?

To mention Perry's "struggle" is to acknowledge that the MCC's ideology is not solely conservative. Beginning in 1972, under the prodding of its articulate women clergy, the UFMCC committed itself officially to gender equality and adopted inclusive language first for the officers specified in its by-laws and later for use in worship. The 1976 General Conference adopted "Once to Every Soul [instead of "Man"] and Nation" as its theme hymn, and in 1981 the General Conference adopted inclusive language as denominational policy. Now, by local congregational option, the Lord's Prayer may be addressed to "Our Creator" or "Our Sustainer" and the Gloria Patri has become "glory be to our maker" (Enroth and Jamison 1974, 82–84; Birchard 1977; UFMCC 1991; author's field notes).[13] These innovations were seen by Perry in evangelistic terms: "I came to the decision that . . . whatever language will reach the largest number of people is the language Metropolitan Community Church will use" (Perry and Swicegood 1990, 308; cf. Iannaccone and Miles 1990).

At first, lesbians, whose population numbers perhaps one-third to one-half as many as gay men in the United States, were severely underrepresented in MCC congregations. Near the end of the first decade of the church's existence, a lesbian critic could say that the "MCC has made progress toward grooming a number of women pastors of real competence, but in general Lesbians are few and far between and those who are attracted are not usually women who would identify themselves as Lesbian-feminists" (Krody 1977, 151). Some of the early women clergy identified more with older lesbian categories like "butch" than with newer feminist sensibilities. But in recent years, lesbians, including feminists, are becoming more prominent in the MCC, partly through the efforts of those very competent pastors Krody refers to, and partly because of the toll wrought by AIDS on the numbers of male MCC members and clergy. Reportedly, women now number 40 percent of MCC clergy and 30 percent of members (Eastman 1989).

Inclusive language represents the MCC's collective attempt to bridge a gap that plagues homophile organizations even more than straight ones, the fact that the "gay-and-lesbian" conjunction is a product of social construction and movement politics, but not of folk culture, let alone any essential reality. Since the development of homosexual cultures after World War II, gays and lesbians have had separate spaces—their own bars—and very different manners. In ideology, lesbian feminists uphold values of cooperation and equality in contrast to masculine values of dominance. Lesbians are more likely than gay men to have no religious affiliation or to identify with a "personal spirituality" or other non-Christian religion. Women in the MCC are more likely than men to describe themselves as theologically liberal. Lesbians are far more likely to be monogamous than gay men. Pornography is more important for gay men than for lesbians, and increasingly so as a means of safe sex in the world of AIDS. A lesbian is more likely to identify as such when she is already in love with another woman or because of a belief in women's solidarity, a gay man because of generalized attraction for persons of the same sex. Furthermore, women coming to lesbianism since Stonewall are likely to have done so within the context of supportive political groups and therefore do not have the problem with guilt and self-hatred that many gay men do. Constructionist theory is therefore closer to lesbian than to gay male experience. (This paragraph based on Adam 1987a; Altman 1982, 45–47; Cherry 1992; Esterberg 1990; Faderman 1984; FitzGerald 1986, 35, 56–57; Herek 1985; McKirnan and Peterson 1987; Neitz 1988; Reback 1988; Risman and Schwartz 1988; Ruse 1988, 9–10; and author's field notes).

Take "Goddess" language, for example. Perry does not approve of it, and he so expressed himself in a pastoral letter to the UFMCC membership in 1989. Yet the pastor of SisterSpirit, a hybrid pagan-MCC congregation in Oregon, does use Goddess language, and for several years in the 1980s De Colores, a multiethnic feminist group at UFMCC headquarters, experimented with God languages. There was something of a showdown on the issue at the General Conference of 1989, held in Minneapolis, when Nancy Wilson and five other women visited Perry in his suite to protest his pastoral letter. Herself deeply ambivalent about Goddess language, Wilson led the group in solidarity with those for whom it is empowering. According to Wilson, Perry backed down a bit from the position taken in his letter and said that his letter was just an expression of his "opinion." "When you say something, people listen," Wilson recalls telling him. "So please be more careful if it's just an opinion" (Wilson interview, 1989).

The MCC today is increasingly gender integrated as a denomination, but there tends to be intercongregational gender differentiation. For example, the Mother Church, Perry's own first MCC pulpit, is now majority lesbian under its second woman pastor (Wilson interview and author's field notes). Not all lesbians have the same religious needs and not all are theologically liberal; Dusty Pruitt, former naval officer and later pastor of MCC Long Beach, prefers the original Pentecostally inspired MCC spirituality to Goddess worship (interview with Dusty Pruitt, Princeton, New Jersey, October 2, 1993). Nonetheless, in some congregations, feminist lesbians are bringing New Age spirituality, Goddess worship, and universalism into the originally Pentecostal and trinitarian MCC mix. The unsettled relationship and ideological differences between gays and lesbians is without doubt the main internal source of change in the UFMCC today.

NOTES

For comments on a previous draft, I am indebted to Michael Gorman, Mary Jo Neitz, Leonard Norman Primiano, and Scott Thumma.

1. According to Enroth and Jamison (1974, 75-76), MCC members were split over dispensationalist fundamentalism versus Pentecostalism, but Perry is thoroughly Pentecostal.

2. For conservative evangelical responses to Perry's efforts, see Enroth and Jamison 1974, 39—60; cf. Bartlett 1977. Many gay Christians harbor the notion that Paul was a celibate homosexual; such was the "thorn" in his flesh (Boyd 1986, 24). The French Catholic society for gays is called David et Jonathan (Adam 1987a, 137). For a survey of claims about homosexuals in scripture, see Boswell 1980.

3. By provision of the by-laws, Perry is elder-for-life, subject to removal only for dereliction of duty.

4. Swicegood (1974, 307—309) reports that only 122 of 300 regulars showed up for this meeting. Of those, the vote was overwhelmingly in Perry's favor, and at the same meeting, he was voted a salary increase. But the relatively low turnout may indicate a widespread lack of interest in political activism.

5. Data for this paragraph come from the feature "Top 20 Tithes" in monthly issues of the UFMCC newsletter, *Keeping in Touch*, for 1993. The concentrated "lavender ghettoes" of New York and San Francisco in the late 1970s were in some measure an alternative source of the "safe space" and psychic exhilaration that the MCC provided. For men from midwestern fundamentalist backgrounds, coming out in the 1970s in San Francisco's Castro community was "a profound experience . . . something like the evangelical experience of being 'born again': it lifted a huge burden and gave them a fresh start" (FitzGerald 1986, 47). According to theorist Steven Epstein, San Francisco was to gays in the United States what Israel is to Jews in the Diaspora, "a focal point for cultural identity, that functions even for those who are not firmly integrated into the culture" (Epstein 1987, 21). See also Gorman 1980.

6. This section is deeply indebted to Epstein 1987 and Thumma 1987. I have also drawn on Altman 1982, D'Emilio 1983, FitzGerald 1986, Herek 1985, Richardson 1983—1984, Risman and Schwartz 1988, Sullivan 1994, and six years of letters to the editor and opinion columns in the *Windy City Times*, Chicago's gay and lesbian weekly.

7. Years earlier, Talcott Parsons had written of the possibility of collectivization of "deviant" statuses; he liked to say that individual isolation that the American "sick role" imposes tends to prevent the development of "magic-mountain-like" communities of the deviant, an allusion to Thomas Mann's novel.

8. See Warren 1974 for a cultural portrait of gay men in San Diego at a time prior to the hegemony of grassroots essentialism. Regarding the lesbian movement, Judy Grahn recalls: "In the early days of the lesbian/feminist groundswell there was a song going around, and I remember singing it: 'Any woman can be a lesbian.' I suppose that Gay men have had similar doctrines of enthusiasm for a reborn cause. But I have come not to believe it" (Grahn 1984, 274).

9. To some extent, constructionist theorists and grassroots essentialists are talking past one another. The former focus on the construction of conscious *identity* and the latter on the reality of the presumed underlying *orientation*. In fact, Perry's autobiography offers

ample material for a constructionist reading of the process by which he came to recognize his homosexuality. Perry insists only on a rather fanciful account of his essential being. Epstein (1987) does the best job that I have come across of untangling these issues.

10. Wilson recommended to me the work of Judy Grahn, who writes (1984, xii–xiv): "Gay culture is ancient. . . . The gay culture I have set out to describe is old, extremely old, and it is continuous. . . . What gives any group of people distinction and dignity is its culture. This includes a remembrance of the past and a setting of itself in a world context whereby the group can see who it *is* relative to everyone else."

11. "[W]e might predict that constructionists would experience considerable difficulties in leading the gay masses to a state of 'true consciousness,' given that constructionism poses a real and direct threat to the ethnic legitimation: people who base their claims to social rights on the basis of a group identity will not appreciate being told that identity is just a social construct; and people who see their sexual desires as fixed——as 'just the way we are'——are unlikely to adopt a viewpoint that presents 'sexual scripting' as a fluid, changeable process open to intentional redefinition" (Epstein 1987, 22).

In a review of Whitam and Mathy's outspokenly essentialist book (1986), the scientific argument of which she rejects, Barbara Risman (1988, 554) writes:

The authors argue convincingly that anti-gay forces on the New Right use scholarly work in the constructionist and social learning traditions to bolster their argument that homosexuality is a choice, and therefore a sin. . . . Minority-group status seems to be reserved for those groups based on ascribed characteristics. . . . The authors have raised serious ethical issues for sociologists who find their work on homosexuality used to further the New Right agenda. . . . The argument that homosexuality is biologically programmed may be not only more effective but even necessary to win rights for homosexuals in the foreseeable future.

When an approving review of David Greenberg's *The Construction of Homosexuality* (1988) appeared in the Chicago gay and lesbian press, a reader responded that the reviewer "fails to mention the big problem with viewing homosexuality as a social peculiarity. If that's all it is (if we're not 'born that way'), what morally constrains a predominantly heterosexual society from attempting to rid itself of it? On the other hand, if homosexuality will always be with us no matter what we do, wouldn't a wise and compassionate society prevent a lot of agony (and bloodshed) if it made an honest accommodation with it?" (*Windy City Times*, March 2, 1989, 10–11).

12. The church also recognizes two sacraments, baptism and communion, and practices six rites, those of ordination, confirmation of membership, holy union, funeral, laying on of hands, and blessing.

13. Nonetheless, according to MCC pastor Dusty Pruitt, eleven of the twelve largest MCC congregations tend to resist the depersonalization of God that often accompanies inclusive language and instead welcome the expression of Pentecostal gifts of the spirit in their worship. Her own experience has been that Pentecostalism is empowering in the MCC (Pruitt 1993).

REFERENCES

(References to writings of the author are found in a separate listing at the back of the book.)

Adam, Barry D. 1987a. *The Rise of a Gay and Lesbian Movement.* Boston: Twayne Publishers.
———. 1987b. Review of Whitam and Mathy 1986. *Contemporary Sociology* 16 (September): 747–748.
Altman, Dennis. 1973. *Homosexual: Oppression and Liberation.* New York: Avon Books.

———. 1982. *The Homosexualization of America, The Americanization of the Homosexual*. New York: St. Martin's Press.

Arthur, L. Robert. 1982. *Homosexuality and the Conservative Christian*. Los Angeles: Samaritan Theological Institute.

Bartlett, David L. 1977. "A Biblical Perspective on Homosexuality." *Foundations: A Baptist Journal of History and Theology* 20 (April—June): 133—147.

Bauer, Paul F. 1976. "The Homosexual Subculture at Worship: A Participant Observation Study." *Pastoral Psychology* 25 (Winter): 115—127.

Bedell, Kenneth. 1993. *Yearbook of American and Canadian Churches, 1993*. Nashville, TN: Abingdon, for the National Council of Churches.

Bell, Alan P., Martin S. Weinberg, and Sue Kiefer Hammersmith. 1981. *Sexual Preference: Its Development in Men and Women*. Bloomington: Indiana University Press.

Birchard, Roy. 1977. "Metropolitan Community Church: Its Development and Significance." *Foundations: A Baptist Journal of History and Theology* 20 (April—June): 127—132.

Bloom, Jack M. 1987. *Class, Race, and the Civil Rights Movement*. Bloomington: Indiana University Press.

Borhek, Mary V. 1982. "Can the NCC Accept a Gay Denomination?" *Christian Century* 99 (April 14): 461—462.

Boswell, John. 1980. *Christianity, Social Tolerance, and Homosexuality. Gay People in Western Europe from the Beginning of the Christian Era to the Fourteenth Century*. Chicago: University of Chicago Press.

———. 1982—1983. "Revolutions, Universals, and Sexual Categories." *Salmagundi* 58/59 (Fall/Winter): 89—113.

Boyd, Malcolm. 1984. *Take Off the Masks*. Philadelphia: New Society.

———. 1986. *Gay Priest: An Inner Journey*. New York: St. Martin's Press.

Burr, Chandler. 1993. "Homosexuality and Biology." *Atlantic Monthly* 271 (March): 47—65.

Carrington, Christopher. 1990. "Respectability: The Inclusion of Gay Men and Lesbians in the Congregational Life of Liberal Protestantism." Paper presented at annual meeting of the Society for the Scientific Study of Religion, Virginia Beach, Va.

Cherry, Kittredge. 1991. "UFMCC Has Ecumenical Impact." *Keeping in Touch* (UFMCC newsletter), July.

———. 1992. "Survey Reveals UFMCC Women's Needs." *Keeping in Touch* (UFMCC newsletter), March.

Cherry, Kittredge, and James Mitulski. 1988. "We Are the Church Alive, the Church with AIDS." *Christian Century* 105 (January 27): 85—88.

Cleath, Robert. 1970. "The Homosexual Church." *Christianity Today* 14 (September 11): 48—50.

Coleman, Gerald D. 1987. "The Vatican Statement on Homosexuality." *Theological Studies* 48: 727—734.

Coleman, John A. 1971. "The Churches and the Homosexual." *America* 124 (February 6): 113—117.

Cooper, Aaron. 1989—1990. "No Longer Invisible: Gay and Lesbian Jews Build a Movement." *Journal of Homosexuality* 18, 3—4: 83—94.

Cory, Donald Webster (pseudonym for Edward Sagarin). 1951. *The Homosexual in America: A Subjective Approach*. New York: Greenberg.

Dallas, Joe. 1992. "Born Gay?" *Christianity Today* 36 (June 22): 20—23.

Dank, Barry M. 1973. *The Development of a Homosexual Identity: Antecedents and Consequents*. Ph.D. diss., Department of Sociology, University of Wisconsin.

Dart, John. 1969. "A Church for Homosexuals." *Los Angeles Times* (December 8).

———. 1991. "Church for Gays Alters Mainline Religions' Views." *Los Angeles Times* (June 7).

D'Emilio, John. 1983. *Sexual Politics, Sexual Communities: The Making of a Homosexual Minority in the United States, 1940—1970*. Chicago: University of Chicago Press.

Douglas, Mary. 1966. *Purity and Danger: An Analysis of the Concepts of Pollution and Taboo.* London: Routledge and Kegan Paul.

Duberman, Martin. 1993. *Stonewall.* New York: Dutton.

Enroth, Ronald E., and Gerald E. Jamison. 1974. *The Gay Church.* Grand Rapids, Mich.: Eerdmans.

Epstein, Steven. 1987. "Gay Politics, Ethnic Identity: The Limits of Social Constructionism." *Socialist Review* 17 (May–August): 9–54.

Esterberg, K. G. 1990. "Salience and Solidarity: Identity, Correctness, and Conformity in a Lesbian Community." Paper presented at annual meeting of the American Sociological Association, Washington, D.C.

Faderman, Lillian. 1984. "The 'New Gay' Lesbians." *Journal of Homosexuality* 10 (Winter): 85–95.

Fierstein, Harvey. 1988. Playboy Interview, conducted by H. Stein. *Playboy* 35 (August): 43–57.

FitzGerald, Frances. 1986. *Cities on a Hill: A Journey Through Contemporary American Cultures.* New York: Simon and Schuster.

Foucault, Michel. 1980. *The History of Sexuality.* Vol. 1. *An Introduction.* New York: Vintage.

Gagnon, John. 1987. Review of Whitam and Mathy 1986. *American Journal of Sociology* 93 (November): 742–744.

Glaser, Chris. 1988. *Uncommon Calling: A Gay Man's Struggle to Serve the Church.* San Francisco: Harper and Row.

———. 1989. "Gays, Lesbians, and the Church." Talk given at Nassau Presbyterian Church, Princeton, N.J., March 12.

Godfrey, Brian J. 1988. *Neighborhoods in Transition: The Making of San Francisco's Ethnic and Nonconformist Communities.* Berkeley and Los Angeles: University of California Press.

Gorman, E. Michael. 1980. *A New Light on Zion: A Study of Three Homosexual Religious Congregations in Urban America.* Ph.D. diss., Department of Anthropology, University of Chicago.

Grahn, Judy. 1984. *Another Mother Tongue: Gay Words, Gay Worlds.* Boston: Beacon Press.

Greenberg, David F. 1988. *The Construction of Homosexuality.* Chicago: University of Chicago Press.

Griffin, Carolyn Welch, Marian J. Wirth, and Arthur G. Wirth. 1986. *Beyond Acceptance: Parents of Lesbians and Gays Talk About Their Experiences.* Englewood Cliffs, N.J.: Prentice–Hall.

Hanks, T. 1990. Review of Greenberg 1988. *Keeping in Touch* (May): 3–4.

Herek, Gregory M. 1985. "On Doing, Being, and Not Being: Prejudice and the Social Construction of Homosexuality." *Journal of Homosexuality* 12 (Fall): 135–151.

Hewitt, Thomas Furman. 1983. *The American Church's Reaction to the Homophile Movement, 1948–1978.* Ph.D. diss., Department of Religion, Duke University.

Humphreys, Laud. 1972. *Out of the Closets: The Sociology of Homosexual Liberation.* Englewood Cliffs, N.J.: Prentice-Hall.

Iannaccone, Laurence R., and Carrie A. Miles. 1990. "Dealing with Social Change: The Mormon Church's Response to Change in Women's Roles." *Social Forces* 68 (June): 1231–1250.

Krody, Nancy. 1977. "An Open Lesbian Looks at the Church." *Foundations: A Baptist Journal of History and Theology* 20 (April–June): 148–162.

Lucas, Charles. 1972. "Postscript." In *The Lord Is My Shepherd and He Knows I'm Gay: The Autobiography of the Rev. Troy D. Perry as told to Charles Lucas,* 229–232. Los Angeles: Nash.

Lyles, Jean Caffey. 1982. "What's Good for the NCC." *Christian Century* 99 (December 1): 1222–1223.

———. 1983. "The Unity They Seek." *Christian Century* 100 (June 1): 539–540.

McKirnan, David, and Peggy L. Peterson. n.d. [1987.] *General Findings from the Social Issues Survey: Population Characteristics, Substance Abuse, and AIDS Risk among Homosexuals.* Typescript. Department of Psychology, University of Illinois at Chicago.

McNeill, John J. 1987. "Homosexuality: Challenging the Church to Grow." *Christian Century* 104 (March 11): 242–246.

Mollenkott, Virginia Ramey. 1979. "Joyful Worship in the Midst of Danger." *Christian Century* 96 (September 26): 910.

———. 1986. "Gay/Lesbian Gifts to the Church." *Windy City Times* (November 13), 12.

Neitz, Mary Jo. 1988. "Sacramental Sex in Modern Witchcraft Groups." Paper presented at annual meeting of the Midwest Sociological Society, Minneapolis.

Pattison, E. Mansell, and Myrna Loy Pattison. 1980. " 'Ex-Gays': Religiously Mediated Change in Homosexuals." *American Journal of Psychiatry* 137 (December): 1553–1562.

Perry, Troy D. 1972. *The Lord Is My Shepherd and He Knows I'm Gay: The Autobiography of the Rev. Troy D. Perry as told to Charles Lucas.* Los Angeles: Nash.

Perry, Troy D., and Thomas L. P. Swicegood. 1990. *Don't Be Afraid Anymore: The Story of Reverend Troy Perry and the Metropolitan Community Churches.* New York: St. Martin's Press.

Pruitt, Dusty. 1993. "Power and Powerlessness: The Appeal of Charismatic Christianity to the Gay and Lesbian Community." Paper presented to the ISAE Consultation on Pentecostal Currents in the American Church, Princeton, N.J.

Reback, Cathy. 1988. "Lesbian Virgins: A Study of Redefining Identities." Paper presented at annual meetings of the American Sociological Association, Atlanta.

Richardson, Diane. 1983–1984. "The Dilemma of Essentiality in Homosexual Theory." *Journal of Homosexuality* 9 (Winter–Spring): 79–90.

Riley, C. T. 1991. " 'Our God Too': Family Formation and Normalization in the Metropolitan Community Church of Pittsburgh." Paper presented at annual meeting of the Society for the Scientific Study of Religion, Pittsburgh.

Risman, Barbara. 1988. Review of Whitam and Mathy 1986. *Social Forces* 67 (December): 553–554.

Risman, Barbara, and Pepper Schwartz. 1988. "Sociological Research on Male and Female Homosexuality." *Annual Review of Sociology* 14: 125–147.

Roof, Wade Clark, and W. McKinney. 1987. *American Mainline Religion.* New Brunswick, N.J.: Rutgers University Press.

Rueda, Enrique. 1982. *The Homosexual Network: Private Lives and Public Policy.* Greenwich, Conn.: Devin Adair.

Ruse, Michael. 1988. *Homosexuality: A Philosophical Inquiry.* Oxford: Basil Blackwell.

Shilts, Randy. 1987. *And the Band Played On: Politics, People, and the AIDS Epidemic.* New York: St. Martin's Press.

Sontag, Susan. 1988. "AIDS and Its Metaphors." *New York Review of Books* 35 (October 27): 89–99.

Spong, John Shelby. 1988. *Living in Sin? A Bishop Rethinks Human Sexuality.* San Francisco: Harper and Row.

Sullivan, Andrew. 1994. "Alone Again, Naturally: The Catholic Church and the Homosexual." *New Republic* 211 (November 28): 47–55.

Swicegood, Tom. 1974. *Our God Too.* New York: Pyramid Books.

Thumma, Scott. 1987. *Straightening Identities: Evangelical Approaches to Homosexuality.* Master's thesis, Candler School of Theology, Atlanta.

Tobin, Kay, and Randy Wicker. 1972. *The Gay Crusaders.* New York: Paperback Library.

UFMCC. 1991. *Universal Fellowship of Metropolitan Community Churches By-Laws: Revised at General Conference XV.* Los Angeles: UFMCC.

Van Gelder, Lindsy. 1991. "The 'Born That Way' Trap." *MS* (May/June): 86–87.

Warren, Carol A. B. 1974. *Identity and Community in the Gay World.* New York: Wiley-Interscience.

Whitam, Frederick L., and Robin M. Mathy. 1986. *Male Homosexuality in Four Societies: Brazil, Guatemala, the Philippines, and the United States.* New York: Praeger.

Wilson, Nancy L. 1987. "A Gay Witness to Pope John Paul II," *Christian Century* 104 (October 7): 845—846.

Windy City Times: Chicago's Gay and Lesbian Newsweekly. 1985—1991.

Wuthnow, Robert. 1988. *The Restructuring of American Religion: Society and Faith since World War II.* Princeton, N.J.: Princeton University Press.

10

Seeing the Word in a Church for the Deaf (1993)

(WITH JAMES S. PAPPAS)

It's wise to show up on time for the 10:30 Mass in the chapel of St. Francis Borgia Church on Chicago's far west side, where the Roman Catholic Deaf Center meets. On the several occasions we have visited, there have been few extra seats. For most of this century, the Deaf Center, also known as Chicago Catholic Ephpheta (from Mark 7:34) or CCE, has met at one or another parish around Chicago under pastoral leadership of Jesuits or priests of some other religious order. For three years (1969–1972) when CCE had no pastor, Nancy Huber, a hearing laywoman who is now religious education coordinator for the archdiocese's Office of the Deaf, held the group together as a volunteer. Since 1977 the pastor has been a diocesan priest, Fr. Joe Mulcrone, and for the past ten years the Deaf Center has made St. Francis Borgia its home.

Though it's a boxy, plain, small room seating only three hundred, the chapel works. American Sign (ASL) requires visual access to the face, hands, and torso of the speaker, so this arrangement is preferable to the long nave and cruciform plan of Chicago's grand nineteenth-century parish churches and the in-the-round seating of some contemporary ones. Yet, small as the room is, people do not pack into the pews, for they need space for the rapid arm and hand gestures that express liturgical responses, even if "and also with you." What the mouth and ears are to the hearing, the hands and eyes are to the deaf.

Not everyone who attends is deaf: the members of our sociology of religion class last September joined the regular contingent of hearing children of deaf parents and other hearing loved ones, friends and visitors, for whom Father Joe, a hearing person who grew up with deaf grandparents, provides a simultaneous oral/aural interpretation of the proceedings. When a member of the congregation steps forward to begin the service by signing "Good morning" and spelling out the names of the celebrant, the deacon, the lector, the eucharistic minister, the ushers and, on occasion, the members of the choir, Father Joe, seated on the aisle in the second row, speaks to us aloud what the commentator is signing.

On one visit there was indeed a choir, five men and women, who stood facing the congregation (and their director in the first pew) to sign the responsorial psalm and later a closing anthem. Standing farther from one another than would a hearing choir, they signed "the earth and everything in it belong to the Lord" in stately unison with broad, sweeping gestures.

The Mass is by no means silent. Plenty of sound, much of it random, comes from planes landing at nearby O'Hare Airport, restless youngsters, crying babies, deaf persons educated under oralist methods, the clap of hands signing "amen," and the voices of hearing guests. At one point Father Joe jokes bilingually that "sometimes you're lucky to be deaf": you don't have to hear the "singing babies."

Although he is more than cordial to the hearing, Father Joe makes a point of limiting leadership roles to deaf participants. Thus the lectionary reading was presented by a deaf layman, clearly and vigorously signing the passage as it appears in *The Holy Bible: English Version for the Deaf.* We were told that this is the first Bible for the deaf. It is a Protestant edition (omitting so-called apocryphal material), but a Roman Catholic committee is currently using it to develop a lectionary for the deaf.

Standing and kneeling in the service are minimized to maintain visual access, and people do not bow their heads for prayer. Nor do they look at the ceiling. Father Joe likes to say that the deaf congregation is the most attentive he's ever served. The priest is often assisted by a deaf deacon. After Father Joe blessed his hands that they might speak God's truth, Deacon Casey Fronczek signed the Gospel reading and preached the homily, while Father Joe assumed his interpreter's seat in the second row. In his discourse, Deacon Casey posed a number of rhetorical questions, and the parishioners answered him (a pattern of response we were more accustomed to seeing in African American churches).

After the homily, Father Joe returned to the altar for the Eucharist and led the congregation in the Lord's Prayer (the signing of which requires an astonishing amount of communal motion) and the passing of the Peace, which is signed by crossing the palms twice—right over left and left over right—while facing the person one is greeting. (If you are facing in the wrong direction, you may be tapped on the shoulder from behind to gain your attention for the rite. Signing and touching, we realized, directly connect sender and receiver.)

Father Joe pronounces the communion rite simultaneously in ASL and oral English, holding the wafer with one hand while signing with the other. Parishioners reported to us that they find his delivery a satisfying part of the Mass. His signing is smooth and crisp, and the routine of the liturgy allows him to accentuate meaning in three dimensions and extend the words of the institution to add greater depth to the Eucharist. To the hearing, his voice carries warmth and authority.

Announcements usually follow Communion, and on one visit, Father Joe alerted parishioners to the imminent voter-registration deadline and told them where deaf people could get help to register. On the Sunday before Christmas, before concluding the Mass Father Joe invited an honored guest to the lectern: Sister Alverna Hollis, a missionary on vacation from her post in Peru who had served CCE years before. She asked Father Joe to be ready to interpret not only in oral English but also in ASL since she, a hearing person now ministering in another sign language to the deaf, had let her ASL get rusty. She spoke of social conditions in Peru in general and for the deaf in particular. The Chicago congregation presented her with a round of applause (both hands swiveling rapidly above the head) and a $1000 check to further her work.

Father Joe asked Sister Alverna to illustrate some differences between the two sign languages. The word "man" in Peru is signed by touching a finger to the upper lip, as if to indicate a moustache. (In ASL, one says "man" by touching the forehead and chest.) But in both languages, "God" is the same—one arm stretched upward, palm outward, and then brought down in an arc—for, said Sister Alverna, "I taught it to them." Here is another expression of ecumenism: outreach from Chicago Catholic Ephpheta to deaf Christians of the world.

The congregation does not disperse as soon as its members hear that "the Mass is ended." They stay not only for an occasional closing choral anthem but also for the extended coffee hour that follows, where the air is full of the hands of hundreds of deaf people catching up with one another's activities. Father Joe understands the importance of after-church socializing from the experience of an uncle who was pastor in a rural parish in the days before telephones were common. As with those in his uncle's parish, the members of this congregation live in conditions that isolate them. Seeing one another is special. The parish leaders also make sure that a literature table carries publications, religious and otherwise, directed to the concerns of the deaf.

We took the opportunity to converse with several parishioners, who, with Domenica Pappas interpreting, helped us appreciate what we had seen. One hard-of-hearing man, educated in oralist schools and far from fluent in ASL, nonetheless welcomed the opportunity to worship among the deaf, who appreciate with him how much one misses through lip-reading alone. A deaf man told us about the parish's months-long collective effort at growing and selling vegetables to come up with the thousand-dollar contribution for Sister Alverna's work.

Intrigued by the concept of different signs for "man" among sign languages but a transcultural sign for "God," we asked if ASL expresses a gender for God. Huber told us that ASL has no pronouns; thus one does not call God "he" or "she." Father Joe, who always speaks with his hands, adding his voice when addressing hearing persons, noted that deaf Catholics nonetheless are deeply devoted to the Virgin. He explained that, on the basis of studies of deaf spirituality, deaf people tend to be closer to their mothers (who go out of their way to learn sign language) than their fathers (who usually do not, and therefore play a shadowy role in their deaf children's imaginations).

As we looked over the congregational conversation—whites and blacks, Latinos and Asians, young and old, well dressed and casual, raised in English-speaking and non-English-speaking families, the physically able and the lame, people gathered from homes all over the metropolitan area—it occurred to us that deafness, like mortality and sexuality and unlike race and class, is a sociological wild card, confounding rather than mirroring social divisions. Although in one sense the congregation is homogeneous, in another sense it draws people from every background. The Christian celebration of ecclesia, union out of difference, takes on a new meaning in this congregation.

11

Elizondo's Pastoral Theology in Action

An Inductive Appreciation (2000)

> Much of Virgil's best theological work is not published on the printed page. . . . [Elizondo is seen] at his best . . . when he is interacting with people and building on the energy that the group dynamic creates. Unfortunately, we cannot fully present the experience of this living engagement between the two covers of this book. My suggestion is that readers . . . go to San Fernando Cathedral for Holy Week. . . . There you will see, hear, touch, sense, and smell the rich ritual life that illuminates Virgil's . . . pastoral theology in action.
>
> —Timothy M. Matovina, *Beyond Borders*

Introduction

Five years before *Beyond Borders* went to press, I did just what Timothy Matovina recommends, going to San Fernando Cathedral for Holy Week. As an ethnographer, I had been asked to join a team of scholars at the Mexican American Cultural Center who were working on a project to interpret the ritual language employed at the cathedral under the tutelage of its then-pastor, Virgil Elizondo. My host, the project's associate director, was none other than Tim Matovina, a perfectly bilingual active Catholic. Knowing that I was neither Catholic nor bilingual and that I was unfamiliar with Elizondo's work, Tim agreed to serve as an interpreter and informant, and he shared a great deal of his wisdom with me during my three days in San Antonio. But for the rituals themselves we consultants were advised to "lose ourselves among the people"; thus I was often on my own to observe ceremonies whose literal sense I could not understand. So I had to pay heed to a lot of nonverbal messages, and my perspective was that of an outsider.

The text immediately following, including notes 3 through 13, is the bulk of the report I wrote for Tim and Virgil and their project upon my return to Chicago but before I had read any of their writings. In the intervening years, inspired by my experience at San Fernando, I have read many of Elizondo's writings, including those reprinted in this volume, and have testified to his influence on my own work.[1] My report will thus serve as relatively uncoached testimony to the effect that as a pastoral theologian Elizondo practices what he preaches. The field report to follow describes Elizondo's practice as I saw it; the indented quotations, taken from Elizondo's essays as reprinted in *Beyond Borders* and listed at the end of this essay, were added five years later as textual evidence of the preaching that corresponds to the practice I earlier witnessed. The "conclusion," written for the 2000 publication, reflects on Elizondo's pastoral theology in action.

Field Report: An Outsider's Experience of Holy Week Observances at San Fernando Cathedral

I was invited to San Antonio to share my reactions to the Holy Week observances.[2] My hosts particularly wanted me to interpret the ritual language employed in the massive Passion play held on Good Friday—the Via Crucis pageant, in which a young man of the parish appointed for the day to be Jesus drags a heavy wooden cross from "Pilate's palace" in the tourist-oriented Mercado (Mexican market) to "Calvary" in the town plaza a half mile away. I did what I was asked and joined the crowd in the procession down the street—actually named Dolorosa in San Antonio—and witnessed with them the graphically sanguinary reenactment of the Crucifixion. It was a big event, worthy of a front-page photo in the next day's *San Antonio Express-News*, where "Jesus," seen "crucified" on the steps of the cathedral with women mourning at his feet, was identified as Javier Gómez, and the crowd was estimated at eight thousand.[3] For me, it was an unforgettable experience.

> Pilgrimages . . . can definitely be privileged moments in everyone's personal journal of faith, as well as fascinating adventures full of unsuspected experiences. . . . In discovering ourselves to be in community with others, even total strangers, we experience the ultimate reality of the church as the people of a God who has no boundaries and is open to everyone without exception. . . . No one should leave for home as they departed from home ("Pastoral Opportunities," 133, 138–139).

Yet it is not Holy Week, San Fernando Cathedral, or Mexican religious practices that come to the attention of the tourist visiting San Antonio. To those arriving in town, San Antonio proclaims itself to be the site of the Alamo, dedicated to the memory of William Travis, James Bowie, Davy Crockett, and the other "martyrs" of the 1836 war of Texas independence. Photos, paintings, and drawings of the Alamo—one of the top tourist attractions in the United States—are everywhere. The word appears in the names of streets, buildings, and businesses, and the scalloped outline of the building's distinctive façade is an ever-present visual trope. I found no postcards of the cathedral in the airport shops, and even when I did find one later (in the Mercado), the Alamo's façade appeared in outline on the address side of the card, as it does on every postcard in the "San Antonio collection."[4] From the same tourist perspective, San Antonio's Mexican American culture is represented primarily in terms of margaritas and salsa, written in neon lights on cream-colored stucco.

I do not doubt that the Hispanic residents of the city—some descended from Spanish families tracing their roots in San Antonio more than two and half centuries back, long before Mexican independence, and others who have arrived from Mexico in the past decade—are fully conscious of this contradiction. The city is publicly identified by a symbol precisely of its alienation from the country—New Spain or Mexico—of their, or their ancestors', origins, despite the fact that San Antonio is near to the border, historically a frontier town, sometimes called "the northernmost city in Mexico." Yet as Americans, residents, and citizens of the United States, many Hispanics wish also to embrace the values of liberty and courage and the national loyalties that the Alamo is said to enshrine.[5]

San Antonio's Hispanics, who constitute 56 percent of the population of the city,[6] thus live in a public culture that holds them at arm's length. The *San Antonio Express-News*, the city's only daily, is published solely in English, unlike the *Miami Herald*, whose every issue is published doubly, one whole paper in English, the other, editorially identical, in Spanish.[7] Were it not for the fact that 80 percent of San Antonio's Hispanic residents speak English,[8] the *Express-News* would go unread by most residents of the city.

It is in this context that Virgilio Elizondo, as pastor of the cathedral parish of San Fernando, determined to revitalize Mexican religious traditions at the cathedral, to valorize and inculcate Mexican religious culture in the heart of the ninth-largest city in the United States. The Holy Week rituals I was invited to observe there are the climax not only of the liturgical year but also—along with the December 12 feast of Our Lady of Guadalupe—of his program of cultural *mestizaje*. Over the three days of my visit, there were The Last Supper (Ultima Cena) and the candlelit procession to Gethsemane, Oración en el Huerto, on Holy Thursday; the Pasión, Via Crucis, Crucifixion, Las Siete Palabras, and Veneration of the Cross during the day on Good Friday; Pésame, the poignant wake in the company of the grieving Mary, and Servicio del Santo Entierro, burial service, on Friday night; and finally the Resurreción Gloriosa, on Holy Saturday night.

The rituals were vivid and involved all one's senses and faculties.

The pilgrimage is not a time for doctrinal or moralistic catechesis, but rather a time for the catechesis of the heart which will come through new profoundly human experiences of friendships, relationships, wonder, gratitude, peace and joy ("Pastoral Opportunities," 136–137). The authentic inculturation of liturgical celebration . . . implies much more than just singing in the local language and using local materials for the vestments. It implies a deep respect and willingness to accompany the people's faith pilgrimage with the full liturgical celebration of the special events that have marked their life and that form part of their collective memory ("Cultural Pluralism," 81).

On Thursday night, a procession followed the Blessed Sacrament as it was carried through the cathedral and out the door to the plaza across the street, all of us carrying candles and chanting, *caminemos con Jesús*, let us walk with Jesus. Burning candles created islands of heat and wafts of scent all over the church. In the sanctuary leaving the service, everyone was given a small loaf of bread to share with family members. Next day, on the Via Crucis, parishioners dressed as Roman legionnaires flailed Gómez's back, leaving garish marks of red, while pious women in black lace led the people in another chant of contrition, "Perdona tu Pueblo, Señor." A few individuals came forward to bear the cross from Gómez for a block or so. (They were, in fact, Elizondo and fellow clergymen honored with the burden.) Loudspeakers carried the sound of hammer on metal as "spikes" were driven through "Jesus' " hands into the truly heavy wood of the cross, and Gómez's screams echoed all over the plaza. To begin the service of the Seven Last Words, the cross—Gómez still attached, smeared with red, naked to the waist, wearing his crown of thorns—was carried up to the altar of the church. Later in the evening, with a full-size wooden figure of Christ now supplanting the actor, a bier with the body of Jesus was again carried through the church, there to be covered with hundreds of flowers brought forward by congregants.

> For the Indians [of 1531] . . . flowers and music . . . were the supreme way of communication through which the presence of the invisible all-powerful God could be expressed. As the apparition [of Our Lady of Guadalupe] had begun with music, giving it an atmosphere of the divine, it reached its peak with flowers, the sign of life beyond life, the sign that beyond human suffering and death there was something greater-than-life in the dwelling place of the wonderful giver of life ("Our Lady," 122).

A woman representing Mary followed the bier up to the altar, crying out in a heart-wrenching (and superbly performed) Moorish wail, as funeral torches filled the nave with pungent smoke.

Many of these rituals were foreign to me, but I doubt that their strangeness was due only to my Presbyterian background. Surely many of my Irish and German Catholic friends would similarly have been astounded by the vividness and the colorfulness of these Mexicano rites, which seemed to fill the imagination to overflowing, to preclude escape into the merely symbolic. Right in front of us we saw realistically reenacted the suffering and death of Jesus, the cruelty of his tormentors, and the grief of his mother. There was nothing metaphorical, nothing merely figurative, nothing generic about these rites.

Yet, as an Anglo, I did not feel excluded.

> I . . . come to you as a pastor of a very active parish who is learning that the more local we are, the more universal we become. We televise a Sunday liturgy to the entire nation. It is a very Mexican celebration. Yet the appeal

of this mass is far beyond the Hispanics of the United States ("Cultural Pluralism," 72). Even though our basic identity is very Mexican, we work hard at welcoming others ("Benevolent Tolerance," 90).

First of all, the rites were Catholic, and some of them were, to my ear, merely Spanish translations of the universal rites of the Church. Thus, the scripture readings on Holy Thursday were, as elsewhere that night in Catholic churches, taken from Exodus, First Corinthians, and the Gospel According to St. John. The Seven Last Words were the same as those spoken the same day at the ecumenical Protestant service in my hometown, Evanston, Illinois, only in a different language. The melody accompanying the words *caminemos con Jesús* is used with different words at Holy Name Cathedral in Chicago.[9] Some aspects of the ritual that I did experience as different, especially when everyone held hands for the Our Father, those on the aisles stretching out to reach those on the other side, felt warmly welcoming.[10]

Second, Elizondo, who introduced himself to me as Virgil, lives on cultural margins and conducts as much of the liturgy as he can in both English and Spanish. Because they were broadcast internationally on UNIVISION, Las Siete Palabras, it is true, were said in Spanish (except for the closing solo, by parishioner Joe Castillo, of "Were You There When They Crucified My Lord"). And yes, the Passion play itself was proclaimed in Spanish. But Elizondo's narration and commentary at the Mercado and during the Via Crucis were bilingual, and the pageant was preceded by invocations in English from Archbishop Patricio Flores and guest pastor Buckner Fanning, a local Baptist. Whenever Elizondo spoke, he said first a paragraph or two in one language and then, in the other, a rough equivalent plus the next part of the discourse. He would then proceed stepwise through his prayer, his announcement, or his homily, never quite repeating himself, never quite leaving anyone in the dark as to his meaning.

Third, it became clear that Elizondo's inclusiveness was not only hospitality extended to Anglo visitors like me, but a feature of his teaching for Mexican Americans. There are others in the parish who don't know Spanish, and they include young Mexican Americans. I was told that 20 percent of San Antonio's Hispanics are, like me, monolingual English speakers,[11] and in the cathedral I saw Mexican American parents leading their teenage children through the Spanish words on the song sheet that was handed out at the door. The officially Spanish policy of the cathedral is intended not only to accommodate Spanish speakers but to foster them.

Thus it became clear to me over the several observances that Elizondo's cultural mestizaje is not simply a matter of admitting "folk" or "native" religious practices into his church but an intentional engendering of religious and cultural traditions that he feels his parishioners have a right to embrace and to pass on to their children.

Five years later, I encountered his recognition that "catechetics needs to help in the creation of the local tradition of living faith ("Cultural Pluralism," 81).

Elizondo's mestizaje, rather than being a defensive concession to popular ways, is an assertive educational mission. Thus, on Thursday night, as Archbishop Flores prepared to wash the feet of the "disciples" (twelve young parishioners in apostles' costumes), Elizondo in his homily invited the children of the parish—a huge throng—to come forward to watch at the steps of the sanctuary, where they stayed until the Communion rite. Thus also Mary Esther Bernal, director of the cathedral's choirs, led the parishioners through the choruses of the Gloria, set to a catchy, folk-sounding but actually newly composed tune, indicating with her hands not only tempo but also relative pitch. Much of the color of the pageantry is evidently intended to fill the memories of onlookers with indelible religious images. In a society as drenched as ours in symbolic representations, Elizondo wants his own message to have a competitive edge.[12]

San Fernando's parishioners live in a busy city full of distractions. Despite the homespun dress of the "disciples" who showed up in church on Thursday night to have their feet washed by the archbishop, Elizondo knows that his church is not filled with peasants fresh from the fields, but with people who use their showers to make sure their feet are clean before exposing them to the archbishop, people who drive cars to church and who (he hopes) will watch services on television if by chance they can't make it in. So the pastor spoke less as the narrator and more as the prophet when, as he welcomed the crowd on Friday to the passion play in the Mercado, he said that they had come not to be entertained but to engage in an act of prayer. He wanted to use the color and drama of the pageant to teach religious and cultural lessons.

> Fiestas without prophetic action easily degenerate into empty parties, drunken brawls, or the opium to keep the people in their misery. But prophetic action without festive celebration is equally reduced to dehumanizing hardness. Prophecy is the basis of fiesta, but the fiesta is the spirit of prophecy ("*Mestizaje*," 175).

Elizondo, Flores, Bernal, and the other shapers of the events I witnessed know that culture is not bred in the blood and bones. Culture is not tribal, automatically passed on from parent to child. "Hispanics" are made, not born. If it is to survive, a culture must be nurtured and learned.

There are two mixed cultures they are trying to teach at San Fernando, each of which they think is enhanced by the other: Christian, specifically Roman Catholic, and Hispanic, specifically Mexican American. The parish today contains some whose journey across the border is within living memory and whose English is rudimentary. Elizondo's Spanish-language policy serves them. But the parish also contains those well-situated Spanish speakers whose English is fluent, idiomatic, and Texan accented but whose devotion to Catholicism has been sorely tried by the Church's neglect of their heritage. At San Fernando, I met people whose ancestors came to the United States early in this century or late in the last—third-, fourth-, fifth-, and later-generation Mexican Americans whose culture Elizondo ennobles, giving them opportunities to pass it on as a valued legacy to their children.

Such parishioners use their English literacy in San Antonio's public life. They do not need the Mass to be said in Spanish for sheer linguistic comprehension. If they did, and if they wanted the Mexican traditions that often accompany the Mass said in Spanish, they could go to Our Lady of Guadalupe on San Antonio's west side, where the parishioners have been putting on their own Via Crucis for generations, one Andrés Camero playing the part of their Jesus during the year I visited San Antonio.[13]

> [During Elizondo's youth in San Antonio, the neighborhood parish] was the only institution in the city where we felt fully at home, fully free to express ourselves in our own language, our singing, our festivities, our worship ("Hispanic Theology," 278).

The Mexican American pillars of San Fernando that I met prefer to worship at the cathedral, just on the west edge of downtown, catercorner from the century-old Bexar County Court House, and they were honored to have Baptist Bill Thornton, who later became San Antonio's mayor, address the crowd gathered in the Mercado for the passion play, and Robert Green, Bexar County Clerk, serve as one of Jesus' pallbearers on Friday night. To watch a dignified usher signal discreetly to a colleague in the back of the crowded nave that he has two seats available halfway to the front—all while the TV cameras are rolling—is to sense the pride that is conferred by the centrality of the cathedral in the public life of San Antonio.

> Those who had nothing to offer now have the best thing to offer to everyone: new life. It is the rejected and marginated Galileans who receive the Spirit and, without ceasing to be Galileans, now see themselves in a new way as they begin to initiate the new humanity. Everyone is invited, but it is the very ones who had been excluded who now do the inviting ("*Mestizaje*," 172).

It seemed to me that Elizondo intends San Fernando to play for the city's Mexican American west side the civic religious role that the Alamo plays for its Anglo north side.

It would be a mistake to dwell overlong on this theme of ethnic pride. What is celebrated at the cathedral—particularly on these days of Holy Week—is a message of humility. The archbishop washing the feet of twelve young men. (He told me later that he had recently undergone knee surgery.) Pastor Elizondo taking up the cross on the Via Dolorosa, while hundreds chanted in unison, "Perdona Tu Pueblo," forgive thy people. More hundreds of mourners coming forward to kiss the cross. Hooded, anonymous *penitentes* bringing their petitions to the grieving Madre de Dios. The whole congregation on its knees for three long prayers during the afternoon service.

I sensed not only a message of humility this particular weekend but also a culture of humility at San Fernando. The photos, mementoes, hospital bracelets, and miniature arms and legs that people array around the effigies of trusted saints (the black Christ of Esquipulas from Guatemala is a new favorite at San Fernando) to dramatize their petitions and expressions of thanksgiving—these humble artifacts are called *milagritos*, the diminutive of miracles, as if to underscore the diffident yet intimate spirit in which they are offered. Nowhere else have I felt so much sincerity behind the Catholic litany before Communion: "Lord, I am not worthy to receive You, but only say the word and I shall be healed."

The contrast could not have been greater when Reverend Fanning spoke to the crowd in the Mercado before the passion play began. He acknowledged the solemnity of the observance, but he refused to be saddened. He urged his listeners to see the cross not as an instrument of torture but as a gigantic "plus sign," representing God's triumph over death. Notwithstanding the fact that the parish was about to observe a long day of vivid, death-oriented rituals and would await the end of the Saturday-night vigil before returning to an officially festive mood, Fanning, smartly dressed in a business suit, spoke to the crowd in the unamplified, hearty voice of the Baptist preacher. Elizondo, clad in red and white vestments, spoke softly into a microphone. Although at the moment I liked Fanning's message, it seemed by the end of the day radically inappropriate to the drama about to unfold.

> For a people who have consistently been subjected to injustice, cruelty and early death, the image of the crucified is the supreme symbol of life in spite of the multiple daily threats of death. If there was something good and redemptive in the unjust condemnation and crucifixion of the God-man, then, as senseless and useless as our suffering appears to be, there must be something of ultimate goodness and transcendent value in it. . . . *Even if we are killed, we cannot be destroyed* ("Popular Religion," 131).

Later, during the Pésame service, when Elizondo invited people from the congregation to come forward to express their thoughts to the grieving Mary, one of those he recognized was County Clerk Green, who on behalf of the people of Bexar County thanked the parish for the honor of addressing them and thanked Mary for the gracious gift of her Son. His demeanor could not have been more unlike that of the weeping, grief-stricken Mexican American parishioners, whose condolences to Mary were spoken so softly, despite the microphone, as to be nearly inaudible. The flower-bedecked wooden corpse and black lace–draped effigy standing next to it in the sanctuary elicited literally inarticulate but physically palpable emotions from the Mexican American people of San Fernando.

In the ridiculed, insulted and crucified Jesus, we knew that God had not abandoned us for the nice and fancy churches of our society, but that God in the person of the suffering Jesus carrying his cross was right there with us in our struggles. . . . The silent suffering of Jesus had been our way of life ("Hispanic Theology," 288–289).

Lest these points about humility obscure what I said earlier about the intentionality of the observances, I must emphasize this: in speaking of the religiosity of the people of San Fernando, I do not mean to suggest the familiar image of pious huddled masses that is evoked when the news media report that "hundreds of the faithful gathered today to pay homage to their crucified Lord," as if the TV cameras had miraculously come upon Good Friday observances in a nineteenth-century Sicilian village. The religiosity at San Fernando is not naive and unreflective, but neither is it triumphalist. As I sat in a pew next to Esther Rodriguez, dressed in the widow's black that many women of the parish wear as an expression of their Good Friday devotion, it occurred to me that her clothes of mourning were a badge of honor, making a statement simultaneously of genuine humility and pride: humility before the greatness of God and the richness of mestizo tradition; pride that at San Fernando Cathedral she could call these things her birthright.

Popular piety . . . becomes liberating when used as a source of unity and strength in the struggle for dignity and subsequent change against the powerful of society ("Our Lady," 122).

Conclusion

Having experienced Elizondo's pastoring at firsthand five years ago and now having read his work as represented in *Beyond Borders* and elsewhere (particularly his 1983 book *Galilean Journey*), I conclude that (1) the situation of Mexican American culture of which he writes can be perceived by an outside observer; (2) he does as a pastor what he says should be done; (3) at least one element of his pastoral theology is clearer in his practice than from his writing; and (4) full appreciation of his pastoral theology requires access, as Matovina says, to his practice on the ground, as well as to his writing in books and journals.

1. While I was in San Antonio, I experienced at firsthand many things about Mexican America of which Elizondo has written (no doubt partly under his influence and that of his disciple, Matovina). Comparing the culture San Antonio makes known to tourists with the San Antonio I saw in the cathedral and the west-side barrio, Elizondo does not exaggerate when he writes: "Only the white Western way appears as the truly human way of life; all others continue to be relegated to an inferior status" ("*Mestizaje*," 162). The fact that Mexican Americans "were made foreigners in their own lands" ("Benevolent Tolerance," 95), however, does not mean that they belong in Mexico, for, as

Elizondo writes: "The love for the United States and the patriotic spirit of the Hispanics for this country is certainly beyond question" ("Bicultural Approach," 65–66). The truth is that Mexican Americans are made to feel marginated, in the Roman Catholic church as well as in secular American society, as Elizondo confesses in his autobiographical reflections: "As *mestizos*, our flesh and blood identity has consistently marginated us from both parent groups. We have been too Spanish for the Indians and too Indian for the Spaniards, too Mexican for the United States, and too 'Gringo' for our Mexican brothers and sisters" ("Hispanic Theology," 282). Such margination is a critical context within which Elizondo pastors.

2. In the rites of the San Fernando Cathedral parish, I saw Elizondo practicing things I later read him saying. In the face of Alamo symbolism and mestizo margination he firmly decentered WASP hegemony:

> In the United States we cannot ignore the strong weight of the dominant and righteous WASP culture with its racism and ethno-centrism. Special emphasis must be made throughout the catechetical texts to attack every notion that consciously or unconsciously promotes white western culture as superior and normative for all others. . . . We must become clearly aware of this and counter it in every way possible ("Cultural Pluralism," 84).

Yet Elizondo carried out this attack in ways that were inclusive rather than exclusive, inviting rather than alienating. Five years ago, I recognized a number of ways in which Elizondo's verbal messages were directed to speakers of English as well as Spanish, but only later did I recognize the importance for his practice of inclusiveness of nonverbal modes of communication, especially music and motion.[14] Elizondo's "catechesis of the heart" transcends linguistic boundaries, but for this to be possible it must be rooted in real human experience, not only in texts.

> The ultimate success or failure of a truly multicultural religious education program depends on the personality of the local congregation, the person of the religious educator, and the total environment of the church—its people, ministers, decorations, music, church order, and celebrations ("Benevolent Tolerance," 90).

As did early Christianity, the ritual practice at the Cathedral of San Fernando drew on the experience of marginated people to "affirm rootedness while destroying ghettoishness" ("Popular Religion," 127).

3. I have encountered in Elizondo's writings only oblique references to what I witnessed as a key component of his pastoral practice, namely a cultural catechesis that inculcates Mexican American culture as well as affirming its value. His writings often acknowledge the contingent quality of racial/ethnic identity, the fact that, in the Mexican American case, people experience

themselves in between opposed cultural forces and many are drawn to one side or the other, some wishing to assimilate to the dominant WASP model, ignoring the lesson that "simply to assimilate would be a sell out, an insult to our ancestors and a betrayal of our faith" ("Bicultural Approach," 66).[15] Elizondo's lesson—that "for a colonized/oppressed/dominated group, [popular expressions of the faith] are the ultimate resistance to the attempts of the dominant culture to destroy them as a distinct group either through annihilation or through absorption and total assimilation" ("Popular Religion," 126)—must be understood as prescriptive as well as descriptive. "Through the pains and frustrations of trying to be what we are not, the uniqueness of our own proper identity begins to emerge" ("*Mestizaje*," 164). As a priest, Elizondo does not merely accept the people's culture into the church, he teaches an inculturated faith.

4. Yet it was necessary for me to read Elizondo to understand how the religion he preaches and practices combines the themes of what five years ago I awkwardly called humility and pride, how he encourages a faith that is reflective but not triumphalist. With respect to people of my background he says: "White Western Christians need to convert from their sins of arrogance and pride. Their righteous sense of superiority has blinded them to their own inadequacies and sinfulness and has kept them from appreciating the treasures God has bestowed on the peoples of the other races and cultures of the world." His own liturgical practice helped me recognize some of those treasures. To fellow mestizos he says: "On the other hand, those who have been marginated, brutalized, abused, segregated, put down, ridiculed, or merely tolerated need also to recognize their sin: the sense of inferiority that some come to believe and accept. . . . Attitudes of docility, embarrassment of color or heritage, and the many negative and self-destructive feelings grow out of the inner sense of shame at being who one is" (quotations in this paragraph from "Benevolent Tolerance," 92). Five years ago, I sensed that such a sin had been put behind them by San Fernando's parishioners, who had come to a deep understanding of what Elizondo calls "biblical humility," which

does not mean putting ourselves down as if we were worthless. We are simply one of the fellowship. This biblical humility means that we accept ourselves as we are—historically and culturally conditioned. This is both our originality and our limitation. As original, we have much to offer; as limited, we have much to learn. It is in this same spirit that we accept all others—neither as superior or inferior, masters or students. It is this *humility* which gives us the spontaneous willingness to offer what we have without apologies and to receive from others without a sense of shame.[16]

It was biblical humility that I witnessed at San Fernando. I pray that I can learn to practice it.

Reprinted by permission of Orbis Books from *Beyond Borders: Writings of Virgilio Elizondo and Friends*, edited by Timothy Matovina.

NOTES

For their comments on the field report contained in this essay, I am indebted to Nancy Ammerman, Joy Charlton, Shoshanah Feher, Luin Goldring, Anne Heider, Luis León, Timothy Matovina, and Olga Villa Parra. For the project as a whole, I am deeply indebted to Timothy Matovina for advice and encouragement and to Virgil Elizondo for inspiration.

1. R. Stephen Warner, "Religion, Boundaries, and Bridges," *Sociology of Religion* 58 (Fall 1997): 217–238.

2. The first draft of the field report was written on Easter Sunday (April 3) 1994, within forty-eight hours of the events described, and before I had read any of the writings of Elizondo or Matovina. This revision contains corrections, including endnotes, made before August 1994, primarily on matters of fact and writing style; it also eliminates some extraneous material. New, indented quotations reference those of Elizondo's writings that are reprinted in *Beyond Borders*.

3. J. Michael Parker, "Jesus's Cross Called 'Plus Sign for Life' by Baptist Pastor," *San Antonio Express-News* (April 2, 1994).

4. Never mind that that very façade was added to the building years after the fabled events of 1836.

5. Early on Good Friday morning, near the Alamo, I saw a recent sculpture of Toribio Losoya, one of nine officially recognized Tejano heroes of the Alamo who died alongside Travis, Bowie, and Crockett at the hands of Mexican general Antonio López de Santa Anna. True, the Tejanos fought more in protest of Santa Anna's abrogation of the Mexican Constitution of 1824 than for Texan independence; nonetheless, the statue proclaims, despite the Daughters of the Texas Republic, that the Alamo is not the Anglos' alone.

6. From the 1990 U.S. Census.

7. From author's observations, confirmed by Professor Thomas A. Tweed. In this sense, whereas Miami is a bilingual city, San Antonio is a city of bilinguals.

8. A figure reported to Timothy Matovina by San Antonio market researcher Lionel Sosa.

9. According to J. Michael Thompson, director of music at St. Peter's Church in Chicago, the melody, as I sang it to him, is a variation on Gregorian Psalm Tone 1 in the Dorian Mode. For details on the chant, see Warner, "Religion, Boundaries, and Bridges," 226–227, and Chapter 5 in this volume.

10. I have since experienced this ritual—holding hands across the aisle for the Our Father—in Mexican American Catholic churches in Los Angeles, San Francisco, and Chicago.

11. From Lionel Sosa and Associates, Market Researchers, as reported by Timothy Matovina.

12. Friday morning in the *Express-News*, columnist David Anthony Richelieu anticipated the irony of the day to come when, recalling previous years' Via Crucis pageants, he wrote: "Nowhere else can Christ's anguished cry, 'Father forgive them, for they know not what they do,' echo across a crowded plaza as nearby, a meter maid slips a parking ticket under the wiper of a TV minicam van blocking traffic." David Anthony Richelieu, "How Tradition Makes Symbols Come Alive," *San Antonio Express-News* (April 1, 1994).

13. Parker, "Jesus's Cross."

14. Warner, "Religion, Boundaries, and Bridges," 226–233, and Chapter 5 in this volume.

15. In the wake of the conquest by the United States of northern Mexico, "the Churches demanded that we break radically from the religious ways of our ancestors. Some of our

people have tried and have found it very painful, others have managed to survive while still others have just given up altogether" ("Hispanic Theology," 285). "In the first stages of the struggle to belong, the *mestizo* will try desperately to become like the dominant group, for only its members appear to be fully civilized and human" (*Mestizaje*, 163).

16. Virgil Elizondo, "Conditions and Criteria for Authentic Inter-Cultural Theological Dialogue," *Different Theologies, Common Responsibility: Babel or Pentecost?* ed. Virgil Elizondo, Claude Geffré, and Gustavo Gutiérrez (Edinburgh: T and T Clark, 1984): 22–23.

Cited Works of Virgilio Elizondo

Listed here are Elizondo's works as reprinted in *Beyond Borders: Writings of Virgilio Elizondo and Friends*, ed. Timothy Matovina (Maryknoll, N.Y.: Orbis Books, 2000), to which the page numbers refer.

"Benevolent Tolerance or Humble Reverence? A Vision for Multicultural Religious Education" (1997), 87–97.
"A Bicultural Approach to Religious Education" (1981), 62–71.
"Cultural Pluralism and the Catechism" (1994), 72–86.
"Hispanic Theology and Popular Piety: From Interreligious Encounter to a New Ecumenism" (1993), 278–291.
"*Mestizaje* as a Locus of Theological Reflection" (1983), 159–175.
"Our Lady of Guadalupe as a Cultural Symbol" (1977), 118–125.
"Pastoral Opportunities of Pilgrimages" (1996), 133–139.
"Popular Religion as Support of Identity" (1986), 126–132.

12

Pentecostal Immigrants and the Making of the Sun Belt (1993)

When Dan Morgan's Tatham family chronicle *Rising in the West: The True Story of an "Okie" Family from the Great Depression Through the Reagan Years* appeared last fall, it was reviewed and found wanting as a sequel to John Steinbeck's *Grapes of Wrath*. Morgan's protagonists didn't appeal to Steinbeck fans. Tathams weren't Joads, they supported Pentecostal churches instead of labor unions, and they eventually flourished in California, some becoming multimillionaires. The critics disapproved, and the book quickly dropped from journalistic sight. That is a shame, for the book is rich in social and religious history. In particular, it helps explain the now nationwide reach of southern-style religious and political populism.

It must be said that Morgan invited the comparison with Steinbeck, for he originally set out to explore the destinies of the novelist's dust-bowl refugees. He had read *The Grapes of Wrath* as an undergraduate in 1955 and spent the following summer on the road in the company of a pair of Okie farm workers. Although he never saw them again, he kept wondering, long after he had become a reporter for the *Washington Post*, what had happened to them and their people. Finally, in 1984, he took time off to go to Sallisaw, Oklahoma, the Joads' point of departure, where he got some names to track down in California. He settled on the extended family of Fresno, California, resident Oca Tatham (b. 1911), who, along with fifteen others crowded on a Chevy flatbed truck, made the famous trek on U.S. 66 from Sallisaw to the San Joaquin Valley in August of 1934. The book is decorated with an endpaper map showing the near-identical itineraries of the Joads and the Tathams.

Morgan scoured archives, interviewed survivors, and used his own eyes and ears, historical imagination, and narrative skill to fashion a vivid account of these long-ago events in Oklahoma, California, and the fifteen hundred miles between. Oklahoma land is poor, jobs are intermittent, and word is that things are better in California. The men worry whether the truck, which Oca had bought for fifty dollars, can make the distance with its human overload, some of them strangers taken on just to help buy gasoline. The truck overturns in New Mexico, and Oca and his mother, Cora, are injured. Local farmers, nurses, and bus drivers lend a hand, and the truck gets underway again with engine intact but no windshield. As they approach the Colorado River crossing the brakes fail, and the whole company walks the last few miles into California.

At this point, however (page 55), Morgan's book has barely begun, and the parallels with Steinbeck's story become ever fewer as we read on. Indeed, Morgan becomes increasingly skeptical of Steinbeck's historical veracity. Sallisaw is in humid Eastern Oklahoma, nowhere near the dust bowl of the Panhandle. Its people were not yeomen but a floating rural proletariat who made their living as miners and mill workers as well as sharecroppers. Few of the tens of thousands who made their way west during the Great Depression were refugees, whether from harsh nature or rapacious capitalists. Not all of them were victims in California, and many prospered. Morgan comes to these conclusions partly on the witness of his Tatham family oral histories, but primarily on the strength of contemporaneous documents, 1940s congressional hearings, and recent historical monographs, for like Steinbeck but with more documentation, Morgan frequently pulls back from his protagonists to reflect on the broader trends they represent.

The final, and theoretically significant, break with Steinbeck comes when Morgan decides that the Okies, Joads notwithstanding, were not refugees at all but immigrants. They came to California in search of opportunity, and most found it. Like other immigrants, they came in waves, a few individuals, typically younger men, or families, like the Tathams, paving the way for relatives and friends. They trusted in family. They maintained ties to Oklahoma kin and took back gifts when they went to visit; a few of them went back for good. Some who had intended merely to sojourn in California wound up settling when it became clear that their children were at home there.

Like other immigrants, they were stigmatized. In front of bosses, they toned down their accents and avoided Oklahoma idioms. ("Okie" was the nastiest ethnic slur I can recall from my own youth in rural California in the 1940s and '50s.) Like other immigrants, they suffered heartache: we see a 1936 group snapshot with three young Okie mothers holding their babies, and right below it is another photo of those three babies' graves a few months later. Like other immigrants, they had to improvise to make ends meet. While his wife, Ruby, and most of the other family members started out picking cotton, Oca, his arm broken in the New Mexico accident, became a brilliant "horse trader" in potatoes, cast-off parts, and anything else he could buy cheap and sell dear, sometimes doubling his capital overnight. He thus replicated the "well-known pattern of immigrant ascent in the United States: filling a niche in the market that was beneath the dignity of established businessmen" (213).

Like other immigrants, they brought their culture and the rudiments of their institutions to their new homeland, above all, their religion. In their case, the homeland—the Ozark plateau area of Missouri, Arkansas, and Oklahoma—was itself, like a third-world country, a place of ongoing political, economic, and religious development at the turn of the century, where, in default of mainline Protestants, people had been religiously organized by Holiness and Pentecostal evangelists. Their religion insisted that adherents set themselves apart from "the world," and its demands were always too rigorous for Oca's father, Walter. But shortly before the move to California Oca himself left bootlegging and womanizing to follow Cora and Ruby into the Pentecostal fold, and Morgan attributes the Tathams' fortitude to their conversions. "They were moving toward a different future, one that they would come to share comfortably with millions of other Americans, but they recognized that surviving the journey would require a concentrated inner focus, a marshaling of inner resources. The paradox of holy roller religion was that it instilled the self-confidence to master the world even as it held it suspect and apart" (18).

It was an individualistic, democratic, optimistic, low-overhead religion that they adopted. Whatever a person's background, anyone could be a convert and anyone could pray for a miracle. Looking to God for healing (and Tathams testify to many), people were practical and also called the doctor. They came to each other's aid in times of crisis. Their institutions, rooted more in family and other social networks than in geographical places, were portable. Using salvaged materials and volunteer labor, Oca and others built themselves the Pentecostal Church of God of McFarland, California, within two years of their arrival. One of their number, Jay Fuller, was their pastor (and is one of many religious entrepreneurs whose careers Morgan chronicles). By the end of the 1930s, PCOG congregations had sprung up throughout the San Joaquin, Imperial, Salinas, and Santa Clara valleys. Soon, California Pentecostals were using the radio to get their message across.

Oca prospered as a trader and trucker, especially in the war boom of the 1940s. Since he followed opportunities up and down the U.S. 99 corridor and used nearly every dollar in earnings to buy something else to sell, the Tatham family did not enjoy the trappings of wealth and the children were seldom in the same school two years in a row. But by the end of the war, Oca, Ruby, and their six children had settled in Fresno. Although Morgan does not stress the point, he provides one clue to Pentecostal growth in the Tathams' record of early marriages and high birth rates. At the time of her death, Cora Tatham (1881–1976), was survived by four children (two had predeceased her), seventeen grandchildren, and thirty-two great grandchildren. Fifteen years later, as he was interviewing the Tathams for the last time, Morgan records that Cora's grandson Dick (who had been an infant on the 1934 trek) himself had six children and nine grandchildren.

The children grew up with a double stigma, Okie and Holy Roller, and, as is the case with children of immigrants and converts, they could attribute their marginality to decisions made by their parents. "Oca and Ruby had joined the Pentecostal church voluntarily, but [their children] had been *born* into it, an altogether different experience" (184). Morgan traces in detail the tensions in the children's and grandchildren's lives between the church's attempt at encapsulation and the attractions of wider worlds, and we read of son Bill's fierce (and successful) drive to material success and granddaughter Cindy's determination to homeschool her own children.

What the first generation's religious world offered the children was a place to meet other young people, a forum for their talents, and a hope-centered world-view. "Tathams were part of a vast non-Freudian America" (367) where doubt was denied and despair repressed. Struggle, not insight, pointed the way. Without much help from Oca, four of his children attended Assemblies of God Bible colleges, but he did encourage them as teenagers to try their hand at business. "The children grew up feeling that they could *do* things, not that they *knew* things" (257), and the resulting self-confidence accentuated their native individualism. Although neither equally affluent nor uniformly pious, most Tatham offspring turned out as adults to be morally conservative individualists, with multiple ties to Pentecostalism.

Religious networks linked the flourishing clan to cultural currents. Fresno was on the itinerary of Oral Roberts's healing ministry, and Oca was a sometime usher and regular contributor. On one of Roberts's visits, in 1951, a breakfast in his honor was hosted by dairyman Demos Shakarian, and Oca joined other contractors, truckers, developers, retailers, and real estate and insurance men as charter members of the Full Gospel Business Men's Fellowship, a kind of Pentecostal Rotary club for self-made men. The agenda was religion and business, but the outcome was eventually political. "Roberts did not support political candidates or promote partisan causes. Yet like so many religious leaders before him, he rallied people and prepared them for broader involvement, participation, and engagement. His large grass-roots following, stretching from Georgia to the central valley of California, was one of the first culturally cohesive Sun Belt communities" (225).

Although most Okies were Democrats and voted in large numbers for Harry Truman in 1948, by 1964 Oca was a Goldwater activist, attracted to the Arizonan's anti-Communism and his individualistic ethic of enterprise over credentials. Decisions by the Supreme Court in the 1960s to prohibit public school prayer and by the Internal Revenue Service in the 1970s to deny tax exemptions to segregated Christian academies pushed Oca further to the political right. Oca's daughter Doris fought countercultural currents in the public schools of her Bay Area town in the 1960s. By the late 1980s, most Tathams were solidly behind Pat Robertson's campaigns.

Morgan does not spare his protagonists an inquiry into their political self-contradictions. "One might have thought," he writes (219), that they "would have been grateful to government." During the first winter in California (1934–1935), the family had survived on federal and state relief. Oca had prospered in war-related trucking and later, with Bill, in Medicare-subsidized nursing homes. The affluence of California's Central Valley, the economy they flourished in, rested on gigantic public water projects. "The Okies were the beneficiaries of the greatest infrastructure program ever undertaken by the federal government and probably by any government in the history of the world" (136). But Oca fumes at government regulations, and Bill curries favor with conservative politicians.

It is probably to provide contrast to the Tathams' right-wing bent that Morgan sought out another Okie family, the Tacketts, for balance. The Tacketts remembered the help they had received from government and remained in the Democratic column. Eldon Tackett, a member of Oca Tatham's generation, worked for one of the municipal irrigation districts and saw how water projects subsidized wealthy farmers. His son Gene, a Peace Corps veteran, served two terms on Kern County's Board of Supervisors, running in 1976 on a mildly environmentalist platform. Yet even Eldon, critical of the welfare system, voted for Ronald Reagan in 1980, and Gene's elective career was over in 1984 after he was defeated twice as Democratic candidate for Congress and state assembly in the early 1980s. The conservative tide seems overwhelming, and the Tackett narrative, three chapters out of twenty-five, feels like an afterthought in the book.

Morgan is much more engaged when he returns to the Tathams, as he does time and again. Although, from a social science point of view, Morgan is reticent about his methods, he must have taken huge chunks of time off from his job at the *Post*, for he eventually spent parts of five years (1985–1990) interviewing family members. It seems likely that he was present for some of the occasions he relates, and this might explain his dwelling on stories that seem peripheral to his main narrative. (For example, he did not lead me to care about the costly, protracted, and ultimately futile attempt of Bill Tatham and his son Billy to turn their U.S. Football League Tulsa and Phoenix franchise into an NFL one.) But Morgan's time was well spent with Oca and his second wife, Ona (Ruby died in 1982), and with Doris and Renee, Oca's oldest and youngest children. Oca and Ona drive east in 1985 to see Jim Bakker's and Pat Robertson's opulent headquarters (which leave them cold) and go to Mexico to help build a Pentecostal mission (where Oca feels his gifts are needed). Doris's marriage goes through a crisis, which Morgan relates in painful, raw detail, and Renee, single well into her forties, her airline-based employment jeopardized by deregulation, adopts a Chinese child.

Despite their moral conservatism, the Tatham children and grandchildren are vulnerable to divorce and what baby-boomer Renee, speaking of her own history, calls "ungodly things" (371). But most of them remain connected to Pentecostal (and, by the 1960s, Charismatic) fellowships. Through Morgan's eyes, we see how their needs are addressed by a new cohort of religious entrepreneurs and a new type of church. What people like Renee wanted in religion, he writes

> was what they were missing in their careers, communities, and homes: a feeling that their lives were meaningful; companionship; and help raising children in a turbulent time. . . . In many respects, the big, new churches of the Sun Belt were doing what the little Pentecostal works and storefronts had once done: serving as bridges for people in transition. What was the

landscape of modern America? Divorce, drugs, corporate mergers, job insecurity. Millions felt that they were losing control over their lives, children, and economic destinies. Doris and Renee had advanced their material position only to find that the place they had reached was a shaky platform. Companies vanished, and people changed jobs, houses, places of residence—even wives. Those grappling with the changes formed a vast pool of potential converts to the new religions. (394)

In his preface, epilogue, and acknowledgments Morgan tells us a little about his method. He drove I-40, the successor to U.S. 66. He sought out the counsel of noted historians specializing in Oklahoma, California, and Pentecostalism. He drew on family genealogies and photo albums. Most important, he got what sociologists call entrée to the Tathams from Bill Tatham, the wealthiest, most powerful member of the family in the 1980s, and he agreed to show them his manuscript before it went to press. At their request he made what he characterizes as two minor changes. In the end, he insists, *Rising in the West* is "their story, but it is my book."

Reviewers in the *New York Times* and *Los Angeles Times* complained that Morgan got too close to his subjects, and indeed there can be no mistaking the affection he feels for some (by no means all) of them. In the epilogue, he even admits that they prayed for him! Yet few social historians would touch such a research project until the principals were deceased, and a social scientist would have had to disguise their names and the places they lived. (If written by one of my colleagues, the book undoubtedly would have analyzed the immigration experiences of an anonymous kinship network between their place of origin, a distressed agricultural and extractive industrial area of the mid-south-central region, and their destination, a rapidly developing agricultural and food-processing area of the Pacific region.) Morgan should be warmly congratulated for this historically informed, richly textured, thoughtful, and humane record of a half century in the life of a major American ethnoreligious group.

13

Religion and New (Post-1965) Immigrants

Some Principles Drawn from Field Research (2000)

From the Puritans and padres onward, religion has been a central topic for Americanists, and now, as often in the past, the world of religion in the United States is undergoing dramatic change. This paper relates some of what I have learned about "new immigrants" and their religions over the past decade (Warner 1991a, 1993a, 1994a, 1997c, 1998b, 1998c, 2001c). Already, it has become increasingly difficult for an American to tell what "a Christian" or "a Buddhist" or "a Muslim" looks like. American Christians, Buddhists, and Muslims come in all colors and speak a babel of languages. Race, ethnicity, and religion are no longer, if they ever were, hard linked to one another. Moreover, places of worship decreasingly fit old cultural molds: a small-town Protestant church—red brick walls, high-pitched roof, and white steeple—may be packed with Asians; those who sit for meditation at a Buddhist temple today are quite likely to be white Americans; and Muslim students gather for Friday prayer on the campuses of colleges where attendance at Christian chapel was once required. Much of this racial-religious uncoupling is due to the new immigration, a huge topic on which, with respect to religion, research is just now beginning.[1]

After a forty-year hiatus between the restrictive laws passed at the end of World War I and the statutory reforms of 1965, legal immigration to the United States has returned to its historically high levels and is now running at the rate of about one million per year, making the United States once again a nation of immigrants. (See Warner 1998b for details on the following sketch.) What is particularly "new" about the post-1965 immigration, distinguishing it from the similarly sized stream coming at the turn of the last century, is that most of the new immigrants come from parts of the world other than Europe, especially from the former "third world" of Latin America, the Caribbean, East and South Asia, and the Middle East and Africa. (Chicago, where I teach, has substantial recent immigration from Europe, including Ireland, Poland, and the former Soviet and Yugoslav republics.) Only 13 percent of the five million immigrants who came to the United States between 1985 and 1990 were born in Europe, Canada, Australia or New Zealand. The new immigration is more truly global than ever before.

Much of this demographic diversification is attributable to the Immigration Act of 1965, which abolished discriminatory 1920s-era country-of-origin quotas and substituted occupational preference and family reunification provisions, by means of which the legislators had looked forward to an infusion of skilled workers into the U.S. economy and an end to decades-long separation of families with one branch in Europe and the other in the United States. What we now recognize to be among the main effects of the law—especially the brain drain of professionals from Asia and subsequent reunification of their families in the United States—was largely unanticipated. But for many reasons the de-Europeanization of the new immigration is only partly attributable to the 1965 reforms: not all newcomers from abroad are technically "immigrants" nor are all legal, and not all people from the "third world" are recent arrivals. During the forty-year immigration hiatus and especially after the Great Depression, guest workers were imported from Mexico at the behest of western agricultural interests in the "Bracero Program" of 1942–1964, and the stream of Mexicans seeking work in the United States has scarcely abated since. From the 1860s through the turn of the century, sugar and railroad interests imported workers from East Asia to the plantations of Hawaii and the hills and valleys of California. West Coast Chinatowns, Buddhist temples, and Japanese and Korean Protestant churches founded a century or more ago served many years later as community nuclei for post-1965 Asian immigrants. The U.S. conquest of the Philippines and Puerto Rico in the war with Spain eventually led to several streams of migration from these countries. At 1.4 million in the 1990 census, Americans of Filipino origin are the second-largest Asian population in the United States; Puerto Ricans—legally citizens, not immigrants—reside in the States by the millions; Mexicans have come to the United States in several waves since the mid–nineteenth century, many to augment communities incorporated into the United States by the 1848 Treaty of Guadalupe Hidalgo. Hundreds of thousands of U.S. allies from lost Cold War causes in China, Cuba, and Vietnam have gained asylum over the past half century, and they have established solid enclaves in San Francisco, Miami, and Orange County. Hundreds of thousands of other victims of Cold War conflicts in Central America, having sought asylum unsuccessfully because they were not on the U.S.-backed side, have nonetheless taken long-term refuge in Los Angeles, and thousands of their children are U.S. citizens. In countless ways, the globalization of the U.S. population in the past third of a century is the result of very old chickens come home to roost (Warner 1998b, 8).

As we shall see, many of these immigrants (as I shall refer to them generically) are deeply involved in their religions, but we know a lot less than we should about their religious identities, participation, and institution building (Christiano 1991). It would be reasonable to expect that, for information on religion and the new immigration, we could look to many different research communities, but in my experience such expectations have been mostly disappointed (Warner 1998c). For example, you might think that demographers would be interested in the topic, but that seems not to be the case, probably because the official governmental statistics with which demographers work, especially the U.S. Census, do not include information on religion. (For an attempt by demographers to overcome these limitations, see Hofrenning and Chiswick 1993.)

Because the new immigrants are so diverse racially and ethnically, and so different from the dominant Euro-American population, ethnic studies scholars should have a lot to report about their religious identities and involvements, but, sadly, such is not the case. For many reasons—disciplinary anticlericalism among them—ethnic studies scholars in the United States, with the exception of a few of those in Asian American Studies, have had little to say about the religious institutions of new immigrants (Yoo 1996).

My own colleagues in sociology of religion have done little better, not because of anticlericalism but because, as predominantly white Protestants, Catholics, and Jews, we tend to lack both the personal cultural capital to have easy entrèe to immigrant communities and the compelling personal interest to want to study their religious lives. As a field, we have spent far more time studying the involvement of a few thousand of our coethnics in so-called new religious movements than that of millions of immigrants in their mostly conventional religions.

Comparative religion is another field that we ought to be able to look to, and here there have been significant research reports from Raymond B. Williams on the religions of South Asians in the United States, from Paul Numrich on Buddhists and Muslims, from Diana Eck's Pluralism Project, especially on non-Christian religions, and from the work of Gary Laderman and his associates on the immigrant component of the new religious diversity of Atlanta (Williams, 1988, 1996; Numrich 1996, 2000a, b; Eck 1996, 1997; Laderman 1996). By and large, though, to judge from papers presented at the annual meetings of the American Academy of Religion, comparative religionists are too text oriented to bother with the difference it makes when a group carries its religion across borders and oceans (Laderman's project, sponsored by the AAR, is a notable exception).

One can look to the various denominations to find how they are ministering to new immigrants, or to metropolitan interfaith groups to connect with those predominantly immigrant communities that are represented among them (e.g., Hindus), but the result will be a biased sample of those groups that are organized in these ways, neglecting nondenominational congregations (common among Chinese Protestants) and those who are not ecumenically minded. Thus, the wonderful religious diversity manifested at the 1993 Parliament of the World's Religions in Chicago severely underrepresented one of the largest sectors of immigrant religion—that of Pentecostal and evangelical Christians from Latin America and East Asia.

To fill these lacunae was the goal of the New Ethnic and Immigrant Congregations Project (NEICP), which, with funding from the Lilly Endowment and the Pew Charitable Trusts, I directed from 1992 to 1997, leading to the publication in

1998 of *Gatherings in Diaspora: Religious Communities and the New Immigration* (Warner and Wittner 1998a). NEICP was a research training and support program open to graduate students and postdoctoral scholars across the United States that was intended both to augment the research literature and to nurture a new generation of researchers. We wanted especially to encourage scholars with roots in new immigrant communities to study their own traditions, as has been the source of many studies of religion in U.S. history (Warner 1998b, 11). As it happened, half of the twelve fellows chosen by NEICP from among the fifty applicants were more-or-less "native anthropologists," members of the linguistic, religious, or national-origin groups whose religious institutions they proposed to study, whereas the others either had less in common with them (language or religion but not both) or were in the situation of the classical anthropological "outsider." (For a discussion of complexities surrounding the concept of the "native" anthropologist, see Narayan 1993.)

In order to orient the work of the fellows, NEICP drew on the scant literature extant at the time our proposal was written (1992), but as project director I also had a more particular, less public grounding for knowledge on new immigrant religion, namely, insights gained from field trips I have taken to religious institutions with students in my sociology of religion classes at the University of Illinois at Chicago (UIC) since 1978. UIC is an urban state university with fairly demanding entrance requirements that especially serves students who are of the first generation in their families to attend university (or to have grown up in the United States). According to the *US News and World Report* publication "America's Best Colleges," UIC is the fifth most diverse of 228 institutions of higher learning in the United States (Burton 2000), a "minority-majority" campus with significant representation of students of Latino, East Asian, South Asian, and Middle Eastern, as well as African American, backgrounds. It is largely because of my students' invitations to their houses of worship that I know as much as I do about Catholics and Pentecostals from Latin America, Protestants from Asia, Hindus, and Muslims from India and the Arab world.

For this article, I draw on my own observations and the previously extant literature, the now completed researches of the NEICP fellows, and a newly growing literature (e.g., Ebaugh and Chafetz 1999; Ebaugh, O'Brien, and Chafetz 2000) to develop five general principles about new immigrant religion, which I will illustrate with specific examples. My thesis is that those of us who track the ramifications of new immigrant religion in the United States must be mindful of both differences and similarities. Thus we should neither blandly assume that, for religious purposes, the new immigrants are just like those who came at the turn of the last century, but at the same time we should not accept the facile view that they bear nothing in common with their predecessors. (Indeed, in the controversies developing within the new literature, I side with those who stress how much we have to learn from the historians who study the last "new immigration" of a hundred years ago [Warner 1998b, 14–15].) Thus, for example, we should recognize that the extent of the new religious and racial diversity in the United States is unprecedented but also not forget that *most of the new immigrants are Christian.* I will return to this matter.

Principle I: *Religion is typically salient for migrants.* This is so for several reasons:

A. Migration promotes reflection on the meaning of the group's history; in the words of Timothy Smith (1978), it is a "theologizing experience." Reflective people among immigrants ask of their presence in the United States, "Why are we here?" Theologian Sang Hyun Lee, of Princeton Theological Seminary, has especially articulated a "theology of liminality," giving theological reasons why Korean immigrants find themselves in a new and strange land and a mission for them to live out (Lee 2001). Under this concept, Lee urges Korean Americans to recognize their own situation in the biblical story of sojourners from Abraham onward. Such awareness gives them a perspective from which to judge the theological, social, and cultural imperfections of the society in which they find themselves and to join with other marginalized people to create a more just society.

B. Religious institutions are "free social spaces" under the American system of religious disestablishment. Unlike their experience in workplaces and schools, immigrants in their own mosques, temples, and churches are not subject to outside pressure to speak English and conform to American ways. Homesick immigrants find in religious institutions a place that feels a bit like home, a little piece of Zion in the midst of Babylon. Will Herberg's portrayal of American religion in the 1950s can be faulted on several grounds but not on his appreciation of its deep roots in the immigrant experience (Herberg 1960, 27–28):

Of the immigrant who came to this country it was expected that, sooner or later, either in his own person or through his children, he would give up virtually everything he had brought with him from the "old country"—his language, his nationality, his manner of life—and would adopt the ways of his new home. Within broad limits, however, his becoming an American did not involve his abandoning the old religion in favor of some native American substitute. Quite the contrary, not only was he expected to retain his old religion, as he was not expected to retain his old language or nationality, but such was the shape of America that it was largely in and through his religion that he, or rather his children and grandchildren, found an identifiable place in American life.

To a great extent, today's immigrants also find their place in American society through their own religion, although, as we shall see, immigrants do not simply "retain" their religion as regards its institutional structure.

C. As their children enter school, immigrants often find that the language and discourse of religion as well as religious rituals themselves are a key to cultural reproduction, a vehicle through which to inculcate the children into their cultural heritage, to give them grounds to understand the differences they experience between themselves and their classmates, differences that at some stages of their upbringing they often wish they could forget. Religion, especially the religious specialists immigrants find in their churches, mosques, and temples, helps immigrant parents answer their children's pained "why?" questions.

D. For many immigrants who suffer indignities in the jobs that they are forced to accept in the new country, the social roles that are made available to them in their religious communities—for example, holding church office—can help them reclaim honor denied in the host society. Election to church offices is thus often an honor to be eagerly sought, rather than an obligation to be borne stoically. This is one reason that "politics," in the narrow sense of who runs the show, is a serious issue in many immigrant churches, often leading to schism (Shin and Park 1988; Hurh and Kim 1990; Min 1992).

E. For those experiencing demands for adjustment to new circumstances, a new religion or newly understood religion may facilitate personal transformation. Thus, born-again Christianity smoothes the break from their parents' culture that the mobility aspirations of Korean American youth demand (Yep et al. 1998); observant Islam helps second-generation Indo-Pakistani college students find a place in America that is both proudly different from the perceived corruption of the host society and autonomous from the patriarchal demands of immigrant parents (Warner, Martel, and Dugan 2001e); and contemplative Buddhism, brought here by monks who minister to immigrant communities, allows European Americans also to transcend the banality of the society in which they were raised even as it allows them to keep on living here (Numrich 2000b).

In general, in U.S. history, religion has mediated difference. Religious difference in the United States is the most significant group difference our society allows. Thus for immigrants religion is a public space, not just a psychological fact. Hence there are thousands of new immigrant churches and other religious institutions and worship centers in the United States. To give a few widely cited counts and estimates (see Warner 1998b, 5), there are about 3,000 Korean Protestant congregations, 700 Chinese Christian churches, and perhaps 7,000 Latino Protestant churches (most of the last-named very small) now in the United States. About 3,500, or one-sixth, of all Catholic parishes in the United States, celebrate the mass in Spanish (and more do so in other languages such as Portuguese, Vietnamese, Kannada, Tagalog, Kreyol, Polish, and Lithuanian); most of these parishes are very large. There are some 1,200–1,500 Islamic centers in the United States, including Muslim Student Association chapters on scores of college campuses, as well as hundreds of Buddhist and Hindu temples and centers. There are also Jain, Sikh, Zoroastrian, and Rastafari centers, as well as countless home altars and house meetings for the practice of Hinduism, popular Catholicism, Vodoun, and Santeria. Of course not all of these are new immigrant institutions, but most are, and very few have received the scholarly attention that is their due.

As NEICP anticipated, several applicants to our program were anthropologists who had been unable to arrange travel abroad to their proposed field sites, but had found a community of the same culture in the United States, centered in, of all places, a church. It was in religious institutions that these anthropologists' "people," whoever those people were, had gathered. These anthropologists had discovered what Smith, Herberg, and other scholars had known, that *religion is typically salient for immigrants.*

Principle II: *Migration is not random with respect to religion* (Warner 1998c).

Although the lack of census data makes it difficult to estimate religious demography, the information we do have suggests that the immigrants who come to the United States from any particular country often represent a religiously (as well as socioeconomically) skewed sample of its population. For example, (South) Korea now is approximately 25 percent Christian, but 50 percent of emigrants from that country to the United States are Christian at the point of embarkation, and half of the remainder join Christian churches as they settle into the United States. The result is that approximately 75 percent of Korean immigrants in the United States are Christian (Kwon, Kim, and Warner 2001a). Vietnam is another historically Buddhist country with a minority of Christians, stemming from relatively recent Western colonialism and proselytization, many of whom had good reason to leave with the communist victory in their homeland. Thus many Vietnamese in the United States are Catholic (Rutledge 1992; Zhou and Bankston 1998). Similarly, India is about 2 percent Christian, 12 percent Muslim, and 85 percent Hindu, but it is very doubtful that the Asian Indian population in the United States simply mirrors these percentages. Raymond Williams (1996) estimates that 10 percent of Indians in the United States are Christian, and it is clear in places like Chicago that Indian Muslims are a major presence in the United States as well, although I haven't heard a reliable estimate of their numbers. For understandable if regrettable reasons, immigrants from the Levant—Lebanese, Jordanians, and Palestinians—are also disproportionately Christian, just as those from the former Soviet Union are disproportionately Jewish and those from Iran are disproportionately Christian and Baha'i as well as Jewish. Both in regard to "pull" factors in migration—the presence of welcoming coreligionists and coethnics as well as jobs in the United States—and "push" factors—targeted persecution and discrimination as well as poverty—religion is one of many variables that must be taken into account if we are to understand who comes to the United States and why.

The internal complexity of sending countries must be taken into account in our attempt to understand the religious factor in immigration. For example, one of the important categories of immigrants who came in response to the occupational preference provision of the 1965 law was nurses from such countries as the

Philippines, Korea, and India. Because in India Christians tend to be concentrated in states like Kerala, with its high levels of education, and because Christian women in India are less subject to Hindu-based strictures against "polluting" occupations, Indian nurses are very likely to be Christian. It is largely for these reasons that Indian Christians are an important presence in the United States (George 1998; Williams 1996). Cubans in America are largely self-selected refugees from a communist regime and thus represent a disproportionately middle-class, white, and conventionally religious (i.e., Roman Catholic) slice of the home island's religious, racial, and social class diversity (Tweed 1997). To take another example, judging from their crowded pews, Catholic churches in Chicago's Mexican neighborhoods appear to be flourishing, despite gloomy prognostications about Latinos' fading loyalty to the Catholic Church. One reason may be that so much of Chicago's Mexican population stems from religiously conservative regions in central Mexico, especially the state of Michoacan, rather than from the more secularized north.

Because a disproportionate share of Asians in the United States (almost all Filipinos, half of Koreans, many Vietnamese, some Indians), as well as almost all Latin Americans, immigrate as Christians and others (a growing number of Chinese) convert after arrival, *the great majority of new immigrants are at least nominally Christian*. Thus the new immigration is bringing about *not the de-Christianization of the United States* (which, if it has happened, has causes internal to Christian denominations [Warner 1999a]), *but the de-Europeanization of American Christianity* (Hernandez 1995; Williams 1996). This is especially apparent on college campuses today, where those who attend well-publicized Bible study groups and those who hand out religious tracts in student unions are likely to be Asian American students, especially Korean, Chinese, and Filipino Americans.

By the same token, America is seeing the de-Asianization of Buddhism because of the participation of so many middle-class whites in Buddhist institutions (Numrich 1996, 2000b), many of which were founded by expatriate and immigrant monks (Fields 1992). Immigration is also implicated in the Sunnification of American Islam through the convergence of African American Muslims and immigrant Muslims, a process underway long before the recent dramatic rapprochement in Chicago between Minister Louis Farrakhan and Imam Warith Deen Mohammed ("Nation of Islam" 2000; Kloehn 2000). These are among the reasons that racial phenotype and ethnic identity are decreasingly reliable indicators of religious affiliation, an observation that leads to the third principle.

> Principle III: *Identities—individual and collective—aren't primordial* (such that what you were in the home country is what you will be or become in the united states) *but "negotiated."*

Religious identities, to use other language, are "constructed" or "transmuted" (in Will Herberg's term) on the basis of home-country materials (especially including religion and language) and group alignments in the receiving country (especially preexisting social groups and categories and the presence or absence of critical masses of coethnics).

As was true a century ago of "Italians" and "Poles" (some of whom had previously been Sicilians and Galicians), so today "Asian Indian," "Indo-Pakistani," "Soviet Jew" (as a religious category), "Afro Caribbean," "African American," "Asian," "Pacific Islander," and "Hispanic" (or "Latino") are identities "made in the U.S.A." (as Raymond Williams [1988] puts it). I think and hope that we have gone beyond sterile either/or debates over "assimilation" versus "the persistence of difference" and can now look dispassionately at the way such changes are occurring today among new immigrants.

As between religious, national origin, and language identities, some become more salient than others in the new country, and, for example, many second-generation Korean Americans seem more eager to be known as "Christian" than "Korean" (Yep et al. 1998). Muslim Pakistanis and Indians in the United States—at least in Chicago—seem more interested in centering their collective life in Islamic centers than are Muslim Arabs, probably because the crosscutting Palestinian identity links many Muslim and Christian Arabs. Evidently, some Asian Indians feel torn between loyalties to their language group (Hindi, Urdu, Gujarati, Punjabi, Telugu, Tamil, Malayalam) and their religion (Hindu, Jain, Sikh, Muslim, and Christian), and it is not clear which identity will prevail (Williams 1988). Nonetheless, Indians in the United States seem concerned to project a *religious* identity rather than one that locates them in the American *racial* hierarchy corresponding to the color of their skin (Kurien 1998), a strategy that some black West Indians employ but with less success (Waters 1999). Thus *"race" is both a conditioning factor in these negotiations and is itself conditioned by them* (McAlister 1998; Wittner 1998; Mittleberg and Waters 1992). American Jews expect Jews from Russia to join synagogues, but many Russian emigrès do not experience their Jewishness as a religious identity (Gold 1987), and they may wind up abandoning it. By contrast, according to Shoshanah Feher (1998), the longer the Islamist regime in Iran persists, the more willing Persian Jews in Los Angeles are to abandon their Persian identity in favor of their Jewish one.

Some immigrant groups, notably Chinese, according to the research of Fenggang Yang (1999), evidently find in Christianity a way of maintaining their homeland identities even as they adjust to life in the United States. Not so much converts—they previously had no religious affiliation at all—as recruits, Chinese Christians find in the independence of their typically nondenominational churches and in the family-oriented teachings of the conservative evangelicalism to which most of them adhere a social space conducive to the expression of Confucian values. The related pattern for Korean Christians has been called one of "adhesive assimilation" by sociologists Kwang Chung Kim and Won Moo Hurh (Kim and Hurh 1993): through their churches, Korean immigrants maintain their Koreanness even as they become American. Although many of their children elevate their

"Christian" over their "Korean" identities, they do so in the context of over-whelmingly Korean youth groups, where they find a comfort zone between the tra-ditionalism of their parents and the racism of American society (Park 2001).

In their study of Vietnamese American youth in New Orleans, Min Zhou and Carl Bankston apply the theory of "segmented assimilation" to show how religion helps these young people grasp one ingredient of assimilation to the American success story—academic achievement—even as they maintain their Vietnamese cultural and linguistic heritage. The more time they spend in church (Zhou and Bankston's site is a Catholic church, but that may be incidental to the story), the more likely they will respect their parents' conservative values and the less likely they will fall under the influence of the alienated American youth who live along-side them in their poverty-ridden community. Over time, these Vietnamese youth may succeed in becoming middle-class Americans even as they continue to be Vietnamese. In this case among others, religion plays a key role *both* in promoting adjustment to the United States *and* in preserving old-country heritage.

The study of "segmented assimilation" is a research frontier (Portes and Zhou 1993) especially in ethnic studies fields, where it is usually employed to look at race- and class-conditioned identities ("black," "Chicano") but not at religious ones. Except for the scholars I have just cited, this literature (e.g., Portes 1994; Rumbaut 1994) has mostly ignored the role of religion in the process of segmented assimilation. Indeed, two recent reviews of Zhou and Bankston's book (in the *International Migration Review* and the *American Journal of Sociology*) mention the role of religious institutions, which is central to their analysis, not at all (Goyette 1999) or only in passing (Chong 1999).

For understanding the negotiation of identity, the role of religion—both as an identity immigrants bring from the home country and a mode of social participa-tion in the host country—cannot be neglected without distorting the processes under study. But this doesn't mean that religious identities automatically tri-umph, or even automatically survive. *In the United States, a society of chronic social change, religion has to be worked at.* It can't be taken for granted (Warner 1991a). That is something that immigrants discover, especially when their children start school. Religion may be thought of as a form of cultural capital, but capital is the result of investments. This leads to the fourth principle.

Principle IV: *Religion in the United States is subject to processes of institutional isomorphism toward congregationalism.*

However the religious group is organized in the home country, there is a ten-dency for religious institutions in the United States to assume a "congregational" form (Warner 1994a), just as formal organizations tend toward the isomorphism of "bureaucracy" (DiMaggio and Powell 1983). The religion may have been temple centered in the old country, where families came at times special or convenient to them to receive the ministrations of monks or priests. But temples do not spontaneously dot the U.S. landscape. Someone has to build them. The religion may have been home centered in the old country, where mother attended a home altar and grandmother provided religious instruction. But U.S. immigration law is biased toward nuclear families, not extended ones, mothers are often busy at work, and grandmothers are in short supply. The very air in the home country may have been suffused with religion, so that children as they grow up see and hear about their families' religion in the street, at school, and at the marketplace. But in the United States, immigrant children have reason to wonder whether their families' customs are simply arbitrary and weird. To bring those children together with those of other families is a way their parents have of providing answers to questions that the children may not even know how to ask and that the parents, as typically hardworking lay people struggling to survive in the new society, most likely would not know how to answer.

The "congregation" is a form of religious organization indigenous to and de jure with Baptists and Jews as a tried-and-true way of concentrating religious energies in a society that approves of religion in general but doesn't provide it as a public service (see Warner 1994a). So the "congregational" form is increasingly adopted "de facto" by other groups, where the religious community becomes (1) a voluntary membership association whose identity is (2) defined more by the people who form it than by the territory they inhabit (cf. the "parish" form of organization). Therefore it is common, though not universal, that immigrant families travel long distances to their places of worship. This is particularly true of Hindus and East Asian Protestants (although less true of Latinos and Muslims [Ebaugh et al. 2000]). A congregation typically features (3) lay leadership (a board of elders, directors, deacons, etc.) and (4) systematic fundraising and a system of trustees (who may overlap with the leadership board) with eventual incorporation for tax purposes as a nonprofit entity, which is often, though not always, independent of any larger "denomination." Because of its lay leadership and voluntary funding, there is (5) a tendency for clergy to be professionals hired as employees. Many immigrant congregations are wracked by conflict between those who exercise religious authority under home-country expectations and those who control the power of the purse in the adopted country (Saloutos 1964, 129; Numrich 1996). Because of its voluntary, self-determined nature, the congregation also has (6) a tendency to ethnic exclusiveness. Because the people who establish the congregation have multiple needs, there is (7) a tendency for it to be multifunctional (featuring more than religious "worship," including educational, cultural, social, political, and social service activities). Because families tend to have the day off on Sunday, there is (8) a tendency for these activities to be brought together under the roof of the institution on Sunday, whatever the particular sacred day of that tradition.

One of many possible examples of such congregationalism is the "Chinese Fellowship Church" studied by Fenggang Yang (1998, 1999). CFC is a nondenominational evangelical church with a big parking lot, run by a lay board jealous of its perquisites and a tradition of keeping its senior pastor on a short leash. Church activities consist of much more than worship, and many of them, including a regular congregational supper, take place on Sunday. Although they represent a wide array of the linguistic and national-origin identities of Chinese Americans, the members (but not the clergy) are exclusively Chinese. Yang's church is Protestant, so we are not surprised that it takes a congregational form.

More surprising is the Church of Haile Selassie I in New York, whose story Randal Hepner (1998) has told. Stemming from the diffuse and liminal Rastafari movement, the CHSI is a settled congregation with a storefront location, regular worship services, a women's organization, Sunday school for the children, counseling services, social events, and a prison ministry. This is a remarkable transformation for a movement founded in Jamaica on the idea that Africans in the diaspora should repatriate to Ethiopia and in the meantime live as sojourners in rural camps. Celebrating weddings, baptisms, and funerals, as well as Sunday services, the CHSI is a far cry from the originally anarchic and egalitarian but masculinist Rasta movement, whose typical gatherings were in public parks and dance halls and whose protagonists followed scripture in letting the dead bury their dead (Hepner 1998, 217). Not a lay-led organization, CHSI is the particular creation of its founder, the Jamaican-born Abuna Asento Foxe, who moved back and forth between Kingston and London and between radical and conservative readings of Rastafarianism before bringing the CHSI to New York in 1990, where he found a receptive audience for his vision of institutionalized religion.

Another example of de facto congregationalism is provided by an earlier study of the Japanese-origin, West Coast–centered Buddhist Churches of America. Tetsuden Kashima (1977) shows how the BCA, partly under World War II–era pressure to look "American" and partly because of constituent demands, came to look less like a lineage of Japanese Buddhist temples and very much like a denomination of American Protestant churches, with men's groups, women's groups, drum corps, professional clergy, weddings, and church suppers.

Catholics in the United States are still organized for the most part into geographical parishes and for much of this century have managed to have ethnically distinct congregations primarily because of their concentration in neighborhoods, which is why I can talk about a sizable number of "Mexican Catholic churches" in Chicago. Yet informally designated "magnet parishes" have appeared all over the country, where people commute from the suburbs into a parish in their old neighborhood or at the intersection of major expressways (Wedam 2000). When the local parish doesn't quite suit them culturally, other Catholics keep their traditions together in saints' associations that meet in private homes. A telling example of how one group of immigrant Catholics do this is provided in Nancy Wellmeier's (1998) study of Mayan Indian refugees from Guatemala living in Los Angeles. They encounter a Catholic archdiocese whose determination to serve the masses of Mexican-origin and other Hispanic Catholics now resident in that city they perceive as an insensitive imposition of an unwanted mixed European-indigenous identity on people who are proud to be Indians.[2] While they do attend mass on Sunday, their religious life really centers on Friday-night home-based meetings of an association devoted to the patron saint of their highland Guatemala village, where they read scripture, discuss its implications, pray communally, share bread and their favorite soft drink, catch up on the news, and play a room-sized marimba that is their most powerful reminder of the homeland many have not seen in years. Although they are lay led and have no professional clergy, they are formally organized, with a board of trustees and elected officers.

Depending on the availability of subcultural critical masses, Hindus in America do similar things. Hindus in America have built huge ecumenical temples with donations from community members that are overseen by professional administrators and usually situated near expressways in the suburbs. (I have visited Hindu temples meeting this description in the New York, Pittsburgh, Nashville, Chicago, and Los Angeles metropolitan areas.) In order to realize economies of scale as well as to help unite the community, such temples often make room for the worship of Gods who in India would not be found in the same space; they are ecumenical temples, and in that respect they are not ethnically exclusive. But in order to socialize their children into their particular language and traditions, members of a Malayalee-speaking Hindu group in Southern California meet in members' homes to offer *pooja* to their own Gods, sing their own *bhajans*, and instruct their own children in their idea of Hindu essentials (Kurien 1998). When, in the company of Prema Kurien, I joined them one evening, a member explained to me that their home-based gatherings were an "experiment"—he used that word—intended to reproduce the tradition in the younger generation.

Of course, in theological terms, a house of worship belongs to God, not to this or that group, and for that reason congregationalism is offensive to many deeply religious people. Islam and Christianity in particular make much of their principled universalism, that people of all races, languages, and nationalities are welcome. Many mosques in the United States, including the Islamic Mission (Brooklyn), approximate this ideal on Friday, when the congregation, those gathered for *jum'ah* prayer from their nearby places of work, tends to be multiethnic. But things are different on Sunday, when the gathering tends to be an ethnically distinct one of families taking the day off (Abusharaf 1998). (For a recent explicit application of the concept of de facto congregationalism to two different immigrant religious communities, see Bankston and Zhou 2000.)

> Principle V: *Congregations* (and other religious institutions) *become vehicles for or venues of intragroup dynamics*, places where relations between generations, genders, and immigrant cohorts are worked out. I will mention three such dynamics.

> A. *There is an immigrant generational gap.* Despite cultural flows from the home country, the American-raised and American-born second generation of most new immigrant groups are for the most part acculturating very rapidly, becoming English dominant and losing fluency in their parents' native tongues. At a minimum, they often find immigrant religious activities incomprehensible

and boring, and many first-generation leaders are worried that their children will leave the fold. One answer is religious instruction in English, and a further development—seen among Korean, Chinese, Filipino, and pan-Asian Protestant groups as well as Muslim Student Association chapters—are English-language worship services. Especially among Asian American youth, these rites are *very* different from those of the parental generation (Chai 1998, 2001), informal where their parents' are formal, using keyboards and drums instead of organs, and overhead projectors instead of hymnals. One question is whether the older generation will cede space for such rites to take place within the precincts of the immigrant congregation—with generational succession only a few years down the road (Goette 2001)—or whether independent and, in principle, panethnic second-generation churches will become the norm. (I hear that such congregations consisting of Korean, Chinese, and Filipino young adults are flourishing in Chicago.) Nonetheless, we can expect generational conflict, because the first generation typically wants the religious institution to be a reminder of what they left behind in the country of origin, a reminder their children don't need in the same way and often don't want.

I would like to see the study of second-generation religion become a research frontier, as is true of the study of the "new second generation" in general (Portes and Zhou 1993; Portes 1994), but that is unlikely to happen until immigrant religion begins to be studied by immigrant communities themselves (especially by members of their own second generation), rather than being monopolized by white anthropologists or expatriate scholars, who are more inclined to focus on "difference."

B. *Gender relations change.* One way that second-generation-led religious groups typically differ from those of the first generation is the higher status assigned to women in formal religious roles: women are likely to serve on boards of directors and even to be worship leaders. But the elevation of women's status happens even among the first generation. So, for example, women are more a presence in many American mosques than they are in mosques in the countries of origin (Haddad and Lummis 1987). I recall the first time I visited New York forty years ago, when, as an undergraduate, I saw Bernstein's *West Side Story* on Broadway and its vivid portrait of immigrant gender relations in the banter that introduces the song-and-dance number "America." Men are often the movers, crossing the ocean in search of better opportunities. But women are typically the settlers and stayers, who find unanticipated freedoms in the new land, even the freedom for a Puerto Rican woman to flout the wishes of her patriarchal family and date a "Polack," while the men dream of going back home crowned with material symbols of their sojourn in America—a Cadillac, a television, and a king-sized bed ready for women who still know their place (Laurents et al. 1958, 45–54).

With such expectations, I was not surprised by Randal Hepner's (1998, 215–217) story of the Daughters of Zion, the organized women of the Church of

Haile Selassie I, who, with evident church blessing, proclaimed emancipation from the "colonial," "medieval," and male-centered conception of themselves as "Rastawomen," insisted on monogamy and the ritual exclusion of the men's "extra wives and girlfriends," and declared the family, no longer the brotherhood, to be the "cornerstone of society." I had suggested to the NEICP fellows that they be on the lookout for such developments.

That makes the story told by NEICP fellow Sheba George (1998) all the more remarkable. George's site was an Indian Orthodox Christian church, peopled primarily by families of nurses from Kerala who, as I have related, came to the United States under the occupational preference provisions of the 1965 immigration law. These women got good jobs in the United States, securely establishing themselves before bringing their husbands and children over some years later. The husbands sought what work they could find, but they often remained underemployed in comparison to the positions they had held in India. It was the husbands who then found in the church a space to reassert their patriarchal authority in the face of the diminution of status they experienced in both the workplace and their homes in the United States. In an unforgettable story, "Caroling among the Keralites," George narrates the tragedy of the men's rejection of their daughters' offer to join them in their joyous Christmas custom of peripatetic caroling through the Indian community of the metropolitan area, when they sing religious texts in Malayalam set to popular Indian movie tunes. The men didn't want their special turf—for years they had gone caroling house to house without members of their families tagging along, frequently indulging in alcoholic beverages illicit in their culture—traipsed upon by yet another reminder of the power of women. Indira Gandhi and their well-employed wives were enough. Thus, the renegotiation of gender roles in the immigrant congregations is not always to the advantage of women. On the basis of their Houston-based RENIR research, Ebaugh and Chafetz (1999, 608) propose this general rule: "To the extent that male congregants perceive themselves to have suffered status loss in the process of immigration, they try to recoup their sense of worth through incumbency in prestigious congregational roles."

Moreover, when women *have* managed to carve out for themselves a new space in the transplanted religious institution—they may be Sunday school or Arab language teachers, even religious day school principals; they may run the bookstore or the media ministry—a new, more religiously conservative cohort of immigrants may arrive and put a halt to such instances of perceived Americanization. That brings me to the third and last occasion for intragroup conflict that I will speak of.

C. *Relations between older and newer cohorts of immigrants may occasion conflict* in religious communities. Fenggang Yang's (1998, 1999) study of a Chinese Christian church in an East Coast city shows how this evidently typical Chinese church renews its ethnicity by successfully incorporating wave after wave of immigrants from an astonishing array of diasporic Chinese communities: speakers of Mandarin, Cantonese, Hakka, and other dialects; nationals of the People's Republic of China, Taiwan, Hong Kong, Singapore, Indonesia, Malaysia, and other countries; fierce anticommunists and those who before coming to the United States had never known a political system other than communism. According to Yang, this diverse array was kept together both by Christian and Confucian ideals of unity and a frequently adjusted system of smaller "fellow-ship groups" to facilitate the ethnically distinct social relations members wanted.

Yet it is not uncommon for newcomers to reject what their predecessors have shaped. When the NEICP fellows convened for our six-week summer training institute in 1994, each of them was assigned as an ethnographic intern to a Chicago-area institution corresponding religiously to the one they had proposed to study in their home site. Rogaia Abusharaf, an emigrè Sudanese Muslim anthropologist, was assigned to a local mosque where I had reason on the basis of previous field trips and personal contacts to believe that she would be welcomed as a scholar and ethnographer. But in the few years since I had been there, newer Islamist activists at the mosque had reintroduced stricter gender roles—including restrictions on women's free-dom of movement within the mosque—that earlier leadership had relaxed. Abusharaf's assignment was less comfortable than I had expected, yet it helped prepare her for a similar phenomenon she encountered at the Brook-lyn mosque that was her research site. In the Brooklyn case, newer immi-grants from another part of the Arab world, namely Yemen, were far less welcoming to women's participation than had been previous groups at the mosque, including Abusharaf's Sudanese countrymen (Abusharaf 1998).

Difference, even antagonism, between cohorts of immigrants is an old story in American immigration history, from the reaction of settled German Reform Jews to the arrival of Eastern European Jews at the end of the nine-teenth century (Herberg 1960) to the grudging welcome extended to new Pol-ish and Lithuanian immigrants in Chicago by those long settled there who fled Soviet regimes after World War II (Erdmans 1998; Kuzmickaite 2003). Religious institutions are one important place that these dramas are played out. In providing themselves a religious space, new immigrants may address one set of problems only to open up new ones.

Conclusion

On the basis of the small literature I have surveyed, the unsystematic site visits I have taken with my students in Chicago, and the advisory role I have played with the out-standing scholars whose work was funded by the New Ethnic and Immigrant Con-gregations Project, I have offered five generalizations about the religious activities and organizations of post-1965 immigrants (and other newcomers to this country) and have been bold enough to call them "principles" that pertain at least to immigrants and their religions in the United States: (1) religion is salient for migrants; (2) migration is not random with respect to religion; (3) identities aren't primordial but "negotiated"; (4) religious institutions tend toward congregationalism; and (5) congregations become venues of intragroup dynamics between parents and children, men and women, and earlier and later cohorts of immigrants. I hope that these principles and the observations abstracted by them may help make sense of glimpses readers may gain of new immigrant religion from local newspapers and public radio stations, among the few media that I have found to pay attention, and that they might serve future scholars as points of departure, "sensitizing concepts" or "hypotheses," for their own research. (One such concept I hope scholars will take up is the idea that we are in the midst of a process of the de-Europeanization of American Christianity, not the de-Christianization of American society.) But more than anything, I hope to have stimulated the demand and the appetite for more research and more literature on a huge, still largely neglected world.

In fact, new research is very much in the offing. The Pew Charitable Trusts, having funded Houston's RENIR project, have promoted that project as a model for grants to projects on religion, immigration, and civic incorporation in a selection of what they call "gateway cities." In contrast to the NEICP's close focus on ten "congregations" scattered about the United States, Helen Rose Ebaugh and her RENIR associates took the city of Houston as the ecological unit of analysis, and they were thus able to propose comparisons across and linkages among individual religious institutions (Ebaugh and Chafetz 1999, 2000; Ebaugh et al. 2000). As of July 2000, six additional large-scale "gateway cities" projects had been funded by Pew, in New York, Los Angeles, Chicago, Miami, Washington, and San Francisco, and results should begin to appear before the middle of the decade.[3] With the city instead of the congregation as the focus and with generous funding for scholars working together on interrelated issues, it should be possible to learn more from the gateway-cities projects how immigrant religious institutions are linked to other local nonreligious institutions, to each other in local ecumenical associations, to such large and important national denominations as the Catholic and Southern Baptist Churches, and to religious and other communities in the countries of origin. NEICP will have helped pave the way by bringing the attention of immigrant religion to funders and scholars and by nurturing a new generation of scholars eager to work on the topic.

NOTES

1. The occasion for the address on which this article is based was the inauguration of the project on Religion and Immigrant Incorporation in New York (RIINY), housed in the International Center for Migration, Ethnicity, and Citizenship at New School University and funded by the Pew Charitable Trusts. Pew had earlier funded RENIR (the Religion, Ethnicity, New Immigrants Research project) at the University of Houston (see Ebaugh and Chafetz 1999;

Ebaugh et al. 2000) after helping fund the NEICP (New Ethnic and Immigrant Congregations Project) at the University of Illinois at Chicago (see Warner and Wittner 1998a).

2. See Warner 2000a (Chapter 11 in this volume) for a sympathetic portrayal of the efforts of Virgilio Elizondo to serve the religious education needs of a culturally and racially mixed (mestizo) immigrant and ethnic population in San Antonio, another major center of migration from Mexico.

3. The author is an advisor for RICSC, the Chicago gateway-cities project Religion, Immigration, and Civil Society in Chicago, housed in the MacNamara Center for the Social Study of Religion at Loyola University of Chicago, the coprincipal investigators of which are Dr. Paul Numrich and Professor Fred Kniss.

REFERENCES

(References to writings of the author are found in a separate listing at the back of the book.)

Abusharaf, Rogaia Mustafa. 1998. "Structural Adaptations in an Immigrant Muslim Congregation in New York." In *Gatherings in Diaspora: Religious Communities and the New Immigration*, ed. R. Stephen Warner and Judith G. Wittner. Philadelphia: Temple University Press.

Bankston, Carl L., III, and Min Zhou. 2000. "De Facto Congregationalism and Socioeconomic Mobility in Laotian and Vietnamese Immigrant Communities: A Study of Religious Institutions and Economic Change." *Review of Religious Research* 41 (June).

Burton, Bill. 2000. "UIC Honored for Campus Diversity by National Student Affairs Group." *UIC News* (March 1).

Chai, Karen J. 1998. "Competing for the Second Generation: English-Language Ministry in a Korean Protestant Church." In *Gatherings in Diaspora: Religious Communities and the New Immigration*, ed. R. Stephen Warner and Judith G. Wittner. Philadelphia: Temple University Press.

———. 2001. "Beyond 'Strictness' to Distinctiveness: Generational Transition in Korean Protestant Churches." In *Korean Americans and Their Religions: Pilgrims and Missionaries From a Different Shore*, ed. Ho-Youn Kwon, Kwang Chung Kim, and R. Stephen Warner. University Park: Pennsylvania State University Press.

Chong, Kelley H. 1999. Review of Zhou and Bankston 1998. *American Journal of Sociology* 104 (March).

Christiano, Kevin J. 1991. "The Church and the New Immigrants." In *Vatican II and U.S. Catholicism: Twenty-Five Years Later*, ed. Helen Rose Ebaugh. Greenwich, Conn.: JAI Press.

DiMaggio, Paul, and Walter W. Powell. 1983. "The Iron Cage Revisited: Institutional Isomorphism and Collective Rationality in Organizational Fields." *American Sociological Review* 48 (April).

Ebaugh, Helen Rose, and Janet Saltman Chafetz. 1999. "Agents for Cultural Reproduction and Structural Change: The Ironic Role of Women in Immigrant Religious Institutions." *Social Forces* 78 (December).

———. 2000. "Dilemmas of Language in Immigrant Congregations: The Tie That Binds or the Tower of Babel?" *Review of Religious Research* 41 (June).

Ebaugh, Helen Rose, Jennifer O'Brien, and Janet Saltman Chafetz. 2000. "The Social Ecology of Residential Patterns and Membership in Immigrant Churches." *Journal for the Scientific Study of Religion* 39 (March).

Eck, Diana. 1996. "Neighboring Faiths: How Will Americans Cope with Increasing Religious Diversity?" *Harvard Magazine* 99 (September–October).

———. 1997. *On Common Ground: World Religions in America*. CD-ROM. New York: Columbia University Press.

Erdmans, Mary Patrice. 1998. *Opposite Poles: Immigrants and Ethnics in Polish Chicago, 1976–1990*. University Park: Pennsylvania State University Press.

Feher, Shoshanah. 1998. "From the Rivers of Babylon to the Valleys of Los Angeles: The Exodus and Adaptation of Iranian Jews." In *Gatherings in Diaspora: Religious Communities and the New Immigration*, ed. R. Stephen Warner and Judith G. Wittner. Philadelphia: Temple University Press.

Fields, Rick. 1992. *How the Swans Came to the Lake: A Narrative History of Buddhism in America.* 3d ed. Boston: Shambhala.

George, Sheba M. 1998. "Caroling with the Keralites: The Negotiation of Gendered Space in an Indian Immigrant Church." In *Gatherings in Diaspora: Religious Communities and the New Immigration*, ed. R. Stephen Warner and Judith G. Wittner. Philadelphia: Temple University Press.

Goette, Robert. D. 2001. "The Transformation of a First-Generation Church into a Bilingual Second-Generation Church." In *Korean Americans and Their Religions: Pilgrims and Missionaries from a Different Shore*, ed. Ho-Youn Kwon, Kwang Chung Kim, and R. Stephen Warner. University Park: Pennsylvania State University Press.

Gold, Steven J. 1987. "Dealing with Frustration: A Study of Interactions Between Resettlement Staff and Refugees." In *People in Upheaval*, ed. Scott M. Morgan and Elizabeth Colson. New York: Center for Migration Studies.

Goyette, Kimberly A. 1999. Review of Zhou and Bankston 1998. *International Migration Review* 33 (Fall).

Haddad, Yvonne Y., and Adair T. Lummis. 1987. *Islamic Values in the United States: A Comparative Study.* New York: Oxford University Press.

Hernández, Edwin. 1995. "The Browning of Adventism." *Spectrum* 25.

Hepner, Randal L. 1998. "The House That Rasta Built: Church-Building and Fundamentalism among New York Rastafarians." In *Gatherings in Diaspora: Religious Communities and the New Immigration*, ed. R. Stephen Warner and Judith G. Wittner. Philadelphia: Temple University Press.

Herberg, Will. 1960. *Protestant, Catholic, Jew: An Essay in American Religious Sociology.* 2d ed. Garden City, N.Y.: Doubleday

Hofrenning, Stella Koutroumanes, and Barry R. Chiswick. 1999. "A Method for Proxying a Respondent's Religious Background." *Journal of Human Resources* 34, 1.

Hurh, Won Moo, and Kwang Chung Kim. 1990. "Religious Participation of Korean Immigrants in the United States." *Journal for the Scientific Study of Religion* 29 (March).

Kashima, Tetsuden. 1977. *Buddhism in America: The Social Organization of an Ethnic Religious Institution.* Westport, Conn.: Greenwood Press

Kim, Kwang Chung, and Won Moo Hurh. 1993. "Beyond Assimilation and Pluralism: Syncretic Socio-cultural Adaptation of Korean Immigrants." *Ethnic and Racial Studies* 16 (October).

Kloehn, Steve. 2000. "Islam's Farrakhan, Mohammed Pledge Support, End to Rivalry." *Chicago Tribune* (February 26).

Kwon, Ho-Youn, Kwang Chung Kim, and R. Stephen Warner, eds. 2001. *Korean Americans and Their Religions: Pilgrims and Missionaries from a Different Shore.* University Park: Pennsylvania State University Press

Kurien, Prema. 1998. "Becoming American by Becoming Hindu: Indian Americans Take Their Place at the Multicultural Table." In *Gatherings in Diaspora: Religious Communities and the New Immigration*, ed. R. Stephen Warner and Judith G. Wittner. Philadelphia: Temple University Press.

Kuzmickaite, Daiva. 2003. *Between Two Worlds: Recent Lithuanian Immigrants in Chicago (1988–2000).* Vilnius, Lithuania: Versus Aureus.

Laderman, Gary, ed. 1996. *Religions of Atlanta: Religious Diversity in the Centennial Olympic City.* Atlanta: American Academy of Religion.

Laurents, Arthur, Leonard Bernstein, Steven Sondheim, and Jerome Robbins. 1958. *West Side Story: A Musical.* New York: Random House.

Lee, Sang Hyun. 2001. "Pilgrimage and Home in the Wilderness of Marginality: Symbols and Context in Asian American Theology." In *Korean Americans and Their Religions: Pilgrims and Missionaries from a Different Shore*, ed. Ho-Youn Kwon, Kwang Chung Kim, and R. Stephen Warner. University Park: Pennsylvania State University Press.

Léon, Luis. 1998. "Born Again in East LA: The Congregation as Border Space." In *Gatherings in Diaspora: Religious Communities and the New Immigration*, ed. R. Stephen Warner and Judith G. Wittner. Philadelphia: Temple University Press.

McAlister, Elizabeth. 1998. "The Madonna of 115th Street Revisited: Vodou and Haitian Catholicism in the Age of Transnationalism." In *Gatherings in Diaspora: Religious Communities and the New Immigration*, ed. R. Stephen Warner and Judith G. Wittner. Philadelphia: Temple University Press.

Min, Pyong Gap. 1992. "The Structure and Social Functions of Korean Immigrant Churches in the United States." *International Migration Review* 26, 4.

Mittelberg, David, and Mary C. Waters. 1992. "The Process of Ethnogenesis among Haitian and Israeli Immigrants in the United States." *Ethnic and Racial Studies* 15 (July).

Narayan, Kirin. 1993. "How Native Is a 'Native' Anthropologist?" *American Anthropologist* 95.

"The Nation of Islam Merges into Islam." 2000. *The Minaret* 22 (February).

Numrich, Paul David. 1996. *Old Wisdom in the New World: Americanization in Two Immigrant Theravada Buddhist Temples*. Knoxville: University of Tennessee Press.

———. 2000a. "Recent Immigrant Religions and the Restructuring of Metropolitan Chicago." In *Public Religion and Urban Transformation*, ed. Lowell W. Livezey. New York: New York University Press.

———. 2000b. "How the Swans Came to Lake Michigan: The Social Organization of Buddhist Chicago." *Journal for the Scientific Study of Religion* 39 (June).

Park, Soyoung. 2001. "The Intersection of Religion, Race, Gender, and Ethnicity in the Identity Formation of Korean American Evangelical Women." In *Korean Americans and Their Religions: Pilgrims and Missionaries from a Different Shore*, ed. Ho-Youn Kwon, Kwang Chung Kim, and R. Stephen Warner. University Park: Pennsylvania State University Press.

Portes, Alejandro, ed. 1994. "Special Issue: The New Second Generation," *International Migration Review* 28 (Winter).

Portes, Alejandro, and Min Zhou. 1993. "The New Second Generation: Segmented Assimilation and Its Variants." *Annals of the American Academy of Political and Social Science* 530 (November).

Rumbaut, Rubén G. 1994. "The Crucible Within: Ethnic Identity, Self-Esteem, and Segmented Assimilation among Children of Immigrants." *International Migration Review* 28, 4.

Rutledge, Paul J. 1992. *The Vietnamese Experience in America*. Bloomington: Indiana University Press

Saloutos, Theodore. 1964. *The Greek in the United States*. Cambridge: Harvard University Press.

Shin, Eui Hang, and Hyun Park. 1988. "An Analysis of Causes of Schisms in Ethnic Churches: The Case of Korean-American Churches." *Sociological Analysis* 49 (Fall).

Smith, Timothy L. 1978. "Religion and Ethnicity in America." *American Historical Review* 83 (December).

Tweed, Thomas A. 1997. *Our Lady of the Exile: Diasporic Religion at a Cuban Catholic Shrine in Miami*. New York: Oxford University Press.

Waters, Mary C. 1999. *Black Identities: West Indian Immigrant Dreams and American Realities*. Cambridge: Harvard University Press.

Wedam, Elfriede. 2000. "Catholic Spirituality in a New Urban Church." In *Public Religion and Urban Transformation*, ed. Lowell W. Livezey. New York: New York University Press.

Wellmeier, Nancy. J. 1998. "Santa Eulalia's People in Exile: Maya Religion, Culture, and Identity in Los Angeles." In *Gatherings in Diaspora: Religious Communities and the New Immigration*, ed. R. Stephen Warner and Judith G. Wittner. Philadelphia: Temple University Press.

Williams, Raymond Brady. 1988. *Religions of Immigrants from India and Pakistan: New Threads in the American Tapestry.* Cambridge: Cambridge University Press.

———. 1996. *Christian Pluralism in the United States: The Indian Immigrant Experience.* Cambridge: Cambridge University Press

Wittner, Judith G. 1998. "A Reader among Fieldworkers." In *Gatherings in Diaspora: Religious Communities and the New Immigration,* ed. R. Stephen Warner and Judith G. Wittner. Philadelphia: Temple University Press.

Yang, Fenggang. 1998. "Tenacious Unity in a Contentious Community: Cultural and Religious Dynamics in a Chinese Christian Church." In *Gatherings in Diaspora: Religious Communities and the New Immigration,* ed. R. Stephen Warner and Judith G. Wittner. Philadelphia: Temple University Press.

———. 1999. *Chinese Christians in America: Conversion, Assimilation, and Adhesive Identities.* University Park: Pennsylvania State University Press.

Yep, Jeanette, Peter Cha, Susan Cho Van Riesen, Greg Jao, and Paul Tokunaga. 1998. *Following Jesus Without Dishonoring Your Parents: Asian American Discipleship.* Downers Grove, Ill.: InterVarsity Press.

Yoo, David. 1996. "For Those Who Have Eyes to See: Religious Sightings in Asian America." *Amerasia Journal* 22 (Spring).

Zhou, Min, and Carl L. Bankston III. 1998. *Growing Up American: How Vietnamese Children Adapt to Life in the United States.* New York: Russell Sage Foundation.

14

Interpreting "Asian American Religion" for a Non-American Audience (2003)

*R*eligions in Asian America: Building Faith Communities, edited by Pyong Gap Min and Jung Ha Kim, is a superb, very much needed collection of original analyses of the many ways that Asians are now (and for a century have been) settling religiously in the United States. It belongs in scholarly libraries and the collections of comparative religionists, and it ought to have widespread classroom use. Yet given the possibility, indeed likelihood, that the title will mislead readers outside the United States, it is necessary to begin with the promises implied in the title (promises on which the book substantially delivers).

First is the matter of what "Asian" means. Large-scale Asian migration to the United States goes back to the 1850s, when Chinese were imported to work in California's mines and railroads. Further migration of Chinese was precluded by law in 1882, whereupon Japanese were brought in, but they in turn were excluded by the "Gentlemen's Agreement" of 1907. Koreans came in 1903–1905 to work the sugar plantations in Hawaii, newly annexed by the United States, until their immigration was prohibited by the Japanese overlords of their country. Then it was the turn of Filipinos, whose homeland was by then a U.S. colony. Asian immigration was cut off entirely by the 1924 laws, but meanwhile many of the Koreans and Filipinos in Hawaii made their way to the mainland, particularly to California. Although the full story is far more complicated than this brief sketch indicates, the upshot is that for its first century Asian migration to the United States was largely a matter of East Asians coming to the West Coast, where the category "Asian" (earlier, "Oriental") referred particularly to Americans of Chinese and Japanese, and to a lesser extent Korean and Filipino, origin. Except for a few thousand Punjabis who fled Canada for California's central valley early in the twentieth century, South Asians came to the United States in large numbers only with the immigration law reform of 1965 (the Hart-Celler Act), and immigrants to the United States from the Middle East, many of them technically from Asia, are not classified as "Asian." Although Pyong Gap Min is careful to point to the simultaneous existence of East Asian and South Asian communities in the United States, "Asian" in the U.S. consciousness still implicitly refers primarily to East Asians, to whose religious communities five of the eight chapters in the book are devoted. (Of the remainder, one is Min's general introduction and one concerns Southeast Asians. Only one is devoted to Indians, and there is no coverage of Pakistanis.) "Asian" has a different meaning in the United States from that in the United Kingdom and elsewhere in Europe.

Second is the question of the composition of "Asian American" populations. Because of the long history of their coethnics in the United States, some post-1965 Asian immigrants, Koreans and Chinese in particular, had preexisting institutions, often religious institutions, as a base on which to build their communities. (There has been very little recent immigration from Japan.) Yet what sociologists call the "new" (i.e., post-1965) immigration from Asia differs substantially from that of the turn of the last century. Typically impelled by the need for labor, U.S. immigration policy after 1965 sought highly educated and skilled workers under so-called occupational preference provisions. Whereas most Asian immigrants of a century ago were manual laborers, many of those coming in the wake of Hart-Celler were professionals. Another provision was for "family reunification," where preexisting communities added relatives to their number. One result is that those Asian Americans populations that stem primarily from post-1965 immigration are disproportionately found near the top of the occupational, and therefore economic, ladder. In the words of Prema Kurien (101): "This explains why Indians are among the wealthiest and most educated foreign-born groups in this country." When such affluent people sponsor their relatives to migrate, the average occupational status of Asian groups tends over time to fall. Nonetheless, Hindus, to take one American religious community, tend to be well off, and there is no obvious reason for Americans to find credible those stereotypes that link Asian religion with backwardness and poverty. As shown in the chapter by Min Zhou, Carl Bankston, and Rebecca Kim, the glaring exception to this pattern are Southeast Asians, the first of whom to come to the United States were war refugees and technically not immigrants, some of the refugees (particularly the Hmong) remaining high-poverty populations. By and large, Asians in America are a success story, often called, to the chagrin of many, "a model minority."

Third is what the "religions" of Asian America are. Because U.S. regulations do not allow questions of religion to be asked by the census, it is difficult to know with certainty what if any religion Americans profess. Yet we do have a knowledge base. For example, migration is not random, so even the relatively evenhanded Hart-Celler provisions do not produce a religious cross section of each sending country among its emigrants. Thus a very large percentage of immigrants from Asia are (or soon become) Christian. According to Min (9), "Filipinos compose the largest Asian immigrant group in the post-1965 era," and, given the history of their country, they are almost all Christian, specifically Catholic. For a variety of reasons, about 75 percent of Korean Americans are Christian, mostly Protestant.

Because those most eager and able to seek refuge from the Communist government of Vietnam after 1975 were Catholics implicated in the French and then American occupations, "Catholics were overrepresented among refugees from Vietnam," at one-third to two-fifths of the refugees, according to Min (5). Many post-1965 Chinese immigrants profess no religion, but many of them convert to Christianity after arrival, with the result, according to Fenggang Yang, that "Christianity appears to have become the largest religion, and Christian churches have, in fact, become the predominant religious institutions among the Chinese in America" (71). Thus, the children of Chinese and Korean immigrants are prominent among evangelical Christians on U.S. university campuses. Even some 10 percent of Indian Americans are Christian, five times their prevalence in their home country. It therefore reflects no bias on the part of the editors that of the space in the book devoted to specific religious communities, far more is devoted to Christians (Catholic and Protestant both) than to those of other religions.

In this light, the coverage of the book is generally representative of Asian American religion, with, in addition to Min's excellent overview of the literature, chapters focused on Southeast Asian (Vietnamese, Cambodian, and Lao) Catholics and Buddhists (Zhou, Bankston, and Kim), Chinese Buddhists and Christians (Yang), Indian American Hindus (Kurien), Japanese American Buddhists and Christians (David Yoo), Filipino Catholics and Protestants (Steffi San Buenaventura), and Korean American Protestants (Jung Ha Kim), and one on the panethnic (East) Asian Christian churches now appearing among second- and later generation Asian Americans in California (Russell Jeung). Yang and San Buenaventura also spend time on elements of folk religion. Two of the chapters are primarily historical, weighted heavily toward the home-country background (San Buenaventura on Filipinos) and on pre–World War II settlements in the United States (Yoo on Japanese Americans). The others are sociological, focusing on the setting of these communities in the present-day United States, their internal dynamic processes, and, in some cases, their relationships with the home country. Notably absent is any treatment of Indo-Pakistani Muslims (indeed any Muslim community) and Thai Buddhists, to mention two groups who seem particularly energetic in the building of religious communities. Someday, I would like to see a chapter on the religiously diverse majority-Asian community of Hawaii. Nonetheless, the efforts of the editors are to be lauded, not blamed. The chapter on Filipinos is one of only a handful on Filipino religion in the United States, and it is difficult to find scholars with the qualifications to conduct sociological research with Muslims in the United States. As Min reminds us, immigrant religion in the United States has until recently been a largely neglected topic, and the outstanding scholars whose work appears in this volume are rare finds.

Some highlights. Southeast Asian refugees were originally scattered around the country in an effort to help them assimilate, but through their remarkable efforts of secondary migration are now concentrated in California, Texas, and Louisiana (Vietnamese and Lao), as well as Wisconsin and Minnesota (Hmong).

According to Zhou, Bankston, and Kim, the authority relations between these laity and their Buddhist monks are conditioned by the relative affluence the various communities have managed to achieve. According to Yang, Chinese Buddhist temples reach out across linguistic, sectarian, and even racial divides, whereas Chinese Christian churches bring together Chinese from a bewildering variety of backgrounds but are themselves sectarian and constrained to exhibit their Chinese identity. Despite the differences between Buddhism and Christianity, David Yoo shows that Japanese Americans called on both to sustain them during the bitter years of World War II when they were removed from their West Coast homes, farms, and businesses to euphemistically named "relocation centers." Readers of Yoo's essay will recognize similarities between the religious struggles of Japanese Americans in the first half of the twentieth century and those of Korean Americans at its end. Hindus in the United States, as already stated, tend to be high caste and upper class. Kurien writes that they have founded religious institutions largely for the benign purpose of passing their traditions on to their children, but these very institutions later serve as a base for the few among them who support the Hindu nationalist movement in India. San Buenaventura documents that Filipinos come to the United States with a background of home-country religious mobilizations (Protestant, Catholic, and indigenous) behind them. Jung Ha Kim usefully divides Korean American history into four periods from 1903 to the present, the fourth being that after the 1988 Seoul Olympics and the 1992 Los Angeles riots, both of which events seemed to make to immigrants the unsettling argument that they would have been better off staying at home. Jeung compares two approaches to the formation of panethnic (especially Japanese American and Chinese American) Protestant churches, those of evangelicals, who see Asian Americans as an ethnic group, and those of the so-called mainline, for whom Asians are a racialized group. The theme of "race"—the claim that the Asian immigrant experience will differ from that of European immigrants of the turn of the last century by reason of racism—is sounded by Min in his introduction and carried throughout most of the chapters.

Reprinted, by permission, from the *Bulletin of the Royal Institute for Inter-Faith Studies (BRIIFS)* 5, no. 1 (Spring/Summer 2003): 210–214. (This reprint is slightly abridged).

15

The De-Europeanization of American Christianity (2004)

As most everyone has heard, immigration is profoundly changing the contour of religion in America. Hundreds of thousands of people, most of them from what used to be known as the third world (relatively few from Europe), stream into the country every year, bringing their religious identities with them. The number of immigrants who have arrived since 1965 exceeds the millions who came at the turn of the last century.

The immigrants' places of worship, identified by signs in strange languages, dot the landscape from coast to coast. Their religious festivals and celebrations are written up in the press. Their children are noticeable on college campuses. Their presence challenges the religious establishment to make room for new partners in interfaith councils and in ongoing debates about the relation between church and state.

All this is true. What many people have not heard, however, and need to hear, is that the great majority of the newcomers are Christian. Some are adherents of other great world religions (including Islam, Hinduism, Buddhism, and Judaism). A larger number profess no religion. A few practice indigenous religions. But most are Christian. This means that the new immigrants represent not the de-Christianization of American society but the de-Europeanization of American Christianity.

The religious sites built by Muslims, Hindus, and Buddhists are surely a dramatic presence. Magnificent Buddhist temples in California and Maryland, ornate Hindu *mandirs* in the outskirts of Los Angeles, Nashville, and Pittsburgh, and grand, austere Islamic centers in uptown Manhattan, outside the Washington beltway, and in the suburbs ringing Chicago—all these offer visible support for the argument of Harvard professor Diana Eck that the United States has become "the world's most religiously diverse nation."

Yet the facts are more complicated. Among countries of historic Christendom, France, Germany, and England have proportionately far more Muslims than does the United States. India, the home of Hinduism, has many more Muslims and Christians than the United States has Hindus and Muslims. South Korea, the historic bridge across which Buddhism traveled to Japan, now has nearly as many Christians as Buddhists. Indeed, a half century ago, the proportion of Jews in the U.S. population was quite a bit greater than the combined proportion of Muslims, Hindus, and Buddhists today. The single paragraph devoted to Christian immigrants by Eck in her much-noticed book *A New Religious America* obscures the fact that the new immigration is bringing about not so much a new diversity among American religions as diversity within America's majority religion.

It should have been obvious all along that most post-1965 immigrants are Christian. The largest single "sending country" is, of course, Mexico, an overwhelmingly Christian nation. Millions of other new immigrants from the Western Hemisphere stem from predominantly Christian countries like El Salvador and Guatemala, the Dominican Republic and Jamaica, Ecuador and Brazil. (Some of the new entrants from these countries to the United States are technically "refugees," not immigrants, but their numbers are included in the totals that concern religious demographers.) Many immigrants from the Eastern Hemisphere also stem from predominantly Christian countries outside Europe, such as the Philippines, ancestral home to the second-largest Asian American population, and Ghana, one of sub–Saharan Africa's several rapidly Christianizing nations. Many also come from Christian sectors of such religiously mixed countries as Korea, Vietnam, India, and Lebanon. Many of the Europeans come from former Soviet bloc countries like Poland, Russia, and Ukraine, which is where the United States gets many of the immigrants who profess no religion, but also the source of Eastern Orthodox Christians (and, of course, Jews).

As a rule, people who leave their country represent a biased, not a representative, sample of their compatriots. The sampling processes, if we can use that term, are complex. In general, younger people are most likely to emigrate. But each country has a different story. The population of South Korea, for example, is about one-quarter Buddhist and one-quarter Christian. (How Christians became so numerous is itself a big story.) But half of those who emigrate from Korea to the United States are Christian, stemming from the more urban, educated, and less settled segment of Korean society. (Many had earlier been refugees from the communist north.) Another half of those who arrive with no religious identity later become Christian. The end result is that 75 percent of Korean Americans are Christian.

As a former French colony, Vietnam had a flourishing Catholic population before the U.S.-backed regime in the south lost its lengthy war with the north. Not surprisingly, many of the first refugees were educated, middle-class Catholics, some previously refugees from the north; these people are disproportionately represented among Vietnamese Americans today.

To cite another example, as a result of the bitter struggle between Israelis and Palestinians, many Christians are leaving the Holy Land. Consequently, Christians are overrepresented among Arab Americans. In yet another instance, America's need for nurses has been answered by immigration from India (among other countries), where, because of both caste taboos and uneven educational opportunities, nurses are especially found among the traditionally Christian people of the state of Kerala.

The same principle of nonrandom selection is responsible for part of the non-Christian presence in the United States. For example, the population of India is about 12 percent Muslim, but because of both "push" factors in India and "pull" factors (especially economic opportunities) in the United States, the proportion of Muslims among Indian Americans is probably higher than that. For the same reasons—push and pull factors—Jews are greatly overrepresented among migrants from the former Soviet Union. Nonetheless, the religiously biased selection principle operates primarily in favor of Christians.

Another factor leading to the diversification of American Christianity is widespread conversion among some immigrant groups, notably the Chinese. Those from mainland China are likely to have no religious identity upon entry. In the United States they encounter ethnic Protestant churches in which several Chinese languages are spoken and family-oriented, Confucian values are taught. Despite initial misgivings, many immigrants find that they can affirm both their traditional Chinese identity and an emerging American identity in such churches. In response to evangelism on the part of fellow Chinese, some Chinese, especially those from Taiwan, reassert their residual Buddhism. But Christian converts predominate to the extent that an estimated one-third of Chinese Americans, across all generations, are now Christian.

The foregoing claims have been qualified with words like "many," "some," and "estimated." Unlike Canada, Great Britain, India, and the Philippines, the United States has no religious census. Sociologists can speak of the age, sex, and racial composition of the U.S. population with some precision, based on government counts. But for religion, researchers have to rely on other sources, each with its own limitations.

One source is the "roll data" kept by religious bodies themselves, which vary in quality from the clearly defined, meticulously updated and publicly available membership records of the Presbyterian Church (U.S.A.) to the much less reliable numbers put forth by many historically African American denominations. Catholic data vary in quality from diocese to diocese.

In the case of Islam, one of its ethical strengths turns out to be a drawback in gathering numbers. A Muslim does not "belong" to a particular mosque, which means that there is enormous racial, ethnic, and class diversity in a congregation that gathers for Friday prayer—in contrast to the homogeneity of most Protestant congregations. But when asked to come up with numbers, Muslim organizations at best can sum up estimates of attendance based on the huge, Easter-sized crowds observing Eid al Fitr at the close of Ramadan. No comprehensive roll data for American Muslims exist.

The other source for religious demography is "poll data" drawn from individuals' answers to questions put to them in surveys. Polls vary greatly in quality. The best data on religion come from the General Social Survey, administered through face-to-face interviews to a representative sample of some fifteen hundred English-speaking adult Americans every other year. The GSS asks hundreds of questions and provides rich information, but the numbers surveyed are insufficient for us to learn much about small immigrant subpopulations.

The opposite extreme was taken by the 2001 American Religious Identification Survey, which asked just a few religion questions of over fifty thousand adult Americans, also English speaking, reached by random telephone dialing. Specialized surveys were taken in 2001 and 2002 of Hispanics and Asians, using Spanish, Chinese, Korean, and Vietnamese for the interviews, and one careful, random-sample survey, asking about religion among other things, was done in 1997 and 1998 based on INS records of legal immigrants in 1996.

Within a reasonable range of error, the poll data tell a consistent story: two-thirds or more of new immigrants are Christian, no more than one-fifth affirm any non-Christian faith, and as many as one-sixth claim no religious identity at all. When these figures are compared to the 75 to 80 percent of the population at large who affirm one or another variety of Christian identity and the roughly 5 percent who are other-than-Christian, it is clear that the new immigration is diversifying American religion. But the case should not be overstated.

In particular, no evidence supports the notion, cited in some newspapers and some pulpits, that there are more Muslims than Presbyterians in the United States. Yes, the number of members claimed by the relatively rigorous counts of all the Presbyterian bodies in the country—around 3.5 million—is less than the 6 or 7 million figure claimed by some Muslim spokespersons. But in surveys, many more Americans call themselves Presbyterian than the Presbyterian churches claim. According to poll data, there are 10 to 11 million Presbyterians. Meanwhile, no national survey shows the Muslim population of the United States to be greater than 1 percent, or around 3 million at most. In other words, while poll data indicate that there are three times as many self-identified Presbyterians as enrolled Presbyterians, there are half as many self-identified Muslims as are claimed by these Muslim leaders.

At the same time, we can reliably estimate from poll data that there are as many Hispanic Protestants in the United States, some eight million, as the number of Jews and Muslims put together. The massive demographic action is found among Christians.

The point is not to celebrate Christian growth or to denigrate Muslims, Buddhists or Hindus, who have become integral constituents of the American religious system. Muslims in particular are a key electoral constituency in such swing states as Michigan (as Jews are in Florida). Any tendency to triumphalism on the part of Christians should be chastened by the equally dramatic, recent defection of millions of American Christians to the ranks of the religiously unaffiliated (not just to the "unchurched," but to the unabashed "no religion" column).

The point is that Christianity is not for European Americans to define, speak for, or even disown. Millions of new immigrants are redefining what it means to be Christian in the United States. They are joining African Americans, who continue to be the American church's sturdiest pillar, in coloring American Christianity.

The impact of immigration is greatest among Catholics, a majority of whom may be Hispanic at some point later in this century. (To a remarkable extent, immigrants are replacing native-born defectors.) Not only are masses said in Spanish in thousands of American parishes, but some parishes are influenced by Latino religious styles. The piety is more devotional, more home-centered, and less parish-centered, more visual and less verbal than the rites inspired by Vatican II. Mexican American public celebrations—from the December 12 feast day of the Virgen de Guadalupe through Good Friday Via Crucis pageants to the observance of El Día de los Muertos in early November—give Catholics a new presence in local newspapers and television. Because the Virgin has appeared to the faithful in many countries at many times, she is celebrated somewhere in the United States throughout the year—in February among Maya Indians in Los Angeles, in July among Haitians in New York, in September among Cubans in Miami.

Catholic scholars have referred to such rites and feast days as reflecting the "inculturation" of pre-Christian symbols and traditions. In cultures influenced by African religiosity, the inculturation of pre-Christian elements is particularly profound. In Haitian vodou, African-origin deities "walk with" the Virgin Mary or another Christian saint, the venerated person having two cultural sides.

Since surveys typically allow only one answer to the religion identification question "Are you Protestant, Catholic, or Jewish?" poll data surely underestimate the number of American practitioners of Afrocentric religions like vodou and Santeria. But because such religions are inextricably mixed with Christian traditions—most Haitians, for example, are located somewhere on a vodou Catholic continuum—the number of Christians is not at the same time overestimated. These people can be said to practice two religions.

Protestants differ on the legitimacy they are willing to accord to the practice of inculturation. Haitian evangelicals reject vodou out of hand, while some Mexican Pentecostal services feature mariachi bands and images of the Virgin. Pentecostalism appears to have been rapidly indigenized in Latin America, Africa, and Asia precisely because of its capacity to absorb and express local cultures—which are then brought to the United States by Pentecostal immigrants.

More broadly, immigrant Protestant congregations are carriers of home-country cultures in matters of music, language, dress, and food, if not in specific religious symbols. Even the typically dignified worship of Chinese evangelicals is distinctly Chinese. Although some immigrant Christians of color descend from people originally evangelized by Europeans, in most cases the faith has been long carried by indigenous communities. White American Protestants might learn from the example of Latin American, Asian, and African ways of being Christian how inculturated their own religious observances are—for example, how European are their celebrations of Christmas and Easter. Such Christians can learn from immigrant Christians how universal is the faith and how relative is one's embodiment of it.

Immigrant Christians tend to be conservative in matters of religious and moral culture. Among Protestants, the influx of Pentecostals and evangelicals greatly outnumbers the adherents of mainline (or, better, "historical") denominational traditions. Many Catholics come from countries little affected by Vatican II liturgical reforms. Eastern Orthodox Christians come from "autocephalous" national churches deeply interwoven with local traditions. Family practices, gender attitudes, and sexual mores are typically more supportive of parents' prerogatives, less in tune with feminist assumptions, and decidedly less accepting of homosexuality than is the case for many white American religious communities.

Yet it is a mistake to equate religious conservatism with political conservatism. A recent study of Hispanic churches revealed a consistent pattern among this group (the largest of America's minority groups, one continually replenished by immigrants): Hispanics, whether Catholic or Protestant, tend to be conservative on issues of sexual morality but liberal on issues of the economy and minority rights. They are less likely than African Americans to identify with the Democratic party, but most vote Democratic. Hispanics—who, strictly speaking, are an ethnic rather than a racial group, composed of people who self-identify as white, black, mixed, and "other"—are historically linked to colonized and subordinated peoples and are unlikely to be complacent about governmental provision of social services. Across the board, new immigrants bring a more communal, less individualistic perspective to our society. Therefore, Americans who struggle for economic justice should not regard these religious conservatives as their enemies. If they do, they will wall themselves off from potential allies.

Above all, the new immigrants make it decreasingly plausible for Americans to think of Christianity as a white man's religion. Both immigration and selective conversion are decoupling religion and race. American Buddhists are as likely to be white as Asian. The U.S. Muslim community mixes African Americans, Bosnians, South Asians, and people from the Middle East. And although it may not be apparent in many congregations, American Christians are increasingly people of color.

16

Changes in the Civic Role of
Religion (1999)

Modernity urgently needs to be saved from its most unconditional supporters.

–Charles Taylor

Contrasting the Civic Role of Religion in 1960 and 1996

By the end of the 1950s the United States had achieved a working consensus on the place of religion in society, consisting of two aspects. First, religious *identity* was relegated to a "private" realm, to be left uncontested and largely unexamined. Another way of putting this is that religion was considered a legitimately "ascribed" category. As Will Herberg (1960) put it, to be a Protestant, a Catholic, or a Jew were three equally acceptable and morally unquestionable ways of being a good American. Indeed, so legitimate was religious identification that no one disclaiming a personal religion was likely to receive a public hearing, and those affirming no religious preference in opinion polls were, in fact, largely marginal members of society.

Second, however, it was also considered entirely proper for religious institutions, especially the National Council of Churches, to make pronouncements on matters of national public policy, with the guiding assumption that, on fundamental matters of *ethics and morality*, all religion speaks with one voice. If religious identities were ascriptive, religion's teachings were universalistic. This was the ethnographer's (if not the philosopher's) wisdom behind Dwight Eisenhower's often quoted remark: "Our government makes no sense unless it is founded on a deeply felt religious faith—and I don't care what it is" (Herberg 1960, 84).

There were limits on this consensus. It did not extend to those other than Christians and Jews, it included some under its umbrella (particularly Catholics and Jews) only at the cost of their adopting Protestant manners (Cuddihy 1987), it was not shared by fundamentalist Protestants (Ammerman 1987), and it depended to some extent on an external enemy, a shared anticommunism. The public space allowed for religion was also a highly gendered space, a masculinist version of "public," a matter to which I will return in the conclusion.

But the consensus was nonetheless real. It passed tests and made differences. The electoral margin of John Kennedy in 1960 was razor thin, but his victory dealt a heavy blow to politically acceptable anti-Catholicism. In the years surrounding the Kennedy presidency, religious leaders successfully (not without challenge and not without great courage) mobilized the legitimacy of religion in support of the civil rights movement and civil rights legislation (Wood 1981). Dr. Martin Luther King, Jr.'s career depended on a religious consensus he both invoked and helped to build.

To speak of such a religious consensus today—of the great moral authority exerted by King in his "Letter from Birmingham Jail"—is to speak about a bygone era. Today, religious proclamations, especially at the national level, are more likely to appear divisive than morally commanding. "Ecumenical" bodies like the National Council of Churches "can no longer plausibly claim to be the primary, privileged vehicles of Christian unity" (Heim 1996, 781) let alone of the national conscience, and at the opposite pole, the claims of Ralph Reed's Christian Coalition are widely understood as partisan pleading.

Forty years ago, in order to allay suspicion and claim respectability, King and his colleagues gathered under the banner of the Southern *Christian* Leadership Conference, invoking both the unifying label of Christianity and the prestige of the ministry as a profession in American society at large and African American society in particular in the 1950s. By contrasting example, the new journal *Books and Culture*, appearing in a format and size virtually identical with the New York Review of Books, announces itself "a *Christian* Review" in self-conscious recognition of its alternative, outsider status, insinuating itself with allies as a welcome cry in the wilderness and virtually daring adversaries to take offense.[1]

Badges of religious identity—from the "Christian" label to the crosses, yarmulkes, and *hijab* coverings worn by today's college students—are increasingly asserted in order to invite recognition from the like-minded, embolden comrades, confound enemies, and invite inquiries from those open to persuasion. Although symbols of this kind may be no more than assertions of the individual identities of their bearers, many onlookers experience them as unwanted efforts at proselytization; some, especially the Christian and Muslim ones, may indeed be so intended. In these and other ways, religious identities have become not only more assertive but also more contested. Instead of having one's religious identity be taken for granted, one may now be expected to defend and claim it. Likewise, if one's religious identity doesn't suit, change to a more suitable one is not out of the question.

Change may be to a deeper embrace of one's ascribed religion (as in the "return" of Jewish youth to an orthodoxy they'd never known [Davidman 1991] and the head coverings increasingly adopted by second-generation Muslim college students), conversion to a different religion, or, with hardly a ripple of social sanction in much of the middle class, the abandonment of religion altogether. Thus, in my current undergraduate sociology of religion class in (ascriptively) Catholic Chicago, I have substantial proportions of students who, baptized Catholic, claim to have left that identity to become "Christian," as well as those who, baptized Catholic, now affirm no religion.[2]

It is not that the American religious order has collapsed. Sociologists of religion are divided on the "secularization thesis," some (e.g., Roof and McKinney 1987; Hadaway et al. 1993) arguing that there has been substantial erosion from a more sacralized past, others (e.g., Greeley 1989; Finke and Stark 1992) insisting that today's patterns are continuous with the past, with religious involvement remaining high. Yet no one disputes the enormous size and significance of religious institutions in the United States, the more than three hundred thousand local congregations, the billions of contributed dollars, the countless hours of volunteer time, the one-third of Americans (more or less) who attend church or religious services every week (see, for details, Hodgkinson and Weitzman 1993; Gallup 1996). Thus, there is far more volatility in *perceptions of religion's influence than in self-reported church attendance* (Gallup 1996, 28–29, 54–55; Warner 1988a, 179–180).

For the sake of argument, I shall overdraw the change in religious culture: whereas a generation ago religious identities were taken to be ascribed and religion's teachings to be universalistic, today religion appears to be particularistic but religious identities appear to be achieved. (For a more developed but also more circumscribed statement, see Warner 1988a, esp. 52–53.) It is the implications of this admittedly overdrawn scheme of change—religion is no longer taken for granted but it is also no longer unifying—that I will explore in this paper.

Changes in Religious Infrastructure since 1960: The Watershed Year of 1965

Although there are many sources of the huge changes experienced by our society since 1960, not least of them the Vietnam War, let us look at the roots of this cultural change in specifically religious institutions, focusing on one watershed year, 1965. Nineteen sixty-five was not only the year that Lyndon Johnson dramatically escalated the war in Vietnam, it was also the year that membership rolls peaked and began to decline in almost all of the mainline Protestant denominations—Presbyterian, Methodist, Northern Baptist—and also the year that Oral Roberts University opened in Tulsa, Oklahoma. By 1972, as conservative bodies like the Assemblies of God and the Southern Baptist Convention continued to grow and the more liberal mainline Presbyterians, Methodists, and Episcopalians to decline, National Council of Churches executive Dean Kelley (1977) caused a ruckus with his scathing analysis of liberal malaise, *Why Conservative Churches Are Growing*. A quarter century later the trend of mainline decline and conservative growth continues.

Sociologists of religion have refuted the notion that the decline of the mainline churches was the result of their outspoken stance in favor of civil rights (Hoge and Roozen 1979). It had deeper demographic causes, being characterized more by a failure to recruit newcomers than by a loss of erstwhile adherents. More controversial is whether their decline was in other ways brought about by the churches' own actions (Finke and Stark 1992) or by factors beyond their control (Hoge and Roozen 1979; cf. Iannaccone 1996). Uncontested is that the decades of mainline decline have meant a dramatic loss of the confidence felt by their predecessors that they spoke for the whole society.[3]

In sheer numbers of local churches, the mainline Protestant decline has been matched by conservative Protestant growth—evangelical, fundamentalist, Pentecostal, and charismatic (Warner 1994a, 56). But this does not mean that the mainline "place" has been taken by the conservatives, for it is a place Protestants no longer occupy. It is a mistake to see in the vociferousness of the organized "Religious Right" a mere protest against and attempt to reverse the Protestant displacement of the 1960s (a period that has been called the "third disestablishment" of religion in America [Roof and McKinney 1987]), for the conservatives had suffered their own great defeat a half century before, in the fundamentalist-modernist battles of the 1920s (Longfield 1991). For them, the mainline debacle of the 1960s was a vindication and a so-far-unrealized opportunity to grab the mantle of American moral stewardship, not to recapture a hegemony that, in fact, they had not known for generations. Yet the conservatives were surely emboldened by the mainline decline.

Corresponding changes in the institutional structure of American Protestantism have been analyzed by Wuthnow (1988) and others. (1) The historic denominations—the Presbyterian Church (USA), the United Methodist Church, the United Church of Christ—have been greatly weakened, partly because of internal divisions, both as organizations and as centers of identification. (2) Policy preferences have been increasingly articulated by religious "special-purpose groups," from the Christian Coalition through Bread for the World and People for the American Way to Clergy and Laity Concerned. (3) Material, human, and moral resources have increasingly devolved to the level of the local church, which in turn has become the focus of much religious loyalty and identity, in a widespread pattern I call "de facto congregationalism" (Warner 1994a, 73–82).

Nineteen sixty-five also saw the conclusion of Vatican II. If any religious voice has made a credible bid for the role of conscience of American society formerly occupied by the National Council of Churches, it is the National Conference of Catholic Bishops, whose pronouncements on war and the economy have won admiration, respect, and serious commentary far beyond the already wide confines of the communion for which the bishops claim to speak (Burns 1992). Yet vocal dissension within the Church—on the part not only of those on the left, who think the Church insufficiently progressive on issues of gender, but also those on the right, for whom the bishops are too radical on disarmament and redistribution—undermines the bishops' claim to be speaking for all Catholics. Meanwhile, their "consistent ethic of life" stance (against abortion but also against the death penalty) sits astride the conservative-liberal divide in American politics. As such it might promise to mediate left-right conflict but instead seems to provoke suspicion and distrust among potential allies on both sides (Wedam 1997).

Two events of 1965 had major implications for the civic role of religion in the black community. First was the passage of the Voting Rights Act, the crowning legislative achievement of the civil rights movement. The 1965 act fully enfranchised African Americans for the first time, with the consequence that politics as a career became more open than ever before to African Americans. One result was to weaken the relative monopoly on leadership that had previously been enjoyed by African American clergy, even though religious institutions continue to play a more important role in African American society than in most other sectors of the United States. Later applications of the Voting Rights Act, now under assault in the courts, have meant that the interests and grievances of African Americans were more likely to be articulated directly by legislators representing majority African American constituencies; thus the black church was no longer the only institutional sphere for the direct expression of group interests.

But 1965 was also the year of the assassination of Malcolm X, soon to assume the status of hero-martyr. Many in the diverse Muslim movements among African Americans, from Louis Farrakhan to Warith Deen Mohammed, claim his legacy, and indeed his legacy is ambiguous. Yet part of that legacy is the appeal of Islam to young African American men and a further weakening of the leadership monopoly of African American Christian clergy. Far too radical for most whites, tarnished by anti-Semitic spokesmen, and morally too conservative to make easy alliance with secular liberals, African American Muslims remained isolated for years. Only recently, with the decline of African American confidence in political institutions and a renewed moral conservatism in public African American discourse, has there reemerged a major civic role for two African American religious leaders: Louis Farrakhan and Jesse Jackson (Wills 1996).

We have a situation—liberal and conservative Protestants stalemate each other, one side attracted to African American clergy's claims for economic justice and the other to their critique of ghetto-oriented liquor advertising, pornography, and gangsta rap; Catholics appear unable to present a united front; and Jews remain a small minority without a stable coalition partner—in which there seems little near-term possibility for an institutionalized locus to articulate whatever latent civil religious consensus might emerge from the interchange between the common value system and the end-of-century empirical reality.

I see signs of a reconstruction emerging from another innovation of 1965, one having profound implications for the religious landscape of the United States. For 1965 was also the year that the Immigration and Nationality Law was amended by the Hart-Celler Act and signed into law by President Johnson, with eventual results that would astonish those who deliberated it. Thirty years later, nearly one million immigrants per year enter the United States, most of them legally, most of them from non-European countries. For example, in 1992–1993, the top ten sending countries were Mexico, China, Philippines, Vietnam, the former Soviet Union, the Dominican Republic, India, Poland, El Salvador, and the United Kingdom (Ungar 1995).

Contrary to stereotype, however, the religious effect of the new immigration is not so much an increasing de-Christianization of America as the de-Europeanizing of American Christianity and the intensification of religious identification. The great majority of new immigrants are Christian (mostly Catholics, evangelicals, and Pentecostals); they are, after all, disproportionately from Latin America. Those from Asia, particularly Korea and Vietnam and even from India and overwhelmingly from the Philippines, are disproportionately self-selected from already Christian segments of the sending countries' populations. The many Muslim immigrants have, among other things, helped shape African American Islamic movements in orthodox directions. Immigrant Buddhist temples provide an institutional home for European-American converts (Numrich 1995). Immigrant Hindus are learning to be religious in their own American way (Williams 1988; Kurien 1998). I will explore the religious implications of the new immigration in the next section.

From Societal Conscience to Cultural Reproduction

The picture I have drawn is a centrifugal one of increasing complexity and decreasing centralization. It is not, however, a picture of fragmentation or entropy. There are signs of systematization, but to appreciate them it is necessary to turn one's gaze away from the demoralized mainline Protestants and the alternatively brash and defensive conservative Protestants to smaller minorities, particularly African Americans, Jews, and new immigrants. For the sensibility that today informs efforts at religious reconstruction is not that of the bearer of the collective conscience but that of the sojourner.

My interpretation of the crosses, yarmulkes, and *hijab* coverings seen on college campuses today is that they represent efforts to build morale internally more than efforts to threaten or persuade others externally. The energies behind the politically oriented Christian Coalition are dwarfed by the culturally oriented energies going into the new "megachurches" (Trueheart 1996; Eiesland 1998), popular, local assemblies that mobilize generous tithes and volunteer labor. In congregations new and old, in midweek campus Bible studies, and in Muslim Student Association Friday prayers, participants learn and tell each other what they have (and are supposed to have) in common, particularly religious narratives and group ritual; in group discussions, they adapt inherited principles to contemporary realities (Livezey 1998); they enjoy the power of singing, moving, and eating together (Warner 1997c); they bear each other up; they find places where their individual gifts can be put to good use; and just by being together they affirm the ways in which they are different—perhaps in their attire, their facial features, their skin color, their language, their ritual, or their moral code (Ammerman 1987)— from those outside the space in which they gather.

Yes, aggressive religious rhetoric is abundant. As a white, European-American Christian with mainline Protestant affiliations, I hear aggressive-sounding talk issuing from conservative Protestants and some Muslims, although I am sure that differently situated observers would perceive aggression to be issuing from different sources. But even so, I argue that Promise Keepers and the Million Man March are primarily efforts at cultural reproduction—on a national scale. To be sure, the march was also intended to demonstrate to Congress the potential power of a mobilized African American constituency, but the motivation of most participants— and the memory they carried away—was to experience the exhilaration of gathering with so many like-minded and like-appearing others.

A month before our meeting at Stanford, I attended a gigantic four-hour-long Christian "crusade" rally, sponsored by one of Chicago's largest African American churches but held, presumably to address the city at large, in the ten-thousand-seat pavilion on my public university campus.[4] Featured were a Grammy-winning Gospel troupe, the church's four-hundred-voice choir, the enthusiastic singing and clapping of thousands of worshippers, and a forty-minute sermon by the church's distinguished, widely honored, and politically influential pastor. His manifest message was that our society needs Jesus, and the integrity of such an event requires both theologically and sociologically that there may be in the assembly one or more who do not already recognize that. Yet the overwhelming effect was to celebrate, reinforce, and nurture the commitment of the multitudes attending, who must have been encouraged by the number turning out and the enthusiasm of their response. It isn't foolish anymore to preach to the choir.

Jews, African American Christians, and immigrants set the tone for religion in America today. As sojourners, they know that religion cannot be taken for granted but must be actively produced, renegotiated, and reproduced into the next generation (Feher 1998; Kurien 1998; León 1998; Wellmeier 1998; Yang 1999). As unmistakable minorities, they do not assume that their beliefs and mores will be supported by messages coming from the surrounding society, so they actively teach their children—and remind themselves—what they are supposed to value and how they are supposed to behave.[5] In Stephen Carter's recent essay on behalf of religious seriousness, he was most passionate about what I call the right of religious reproduction. "No nation that strips away the right of parents to raise their children in their religion is worthy of allegiance" (Carter 1993, 192; Warner 1994–1995).

Even churches of the old Protestant main line have taken to using the "children's message" or "children's sermon" as the pastor's means of speaking over the heads of the young ones to impart to their elders first principles of theology that it would be embarrassing for all concerned to acknowledge that they have forgotten or never learned in the first place. Jettisoning the "cultural invisibility within which the North American upper middle class hides itself from itself" (Rosaldo 1989, 203), wise clergy recognize that even mainline Protestantism is today a counterculture.

Subcultural religious reproduction does not require antagonism toward one's neighbor. In the United States, religion is the preeminent institution for the mediation of cultural difference. In the United States, religious difference is the most legitimate cultural difference (Herberg 1960; Williams 1988; Warner 1993a), and in our history religion has tended to moderate difference (Hepner 1998). Therefore the softening of manners or liberalization of social mores, a characteristic of America Tocqueville noticed a century and a half ago, can advance along with religious particularism.

Religious particularism primarily takes not a political but a constitutive form, in which the differences that are emphasized are the founding myth (e.g., scriptural narrative, stories of the prophets) and the distinctive religious style (e.g., liturgy, music, dress, language). For example, Jewish services, even in Reform synagogues, now emphasize the use of Hebrew and the wearing of yarmulkes to a degree unknown a generation ago, thus accentuating their Jewishness (Wertheimer 1993, 95–113). That we are not talking about across-the-board conservatism or a mere "return to tradition" is clear when we recognize that many Reform Jewish women, as well as men, now wear yarmulkes. To cite another example, many churches that are open to gay men feature the "highest," most arcane liturgy (Reed 1989; Warner 1995, 94). Social liberalism and religious conservatism can go hand in hand.

Both to ensure their own survival as communities and to meet the needs of their individual and family constituents, today's religious institutions put at least as much of their energy into articulating their particularities as they do into addressing, whether in a civic, evangelistic, or antagonistic spirit, those outside.

Implications for Society at Large

In concluding, I briefly address two issues: first, whether the new particularism I have outlined threatens civil order and, second, whether it represents a retreat from societal responsibility. I answer both questions in the negative.

In a society historically less open, less mobile, less tolerant, less deeply individualistic, and less affluent than ours, the kind of particularism I have claimed prevails in American religion today might well be worrisome. But in the United States, motion across communal boundaries is to be expected and is very often positively valued (which is precisely why groups stress their differences). Religious switching and racial-ethnic intermarriage are commonplace (the former very frequent among liberal and conservative Protestants [Roof and McKinney 1987, 164–170] and the latter among Asians and Hispanics [Farley 1999].) Mass media–driven and peer youth cultures are hugely pervasive (Denby 1996; Dyson 1996), and the children of immigrants are increasingly unable to speak the first language of their parents (Chai 1998; George 1998). Despite divisive battles over abortion, sexual orientation, and women's ordination, increasing tolerance and liberalism on racial and gender issues pervade our society (DiMaggio et al. 1996). Those who formally reject the standards of secular society are drawn by the allure of its honors (I have in mind the respect paid to academic credentials by the most outspoken of conservative Protestants). Although incomes are highly unequal, unemployment is low.

It is doubtful that we can rely much longer on the older religious regime to shore up the civil values that legitimate such liberal social values.[6] Meanwhile, the religious cultural reproduction of the sort that I see promoted in black churches, white evangelical churches, Hispanic/Latino churches, synagogues, and immigrant congregations presupposes at least implicitly what mainline churches proclaim explicitly: that society is worth the church's while. It is worth the effort to raise children so that they can have a decent life in it and can raise their children in turn to have a decent life. The successful formula that Jews are perceived to have concocted—being simultaneously different and assimilated—is invoked as a model by immigrant Hindus and Chinese Christians, as I discovered on site visits to their communities for the New Ethnic and Immigrant Congregations Project. Religion as an identity of esteemed difference is recurrently being rediscovered by other new Americans (Feher 1998; McAlister 1998).

This perhaps cyclical religious emphasis on subcultural reproduction does not represent a retreat from societal responsibility; instead it is an effort to repair structural and cultural underpinnings of society beginning at home, a religious form of thinking globally but acting locally.

Although religion's public face is less visible and less unifying at the national level today than a generation ago, local religious communities, individually or through local ministerial alliances, still make themselves felt to their neighbors. They promote charitable causes, from providing meals to elderly shut-ins to housing the homeless. They provide services, including resale shops, family counseling, after-school tutoring, and courses in English as a second language. They host concerts and community meetings. They lobby city hall to collect the garbage, close down crack houses, and award development contracts to socially responsive builders.[7]

Perhaps the most important way local religious communities—"congregations"—contribute to the social order is through the development of "social capital," the "network of skill and trust that makes civic life possible" (Ammerman 1997, 347). Churches are places of meeting for diffuse purposes outside the family, places where relationships of trust are built up with people who, while perhaps not strangers, are also not kin. They are arenas where skills of leadership and discussion are inculcated. Robert Putnam (1995) has argued that many middle-class-based voluntary associations are in steep decline, but an important exception to his rule is found is American congregations, *and especially the congregations of racial, ethnic, and cultural minorities.* The black church is the classic nursery of African American oratorical skills, and for many subordinate ethnic groups the Pentecostal and evangelical movements' emphasis on "testimony" provides a legitimate occasion for rank-and-file public speaking. "Because people of all economic and educational levels belong nearly equally to congregations (whereas other voluntary associations are disproportionately middle and upper class), congregations are the single most widespread and egalitarian providers of civic opportunity in the United States" (Ammerman 1997, 364).

But the new religious particularism may also help repair our culture. The theory of modern culture I depend on here is broadly that of Talcott Parsons (1951), that the universalistic and individualistic, justice- and achievement-oriented (and often masculine) "gesellschaftlich" values of the modern American "public sphere" depended intimately on an infrastructure of particularistic and collective, relational and ascriptive (and often feminine) "gemeinschaftlich" values of the "private sphere." Parsons articulated this theory in his AGIL and pattern-variable schemes, where he tried to make clear that one side always needed the other,[8] that A and G (economy and polity) always needed I and L (societal community and fiduciary), or, in terms of the 1950s, that Dad always needed Mom. For Parsons, modern society involved a system of role differentiation into two spheres. Thus, the modern occupational sphere required for its balancing—indeed for its completeness—the modern family. Tocqueville had seen the same thing about the United States a century ahead of Parsons.[9]

But Parsons's insight, and the societal balance it articulated, was lost sight of in the 1960s (Warner 1988b). What happened is that public culture took public values all too much at face value.[10] An example is the early career of renowned theologian Reinhold Niebuhr, whose peripatetic lecturing depended intimately on a pastoral household (in Detroit) that his widowed mother effectively ran (Fox 1985, 69). What seems to have happened from mid-century onward was that American middle-class culture in general and mainstream Protestantism in particular increasingly lost sight of its necessary grounding in nurturance, which was relegated to lesser status and lesser urgency. By the 1950s, public intellectuals positively dismissed community building and nurturance ("suburban captivity") as unworthy of the churches (Winter 1962). In an odd way, this self-styled prophetic rhetoric represented just as much the triumph of a masculinist perspective as did the adolescent fixations of *Playboy* and the beats and hippies (see Barbara Ehrenreich, *The Hearts of Men*). In fleeing from the claims of family and parish to the greater good of the "public sphere," too many intellectuals lost sight of the classical wisdom, recently restated by Charles Taylor (1989, 511), that "a dilemma doesn't invalidate the rival goods. On the contrary, it presupposes them."

It must be said that public intellectuals did not alone trivialize the private sphere. Social processes did that too. The suburbs were far more removed from the "public" world than had been true of the urban neighborhood: work was farther away, the commute was longer, and the bedroom community was more isolated.[11] Meanwhile, it had always been part of the formula that those responsible for child rearing should be educated, and these educated women had longer life expectancies and greater aspirations. Betty Friedan (1963) articulated their anger and bewilderment a generation ago, but today a broad spectrum of American subcultures wants to renew attention to nurturance.

Those who were less enmeshed in urban, middle-class life were less affected by postwar privatizing trends. Hence, African Americans, working-class Americans, rural Americans (the mid-century heartland of evangelicalism), and, of course, those who had not yet come to the United States were less affected by the decay of attention to the "private sphere." Their religious institutions and cultures had not yet forgotten that new generations need to be nurtured. It is the sociological wisdom of their religious institutions that is setting the tone for the cultural role of U.S. religion at the end of the twentieth century.

Reprinted by the permission of Princeton University Press from DIVERSITY AND ITS DISCONTENTS, edited by Neil J. Smelser and Jeffrey C. Alexander, 1999.

NOTES

An earlier draft of this paper was presented at the conference on Common Values, Social Diversity, and Cultural Conflict, Stanford, California, October 17–19, 1996. For comments and suggestions, I am indebted to Nancy Ammerman, Anne Heider, Frank Lechner, Lowell Livezey, Robert V. Robinson, Frank Senn, Michael R. Warner, Elfriede Wedam, Robert Wuthnow, Feng-gang Yang, and my fellow participants in the Stanford conference. For the stimulus to write this paper, I thank Neil Smelser and Jeffrey Alexander.

1. *Books and Culture: A Christian Review* 2, 4 (July/August 1996), features essays by Eugene Genovese, Eric Metaxas, and Harry Stout, among others. Along with Stout, the masthead lists Nathan Hatch, George Marsden, Mark Noll, and others as editors.

2. This was written during the fall semester of 1996.

3. The essays and particularly the photographs collected by historian William Hutchison (1989) speak eloquently about that vanished confidence.

4. Specifically the Apostolic Church of God, whose guiding spirit and senior pastor is Rev. Arthur Brazier. For extensive analysis of Brazier and his ministry, see Browning 1991. The date of the rally was September 13, 1996.

5. Liberal critic David Denby (1996, 48-49) shares their outrage at the culture's effect on children but cannot bring himself to apply the authoritarian measures of religious conservatives. Speaking of his children and the media with exasperation, he cries: "There is so much to forbid-perhaps a whole culture to forbid! . . . How can you control what they breathe?"

6. "We agree surprisingly well, across great differences of theological and metaphysical belief, about the demands of justice and benevolence, and their importance. . . . So why worry that we disagree on the reasons, as long as we're united around the norms? It's not the disagreement which is the problem. Rather the issue is what sources can support our far-reaching moral commitments to benevolence and justice. . . . The question . . . is

whether we are not living beyond our moral means in continuing allegiance to our standards of justice and benevolence" (Taylor 1989, 515, 517).

7. This paragraph and the one following draw for orientation and illustrative material on a number of recent and ongoing research projects on the role of religious institutions in local community life, including the Springfield Project (Demerath and Williams 1992) and the Program on Non-Profit Organizations (Hall 1997), but especially the Congregations in Changing Communities Project (Ammerman 1997; Becker 1999; Eiesland 1999) and the Religion in Urban America Program (Livezey 1996, 1998), to both of which I am deeply indebted.

8. See the dedication of *The Social System* to his wife, Helen, the "indispensable balance-wheel" (Parsons 1951, v).

9. "The Americans have applied to the sexes the great principle of political economy which now dominates industry. They have carefully separated the functions of man and of woman so that the great work of society may be better performed" (Tocqueville 1969, 601). With the advance of technology and the increased salience of specific skills, gender ascription becomes less functional (Marwell 1975). That the "private sphere" need no longer be "women's place" nor the "public sphere" men's is one progressive perception I attribute to such movements as Promise Keepers and the Million Man March, for whom concerns of parents are once again to be brought into the quasi-public arena of football stadiums and the Washington Mall. Yet the various functions, I and L as well as A and G, or however one wishes to classify them, continue as needs of the society.

10. Because I see the new particularism strengthening these essential I and L activities, my interpretation of religious conservatism necessarily parts company with that of Lechner (1985), for whom "fundamentalism" represents "dedifferentiation." Yet Lechner recognizes that those who "retreat to . . . traditionalist security bases" thereby add complexity to their lives and thus become even more "quintessentially modern" (167).

11. "[A] man's job, is usually related, directly or indirectly, to large organizations of industry and union which have considerable influence on the national life; by contrast, his neighborhood, life with family, at church, or in a local association has little or no connection with his job or even with the interests and problems which fill his mind during the day. . . . The sphere of residential activities . . . (family problems, nurture of the young, neighborhood interests, informal association, and general consumer activities) . . . is a very private aspect of modern life" (Winter 1962, 156–157).

REFERENCES

(References to writings of the author are found in a separate listing at the back of the book.)

Ammerman, Nancy Tatom. 1987. *Bible Believers: Fundamentalists in the Modern World*. New Brunswick, N.J.: Rutgers University Press.
———. 1997. *Congregation and Community*. New Brunswick, N.J.: Rutgers University Press.
Becker, Penny Edgell. 1999. *Congregations in Conflict: Cultural Models of Local Religious Life*. New York: Cambridge University Press.
Browning, Don S. 1991. "Congregational Care in a Black Pentecostal Church." In *A Fundamental Practical Theology: Descriptive and Strategic Proposals*, 243–277. Minneapolis: Fortress.
Burns, Gene. 1992. *The Frontiers of Catholicism: The Politics of Ideology in a Liberal World*. Berkeley: University of California Press.
Carter, Stephen L. 1993. *The Culture of Disbelief*. New York: Basic Books.
Chai, Karen. 1998. "Competing for the Second Generation: English-Language Ministry in a Korean Protestant Church." *In Gatherings in Diaspora: Religious Communities and the*

New Immigration, ed. R. Stephen Warner and Judith G. Wittner, 295–331. Philadelphia: Temple University Press.

Cuddihy, John Murray. 1987. *The Ordeal of Civility*. 2d ed. Boston: Beacon.

Davidman, Lynn. 1991. *Tradition in a Rootless World: Women Turn to Orthodox Judaism*. Berkeley and Los Angeles: University of California Press.

Demerath, N. J., III, and Rhys H. Williams. 1992. *A Bridging of Faiths: Religion and Politics in a New England City*. Princeton, N.J.: Princeton University Press.

Denby, David. 1996. "Buried Alive: Our Children and the Avalanche of Crud." *New Yorker* 72 (July 15): 48–58.

DiMaggio, Paul, John Evans, and Bethany Bryson. 1996. "Have Americans' Social Attitudes Become More Polarized?" *American Journal of Sociology* 102 (November): 690–755.

Dyson, Michael Eric. 1996. *Between God and Gangsta Rap: Bearing Witness to Black Culture*. New York: Oxford University Press.

Eiesland, Nancy L. 1999. *A Particular Place: Exurbanization and Religious Response in a Southern Town*. New Brunswick, N.J.: Rutgers University Press.

Farley, Reynolds. 1999. "Racial Issues: Recent Trends in Residential Patterns and Intermarriage." In *Diversity and Its Discontents: Cultural Conflict and Common Ground in Contemporary American Society*, ed. Neil J. Smelser and Jeffrey C. Alexander, 85–128. Princeton, N.J.: Princeton University Press.

Feher, Shoshanah. 1998. "From the Rivers of Babylon to the Valleys of Los Angeles: The Exodus and Adaptation of Iranian Jews." In *Gatherings in Diaspora: Religious Communities and the New Immigration*, ed. R. Stephen Warner and Judith G. Wittner, 71–94. Philadelphia: Temple University Press.

Finke, Roger, and Rodney Stark. 1992. *The Churching of America, 1776–1990: Winners and Losers in Our Religious Economy*. New Brunswick, N.J.: Rutgers University Press.

Fox, Richard Wightman. 1985. *Reinhold Niebuhr: A Biography*. New York: Pantheon.

Friedan, Betty. 1963. *The Feminine Mystique*. New York: W.W. Norton.

Gallup, George H., Jr. 1996. *Religion in America, 1996*. Princeton, N.J.: Princeton Religion Research Center.

George, Sheba M. 1998. "Caroling with the Keralites: The Negotiation of Gendered Space in an Indian Immigrant Church." In *Gatherings in Diaspora: Religious Communities and the New Immigration*, ed. R. Stephen Warner and Judith G. Wittner, 265–294. Philadelphia: Temple University Press.

Greeley, Andrew M. 1989. *Religious Change in America*. Cambridge: Harvard University Press.

Hadaway, C. Kirk, Penny Long Marler, and Mark Chaves. 1993. "What the Polls Don't Show: A Closer Look at U.S. Church Attendance." *American Sociological Review* 58 (December): 741–752.

Hall, Peter Dobkin. 1997. "Founded on the Rock, Built upon Shifting Sands: Churches, Voluntary Associations, and Non-Profit Organizations in Public Life, 1850–1990." Working paper of the Program on Non-Profit Organizations, Yale University.

Heim, S. Mark. 1996. "The Next Ecumenical Movement." *Christian Century* 113 (August 14–21): 780–783.

Hepner, Randal L. 1998. "The House That Rasta Built: Church-Building among New York Rastafarians." In *Gatherings in Diaspora: Religious Communities and the New Immigration*, ed. R. Stephen Warner and Judith G. Wittner, 197–234. Philadelphia: Temple University Press.

Herberg, Will. 1960. *Protestant, Catholic, Jew: An Essay in American Religious Sociology*. 2d ed. Garden City, N.Y.: Doubleday.

Hodgkinson, Virginia A., and Murray S. Weitzman. 1993. *From Belief to Commitment: The Community Service Activities and Finances of Religious Congregations in the United States*. Washington, D.C.: Independent Sector.

Hoge, Dean R., and David A. Roozen, eds. 1979. *Understanding Church Growth and Decline, 1950–1978*. New York: Pilgrim.

Hutchison, William R., ed. 1989. *Between the Times: The Travail of the Protestant Establishment in America, 1900–1960*. Cambridge: Cambridge University Press.

Iannaccone, Laurence R. 1996. "Reassessing Church Growth: Statistical Pitfalls and Their Consequences." *Journal for the Scientific Study of Religion* 35 (September): 197–217.

Kelley, Dean M. 1977. *Why Conservative Churches Are Growing*. 2d ed. San Francisco: Harper and Row.

Kurien, Prema. 1998. "Becoming American by Becoming Hindu: Indian Americans Take Their Place at the Multicultural Table." In *Gatherings in Diaspora: Religious Communities and the New Immigration*, ed. R. Stephen Warner and Judith G. Wittner, 37–70. Philadelphia: Temple University Press.

Lechner, Frank J. 1985. "Modernity and Its Discontents." In *Neofunctionalism*, ed. Jeffrey C. Alexander, 157–176. Beverly Hills, Calif.: Sage.

León, Luís D. 1998. "Born Again in East LA: The Congregation as Border Space." In *Gatherings in Diaspora: Religious Communities and the New Immigration*, ed. R. Stephen Warner and Judith G. Wittner, 163–196. Philadelphia: Temple University Press.

Livezey, Lowell W. 1996. "Congregations and Their Publics." Address presented to a conference on "Leading Congregations That Matter" at the Louisville Institute, October 10–11.

———. 1998. "Family Ministries at Carter Temple CME Church." In *Tending the Flock: Models of Congregations Family Ministries*, ed. K. Brynford Lyon and Archie Smith, Jr., 10–39. Louisville, Ky.: Westminster/John Knox.

Longfield, Bradley. 1991. *The Presbyterian Controversy*. New York: Oxford University Press.

Marwell, Gerald. 1975. "Why Ascription? Parts of a More or Less Formal Theory of the Functions and Dysfunctions of Sex Roles." *American Sociological Review* 40 (August): 445–455.

McAlister, Elizabeth. 1998. "The Madonna of 115th Street Revisited: Vodou and Haitian Catholicism in the Age of Transnationalism." In *Gatherings in Diaspora: Religious Communities and the New Immigration*, ed. R. Stephen Warner and Judith G. Wittner, 123–160. Philadelphia: Temple University Press.

Numrich, Paul David. 1996. *Old Wisdom in the New World: Americanization in Two Immigrant Theravada Buddhist Temples*. Knoxville: University of Tennessee Press.

Parsons, Talcott. 1951. *The Social System*. Glencoe, Ill.: Free Press.

Putnam, Robert. 1995. "Bowling Alone: America's Declining Social Capital." *Journal of Democracy* 6, 1: 65–78.

Reed, John Shelton. 1989. " 'Giddy Young Men': A Counter-Cultural Aspect of Victorian Anglo-Catholicism." *Comparative Social Research* 11: 209–236.

Roof, Wade Clark, and William McKinney. 1987. *American Mainline Religion: Its Changing Shape and Future*. New Brunswick, N.J.: Rutgers University Press.

Rosaldo, Renato. 1993. *Culture and Truth: The Remaking of Social Analysis*. Boston: Beacon.

Taylor, Charles. 1989. *Sources of the Self: The Making of Modern Identity*. Cambridge: Harvard University Press.

Tocqueville, Alexis de. 1969. *Democracy in America*. Edited by J. P Mayer and translated by George Lawrence. Garden City, N.Y.: Anchor.

Trueheart, Charles. 1996. "Welcome to the Next Church." *Atlantic Monthly* 278, 2 (August): 37–58.

Ungar, Sanford J. 1995. *Fresh Blood: The New American Immigrants*. New York: Simon and Schuster.

Wedam, Elfriede. 1997. "Splitting Interests or Common Causes: Styles of Moral Reasoning in Opposing Abortion." In *Contemporary American Religion: An Ethnographic Reader*, ed. Penny Edgell Becker and Nancy L. Eiesland, 147–168. Walnut Creek, Calif.: Altamira Press.

Wellmeier, Nancy J. 1998. "Santa Eulalia's People in Exile: Maya Religion, Culture, and Identity in Los Angeles." In *Gatherings in Diaspora: Religious Communities and the New Immigration,* ed. R. Stephen Warner and Judith G. Wittner, 97–122. Philadelphia: Temple University Press.

Wertheimer, Jack. 1993. A *People Divided: Judaism in Contemporary America.* New York: Basic Books.

Williams, Raymond Brady. 1988. *Religions of Immigrants from India and Pakistan: New Threads in the American Tapestry.* Cambridge: Cambridge University Press.

Wills, Garry. 1996. "A Tale of Three Leaders." *New York Review of Books* 43, 14 (September 19): 61–74.

Winter, Gibson. 1962. *The Suburban Captivity of the Churches: An Analysis of Protestant Responsibility in the Expanding Metropolis.* New York: Macmillan.

Wood, James R. 1981. *Leadership in Voluntary Organizations: The Controversy over Social Action in Protestant Churches.* New Brunswick, N.J.: Rutgers University Press.

Wuthnow, Robert. 1988. *The Restructuring of American Religion: Society and Faith since World War II.* Princeton, N.J.: Princeton University Press.

Yang, Fenggang. 1999. *Chinese Christians in America: Conversion, Assimilation, and Adhesive Identities.* University Park: Pennsylvania State University Press.

Prospect

Looking Forward and Outward

The battle for the new paradigm is all but over. Most scholars, whether or not they use the language of "paradigms," have come to agree that religion in the United States is fundamentally different from religion in Europe, the source of sociology of religion's previously dominant paradigm (Davie 2002). Unlike religion in Europe, where an established church looms in the near or far background, religion in the United States has been disestablished from the beginning, which made it possible for it to accommodate cultural pluralism. For two centuries, American religion has flourished as a set of popular social institutions because of, not in spite of, being constitutively disestablished. Religion may provide one source of American social cohesion, but first of all it gives members of each of America's many constituent subgroups an identity (Lindsay 2003). Thus, unlike the European case, early nineteenth-century American movements for social change had primarily religious roots rather than political ones (Young 2002). Peter Berger, whom I identified in 1993 as the leading proponent of the old paradigm, has himself come to recognize that the European experience is not an appropriate general model on which to build sociology of religion (2001).

Issues for the New Paradigm

However, to say that there has been a paradigm succession is not to say that all issues surrounding the new paradigm have been settled. Nor is it to deny that much progress remains to be made in understanding American religious communities. With respect to the new paradigm, sociologists of religion are divided on how to assess the extent and causes of the recent decline in participation in U.S. religion. If not European-style secularization, what is going on? If it is agreed that U.S. religion is at once diverse and disestablished, how are these qualities connected? More broadly, what institutional and psychological processes underlie the American religious system? Does economic, or "rational choice," theory suffice for that foundation? Or should we work on other theories? Debate on these issues has generated valuable light as well as distracting heat.

Religious Decline

Surveys reveal that more and more Americans claim no religious affiliation, and comparison of poll data and on-the ground attendance counts suggests that many Americans overstate the regularity of their religious observance. Whereas only 2–3 percent of Americans acknowledged no religious affiliation in the 1950s, today the "nones" amount to some 14 percent (Hout and Fischer, forthcoming). Whereas one-third to two-fifths of Americans claim to be in church (or some other religious service) every week, reports from religious institutions themselves argue that only one quarter actually are. Some religious leaders themselves are convinced that ours is becoming a "post-Christian," even pagan, society.

Religious jeremiads are easy to deal with: the new paradigm suspects that from the point of view of religious establishments, change always appears to be devolution. Discrepancies between claimed and actual attendance, however, cannot be dismissed, even if their extent and meaning are subject to debate ("Symposium" 1998). Do Americans overstate their attendance by 100 percent, or 50 percent, or less? Is it the case that those who say they were in church within the last seven days actually mean the last two weeks? If Americans exaggerate their religious faithfulness, have they only begun to do so in the past generation? The claim has been made that precisely in the amount that their church attendance has actually declined, Americans inflate their claims in response to interviewers. According to this line of argument, 40 percent did attend every week a generation ago, but only 25 percent do so now and another 15 percent erroneously claim to have done so. Is this the case? Just as plausible is that Americans have exaggerated their attendance ever since the advent of polling a half century ago. So far, the compelling evidence put forth that Americans' self-reported church attendance is exaggerated does not directly address the question of religious decline.

More significant is the undoubtedly growing category of "nones." As younger cohorts enter the adult population, more and more of them claim to have no religious affiliation. Moreover (and this is a distinct change from a claim I made in the 1993 article), those raised with no religion are now as likely as those raised with a religion to maintain the religious, or irreligious, status of their upbringing (Hout and Fischer, forthcoming). New in American history, "nones" are reproducing themselves as a growing minority that is unlikely to disappear.

We are learning more about what is driving people from (or failing to keep them attached to) religion. Studies show that nones derive disproportionately from mainline Protestants and from Catholics (Smith and Kim 2004). These defections aggravate the continuing demographic decline of the former group, whereas in the Catholic Church, defectors are largely being replaced by immigrants. Mainline Protestant defections seem to result from blurred boundaries between their churches and the environing society, such that it matters less and less for offspring of liberal Protestants whether or not they belong to the churches they were raised in (Hoge et al. 1994). Catholic defections, on the other hand, seem to be due to active dissatisfaction with the policies of the Church (Hout 2000). Both kinds of defectors are saying, in different ways, that their former churches no longer speak for them.

Apathy and anger, not enlightenment and education, are the primary factors behind the current falloff of religious identification in the United States. This is not what sociologists of religion had been led to expect by the old paradigm. Reflecting on religion in Europe, influenced by the writings of Weber and Durkheim, old-paradigm theorists had expected that people would decreasingly believe in and feel drawn to the supernatural and mystical forces presupposed by religion. These theorists thought that this inexorable rationalization and disenchantment (literally, "de-magicification") would sooner or later empty the churches.

Unchurched Americans, however, are not notably unbelievers. Quite the contrary. It is not disbelief but organizational disaffiliation that leads an increasing proportion of Americans to say that they have "no religion." Many, in fact, say they are "spiritual but not religious." Supernatural and spiritual beliefs remain exceedingly popular in the United States, even among those who do not go to church. Thus, the category of persons least trusted by their fellow Americans is not homosexuals, people of color, Arabs, or Muslims; it is "atheists." Americans are still overwhelmingly believers.

Moreover, the falloff in participation has affected nearly every kind of membership organization in the United States—bowling leagues, service clubs, professional societies, veterans' organizations, Masonic lodges, the League of Women Voters—and these other organizational declines are typically worse than those involving religion (Putnam 2000). In all, the evidence suggests that the decline in church attendance and religious identification is part of a broader organizational process, not a specific process of secularization (Wuthnow 1998). Perhaps a widespread organizational restructuring is under way that is yet to be fully understood. Sociologists of politics and education as well as religion need to track the emerging modes of participation through which Americans express their continuing interests and convictions in these fields.

The Correlation of Variety and Vitality

The old paradigm thought that the viability of religion rested on the absence of alternatives. Ideological monopoly was religion's supposed natural state. But it is now clear to all observers that there has been no religious monopoly in the United States from the ratification of the Constitution onward. Instead, religious participation and religious pluralism have grown together across two centuries of U.S. history. At every step of the way—as first the oligopoly of Congregationalists, Presbyterians, and Anglicans was broadened to include the Methodists and Baptists and broadened again later as Catholics and Jews were added to the American religious mix—the variety and vitality of American religion increased hand in hand, at least until the 1960s.

Reflection on that correlation was one source of inspiration for the formulation of the new paradigm. Cosmopolitan secular intellectuals found it plausible that the social heterogeneity of cities would be inimical to religion, but that obvious idea did not work when applied to cities in the United States. It was similarly plausible that countries with an uncontested, taken-for-granted sacred canopy would offer the most favorable ground for religion. The example of the United States, at once the most religiously diverse and religiously mobilized modern society, refuted this notion. A new idea was called for. If variety and vitality coexisted from the beginning in U.S. religion, the question was why. Midrange theories of all sorts were developed to account for this fact: new-paradigm sociologists said that religion flourishes when lay people have more options to choose from and when clergy must work hard to earn the loyalty of those who can easily go elsewhere.

Much of this theorizing was framed in terms of the proposition that religious pluralism promotes religious participation, a proposition that was hotly contested from the outset. Is it, or is it not, the case that within a given unit—a city, county, state, or nation—the more different religious bodies there are, the higher the proportion of the residents who will participate in religion? Even in 1993, I wrote that the supposed positive effect of pluralism on religion was a matter of dispute, and in the intervening years that already burgeoning literature boomed, with mixed results (Chaves and Gorski 2001). Some said that although pluralism and participation seemed to coexist in American religion, they were not causally related, at least not positively. But eventually, careful methodological analysis by Voas, Olson, and Crockett (2002) showed that the entire research effort—both the supposed proofs and the refutations of the pluralism/participation hypothesis—was fatally flawed by the impossibility, given current measurement techniques, of operationally distinguishing the independent and dependent variables.

Efforts continue to explain why it is that variety and vitality coexist in American religion (and whether the correlation pertains to other societies). One promising idea is that the two factors are separately caused by an underlying third factor, which in my formulation of the new paradigm is the constitutive disestablishment of religion. Recently, Stark and Finke (2000) have expanded their concept of religious diversity beyond the strictness/laxness dimension, itself inspired by sect/church theory, that had long been central to their and their associates' work. They now conceptualize a multitude of "niches" of demand for religion that can be filled by unfettered religious suppliers. Daniel Olson (2002) has systematically investigated claims that religious competition, set in place by the lack of public support for or regulation of religious bodies, may lead religious leaders to work harder and their rank and file to contend more energetically for religious identities. Mark Chaves (2004, 127–165) models the way that the competitive American religious system systemically promotes innovation in worship styles, making religion attractive to those on the cultural frontier. Explaining just why American religion is both varied and vital is a wide-open field.

Not to deny the cogency of other explanations, my own view is that the connection of disestablishment, diversity, and vitality in American religion is so complex as to be effectively unique. American religion was disestablished from the outset of the Republic not because of antireligious sentiment but because the exuberant cacophony of religions (Butler 1990) was incompatible with official recognition of any one. Although little love was lost between advocates for one or another theology—Calvinists and Arminians, for example—the answers they offered readily became alternatives to one another for the people they tried to recruit. In effect, the various evangelical sects competed with one another. Meanwhile, the new political institutions adopted by the founding fathers made no provision for the representation of minorities (e.g., proportional representation). In fact, they hoped to subdue factionalism, and one consequence of the political rules they established was that religion became the most available channel for the public expression of societal differentiation. By the beginning of the nineteenth century, a flourishing open market for religion had thereby been created. As immigration, conquest, and economic growth brought more and more cultural diversity into a society so organized, newcomers, including their nonevangelical religions, were sooner or later recruited into this diffusely proreligious market. Even Catholic priests led revivals (Neitz 1987).

Given this complicated history, I find it implausible that the various forms of disestablishment now being introduced in western Europe (through the disestablishment of state churches, as in Sweden) and eastern Europe (through the disestablishment of official atheism, as in East Germany) will soon bring about American-style religious markets. The profusion of religions in India—the site of far more profound religious diversity than is found in the United States—is more likely to create severe conflict than peaceful competition, because the religions of India are not seen as substitutes for one another (Olson 2002). Grace Davie (2002) has proposed "conceptual maps" for different religious systems around the world—Europe, South America, Africa, East Asia, as well as the United States—that might be the germ of what I would call particularistic "paradigms" for each culture area (Warner 2004e).

Theoretical Foundations

The new paradigm, which is a framework for understanding American religion, should be distinguished from the theories that explain religious and other social behavior, including rational choice theory. By way of analogy, plate tectonics is the new paradigm in geology that accounts for the particular height of mountain ranges and their particular mélange of rocks, for example, why the Andes rise so abruptly from the west coast of South America or why the Coast Range of California is so lithologically messy (Lamb 2004; McPhee 1998). But new-paradigm geologists use the same elementary theories of physics and chemistry as did their old-paradigm predecessors, drawing different, more compelling pictures using the same basic tools (McPhee 1998, 115–131).

Similarly, the new paradigm in religion, which pictures religion in the United States as constitutively disestablished, can draw on rational choice and other theories but is not identical to any of them. In common with American religious historians, proponents of the new paradigm have found it evocative and fruitful to speak of the efforts of religious entrepreneurs in an open religious market, but not all of us adduce economic theory as the theoretical foundation for the paradigm. New-paradigm sociologists broadly agree with economists that the behavior we are called upon to account for must be understood as rational as opposed to irrational, but not all of us presuppose that the wellspring of this behavior is identical to economic behavior. I have said these things in Chapters 3 and 6.

Ironically, prominent rational choice theorists of religion share with the old paradigm the presupposition that religion is to be approached primarily in its cognitive aspect. Both Peter Berger and Rodney Stark center their understanding of religion on the intellectual, doctrinal side of religion. For Berger's early work (1969), it was the implausibility of religious doctrine that rendered it vulnerable to the doubt that cosmopolitanism would surely induce. Thus, religion in modern society had to be propped up by "plausibility structures." For Stark (2001), it is the promises made by religious doctrines—the relationship between God and humans they propose—that make religion rational. At least for America, a society of believers, Stark is right and the Berger of 1969 is wrong: the theological claims of religion are a source of its strength, not of its vulnerability. In America, religions that stress their theological foundations do better in the market than do those that soft-pedal them.

I shared Berger's and Stark's cognitivist views before I undertook field research in American religion. Trained as a "theorist," steeped in the European theories of Durkheim, Simmel, and Weber and the American theories of Erving Goffman, Harold Garfinkel, and Thomas Schelling, just before going into the field I proposed a cognitive reorientation of Talcott Parsons's theory of action (Warner 1978; also 1970, 1972). I was soon surprised that the religious people I came to know in Mendocino did not seem to have problems with what I found at the time to be the wildly implausible claims of their faith. But I was a professor, subject to the same blindness Robert Wuthnow has since discerned among religious leaders. "Like many other professionals who have spent years in school, clergy too often fall into a pattern of thinking that reality is from the neck up" (Wuthnow 2003, 245; see also Mellor, forthcoming).

Explaining the world—mapping the cosmos, providing meaning for existence—is only one of the things religion does, and perhaps not the most important thing in a pluralistic but young and brash society like the United States. I insinuated as much in 1993 when, in the much-too-cryptic Table 2.1, I contrasted the old paradigm's focus on "explanation, meaning" as the prime function of religion with the new paradigm's focus on "solidarity, morale." From my firsthand research and (by

1993) fifteen years of reading the results of others' research, I had come to see that religion in America is especially important because it provides group identities—"fit[ting] people into their communities and [giving] organization to the differences among them" (Swatos 1981, 223)—and helps them act together in the world (Billings 1990; Pattillo-McCoy 1998; Smith 1998; Wood 2002). In the most robust cases, religion engenders intense solidarity, courage to face adversity, and inspiration to better the group's lot. Understanding the grounds and the significance of such group-formation functions of religion is a research frontier in sociology of religion that is especially central to the new paradigm as I understand it.

Important efforts are under way to understand religion in terms of emotion and ritual. Chapter 5 represents my own contribution, so far, to the understanding of how ritualized action can create and promote solidarity in a largely noncognitive manner, solidarity in the absence of like-mindedness. Because I framed that chapter in response to concerns about religious balkanization, I stressed the building of intergroup bridges. But I might as well have said that I was trying to theorize how groups form in the first place. Making music, moving, and eating together can give people a feeling that they belong together, even if they cannot understand one another's language. That, at least, is how William McNeill (1995) thinks Islam quickly became a world religion in the seventh century: the physical act of praying together five times a day made men from many different tribes into a cohesive force. Recently, Robert Bellah (2003) has surveyed theories of the ritual basis of social order that begin with the seminal but too often neglected insights of Durkheim's *Elementary Forms* and culminate closest to sociology of religion in the work of Randall Collins (2004). Under the right circumstances, beginning with infancy, ritual creates a sense of bounded belonging, mutual moral obligation, and collective energy. These new insights on ritual can and should be developed by sociologists of religion of all persuasions, old and new.

Researching American Congregations

The most undeniable, wide-scale progress in research on contemporary American religion has been made in the broad field of congregational studies. Although, in my opinion, the results of this research substantially support the positions taken in my first contributions to the field (Chapters 2, 7, and 8 and my earlier book on the Mendocino church [Warner 1988a]), I cannot claim credit for this progress. Most of the research findings are consistent with the new paradigm, but most of the research was not inspired by my formulation of it. Instead, a host of religion scholars, religious leaders, and research funders had separately and together decided that it was high time researchers paid attention to the congregational bedrock of American religious activity. I learned of their efforts only after I finished *New Wine in Old Wineskins* and found that my focus on the congregation was not unique. Research was accomplished, under way, or in the offing on one- or two-congregation case studies (e.g., Ammerman 1987; Neitz 1987; Davidman 1991;

Freedman 1993; Dorsey 1995; Wilkes 1994; Numrich 1995; Kostarelos 1995; Feher 1998; Skokeid 1995; Warner and Wittner 1998); on focused, mostly qualitative, comparisons of multiple congregations in one or more locales (e.g., Ammerman 1997; Edgell Becker 1999; Eiesland 2000; Livezey 2000; Ebaugh and Chafetz 2000; McRoberts 2003); on theoretical frameworks for the understanding of congregations (Carroll et al. 1986; Ammerman et al. 1998); and on massive, mostly quantitative national surveys attempting to generalize about America's more than three hundred thousand congregations (e.g., Dudley and Roozen 2001; Chaves 2004; Ammerman 2005). The surge in congregational studies was a case of convergence of consciousness in the face of an undeniable social reality.

It is now beyond dispute that the congregation is worthy of the attention of scholars and religious activists, that "congregation" is a level of organizational analysis distinct from and often carrying more information than "denomination," that congregations may grow as the denominations with which they are affiliated decline (and vice versa), and that using the expression "parent denomination" instead of "the denomination with which the congregation is affiliated" in sentences like this one is often a misnomer (because some congregations predated their denominations and others joined them in midcareer). Denominations do still matter, and congregations that strongly embrace their denominations have distinctive properties (Dudley and Roozen 2001; Ammerman 2005). But we must look to those congregations themselves to understand why and how they embrace their denominational identities.

My concept of "de facto congregationalism" touched raw nerves in ecclesiastical circles and informed research agendas in academic ones. Within formerly centralized denominations rent by internal disputes, "de facto congregationalism" has come to serve as something of a shibboleth to tar opponents alleged to be disloyal to historical commitments of the tradition. Thus liberals use the term to scorn conservatives' foot-dragging on civil rights, and conservatives to condemn congregations that, contrary to churchwide resolutions, persist in ordaining gay and lesbian ministers and celebrating "holy unions." Among researchers, the concept has served less emotionally as a prediction of the form that new religious institutions will take (e.g., Bankston and Zhou 2000; Ebaugh and Chazetz 2000). The results are mixed (e.g., Cadge 2004) and efforts are under way to identify institutional levels between the denomination and the congregation (Ammerman 2005). But, except for those who find congregational adaptations in the United States too much out of step with their historic traditions, the research effort is relatively dispassionate.

The idea that, however they are named, American religious institutions tend to be congregations, defined by those who constitute them, rather than parishes, defined by the territory in which they are located, has also been recognized as itself capturing an undeniable reality (Eiesland 2000; Livezey 2000; McRoberts 2003). For better or worse, any given local congregation has limited influence and no legal authority over its geographical neighborhood. In most cases, when churches do serve their communities, they do so in collaboration with other congregations and/or public social service agencies (Chaves 2004; Ammerman 2005). The emergence of this recognition on the part of researchers may be indexed by comparing the treatments of the congregation in its context found in the two successive editions of the widely used "handbook" produced by the Congregational Studies Project Team. In the first handbook (Carroll et al. 1986), the chapter on "context" contains elaborate, helpful guides to the identification of populations in need in the congregation's proximity but nothing about the fact that, in most American locales, many other congregations will be located in that very proximity, arguably sharing responsibility for the respective populations. Inspired by the ongoing work of Ammerman (1997) and Eiesland (2000), the corresponding chapter on "ecology" in the second handbook (Ammerman et al. 1998) corrects this oversight. From the point of view of widely shared religious ethics, any given congregation ought to pay attention to its surrounding community, but it is the height of arrogance for it to act as if it is the only religious institution in the area.

The literature on congregations largely supports the claim of Chapter 8 that congregations are "functionally diffuse" institutions, doing all sorts of things and engaging their members in sensory as well as cognitive and ethical ways. But the polemic in that chapter against the idea that congregations as voluntary associations can realistically be called upon to devote themselves to specific mission tasks—especially as agents of social change—overstates the central role of "fellowship" in them. Fellowship is indeed important in American churches, but it is not as central as are worship and religious education, a corrective that Edgell Becker (1999) and Chaves (2004) have justly made. Yet just as much as fellowship tends to make congregations particularistic, dedicated to the cultures of their constituents, so also does worship, which is one of the ways that congregations are agents of cultural reproduction (Chaves 2004). And no more than "fellowship" is "worship" easily circumscribed as to the senses it mobilizes or the meanings it evokes. Worship, as much as fellowship, is one of the ways that congregations are incorrigibly diffuse, impossible to confine to a functional box. Especially because of the prominence of worship, education, and fellowship, congregations are not instruments that can be readily applied to specific purposes, whether social service delivery or social issue advocacy.

The extent to which congregations provide social services is a hot issue, although the empirical assessments of careful scholars (Cnaan 2002; Chaves 2004; Ammerman 2005) are not far apart from one another. Most congregations help people in need, although few congregations support large-scale social service programs. Congregations are a historically important part of the welfare system, but their efforts would be wholly inadequate to provide a social safety net were publicly supported programs to be abandoned. Part of the controversy is a matter of perceiving the glass half full or half empty. Given how much partisans of privatization exaggerate what can be expected of congregations, it is important to stress their limitations as service providers and to recognize the relative emptiness of the glass (Chaves 2004). Given the centrality of worship, not social service, in congregational life, it is reasonable to give credit where credit is due and acknowledge how relatively full the social services glass is (Ammerman 2005).

Another issue is whether informal services, often provided for members or affiliates of the congregation rather than for outsiders, should be included within the category of congregational social service provision. Meals for shut-ins. Camperships for children of struggling families. Visits to the hospitalized. Emergency aid for abused women. Hand-me-down clothing for the whole family. True, such help comes with implicit strings attached. Recipients can expect to be called upon to reciprocate. If they signed up with a religious organization in order to qualify for secular help, it is no small matter if the congregation adheres to exclusive, conservative doctrine. Moreover, if such services count as social services, so also, one could argue, should the lunchboxes parents send their children to school with. After all—so the argument goes—the congregation, as a bonded group, is like a family.

On this issue, it is said that acts of care directed internally generate only "bonding," not "bridging," social capital. They consolidate, rather than expand, preexisting social relations (Putnam 2000). Yet even in small congregations it is the case that such services typically extend the circle of human caring well beyond the confines of families, nuclear and otherwise. Moreover, as the literature shows (Warner 1988a; Ammerman 1997; Eiesland 2000), congregations are by no means static entities sealed off from the society. They have porous demographic boundaries even if not symbolic ones. They absorb people newly in town, for whom they renew, and sometimes newly provide, a common identity. This is particularly true of newer congregations in demographically growing areas, which are likely to be theologically conservative. Congregations are one way—historically one of the most important ways—that American society organizes itself beyond the confines of families. In our highly mobile society, where denominational labels are of decreasing salience, students of religion are challenged to map the ways that congregations create solidarities, as well as reinforce them.

In congregational studies, the most rapid progress has been made in mapping and understanding new immigrant religious institutions (see Chapter 13), especially because of the foresight and generosity of the Lilly Endowment and the Pew Charitable Trusts. Funded by both foundations, I did my best to promote the careers of the New Ethnic and Immigrant Congregations Project fellows (as in Chapter 5) and the book that presented their reports (Warner and Wittner 1998a). Findings from the Pew-funded Gateway Cities projects in New York, Los Angeles, Chicago, Miami, San Francisco, and Washington, D.C., have been rehearsed at professional conferences and will soon be appearing in book form. Findings from the Houston Gateway Cities project (Ebaugh and Chafetz 2000) have been informing the field for several years. Studies of Muslim communities are still scarce, although the substantial chapter in Diana Eck's book on non-Christian immigrants (Eck 2001, 222–293), based on the research for her Pluralism Project at Harvard, contributes intimate portraits of both immigrant and convert Muslims at the grass roots. Hispanic/Latino religious communities (as opposed to "Hispanic/Latino theologies") remain underrepresented in the literature, perhaps in part because of the misperception (targeted in Chapter 15) that immigrant religion is primarily non-Christian and in part out of the failure of religion scholars to comprehend how significantly recent immigration is adding to Hispanic/Latino religious activity. A promising and eclectic burst of such literature has recently been or is soon to be published (e.g., Dahm 2004; León 2004; Matovina and Riebe-Estella 2002; Sanchez Walsh 2003; Wood 2002). Keeping up with America's increasing religious diversity—new or unfamiliar religions, new or unfamiliar constituents in seemingly familiar religions—will keep many scholars busy for the indefinite future.

Because of recent, on-the-ground work (e.g., Harris 1999; Nelson 1996; Pattillo-McCoy 1998), the autonomous transformative role of the black church tradition is better understood. In their comprehensive survey of the tradition, Lincoln and Mamiya (1990) theorized how the dominant theological conservatism of the black church was combined dialectically with its progressive social teaching. They thus helped to overcome the old-paradigm-inspired view of the black church as fatally cut off from progressive white theological influences and increasingly irrelevant to modern society. In a similar vein, studies of the gay and lesbian presence in American religious institutions (e.g., Cadge 2005; Primiano 2005; Shokeid 1995; Wilcox 2003; Wilson 1995, as well as Chapter 9 here) show that grassroots activists resist top-down academic social constructionist queer theories and affirm their own "essential" identities to find their place in local congregations. As different as they are, the African American and gay/lesbian communities both exhibit the irreducible impact of the religions of the American people.

FOR THE PAST FIFTEEN years, throughout the writings collected in this book and elsewhere, I have stressed the distinctiveness of American religious communities but also the way that, by and large, they contribute to the well-being of the society. That conviction is the argument of Chapter 16, but it is time to acknowledge, coming to the end of the book, that it is also a matter of my faith as an American and a Christian. I recognize that, daydreams and nightmares about "multiculturalism" notwithstanding, American culture has undiminished assimilative power, although in that regard I would not go as far as Alan Wolfe (2003), who interprets most American religion, especially that of evangelicals, as having capitulated to the culture. In the United States, it is exceedingly difficult for a minority community, religious or otherwise, to remain cut off from the wider society for more than a couple of decades at most (that is, until the emergence of a new generation). Social relations are too fluid and mass media too pervasive for long-term isolation to be possible. Assimilation does not always, or even especially, mean that newcomers will adopt white middle-class manners or succeed in gaining entry to the middle class (Portes and Rumbaut 2001). It means that, over time and generations, they become one or another variety of American. It is possible that these assimilative forces will weaken with growing inequality and the right-wing drive toward privatization that exacerbates both inequality and its consequences. With decreased social provision and a frayed social safety net, it is possible that our society will cut off all the lower rungs on the social ladder by which immigrants and other minorities would come to have a stake in being American. Especially judging by immigrant communities, I do not think we have yet come to that point (Alba and Nee 2003). As a partisan, I do what I can to prevent it.

I also recognize that religion in America is a force, usually for progress, sometimes for regress, although I would not, in general, go as far as Diamond (1996) in that regard. For the past decade, religion has been increasingly seen as a polarizing force, regular churchgoers and the "red states" for the Republicans, secularists and the "blue states" for the Democrats. Myself a churchgoing Democrat, I am one of millions who violate the generalization. More to the point, I argue (in Chapter 15) that if they are to remain the party of the people, the Democrats cannot afford to write off the religious constituency, which is disproportionately composed of people of color. Still more to the point, the bitter political polarization in the United States at the turn of the twenty-first century is the effect not so much of religion (which is one of its markers) as of the positions the two parties have assumed on abortion over the past thirty years. The formerly more libertarian Republicans became the antiabortion party, while the formerly heavily Catholic Democrats became the party of abortion rights (Adams 1997; Evans 2002; Hout 1999). The Republicans' official stance on abortion (which they do very little to implement [Saletan 2003]) having made them the party of the Religious Right, I believe it would be a grave mistake for the Democrats to become the party of the irreligious Left.

Not only are there not enough Americans on the unchurched Left to constitute a majority party, but also the secularist vision is blind to the ways that religion remains a vital presence in our society. This book is an invitation to be on the lookout for perennial stirrings in local, out-of-the-public-eye religious communities where sustained, often quiet, work goes on to nurture the young, inspire the marginalized, empower workers, promote livable cities, and preserve cultural traditions. For the foreseeable future in the United States, religion will remain a force to be reckoned with, but it is much more than a political force.

REFERENCES

(References to writings of the author are found in a separate listing at the back of the book.)

Adams, Greg D. 1997. "Abortion: Evidence of Issue Evolution." *American Journal of Political Science* 41 (July): 718–737.

Alba, Richard D., and Victor Nee. 2003. *Remaking the American Mainstream: Assimilation and Contemporary Immigration.* Cambridge: Harvard University Press.

Ammerman, Nancy T. 1987. *Bible Believers: Fundamentalists in the Modern World.* New Brunswick, N.J.: Rutgers University Press.

———. 1997. *Congregation and Community.* New Brunswick, N.J.: Rutgers University Press.

———. 2005. *Pillars of Faith: American Congregations and Their Partners.* Berkeley and Los Angeles: University of California Press.

Ammerman, Nancy Tatom, Jackson W. Carroll, Carl S. Dudley, and William McKinney, eds. 1998. *Studying Congregations: A New Handbook.* Nashville, Tenn.: Abingdon.

Bankston, Carl L., III, and Min Zhou. 2000. "De Facto Congregationalism and Socioeconomic Mobility in Laotian and Vietnamese Immigrant Communities: A Study of Religious Institutions and Economic Change." *Review of Religious Research* 41 (June): 453–470.

Bellah, Robert N. 2003. "The Ritual Roots of Society and Culture." In *Handbook of the Sociology of Religion*, ed. Michele Dillon, 31–44. Cambridge: Cambridge University Press.

Berger, Peter L. 1969. *The Sacred Canopy: Elements of a Sociological Theory of Religion.* Garden City, N.Y.: Doubleday.

———. 2001. "Reflections on the Sociology of Religion Today." *Sociology of Religion* 62 (Winter): 443–454.

Billings, Dwight B. 1990. "Religion as Opposition: A Gramscian Analysis." *American Journal of Sociology* 96 (July): 1–31.

Butler, Jon. 1990. *Awash in a Sea of Faith: The Christianization of the American People.* Cambridge: Harvard University Press.

Cadge, Wendy. 2004. *Heartwood: The First Generation of Theravada Buddhism in America.* Chicago: University of Chicago Press.

———. 2005. "Reconciling Congregations Bridging Gay and Straight Communities." In *Gay Religion*, ed. Scott Thumma and Edward R. Gray, 31–45. Lanham, Md.: AltaMira Press.

Carroll, Jackson, Carl Dudley, and William McKinney, eds. 1986. *Handbook for Congregational Studies.* Nashville, Tenn.: Abingdon.

Chaves, Mark. 2004. *Congregations in America.* Cambridge: Harvard University Press.

Chaves, Mark, and Philip S. Gorski. 2001. "Religious Pluralism and Religious Participation." *Annual Review of Sociology* 17: 261–281.

Cnaan, Ram A. 2002. *The Invisible Caring Hand: American Congregations and the Provision of Welfare.* New York: New York University Press.

Collins, Randall. 2004. *Interaction Ritual Chains.* Princeton, N.J.: Princeton University Press.

Dahm, Charles W. 2004. *Parish Ministry in a Hispanic Community.* Mahwah, N.J.: Paulist Press.

Davidman, Lynn. 1991. *Tradition in a Rootless World: Women Turn to Orthodox Judaism.* Berkeley: University of California Press.

Davie, Grace. 2002. *Europe: The Exceptional Case: Parameters of Faith in the Modern World.* London: Darton, Longman, and Todd.

Diamond, Sara. 1996. *Facing the Wrath: Confronting the Right in Dangerous Times.* Monroe, Me.: Common Courage Press.

Diaz-Stevens, Ana Maria, and Anthony M. Stevens-Arroyo. 1997. *Recognizing the Latino Resurgence in U.S. Religion: The Emmaus Paradigm.* Boulder, Colo.: Westview Press.

Dorsey, Gary. 1995. *Congregation: The Journey Back to Church.* New York: Viking.

Dudley, Carl S., and David A. Roozen. 2001. *Faith Communities Today: A Report on Religion in the United States Today.* Hartford, Conn.: Hartford Institute for Religion Research.

Ebaugh, Helen Rose, and Janet Saltzman Chafetz. 2000. *Religion and the New Immigrants: Continuities and Adaptations in Immigrant Congregations.* Walnut Creek, Calif.: AltaMira

Eck, Diana. 2001. *A New Religious America: How a "Christian Country" Has Become the World's Most Religiously Diverse Nation.* New York: HarperSanFrancisco.

Edgell Becker, Penny. 1999. *Congregations in Conflict: Cultural Models of Local Religious Life.* New York: Cambridge University Press.

Eiesland, Nancy L. 2000. *A Particular Place: Urban Restructuring and Religious Ecology in a Southern Exurb.* New Brunswick, N.J.: Rutgers University Press.

Evans, John H. 2002. "Polarization in Abortion Attitudes in U.S. Religious Traditions, 1972–1998." *Sociological Forum* 17 (September): 397–422.

Feher, Shoshanah. 1998. *Passing Over Easter: Constructing the Boundaries of Messianic Judaism.* Walnut Creek, Calif.: AltaMira Press.

Freedman, Samuel G. 1993. *Upon This Rock: The Miracles of a Black Church.* New York: Harper-Collins.

Harris, Fredrick.1999. *Something Within: Religion in African-American Political Activism.* New York: Oxford University Press.

Hartman, Keith. 1996. *Congregations in Conflict: The Battle over Homosexuality.* New Brunswick, N.J.: Rutgers University Press.

Hoge, Dean R., Benton Johnson, and Donald Luidens. 1994. *Vanishing Boundaries: The Religion of Mainline Protestant Baby Boomers.* Louisville, Ky.: Westminster/John Knox Press.

Hout, Michael. 1999. "Abortion Politics in the United States, 1972–1994: From Single Issue to Ideology." *Gender Issues* 17 (Spring): 3–34.

———. 2000. "Angry and Alienated: Divorced and Remarried Catholics in the United States." *America* (December 16): 10ff.

Hout, Michael, and Claude Fischer. Forthcoming. "Religious Diversity in America, 1940–2000." In *Century of Difference.* New York: Russell Sage Foundation (2001 Working Paper, Survey Research Center, University of California at Berkeley. http://ucdata.berkeley.edu/rsfcensus/papers/Hout_FischerASA.pdf)

Kostarelos, Frances. 1995. *Feeling the Spirit: Faith and Hope in an Evangelical Black Storefront Church.* Columbia: University of South Carolina Press.

Lamb, Simon. 2004. *Devil in the Mountain: A Search for the Origin of the Andes.* Princeton, N.J.: Princeton University Press.

León, Luis D. 2004. *La Llorona's Children: Religion, Life, and Death in the U.S.-Mexican Borderlands.* Berkeley: University of California Press.

Lincoln, C. Eric, and Laurence Mamiya. 1990. *The Black Church in the African American Experience.* Durham, N.C.: Duke University Press.

Lindsay, D. Michael. 2003. "Explaining the Gap: Religious Commitment in the United States and Great Britain." Paper presented at annual meeting of the Society for the Scientific Study of Religion, Norfolk, Va.

Livezey, Lowell W., ed. 2000. *Public Religion and Urban Transformation.* New York: New York University Press.

Matovina, Timothy M., and Gary Riebe-Estrella. 2002. *Horizons of the Sacred: Mexican Traditions in U.S. Catholicism.* Ithaca, N.Y.: Cornell University Press.

McNeill, William H. 1995. *Keeping Together in Time: Dance and Drill in Human History.* Cambridge: Harvard University Press.

McPhee, John. 1998. *Annals of the Former World.* New York: Farrar, Straus and Giroux.

McRoberts, Omar M. 2003. *Streets of Glory: Church and Community in a Black Urban Neighborhood.* Chicago: University of Chicago Press.

Mellor, Philip A. Forthcoming. "Religion, Culture, and Society in the 'Information Age.' " *Sociology of Religion.*

Neitz, Mary Jo. 1987. *Charisma and Community: A Study of Religious Commitment Within the Charismatic Renewal.* New Brunswick, N.J.: Transaction.

Nelson, Timothy J. 1996. "Sacrifice of Praise: Emotion and Collective Participation in an African-American Worship Service." *Sociology of Religion* 57 (winter): 379–396.

Numrich, Paul David. 1995. *Old Wisdom in the New World: Americanization in Immigrant Theravada Buddhist Temples.* Knoxville: University of Tennessee Press.

Olson, Daniel V. A. 2002. "Competing Notions of Religious Competition and Conflict in Theories of Religious Economies." In *Sacred Markets, Sacred Canopies: Essays on Religious Markets and Religious Pluralism,* ed. Ted Jelen, 133–165. Lanham, Md.: Rowman and Littlefield.

Pattillo-McCoy, Mary. 1998. "Church Culture as a Strategy of Action in the Black Community." *American Sociological Review* 63 (December): 767–784.

Portes, Alejandro, and Rubén G. Rumbaut. 2001. *Legacies: The Story of the Immigrant Second Generation.* Berkeley: University of California Press.

Primiano, Leonard Norman. 2005. "Gay Gods of the City: The Emergence of the Gay and Lesbian Ethnic Parish." In *Gay Religion*, ed. Scott Thumma and Edward R. Gray, 7–29. Lanham, Md.: AltaMira Press.

Putnam, Robert D. 2000. *Bowling Alone: The Collapse and Revival of American Community.* New York: Simon and Schuster.

Saletan, William. 2003. *Bearing Right: How Conservatives Won the Abortion War.* Berkeley and Los Angeles: University of California Press.

Sanchez Walsh, Arlene. 2003. *Latino Pentecostal Identity: Evangelical Faith, Self, and Society.* New York: Columbia University Press.

Skokeid, Moshe. 1995. *A Gay Synagogue in New York.* New York: Columbia University Press.

Smith, Christian, with Michael Emerson, Sally Gallagher, Paul Kennedy, and David Sikkink. 1998. *American Evangelicalism: Embattled and Thriving.* Chicago: University of Chicago Press.

Smith, Tom W., and Seokho Kim. 2004. "The Vanishing Protestant Majority." GSS Social Change Report No. 49, NORC/University of Chicago. http://www-news.uchicago.edu/releases/04/040720.protestant.pdf

Stark, Rodney. 2001. *One True God : Historical Consequences of Monotheism.* Princeton, N.J.: Princeton University Press.

Stark, Rodney, and Roger Finke. 2000. *Acts of Faith: Explaining the Human Side of Religion.* Berkeley: University of California Press.

Swatos, William H., Jr. 1981. "Beyond Denominationalism? Community and Culture in American Religion." *Journal for the Scientific Study of Religion* 20 (September): 217–227.

"Symposium on Religious Attendance." 1998. *American Sociological Review* 63 (February): 111–145.

Voas, David, Daniel V. A. Olson, and Alasdair Crockett. 2002. "Religious Pluralism and Participation: Why Previous Research Is Wrong." *American Sociological Review* 67 (April): 212–230.

Wilcox, Melissa M. 2003. *Coming Out in Christianity: Religion, Identity, and Community.* Bloomington: Indiana University Press.

Wilkes, Paul. 1994. *And They Shall Be My People: An American Rabbi and His Congregation.* New York: Atlantic Monthly Press.

Wilson, Nancy. 1995. *Our Tribe: Queer Folks, God, Jesus, and the Bible.* San Francisco: Harper.

Wolfe, Alan. 2003. *The Transformation of American Religion: How We Actually Live Our Faith.* New York: Free Press.

Wood, Richard L. 2002. *Faith in Action: Religion, Race, and Democratic Organizing in America.* Chicago: University of Chicago Press.

Wuthnow, Robert. 1998. *Loose Connections: Joining Together in America's Fragmented Communities.* Cambridge: Harvard University Press.

———. 2003. *All In Sync: How Music and Art Are Revitalizing American Religion.* Berkeley: University of California Press.

Young, Michael P. 2002. "Confessional Protest: The Religious Birth of U.S. National Social Movements." *American Sociological Review* 67 (October): 660–688.

APPENDIX:
LIST OF AUTHOR'S CITED WORKS

All citations to the work of the author, including coauthorships and editorial collaborations, are listed in chronological order. Unless otherwise indicated, the sole author of each work is R. Stephen Warner.

1970   "The Role of Religious Ideas and the Use of Models in Max Weber's Comparative Studies of Non-Capitalist Societies." *Journal of Economic History* 30 (March): 74–99.

1972   "The Methodology of Max Weber's Comparative Studies." Ph.D. diss., Department of Sociology, University of California at Berkeley.

1976   Neil J. Smelser and R. Stephen Warner. *Sociological Theory: Historical and Formal.* Morristown, N.J.: General Learning Press.

1978   "Toward a Redefinition of Action Theory: Paying the Cognitive Element Its Due." *American Journal of Sociology* 83 (May): 1317–1349.

1979   "Theoretical Barriers to the Understanding of Evangelical Christianity." *Sociological Analysis* 40 (Spring): 1–9.

1981a   Review of *Understanding Church Growth and Decline: 1950–1978*, ed. Dean R. Hoge and David A. Roozen. *Sociological Analysis* 42 (Spring): 73–74.

1981b   "Parsons's Last Testament." *American Journal of Sociology* 87 (November): 715–721.

1983   "Research Note: Visits to a Growing Evangelical and Declining Liberal Church in 1978." *Sociological Analysis* 44 (Fall): 243–253.

1985   "Dualistic and Monistic Religiosity." In *Religious Movements: Genesis, Exodus, and Numbers*, ed. Rodney Stark, 199–220. New York: Paragon House.

1988a   *New Wine in Old Wineskins: Evangelicals and Liberals in a Small-Town Church.* Berkeley and Los Angeles: University of California Press.

1988b   "Sociological Theory as Public Philosophy." Review essay on *The Modern Reconstruction of Classical Thought: Talcott Parsons*, by Jeffrey C. Alexander, vol. 4 of *Theoretical Logic in Sociology. American Journal of Sociology* 94 (November): 644–655.

1989a   Review of *The Restructuring of American Religion*, by Robert Wuthnow. *American Journal of Sociology* 94 (May): 1434–1436.

1989b   "The Metropolitan Community Church as a Case Study of Religious Change in the U.S.A." Paper presented at annual meeting of the Society for the Scientific Study of Religion, Salt Lake City [substantially revised for Chapter 9 of this volume].

1989c   Review of *Reinhold Niebuhr: A Biography*, by Richard Wightman Fox. *Sociological Analysis* 49 (Winter): 447–449.

1990a   "Mirror for American Protestantism: Mendocino Presbyterian Church in the Sixties and Seventies." In *The Mainstream Protestant "Decline": The Presbyterian Pattern*, ed. Milton J. Coalter, John M. Mulder, and Louis B. Weeks, 198–223 and 250–253. Louisville: Westminster/John Knox [Chapter 7 in this volume].

1990b   "The Korean Immigrant Church in Comparative Perspective." Paper presented at colloquium "The Korean Immigrant Church: A Comparative Perspective," Princeton Theological Seminary, Princeton, N.J., February 16–18 [incorporated in Warner 2001c].

1990c   "Woman's Place, Women's Space." Paper presented at annual meeting of the Association for the Sociology of Religion, Washington, D.C., August 9.

1991a   "Starting Over: Reflections on American Religion." *Christian Century* 108 (September 4–11): 811–813 [Chapter 1 in this volume].

1991b   "Oenology: The Making of *New Wine*." In *A Case for the Case Study*, ed. Joe Feagin, Anthony Orum, and Gideon Sjoberg, 174–199. Chapel Hill: University of North Carolina Press.

1992a   "Congregating: Walk Humbly at Rock Church." *Christian Century* 109 (October 28): 957–958.

1992b   "New and Old in Chicago Immigrant Religion." Manuscript. University of Illinois at Chicago.

1993a   "Work in Progress Toward a New Paradigm for the Sociological Study of Religion in the United States." *American Journal of Sociology* 98 (March): 1044–1093 [Chapter 2 in this volume].

1993b   R. Stephen Warner and James S. Pappas. "Congregating: Seeing the Word." *Christian Century* 110 (June 30–July 7): 663–665 [Chapter 10 in this volume].

1993c   "Pentecostal Immigrants and the Making of the Sun Belt." Review essay on *Rising in the West*, by Dan Morgan. *Christian Century* 110 (August 25–September 1): 819–822 [Chapter 12 in this volume].

1993d   Review of *The Churching of America, 1776–1990: Winners and Losers in Our Religious Economy*, ed. Roger Finke and Rodney Stark. *Journal for the Scientific Study of Religion* 32 (September): 295–297 [included in Chapter 4 of this volume].

1994a   "The Place of the Congregation in the American Religious Configuration." In *New Perspectives in the Study of Congregations*, ed. James P. Wind and James W. Lewis, 54–99, vol. 2 of *American Congregations*. Chicago: University of Chicago Press [Chapter 8 in this volume].

1994b   Elfriede Wedam and R. Stephen Warner. "Sacred Space on Tuesday: A Study of the Institutionalization of Charisma." In *"I Come Away Stronger":*

How Small Groups Are Shaping American Religion, ed. Robert Wuthnow, 148–178. Grand Rapids, Mich.: Eerdmans.

1994c   "Mixing It Up in San Antonio: An Outsider's Experience of Holy Week Observances at the Cathedral of San Fernando." Report to San Fernando Cathedral Self-study Project [incorporated in Chapter 11 of this volume].

1994–   "Oh Ye of Little Faith." Review essay on *The Culture of Unbelief*, by Stephen
1995   Carter. *Responsive Community* 5 (Winter): 68–72.

1995   "The Metropolitan Community Churches and the Gay Agenda: The Power of Pentecostalism and Essentialism." In *Sex, Lies, and Sanctity: Religion and Deviance in Contemporary North America*, ed. Mary Jo Neitz and Marion S. Goldman, 81–108. Greenwich, Conn.: JAI Press [Chapter 9 in this volume].

1997a   "Convergence Toward the New Paradigm: A Case of Induction." In *Rational Choice Theory and Religion: Summary and Assessment*, ed. Lawrence A. Young, 87–101. New York: Routledge.

1997b   "A Paradigm Is Not a Theory: Reply to Lechner." *American Journal of Sociology* 103 (July): 192–198 [Chapter 3 in this volume].

1997c   "Religion, Boundaries, and Bridges: The 1996 Paul Hanly Furfey Lecture." *Sociology of Religion* 58 (Fall): 217–238 [Chapter 5 in this volume].

1997d   "'New Paradigm' Churches: Lessons from California." Review essay on *Reinventing American Protestantism*, by Donald E. Miller. *Christian Century* 114 (November 19–26): 1085–1088 [included in Chapter 4 of this volume].

1998a   R. Stephen Warner and Judith G. Wittner, eds. *Gatherings in Diaspora: Religious Communities and the New Immigration*. Philadelphia: Temple University Press.

1998b   "Immigration and Religious Communities in the United States: Introduction." In *Gatherings in Diaspora: Religious Communities and the New Immigration*, ed. R. Stephen Warner and Judith G. Wittner, 3–34. Philadelphia: Temple University Press.

1998c   "Approaching Religious Diversity: Barriers, Byways, and Beginnings." 1997 presidential address to the Association for the Sociology of Religion. *Sociology of Religion* 59 (Fall): 193–215.

1998d   Nancy L. Eiesland and R. Stephen Warner. "Ecology: Seeing the Congregation in Context." In *Studying Congregations: A New Handbook*, ed. Nancy Ammerman, Jackson Carroll, Carl Dudley, and William McKinney, 40–77. Nashville, Tenn.: Abingdon.

1998e   "Religion and Migration in the United States." *Social Compass* 45 (March): 115–126.

1999a   "Changes in the Civic Role of Religion." In *Diversity and Its Discontents: Cultural Conflict and Common Ground in Contemporary American Society*, ed. Neil J. Smelser and Jeffrey C. Alexander, 229–243. Princeton, N. J.: Princeton University Press [Chapter 16 in this volume].

1999b   Review of *Revive Us Again: The Reawakening of American Fundamentalism*,
          by Joel Carpenter. *Social Forces 77* (June): 1662–1664 [included in Chapter
          4 of this volume].

2000a   "Elizondo's Pastoral Theology in Action: An Inductive Appreciation." In
          Beyond Borders: Writings of Virgilio Elizondo and Friends, ed. Timothy Matov-
          ina, 47–57. Maryknoll, N.Y.: Orbis Books [Chapter 11 in this volume].

2000b   "Epilogue: Building Religious Communities at the Turn of the Century."
          In *Public Religion and Urban Transformation*, ed. Lowell W. Livezey,
          295–307. New York: New York University Press.

2000c   Review of *Ordaining Women: Culture and Conflict in Religious Organizations*,
          by Mark Chaves. *American Journal of Sociology* 105 (May): 1797–1799.

2000d   Review of *Southern Cross: The Beginnings of the Bible Belt*, by Christine Leigh
          Heyrman. *Social Forces* 78 (June): 1587–1588.

2000e   "Religion and New (Post-1965) Immigrants: Some Principles Drawn from
          Field Research." *American Studies* 41 (Summer/Fall): 267–286 [Chapter 13
          in this volume].

2001a   Ho-Youn Kwon, Kwang Chung Kim, and R. Stephen Warner, eds. *Korean
          Americans and Their Religions: Pilgrims and Missionaries from a Different
          Shore*. University Park: Pennsylvania State University Press.

2001b   Kwang Chung Kim, R. Stephen Warner, and Ho-Youn Kwon. "Korean
          American Religion in International Perspective." In *Korean Americans
          and Their Religions: Pilgrims and Missionaries from a Different Shore*, ed. Ho-
          Youn Kwon, Kwang Chung Kim, and R. Stephen Warner, 3–24. University
          Park: Pennsylvania State University Press.

2001c   "The Korean Immigrant Church as Case and Model." In *Korean Americans
          and Their Religions: Pilgrims and Missionaries from a Different Shore*, ed. Ho-
          Youn Kwon, Kwang Chung Kim, and R. Stephen Warner, 25–52. Univer-
          sity Park: Pennsylvania State University Press.

2001d   Mary Jean Cravens and R. Stephen Warner. "The High Intensity Youth Min-
          istry at Soul Station: An Exception to the Pied Piper Model." Paper presented
          at annual meeting of the Midwest Sociological Society, St. Louis, April 4.

2001e   R. Stephen Warner, Elise Martel, and Rhonda E. Dugan. "Catholicism Is to
          Islam As Velcro Is to Teflon: Ambivalence about Religion and Ethnic
          Culture among Second Generation Latina and Muslim Women College
          Students." Paper presented at annual meeting of the Society for the Sci-
          entific Study of Religion, Columbus, Ohio, October 19.

2001f   Review of *New Spiritual Homes: Religion and Asian Americans*, ed. David K.
          Yoo. *Journal of the American Academy of Religion* 69 (Fall): 732–735.

2002   "More Progress on the New Paradigm." In *Sacred Markets, Sacred Canopies:
          Essays on Religious Markets and Religious Pluralism*, ed. Ted G. Jelen, 1–29.
          Lanham, Md.: Rowman and Littlefield.

2003a   Rhys H. Williams and R. Stephen Warner. "Creating a Diverse Urban
          Evangelicalism: Youth Ministry as a Model." In *A Public Faith: Evangelicals*

and Civic Engagement, ed. Michael Cromartie, 205–214 and 256. Lanham, Md.: Rowman and Littlefield.

2003b   Review of *Heaven Below: Early Pentecostals and American Culture*, by Grant Wacker. *Journal for the Scientific Study of Religion* 42 (March): 166–167 [included in Chapter 4 of this volume].

2003c   Review of *Religions in Asian America: Building Faith Communities*, ed. Pyong Gap Min and Jung Ha Kim. *Bulletin of the Royal Institute for Inter-Faith Studies* 5 (Spring–Summer): 210–214 [Chapter 14 in this volume].

2003–   "What the Abortion War Costs." Review essay on *Bearing Right: How*
2004   *Conservatives Won the Abortion War*, by William Saletan. *Responsive Community* 14 (Winter): 70–75.

2004a   Review of *All In Sync: How Music and Art Are Revitalizing American Religion*, by Robert Wuthnow. *American Journal of Sociology* 109 (January): 990–992.

2004b   "Coming to America: Immigrants and the Faith They Bring." *Christian Century* 121 (February 10): 20–23 [under a different title as Chapter 15 in this volume].

2004c   "They're OK, We're OK." Review essay on *The Transformation of American Religion: How We Actually Live Our Faith*, by Alan Wolfe. *Books and Culture: A Christian Review* 10 (March–April): 20.

2004d   "Enlisting Smelser's Theory of Ambivalence to Maintain Progress in Sociology of Religion's New Paradigm." In *Self, Social Structure, and Beliefs: Essays in Honor of Neil Smelser*, ed. Jeffrey C. Alexander, Gary T. Marx, and Christine Williams, 103–121. Berkeley and Los Angeles: University of California Press [Chapter 6 in this volume].

2004e   "Religion." In *Encyclopedia of Social Theory*, ed. George Ritzer, 634–639. Thousand Oaks, Calif.: Sage Publications.

2004f   Review of *Coming Out in Christianity: Religion, Identity, and Community*, by Melissa M. Wilcox. *Christian Century* 121 (August 10): 39–40.

INDEX

abortion, 289
Abusharaf, Rogaia, 87, 94, 95, 245, 247–248
achieved recruitment, 44
Adam, Barry D., 186, 194–195, 197, 202
Adams, Greg D., 289
Advocate, 185
affiliation, religious: ambivalence and, 113–114; data on, 22; disaffiliation, 43–48, 73, 111, 162, 279–280; ethnicity and, 238–239; rational choice and, 111–112; unaffiliated, 279
African Americans: empowerment of religion, 40; enfranchisement of, 257; Jehovah's Witnesses, 30; Muslims, 239, 267; in Pentecostal movement, 76, 98. *See also* black church
Afrocentric religions, 261
AIDS, 200
Alba, Richard D., 86, 289
Alford, Robert R., 19, 29, 41
Althauser, Robert P., 39
Althorpe, Frederick (pseudo.), 129, 140
Altman, Dennis, 38, 184, 187, 196, 199, 202
ambivalent religiosity, Smelser's theory of, 114–117, 118, 119
American Buddhist Congress, 169
American Congregations, 147, 151, 160, 161, 168
American Religious Identification Survey, 260
American Sign Language (ASL), 209, 211
American Sociological Association, 105, 110, 114
American Sociological Review, 70
Ammerman, Nancy Tatom, 21, 35, 38, 46, 66, 73, 98–99, 105, 107, 111, 263, 269, 271, 284, 285, 286, 287
antisecularization thesis, 21
Apostolic Church of God, 273n4
apostolic succession, 34
Arab Americans, Christian immigrants, 258–259
Asian Americans: ambivalent religiosity, 112, 113, 115; Christian immigrants, 238–239, 258–259; composition of, 254; immigration history, 253–254; new immigrants, 232, 234, 254; religious affiliations of, 32, 254–255; from Southeast Asia, 255–256. *See also* specific groups
Assemblies of God, 71, 75, 127, 146, 147, 265
assimilation, 97–98, 241, 288–289
Augustine, Saint, 93
Awash in a Sea of Faith (Butler), 22

Baer, Douglas E., 31
Bahr, Howard M., 22
Bainbridge, William Sims, 23, 26, 108
Bankston, Carl L. III, 84, 238, 241, 245, 254, 256, 285
Baptist church: affiliation in, 29, 72; bureaucracy in, 161; congregationalism in, 157, 163; demographic factors in, 23; number of congregations, 146–147; Southern Baptist Convention, 45, 71, 73, 146, 163, 194, 265
Barfoot, Charles H., 43, 47
Bauer, Paul F., 188, 190
Beaudoin, Tom, 117
Bedell, Kenneth, 184
Bell, Alan P., 196
Bell, Daniel, 46
Bellah, Robert N., 26, 44, 117, 284
Bender, Courtney Jane, 21, 37
Berger, Peter L., 5, 15, 18, 20, 24–25, 26, 31, 66, 107, 108, 118, 155–156, 283
Bernal, Mary Esther, 218
Beth Chayim Chadashim, 193
Beyond Borders, 213, 221
Bibby, Reginald, 80
Biesadecki, Carol, 166
Bilhartz, Terry D., 23, 107, 108
Billings, Dwight B., 39–40, 41, 284
Birchard, Roy, 201
Blackburn, Anne, 32
black church, 29, 109; civic role of, 38, 39, 266, 269; food sharing in, 96; number of congregations, 146–147; research on, 288
Blacking, John, 90–91, 92, 93–94
Blau, Judith R., 27
Bloom, Jack M., 195
Books and Culture, 264
Borhek, Mary, 199
Boswell, John, 192, 197
Boyd, Malcolm, 198
Boyte, Harry C., 30
Bozorgmehr, Mehdi, 32, 33
Brasher, Brenda E., 79, 80
Braude, Ann, 66
Bread for the World, 266
Breault, Kevin D., 27, 48
Brereton, Virginia Lieson, 40, 41
Briggs initiative, 192
Bruce, Steve, 105
Brusco, Elizabeth, 42
Bryan, William Jennings, 76

Buddhist Churches of America, 148, 243–244
Buddhists, 32, 37; European American, 239; congregationalism among, 167; interethnic, 169; number of congregations, 148
Bull, Malcolm, 30
Burdick, John, 41
Burns, Gene, 266
Burr, Chandler, 196
Burton, Bill, 235
Butler, Jon, 15, 22, 23, 26, 69, 107, 282

Cadge, Wendy, 285, 288
Caldwell, Thekla J., 43
Calvary Chapel, 79–81, 147
camp meetings, 72
Camp Ramah movement, 169
Cann, David E., 28, 49
Caplow, Theodore, 22, 46, 48, 49
Carpenter, Joel A., 40, 107, 111; *Revive Us Again*, 76–79
Carrington, Christopher, 195
Carroll, Jackson W., 35, 36, 41, 48, 285, 286
Carter, Stephen L., 85, 269
Catholic Church, 3–4, 8–9; affiliation, 23, 70, 72, 112; ambivalent religiosity, 113–114; charismatic groups in, 20; civic role of, 266–267; de facto congregationalism in, 36–37, 164–166, 244; congregation as defined by, 157; converts to, 44–45; Deaf Center, 209–212; disaffiliation, 28, 43, 44, 73, 279, 280; gays and lesbians in, 172, 193, 194, 195; geographic concentration, 27; His-panics/Latinos in, 91–92, 214–221, 239; immigrant churches, 31, 237; parishes (*See* parishes); Spanish-language worship, 217, 218–219, 237, 261; structural adaptability of, 34–35; Vietnamese in, 238; women's empowerment, 42; worship in, 153
centrifugal processes, 35–36
centripetal processes, 35
Chadwick, Bruce A., 22
Chafetz, Janet Saltzman, 235, 247, 249, 285, 287
Chai, Karen J., 86, 87, 245, 271
Chappell, David L., 112
charismatic movement, 20, 37, 42, 72, 132
Charlton, Joy C., 48, 99, 224; history, 253
Chaves, Mark, 28, 35, 44, 48, 49, 109, 281–282, 285, 286, 287
Chazanov, Mathis, 37
Cherry, Kittredge, 194, 202
Chicago Catholic Ephpheta, 209–212
Chinese Americans, 32; Christians, 240–241, 255, 256, 259; cohorts of immigrants, 247; immigration history, 253
Chinese Fellowship Church, 243
Chiswick, Barry R., 234
Chong, Kelley H., 241
Christian Coalition, 264, 266, 268
Christianity Today, 128
Christiano, Kevin J., 21, 27, 31, 34, 36, 109, 233
churches: architecture, English *vs.* American, 13–14; architecture, of immigrant churches, 15–16; attendance, 50n3, 265, 279; geo-graphic mobility and, 163; membership rate, 21–22, 50n2, 69–70; monopolistic, 27;

new-paradigm, 79–81; structural adaptabil-ity of, 34–38. *See also* congregations; denominations
Church of God in Christ, 75, 147, 148, 169
Church of Haile Selassie I, 243, 246
Churching of America, The (Finke and Stark), 69–74
Church of Jesus Christ of Latter-day Saints, 147, 168
Cities on a Hill (FitzGerald), 16
civil rights movement, 38, 39, 264
Clark, Linda J., 92, 93, 98
Cleath, Robert, 194
Clergy and Laity Concerned, 266
Cnaan, Ram A., 286
cohorts, immigrant, 247–248
Coleman, Gerald D., 193
Coleman, John A., 189, 194
Collins, Randall, 109, 284
colonial churches: affiliation rate in, 69–70; disestablishment of, 23; spiritual lethargy in, 22
Comparative religion research, 234
Congregational History Project, 151, 156
congregationalism, de facto, 36–37, 86, 145, 160–168, 193, 242–245, 285; in Catholic Church, 36–37, 164–166, 244; costs to, 168–169, 163; defined, 36, 163; disloyalty charge and, 285; in non-Christian religions, 37, 167–168, 242–245; pressures toward, 163–164
congregationalism, formal, 35, 37, 160–161, 168–169
Congregationalist church, 23, 29, 71, 72, 161
Congregational Studies Project Team, 286
congregations, 8; civic role of, 271–272; con-servative shift in, 147, 266; contrast with denominations, 150–151; countercyclical growth and decline patterns of, 149; for deaf, 209–212; fellowship in, 155–160, 286; function of, 150; geographic mobility of, 163; immigrant (*See* immigrant congrega-tions); local cultures and, 170–172; mission of, 151–152, 154–155; number of, 146–147; religious education in, 154; research on, 284–288; as service provider, 286–287; stewardship of, 155; view of denomination, 151; as voluntary community, 152–153; wor-ship in, 153–154, 286
constructionist theory of homosexuality, 196–198, 202
Cooper, Aaron, 193
Cooper, Lee R., 30
Cornelius, Wayne A., 84, 85
Cory, Donald Webster, 186, 195
Cott, Nancy F., 41
Cowper, William, 139–140
Cravens, Mary Jean, 117
Crockett, Alasdair, 281
Cuban immigrants, 239
Cuddihy, John Murray, 263
cultural boundaries, bridging. *See* solidarity, religious
cultural reproduction role of religion, 85, 269–270, 271

Cursillo de Cristiandad, 98, 135, 152
Curtis, James E., 31

Dahm, Charles W., 288
Dallas, Joe, 198
Daniels, Roger, 43
Dank, Barry M., 186, 187, 189, 190
Dart, John, 34, 186
Davidman, Lynn, 21, 26, 42, 44, 46, 264, 284
Davie, Grace, 278, 282
Davis, James A., 19, 22, 25
Day, Thomas, 156
Deaf, church for the, 209–212
Deane, Glenn, 27
De Colores, 202
D'Emilio, John, 186, 199
Democratic party, 289
Democratization of American Christianity, The
    (Hatch), 22, 80
Denby, David, 85, 270
Denny, Frederick, 31, 32, 37, 167
denominations: affiliation, 22, 72–73; central-
    ized bureaucracy of, 161, 162; centrifugal
    process in, 35–36; centripetal process in,
    35; vs. congregationalism, 169–170; congre-
    gational view of, 151; conservative pressure
    groups within, 162; contrast with congrega-
    tions, 150–151; decentralization of, 162–163;
    disaffiliation and switching, 43–48, 111, 162,
    270, 279–280; disestablishment and, 23;
    function of, 149; for gays and lesbians (See
    Metropolitan Community Churches);
    growth-and-decline curves in, 148–149;
    homosexuality and, 193–195; mainline
    decline, 147, 152, 161–162, 163, 265–266;
    mergers and federations of, 161; new
    church development, 157, 170–171, 172;
    number of, 148; number of congregations,
    146–147; regional, 27, 29; voluntary organiz-
    ation of, 15
Diamond, Sara, 36, 289
Diaz-Stevens, Ana-María, 98
Dignity-Chicago, 172, 193
DiMaggio, Paul J., 35, 167–168, 271
disaffiliation, religious, 43–48, 72, 162,
    279–280
disestablishment, 6, 15, 22, 23, 24, 65, 107, 108,
    282
Dobbelaere, Karel, 105
Dodson, Jualynne E., 96
Dolan, Jay, 23, 31, 37
Dorsey, Gary, 285
Douglas, Bruce (pseud.), 134, 136, 142
Douglas, Mary, 200
Duberman, Martin, 184
Dudley, Carl S., 285
Durkheim, Emile, 5, 65, 90, 280, 283, 284
Dyson, Michael Eric, 98, 270

Eastman, Don, 191
Ebaugh, Helen Rose, 235, 242, 247, 249, 285,
    287
Eck, Diana, 234, 258, 287–288
economy, religious, 6–7, 23–25, 26, 28, 67n1,
    70–71, 77–78, 283

Edgell Becker, Penny, 285, 286
education, religious, 154
Ehrenreich, Barbara, 272
Eiesland, Nancy L., 268, 285, 286, 287
Eisenhower, Dwight, 263
elective parochialism, 1, 8, 46, 83, 106, 134
Elizondo, Virgilio, 86, 91, 92, 97, 99, 213–214;
    Holy Week Rituals of, 215–218, 219–221; pas-
    toral theology of, 221–223; Spanish lan-
    guage policy of, 217, 218–219
Ellison, Christopher G., 39, 40
emotionalism, in religion, 7, 86, 90–91, 93–94
empowerment function of religion, 40–43
English church architecture, 13–14
English-language worship, immigrant, 33, 86,
    245
Enroth, Ronald E., 185, 189, 190, 198, 201
Episcopal church, 25–26, 29, 34, 45, 147, 162;
    gays and lesbians in, 163, 194, 195
Epstein, Barbara Leslie, 41
Epstein, Steven, 186, 196, 197
Erdmans, Mary Patrice, 248
essentialist theory of homosexuality, 196–197,
    198–200
Esterberg, K.G., 202
ethnographic methods, 126
evangelicalism, 16, 111; achieved recruitment,
    44; among Asian immigrants, 255; empow-
    erment of women, 42; Herberg on, 3; insti-
    tutional, 128; in Mendocino Presbyterian
    Church, 125, 126, 127–128, 132–134, 141–142;
    modernism and, 18; new-paradigm
    churches, 79–81. See also Pentecostals
Evangelical Lutheran Church, 146
Evans, John H., 289
Evans, Sara M., 30

Faderman, Lillian, 202
Fanning, Buckner, 217, 220
Farley, Reynolds, 270
Farrakhan, Louis, 239, 267
Feher, Shoshanah, 87, 240, 269, 271, 285
fellowship, congregational, 155–160, 286
Fellowship of Inner-City Word of Faith, 147
Fenton, John Y., 32, 37
Fields, Karen E., 30, 37, 38, 39, 43
Fierstein, Harvey, 197, 200
Filipino Americans, 32, 233, 239, 253, 254, 255,
    256
Finke, Roger, 6, 22, 23, 26, 27, 34, 48, 49, 66,
    105, 107, 108, 109, 110, 111, 118, 265, 266, 281;
    The Churching of America, 69–74
Finney, Charles Grandison, 78, 186
Finney, Henry C., 21
Fischer, Claude S., 34
FitzGerald, Frances, 9, 16, 33–34, 36, 45, 47,
    186, 197, 200, 202
Fitzpatrick, Joseph S.J., 28
Flores, Archbishop Patricio, 217
Flynt, Wayne, 160
food sharing, 96
Foucault, Michel, 196
Fox, Richard Wightman, 272
Foxe, Abuna Asento, 243
Frady, Marshall, 39

Freedman, Samuel G., 99n5, 285
Friedan, Betty, 273
Friedland, Roger, 19, 29, 41
Fronczek, Casey, 210
Fuller Theological Seminary, 128, 132, 133, 137, 163, 170
fundamentalism: Carpenter on, 76–79. *See also* evangelicalism
Furman, Frida Kerner, 26

Gagnon, John, 196
Galilean Journal (Elizondo), 221
Gallardo, Susana, 86, 98
Gallup survey, 19, 20, 22, 25, 44, 148
Garfinkel, Harold, 283
Gateway Cities projects, 287
Gatherings in Diaspora (Warner and Wittner), 5, 235
gay rights movement, 38, 184; radical, 196
gays and lesbians: Catholics, 172, 193, 194, 195; definition of terms, 184; denominations, attitudes of, 193–195; in Episcopal church, 163, 194, 195; Jewish congregations, 193; in religious institutions, research on, 288. *See also* Metropolitan Community Churches
gender roles, immigrant, 246–247, 248
General Social Survey, 260
generation gap, immigrant, 33, 86, 245–246
Gentlemen's Agreement, 253
geographic mobility, 15, 30, 33–34, 47, 157, 163
George, Sheba M., 239, 246, 271
Gerard, Susan Elizabeth, 42
Gibson, Margaret A., 86
Gilkes, Cheryl Townsend, 21, 41, 96, 169
Gilkey, Langdon, 151
Glaser, Chris, 187, 189, 198
Glenn, Norval D., 43
Glesser, John, 165
goddess worship, 202
Godfrey, Brian J., 186
Goette, Robert D., 245
Goffman, Erving, 283
Goizueta, Roberto S., 85, 91–92
Gold, Steven J., 33, 240
Goldman, Karla, 160
Gomez, Leopoldo, 40
Gorman, E. Michael, 21, 189, 194
Gorski, Philip S., 109, 281
Goyette, Kimberly A., 241
Grabb, Edward G., 31
Graham, Billy, 76, 77
Grapes of Wrath, The (Steinbeck), 226, 227
Great Awakening: First, 70; Second, 15, 22, 41, 70
Greek Orthodox Church, 161, 178n59
Greeley, Andrew M., 23, 25, 26, 43, 48, 49, 265
Green, Robert, 219
Greenberg, David F., 192
Griffin, Carolyn Welch, 200
Gulliksen, Kenn, 79
Guth, James L., 38

Habits of the Heart (Bellah), 44
Hackett, David G., 22

Hadaway, C. Kirk, 28, 34, 43, 45, 46, 265
Haddad, Yvonne Yazbeck, 32, 33, 37, 158, 246
Hadden, Jeffrey K., 18, 21, 35, 128
Hammersmith, Sue Kiefer, 196
Hammond, Phillip E., 24, 44, 46, 151, 158
Hanks, Thomas, 199
Hannigan, John A., 38, 39
Harding, Susan, 109
Hargrove, Barbara, 35, 42, 48
Harrell, David Edwin, Jr., 28, 48
Harris, Frederick, 288
Harris, James Henry, 39
Hart-Celler Act, 253, 254, 267
Hatch, Nathan O., 15, 22, 23, 26, 28, 48, 78, 80, 107, 108
Hathout, Hassan, 33
Hathout, Maher, 33
havurot, 152, 172
Heaven Below (Wacker), 74–76
Heilman, Samuel C., 44
Heim, S. Mark, 264
Henry, Carl F.H., 198
Hepner, Randal, 243, 270
Herberg, Will, 2–3, 5–6, 19, 22, 23, 30–31, 35, 40, 85, 128, 236, 240, 263, 270
Herek, Gregory M., 202
Hernández, Edwin, 239
Hewitt, Thomas Furman, 195
Heyrman, Christine Leigh, 109
Hill, Samuel S., 29
Himmelfarb, Gertrude, 64
Hindus, congregational form among, 241, 244–245
Hispanics/Latinos, 32, 84, 239; ambivalent religiosity, 112, 113–114, 116, 117; congregational organization among, 244; cultural mixing (*mestizaje*), 97, 215, 217–218; Cursillo movement, 98; disaffiliation, 43; guest workers, 233; music and ritual, 91–92, 214–221, 261; Pentecostals, 28; Protestant, 148, 237, 260; research on, 288; Spanish-language worship, 217, 218–219, 237, 261
Hodgkinson, Murray S., 265
Hofrenning, Stella Koutroumanes, 234
Hoge, Dean R., 35, 48, 265–266, 280
Hollis, Alverna, 211
homophile movement, 193–194, 195, 200
homophobia, 190, 192
Homosexual in America, The (Cory), 186, 195
Homosexual: Oppression and Liberation (Altman), 196
homosexuality: constructivist concept of, 196–198; essentialist concept of, 196–197, 198–200; homophile movement, 193–194, 195, 200; Perry's teaching of innate gospel of, 40, 43, 187–188, 195–196. *See also* gays and lesbians; Metropolitan Community Churches
Hopewell, James, 154
Hose, John, 186, 191
house-church, 172
Hout, Michael, 289
Howe, Neil, 117
Hsu, Peter (pseud.), 128, 129–130, 134, 136, 140, 142, 152

Huber, Nancy, 209, 211
humility, 220, 221, 223
Humphreys, Laud, 38, 187, 189, 190
Hunter, James Davison, 21, 25, 36, 42
Hurh, Won Moo, 31, 32, 33, 86, 158, 237
Hutchison, William R., 35
Hymns for the Living Church, 163

Iannaccone, Laurence R., 23–24, 26, 27–28, 42, 47, 48, 49, 66, 72, 73, 105, 107, 108, 110, 201, 266
immigrant congregations: architecture of structures, 15–16; of Buddhists, 167; cohorts in, relations among, 247–248; cultural reproduction role of religion, 85–86; de facto, 86, 163–164; fellowship in, 158; gender roles in, 246–247, 248; generation gap in, 33, 86, 245–246; growth of, 147–148; Hispanic/Latino, 214–221; inclusiveness of, 86–90; Korean Presbyterians, 88–90, 148, 163–164; linguistic acculturation of, 33, 86, 245; music in, 91–94; of Muslims, 166–167; numbers of, 237–238; pluralism and, 29, 30–33; research on, 287–288; vigor and variety of, 84
immigrants, 1, 9; affiliation and disaffiliation, 112; Asian migration, 253; Christian, 238–239, 257–262; Christian converts, 259; congregationalism among, 242–245; guest workers, 233; importance of religion, 236–238; Pentecostal Okies as, 227–231; post-1965 migration, 232–233, 254, 257, 267–268; religious conservatism of, 262; religious identity of, 240–241; research on new immigrants, 233–236, 248–249. *See also specific groups*
Immigration Act of 1965, 233, 253, 267–268
Independent Sector, 146, 147
India, religious diversity in, 282
Indian and Pakistani immigrants, 32, 33; Christian, 238, 239, 255, 259; gender roles among, 246–247; Hindus, 244–245; Muslim, 237, 240; occupational status of, 254; religious identity of, 240
institutional isomorphism, 167–168
intermarriage, 47, 270
Iranian refugees, 33
Islam. *See* Muslims
Islamic Mission (Brooklyn), 245

Jackson, Jesse, Sr., 39, 267
Jacquet, Constant H., Jr., 21, 22
James, William, 81
Jamison, Gerald E., 185, 189, 190, 198, 201
Japanese Americans, 32, 167, 256
Jehovah's Witnesses, 30, 147
Jeung, Russell, 255
Jones, Alice M., 21, 22
Jones, Jim, 168
Jorstad, Erling, 36
Judaism: Camp Ramah movement, 169; cohorts of immigrants, 248; congregationalism in, 37, 172; decentralization in, 162; gay and lesbian congregations, 193; *havurot*, 152, 172; Orthodox, 44, 46; pluralism and,

26; religious identity and, 240; religious particularism and, 270; voluntaristic, 47–48

Kandiyoti, Deniz, 41
Kashima, Tetsuden, 37
Kaufman, Debra Renée, 21, 44
Keeley, Charles B., 31
Kelley, Dean M., 72, 73, 128, 265
Kennedy, Paul, 79
Kertzer, David L., 90
Keysar, Ariela, 44
Kim, Jung Ha, 253, 255, 256
Kim, Kwang Chung, 31, 32, 33, 86, 158, 237, 251
Kim, Rebecca, 254
Kimmerly, Mark (pseud.), 128, 130, 132, 136, 140, 142
Kincheloe, Samuel, 149
King, Martin Luther, Jr., 264
Kinsey, Alfred, 196
Kitano, Harry H.L., 43
Kivisto, Peter A., 31, 109
Kloehn, Steve, 239
Koch, Forrest (pseud.), 137, 139, 142
Korean Americans, 32, 33, 43, 237, 253, 256; Buddhists, 148, 167; Christian immigration, 238, 239, 254, 258; church affiliation, 158; Methodists, 172; Presbyterian congregations of, 88–90, 148, 163–164, 169; religious identity of, 240, 241
Korean Presbyterian Church in America, 148, 164
Korean United Presbyterian Church of Los Angeles, 164
Kosmin, Barry A., 32, 44
Kostarelos, Frances, 96, 285
Kovacs, Daniel, 112
Krody, Nancy, 201
Kuhn, Thomas, 63, 64, 66
Kurien, Prema, 87, 240, 244–245, 254, 255, 256, 268, 269
Kuzmickaite, Daiva, 248
Kwilecki, Susan, 42, 48
Kwon, Ho-Youn, 238

Lachman, Seymour P., 32
Laderman, Gary, 234
LaMagdeleine, Donald, 165
Lamb, Simon, 282
Land, Kenneth C., 27
Latinos. *See* Hispanics/Latinos
Laurents, Arthur, 246
Lawler, Edward J., 115
Lawless, Elaine, 42
Lay leadership, 134–135, 140, 141
Lechner, Frank J., 7, 21, 48, 63, 65, 66, 105
Lee, Richard R., 23, 26
Lee, Sang Hyun, 88, 236
Lehrman, William, 40
León, Luis, 87, 98, 269, 288
Leone, Mark P., 23
Lerer, Nava, 44
lesbians: in Metropolitan Community Churches, 169, 201–202. *See also* gays and lesbians
Lewis, James W., 8

Liebman, Robert C., 36, 38
lifestyle enclaves, 44, 171
Lilly Endowment, 287
Lincoln, C. Eric, 39, 40, 288
Lindsay, D. Michael, 278
Lindsell, Harold, 133
linguistic acculturation, 33, 86
Lipset, Seymour Martin, 6, 22, 27
Littel, Franklin Hamlin, 23, 107
liturgical renewal, 152
Livezey, Lowell W., 268, 285
Lockhart, Keith, 30
Longfield, Bradley, 266
Lucas, Charles, 187
Luker, Kristin, 44–45
Lummis, Adair T., 32, 33, 35, 37, 42, 48, 158, 246
Lutherans, 146, 147, 161, 193, 195
Lyles, Jean Caffey, 189, 194

Mamiya, Lawrence H., 39, 40, 288
Marcuse, Herbert, 196
market theories of religion, 27–29, 67n1, 70–71, 77–78
Marler, Penny Long, 28, 34, 43, 45, 46
Marriage Encounter, 152
Marsden, George M., 26, 40
Marty, Martin E., 9, 16, 69, 70, 78, 128, 147, 151, 153
Mathews, Donald G., 22
Mathy, Robin M., 196, 197
Matovina, Timothy, 91, 213, 221, 288
Matters, Michael D., 38, 45
Mauss, Armand L., 44, 45, 48
May, Cheryll, 168
May, Dean, 168
McAdam, Doug, 38, 45
McAlister, Elizabeth, 87, 94, 240, 271
McGuire, Meredith B., 37, 42
McKinney, William, 36, 43, 44, 45, 47, 158–159, 189, 265, 266, 270
McKirnan, David, 202
McNeill, John, 193, 198
McNeill, William H., 94, 95, 284
McPhee, John, 282, 283
McPherson, Aimee Semple, 191
McRoberts, Omar M., 285
Mead, Sidney E., 6, 23, 26, 107
Mellor, Philip A., 283
Melton, J. Gordon, 21
Mendocino Presbyterian Church, 8, 17, 106, 125–144, 146; conflict among evangelicals, 135; demographic change and, 136, 140–141; lay involvement in, 134–135, 140, 141; under liberal pastors, 129–130, 132; membership and attendance, 127, 127, 130–131, 132, 133, 134, 139, 140; mission of, 152; research methods, 125–127; shift to evangelicalism, 125, 126, 127–128, 132–133; social enclaves in, 160; succession crisis at, 136–139; theological diversity of, 138, 141; Underwood's orthodox theology, 133–134, 141–142, 170
mestizaje, 97, 215, 217, 218
Methodist church: affiliation, 29, 71, 72, 73; demographic factors in, 23; gays and

lesbians in, 195; Korean, 172; mergers in, 161; number of congregations, 146, 147
Metropolitan Community Churches, 4, 8, 34, 38, 183–202; background of, 184–185; converts, church of, 44; denomination formation, 190–191; emotional support in, 200; founding of, 170, 183, 185–186; gender equality in, 169, 201–202; innate homosexuality as teaching of, 40, 43, 187–188, 195–196; liturgy of, 170–171, 189; locations of, 193; membership profile, 186; NCC membership and, 192, 194; political activism of, 183–184, 191–192; as social centers, 189–190; stigma redemption through, 190; structure of, 191; theological conservatism of, 20–21, 187, 200–201
Metz, Donald, 152, 161
Mexican Americans. See Hispanics/Latinos
Michaelson, Robert S., 26
migration, internal, 15, 30, 33–34, 47, 227–228
Miles, Carrie A., 42, 201
Miller, Donald, Reinventing American Protestantism, 79–81
Million Man March, 269
Min, Pyong Gap, 237, 253–254, 255, 256
minyan, egalitarian, 37, 47
Mittelberg, David, 32, 86, 240
Miyakawa, T. Scott, 30
mobility: geographic, 15, 30, 33–34, 47, 133, 157, 226–231; religious, 43–48
modernism, fundamentalism and, 78
Mohammed, Warith Deen, 239, 267
Mollenkott, Virginia Ramey, 189, 198
monopoly church, 64–65
Montoya, Alex D., 37
Moody, Dwight L., 78
Moore, Laurence R., 108
Moral Majority, 38
moral reform movement, 41
Morgan, Dan, 9, 226–231
Mormons, 30, 168
Morris, Aldon D., 19, 38, 39, 159
Mulcrone, Joe, 209, 210, 211
Mumford, Bob, 168–169
music, bonding power of, 91–94
Muslims, 32, 33; African American, 239, 267; congregationalism among, 37, 166–167, 245; fellowship role of religion, 158; number of, 259, 260; number of centers, 148, 237; power of ritual, 94–96; religious identity of, 240; women's status, 246, 248; worship of, 153–154; youth, religiosity of, 112, 113, 115–116, 264

Narayan, Kirin, 235
National Conference of Catholic Bishops, 19–20, 28, 266
National Council of Churches (NCC), 19, 35, 161, 162, 263, 266; MCC membership and, 192, 194; Yearbook, 146, 147, 148
Nazarenes, 45, 71, 147
Nee, Victor, 86, 289
Neitz, Mary Jo, 20, 37, 42, 48, 66, 105, 107, 202, 282, 284
Nelson, Timothy J., 90, 288

New Ethnic and Immigrant Congregations Project (NEICP), 83, 84, 86, 94, 234–235, 238, 247, 249, 271, 287

new paradigm analysis: ambivalent religiosity, Smelser's theory of, 114–117, 118, 119; development of, 106–110; economic imagery of, 6–7, 23–25, 26, 28, 67n1, 70–71, 77–78, 283; vs. old paradigm, 24; presuppositional key to, 21–29; rational choice theory and, 110–113, 118, 119, 283; research agenda of, 48–49; shift to, 6, 18–19, 63, 65–67; theoretical foundations for, 282–284

new paradigm churches, 79–81

New Religious America, A (Eck), 258

New Religious Right, 39

New Wine in Old Wineskins (Warner), 1, 8, 125, 127, 133, 139, 140, 145–146, 284

Niebuhr, H. Richard, 5, 31, 33, 35, 73

Niebuhr, Reinhold, 19, 142, 272

Noise of Solemn Assemblies, The (Berger), 155–156

Noll, Mark, 69, 92

Notre Dame Study of Catholic Parish Life, 149

Numrich, Paul David, 31, 32, 33, 234, 237, 239, 268, 285

O'Brien, Jennifer, 235

occupational status, immigrant, 254

Okie Pentecostal migrants, 227–231

old paradigm analysis, 6, 8, 19–21, 64–65, 118–119

Olson, Daniel V.A., 27, 30, 34, 35, 48, 157, 281, 282

Oral Roberts University, 265

Orsi, Robert A., 42

Orthodox Church, 34, 35

Osman, Fathi, 33

Pakistani immigrants. *See* Indian and Pakistani immigrants

Pang, Keng Fong, 87

Papaiouannou, George, 161

Pappas, Domenica, 211

paradigm: defined, 64; new paradigm (*See* new-paradigm analysis); new vs. old, 24; old paradigm, 6, 8, 19–21, 64–65; vs. theory, 63

Parents and Friends of Lesbians and Gays (PFLAG), 200

parishes: concept of, 156–157; consolidation of, 166; "floating" laity, 164–165, 166; magnet, 244; number of, 147; territorial principle in, 165

Park, Hyung, 33

Park, Soyoung, 242

Parliament of the World's Religions, 234

Parsons, Talcott, 20, 109, 110, 153, 272, 283

patriarchy, 40, 41, 42–43

Pattillo-McCoy, Mary, 284, 288

Pattison, E. Mansell, 198

Pattison, Myrna Loy, 198

Peacocke, Dennis, 168–169

Pentecostals, 9, 16, 20; affiliation, 72; founding of, 74–76; inculturation and, 261; Okie

migrants, 227–231; Oral Roberts and, 28, 229; transcultural appeal of, 28, 98; women's empowerment, 42–43

People for the American Way, 266

People's Temple, 168

Perrin, Robin D., 44, 45, 48

Perry, Troy D., 21, 34, 38, 190; background of, 184–185; founding of MCC, 170, 183, 185–186; on Goddess language, 202; on innate homosexuality, 40, 43, 187–188, 195–196, 198; liturgy of, 170–171, 189; political activism of, 183–184, 191–192; theological conservatism of, 187, 200–201

Peterson, Peggy L., 202

Pew Charitable Trusts, 248, 287

Pick, Grant, 166

Pizzorno, Alessando, 111

plausibility structures, 25, 64

plausibility theory, 118

Ploen, Richard, 186

pluralism, religious: adjustment to, 25–26; in competitive religious market, 27–29; immigration and, 29, 30, 30–33; internal migration and, 15, 30, 33–34; proliferation of denominations, 148; social factors in, 29–30; vitality and, 280–282

political polarization, 289

Poloma, Margaret M., 21, 47

Portes, Alejandro, 85, 86, 241, 246, 288

Powell, Walter W., 35, 167–168

Pratt, Henry J., 35

Prell, Riv-Ellen, 21, 37, 47

Presbyterian church: affiliation, 43; autonomy of congregations, 163; decentralization, 162; demographic factors in, 29; gays and lesbians in, 195; Korean congregations, 88–90, 148, 163–164, 169; mergers, 161; number of congregations, 146, 147; theological divisions in, 138. *See also* Mendocino Presbyterian Church

Preston, David L., 21, 37

Primiano, Leonard Norman, 288

Pritchard, Linda, 47

Promise Keepers, 269

Propocki, Thomas, 165

Protestant, Catholic, Jew (Herberg), 2–3, 19

Pruitt, Dusty, 202

Puritans, parishes of, 156–157

Putnam, Robert, 271, 280, 287

Rambo, Lewis R., 88, 94

"Rational and Ambivalent in the Social Sciences, The" (Smelser), 114–117

rational choice theory, 6–7, 23, 66, 105, 108, 109, 110–113, 114, 118, 119, 283

Ray, Melissa, 165

Reback, Cathy, 202

Redding, Kent, 27

Redford, Larry (pseud.), 128, 132, 134, 135, 136, 140, 152

Reed, John Shelton, 270

Reed, Ralph, 264

Reformed church, 29

Reinventing American Protestantism (Miller), 79–81

religion in America: assimilation and, 288–289; civic role of, 38–40, 263–273; comparison to European experience, 13–15, 278; cultural change and, 265–268; cultural reproduction role of, 85, 269–270, 271; demography of, 259–260; diversity of (*See* pluralism, religious); empowerment role of, 40–43; Herberg on, 2–3, 5–6; homophobia and, 192; individualist trends in, 43–48; new paradigm (*See* new paradigm analysis); old paradigm, 6, 8, 19–21, 118–119; political polarization and, 289. *See also* churches; congregations; denominations
Religions in Asian America (Min and Kim), 253
religious education, 154
RENIR project, 248–249
Republican party, 289
Revive Us Again (Carpenter), 76–79
Richardson, Diane, 197
Riebe-Estrella, Gary, 288
Riley, C.T., 189
Rising in the West (Morgan), 9, 226–231
Risman, Barbara, 197, 200, 202
ritual: embodied, 83, 96; inculturation of, 97, 215, 217–218, 261–262; social solidarity through, 90, 94–96, 284
Ritual, Politics, and Power (Kertzer), 90
Roberts, Oral, 28, 186, 229
Roof, Wade Clark, 21, 34, 36, 43, 44, 45, 47, 117, 189, 265, 266, 270
Roozen, David A., 36, 44, 48, 266, 285
Rosaldo, Renato, 270
Rose, Susan D., 21, 46
Rosenberg, Bruce A., 39
Rubinstein, David M., 118
Rueda, Enrique, 38, 193, 196
Rumbaut, Rubén, 84, 241, 288
Ruse, Michael, 196, 197
Rutledge, Paul James, 32, 238
Ryan, Mary, 41, 42, 47

Sacred Canopy (Berger), 66
sacred canopy concept, 15, 26
Saint Benedict the African, 166
Saletan, William, 289
San Buenaventua, Steffi, 255, 256
Sanchez Walsh, Arlene, 288
sanctuary movement, 38, 161
San Fernando Cathedral, Holy Week rituals at, 214–221; pastoral theology, 221–223
Sarna, Jonathan D., 37, 160
Schellenberg, E. Glenn, 92
Schelling, Thomas, 283
Scherer, Ross P., 28
Schumpeter, Joseph A., 18, 63
Schutz, Alfred, 5, 92, 93
Schwartz, Pepper, 197, 200, 202
Scopes "monkey trial," 76
Seventh-Day Adventists, 30, 147
Seymour, William Joseph, 74
shape-note singing, 92
Sharot, Stephen, 21
Sheppard, Gerald T., 43, 47
Sherkat, Darren E., 39, 40, 111
Shilts, Randy, 199, 200

Shin, Eui Hang, 33
Shipps, Jan, 27, 30, 168
Shupe, Anson, 40
Silver, Allan, 35, 157
SisterSpirit, 202
Skokeid, Moshe, 285, 288
Smelser, Neil J., 105, 106, 110, 114–117
Smilde, David, 111
Smith, Adam, 23–24, 27
Smith, Christian, 111, 118, 284
Smith, Chuck, 79, 81
Smith, Timothy L., 30, 31, 32, 33, 35, 88, 157, 236
Smith, Tom W., 19, 22, 25
Smith, Willie, 192
Smith-Rosenberg, Carroll, 41
social change function of religion, 38–40
social services, congregational, 286–287
solidarity, religious, 86–90; assimilation and, 97–98; in food sharing, 96; in music, 91–94; out-group hostility and, 117; in prayer ritual, 94–96, 284
Sollors, Werner, 32
Sontag, Susan, 199, 200
Southern Baptist Convention, 45, 71, 73, 146, 163, 194, 265
Southern Christian Leadership Conference, 264
Spanish-language worship, 217, 218–219, 237, 261
Spong, John Shelby, 199
Sri Lankan Buddhists, 167
Stacey, Judith, 21, 42, 98
Stacey, William, 40
Stark, Rodney, 6, 22, 23, 26, 27, 48, 49, 66, 105, 107, 108, 109, 110, 111, 118, 265, 266, 281, 283; *The Churching of America*, 69–74
Stehlin, Helen V.L., 42
Steinbeck, John, 226, 227
Steinfels, Peter, 69, 70
stewardship, of congregations, 155
Stewart, John A., 64, 66
Storr, Anthony, 92, 93
Stout, Harry S., 48, 107
Strauss, William, 117
Stump, Roger W., 29
subcultures, religious, 30
Sullins, Donald Paul, 45
Sullivan, Andrew, 164, 188, 198
supply-side analysis, 28, 70, 108
Swatos, William H., Jr., 8, 26, 35, 109, 284
Swicegood, Thomas L.P., 21, 38, 40, 43, 185, 186, 187, 188, 189, 190, 192, 195, 200

Takayama, K. Peter, 35
Taylor, Charles, 263, 272
Thomas, George M., 47
Thompson, J. Michael, 92
Thompson, Wayne, 44
Thornton, Bill, 219
Thumma, Scott, 21, 189, 197
Tillich, Paul, 19
Tiryakian, Edward A., 49
Tobin, Kay, 187
Tocqueville, Alexis de, 272

Toledo Islamic Center, 167
Trehub, Sandra E., 92
Trueheart, Charles, 268
Tschannen, Olivier, 18, 21
Tweed, Thomas A., 239

Underwood, Eric (pseud.), 128, 132–135, 136, 138, 142, 154
Unitarian-Universalist church, 171, 193
United Church of Christ, 147, 162, 193–194
United Methodist Church, 146
United Presbyterian Church, 127
Universal Fellowship of Metropolitan Community Churches. *See* Metropolitan Community Churches
University of Illinois at Chicago, 235

Van Gelder, Lindsy, 197
Varieties of Religious Experience (James), 81
Vatican II, 73, 165, 266
Vietnamese: Christian immigration of, 238, 239, 255, 258; religious identity of, 241
Vineyard churches, 44, 79–81, 147, 172
Voas, David, 281
voluntarism, religious, 43–48, 66, 152–153
Voting Rights Act, 267

Wacker, Grant, 26, 27; *Heaven Below*, 74–76
Wagner, Melinda, 162
Walk to Emmaus, 152
Warner, R. Stephen, 1, 5, 9, 21, 23, 29, 31, 32, 34, 35, 36, 37, 40, 42, 44, 46, 63, 64, 66, 70, 83, 84, 85, 86, 92, 95, 98, 105, 106, 107, 108, 109, 110, 111, 113, 116, 117, 119, 193, 194, 232, 233, 238, 239, 265, 266, 268, 269, 270, 272, 283, 284, 285, 287
Wat Dhammaram, 169
Waters, Mary C., 32, 86, 240
Waugh, Earle H., 31, 32, 33, 37
Weber, Max, 5, 65, 75, 280, 283
Wedam, Elfriede, 83, 244, 267
Weinberg, Martin S., 196
Weitzman, Murray S., 265
Wellmeier, Nancy J., 86, 244, 269
Wertheimer, Jack, 37, 42, 270

Wheeler, Barbara G., 86, 90, 154, 159
Whitam, Frederick L., 196, 197
Whitefield, George, 77–78, 186
Why Conservative Churches Are Growing (Kelley), 265
Wicker, Randy, 187
Wilcox, Clyde, 40
Wilcox, Melissa M., 288
Williams, Melvin D., 96
Williams, Raymond Brady, 31, 32, 33, 85, 234, 239, 240, 268, 270
Williams, Rhys H., 116
Willow Creek Community Church, 16
Wills, Garry, 19, 20, 39, 267
Wilson, Bryan, 105
Wilson, Nancy, 192, 194, 199, 200, 202, 288
Wiltfang, Gregory, 38, 45
Wimber, John, 79, 81
Wind, James P., 8
Winter, Gibson, 272
Wittner, Judith G., 5, 83, 235, 240, 285, 287
Wolfe, Alan, 85
women: denominations and, 169; nineteenth-century doctrine of womanhood, 41; in immigrant congregations, 246–247; in Metropolitan Community Churches, 169, 201–202; ordination of, 37, 41–42; in private sphere, 273; religious empowerment of, 42, 246; religious participation of, 40–41
Wood, James R., 35, 264
Wood, Richard L., 284, 288
worship, 153–154, 286
Wuthnow, Robert, 8, 25, 28, 30, 34, 35, 36, 40, 41, 42, 78, 161, 162, 193, 266, 280, 283

Yang, Fenggang, 87, 240, 243, 255, 256, 269
Yep, Jeanette, 237, 240
Yoo, David, 66, 234, 255, 256
Youth and Religion Project, 109, 112–113, 114, 115
Yu, Eui-Young, 32

Zaretsky, Irving I., 23
Zhou, Min, 84, 238, 241, 245, 246, 254, 256, 285
Zikmund, Barbara Brown, 43

ABOUT THE AUTHOR

R. STEPHEN WARNER is a professor of sociology at the University of Illinois at Chicago. In 1989, he received the Distinguished Book Award from the Society for the Scientific Study of Religion for *New Wine in Old Wineskins: Evangelicals and Liberals in a Small-Town Church.*